MODERN STUDIES IN PROPERTY LAW:
VOLUME 4

This book is a collection of papers given at the sixth biennial conference at the University of Reading held in March 2006, and is the fourth in the series Modern Studies in Property Law. The Reading conference has become well-known as a unique opportunity for property lawyers to meet and confer both formally and informally. This volume is a refereed and revised selection of the papers given there. It covers a broad range of topics of immediate importance, not only in domestic law but also on a worldwide scale.

Modern Studies In Property Law

Volume 4

Edited by

ELIZABETH COOKE

Professor of Law,
University of Reading

·HART·
PUBLISHING

OXFORD AND PORTLAND, OREGON
2007

Published in North America (US and Canada) by
Hart Publishing
c/o International Specialized Book Services
920 NE 58th Avenue, Suite 300
Portland, OR 97213-3786
USA
Tel: +1 (503) 287-3093 or toll-free: +1 (800) 944-6190
Fax: +1 (503) 280-8832
E-mail: orders@isbs.com
Website: www.isbs.com

Hart Publishing, 16C Worcester Place, Oxford, OX1 2JW, United Kingdom
Telephone: +44 (0)1865-517530 Fax: +44 (0)1865-510710
E-mail: mail@hartpub.co.uk
Website: http://www.hartpub.co.uk

British Library Cataloguing in Publication Data
Data Available

ISBN-13: 978-1-84113-628-8 (hardback)
ISBN-10: 1-84113-628-X (hardback)

Typeset by Columns Design Ltd, Reading
Printed and bound in Great Britain by
Biddles Ltd, King's Lynn, Norfolk

Preface

The fourth volume of *Modern Studies in Property Law* celebrates the sixth biennial conference of the Centre for Property Law at the University of Reading. It has been a pleasure for me and for my colleagues at Reading, many of whom were involved in the very beginning of this conference series, to see it going from strength to strength. Papers from the earlier Reading conferences were published as: Jackson, P and Wilde, DC (eds), *The Reform of Property Law* (Dartmouth, Ashgate, 1997); Jackson, P and Wilde DC (eds), *Contemporary Property Law* (Dartmouth, Ashgate, 1999); Jackson, P and Wilde DC (eds), *Property Law: Current Issues and Debates* (Dartmouth, Ashgate, 1999); and the first three volumes of *Modern Studies in Property Law* (Oxford, Hart Publishing), which contain papers from the conferences in 2000, 2002 and 2004. All the *Modern Studies* volumes are refereed publications, and as editor I am most grateful to the small team of distinguished, anonymous scholars who have helped select and refine papers for publication, as well as to the authors of the papers for their co-operation with this process.

This volume opens with the keynote address for the conference, given by Martin Partington. His work as a Law Commissioner for England and Wales, and now as a Special Consultant to the Law Commission, puts him in an ideal position to report on the Law Commission's work on the reform of housing law. This has burgeoned into three projects—Renting Homes, Housing Disputes and Responsible Renting. The final Renting Homes report has been published with a draft Bill, while the other two projects, which grew out of it, are in their early stages. All offer exciting prospects for the reform of this vexed area, in addition to expanding the scope of the work undertaken by the Law Commission.

The next section of the book is blandly entitled 'Law and Equity' and covers issues of domestic law, in many cases with an equity flavour. Martin Dixon revisits a long-running discussion in the volumes of *Modern Studies in Property Law* about equitable co-ownership of land, arguing that the courts have all but eliminated the proprietary status of equitable ownership rights, thereby going further than they need in favour of third parties. The subject is one of endless fascination and perennial relevance, not least in the light of the Law Commission's recent consultation paper on cohabitation. Graham Ferris' controversial chapter on the nature of undue influence follows, underlining the complexity of the interaction between judicial law-making and academic analysis. Gary Watt explores the world of mortgages, another favourite field of creativity for equity, and exposes the difficulty involved in dispensing with so many centuries of entrenched fictions.

Robin Hickey turns our attention to personal property law. He asks if our law imposes on the finder of goods any duty to the person who lost them. He concludes that it does not, and points out that in a context where the protection of possessions is a human right, this failing may have to be remedied.

The two final chapters in this section revert to the law relating to homes, but with a public law flavour. Warren Barr looks at rented housing and the possibilities of 'rethinking possession' against vulnerable groups. This is another area—like mortgages and the law relating to equitable co-ownership rights—in which the law endeavours to keep folk in their homes but has to make very difficult choices between individuals and the wider community. The law reform heralded by Martin Partington's chapter will, it is hoped, go some way to solve the problems in this area. Nick Hopkins and Emma Laurie pursue the theme of home in the context of social security law and the concept of ownership, pointing out the different objectives of ownership concepts in social security law and property law and arguing for a reconciling of their different meanings.

The next section of the book contains three chapters that examine the effect of time upon the creation of property rights in land. First, Amy Goymour looks at the many instances in English law when time operates alongside other factors to create rights in land. Because the various doctrines have grown up independently, they are not often examined together; this chapter subjects the muddle to some joined-up thinking, arguing that a coherent pattern can be seen and could be developed further—and indeed that it must be, in the light of the provisions of the European Convention on Human Rights.

One of the most potent effects of possession of land over time is the limitation of actions. Pam O'Connor looks at this in the context of registered land, where decisions have to be taken in order to reconcile the confiscatory effect of adverse possession at common law with the supposed indefeasibility of registered title. Her chapter analyses the different responses found to this conundrum in different jurisdictions. She finds three principal approaches and concludes that the method adopted in the English Land Registration Act 2006 could be substantially improved.

Finally, this section concludes with Bruce Ziff and Sean Ward's analysis of the settlement of land around Alberta in the nineteenth century, which gives this section of the book a historical perspective. Their account of the 'squattocracy' and the transformation of the possession of frontier claims into legitimate ownership also sets the stage for the final section of the book, where we look at those who were dispossessed by this process.

Finally, then, is the section 'Property, Empire and Indigenous Title'. English common law has been exported throughout the world and has been a powerful tool for the oppression of aboriginal communities and the denial of their land rights. Patrick McAuslan shows the origins of this technique in the Norman conquest of 1066 and then in the subjugation of Ireland, and its later development in successive colonisations. Lee Godden and Maureen Tehan then look at native title claims in Australia, examining the process of translating native title into the concepts and language of Western property and then again, even more painfully, into marketable rights. Margaret Stephenson's chapter addresses the same issue but in a different style and with different scope; she examines the numerous different forms of indigenous land tenure in Australia, the USA, Canada and New Zealand, searching for lessons for Australia to assist in the latter's attempts to solve this massive inherited problem. These three chapters together present different aspects of a sorry tale, and we are left reflecting on how very long it will take to heal the damage wrought by the importation of the common law of property along with settlement and colonisation.

This volume thus begins with the protection of rented homes in England and Wales, moves through a huge range of interests and ends with the search for adequate and appropriate protection for the homelands of peoples who have been oppressed and dispossessed. Perhaps more questions are raised than answers; certainly we shall continue asking and answering them for many a year.

There has been a biennial property law conference at Reading for ten years now, and it is time for a change. In 2008 the conference will take place at the University of Cambridge under the expert care of Martin Dixon. As the current editor of this series I should like to thank all the contributors to this volume for their hard work; all who attended the conference for their company and their wonderfully constructive participation; and Martin for taking on the task of chairing the conference and editing the book in 2008.

Lizzie Cooke
University of Reading
Michaelmas Day, 2007

Contents

IV   Property, Empire and Indigenous Title

List of Contributors

Warren Barr is a Lecturer in the School of Law at the University of Liverpool and Director of the Charity Law Unit there.

Martin Dixon is a fellow of The Queen's College and a University Senior Lecturer in the Department of Land Economy at the University of Cambridge.

Graham Ferris is a Senior Lecturer in Law at Nottingham Trent University.

Lee Godden is a Senior Lecturer in the Faculty of Law at the University of Melbourne.

Amy Goymour is a Fellow of Fitzwilliam College, University of Cambridge.

Robin Hickey is a Lecturer in the School of Law at Queen's University, Belfast.

Nicholas Hopkins is a Senior Lecturer in Law at the University of Southampton.

Emma Laurie is a Lecturer in Law at the University of Southampton.

Patrick McAuslan is a Professor of Law in the Law School at Birkbeck College, University of London.

Pamela O'Connor is an Associate Professor of Law and Director of Teaching at Monash University, Melbourne.

Martin Partington is a Special Consultant to the Law Commission for England and Wales and Emeritus Professor of Law at the University of Bristol.

Margaret Stephenson is a Senior Lecturer in Law at TC Beirne School of Law, University of Queensland, Australia.

Maureen Tehan is an Associate Professor in the Faculty of Law, University of Melbourne.

Sean Ward is a graduate of the Faculty of Law, University of Alberta and a member of the Law Society of Alberta.

Gary Watt is a Senior Lecturer at the School of Law, University of Warwick.

Bruce Ziff is a Professor of Law at the University of Alberta.

Table of Cases

United States

Social Security Commissioner Decisions

Table of Legislation

Primary Legislation

Table of International Treaties and Conventions

I

Keynote Address

1

Reforming Housing Law: A Progress Report

MARTIN PARTINGTON*

INTRODUCTION

WHEN I WAS asked to deliver the lecture on which this chapter is based, I was anticipating the end of my term of office as a Law Commissioner for England and Wales. I thought it might give me the chance to reflect on the Law Commission's work on the reform of housing law and to put it into a more academic context. Things have not worked out like that. I was asked to stay on at the Commission as Special Consultant. The opening months of 2006 were a period of intense activity with the publication of two major reports and a draft Bill, as well as the launch of a new round of consultations and workshops on the Commission's continuing work on disputes and regulation. Time for reflection has been at a premium.

Nevertheless, given the stage that the Law Commission's work has reached, an account of what has been achieved so far and what is still to come will, I hope, be of interest to readers of this volume, even if it is more in the nature of an interim rather than a final analysis. This chapter therefore offers a personal view of the Law Commission's housing law reform programme to date.[1] It seeks to give some of the flavour of what the Commission has been striving to achieve in its work. It starts with a brief overview of the programme and then gives more detail about progress on each of the individual projects that make up the programme and offers some views on possible further developments.

---

* The views expressed in this paper are personal to the author; they do not represent the collective views of the Law Commission for England and Wales.
[1] For a fuller discussion of the development of housing law and a consideration of how it may develop, see A Arden and M Partington, 'Housing Law: Past and Present' in S Bright (ed), *Landlord and Tenant Law: Past, Present and Future* (Oxford, Hart Publishing, 2006).

THE LAW COMMISSION'S PROGRAMME

Under the general umbrella of housing law reform, the Law Commission is engaged in three distinct but inter-related projects: the Renting Homes project; the Housing Disputes project; and the Responsible Renting project.[2] The broad objectives of each, and how they relate to each other, are as follows.

1. The **Renting Homes** project is designed to make the basic legal structure for renting homes simpler and more flexible, not just to simplify the law, but also to facilitate the delivery of housing policy.[3]
2. The **Housing Disputes** project accepts that however rational and clear the underlying law may be, disputes between landlords, occupiers and others will continue to arise. This project explores the extent to which people with housing problems can find easier ways to resolve them—whether or not reform of the underlying law occurs.
3. The **Responsible Renting** project looks more broadly at the application of different forms of regulation to the rented housing market, in particular the private rented sector. It moves beyond traditional lawyers' views of the function of law, which tend to focus on the sanctions to be imposed on those who have broken the law. Instead, it considers how law may be used to incentivise all those involved in the renting of accommodation, both landlords and occupiers, to manage their affairs better, thereby preventing problems arising in the first place.

THE RENTING HOMES PROJECT

The Renting Homes project is at the most advanced stage. Following the publication of two consultation papers[4] and an intense period of consultation,[5] the Law Commission published both a report and a final report, which included a draft Bill.[6] The second (final) report also contains drafts of two model occupation contracts that are a central feature of the Commission's recommendations.

---

[2] The Terms of Reference to which the Law Commission originally worked did not set the projects out in exactly this way. See Law Commission, 'Renting Homes' (Law Com No 284, 2003) [2.6]. However, they were drafted to allow flexibility; they have thus as the programme has developed.

[3] See M Partington, 'Five Years After' (July/August 2006) *Roof Magazine* 36.

[4] Law Commission, 'Renting Homes 1: Status and Security' (Consultation Paper No 162, 2002); Law Commission, 'Renting Homes 2: Co-occupation, Transfer and Succession' (Consultation Paper No 168, 2002).

[5] See the description in M Partington, 'The Relationship between Law Reform and Access to Justice: A Case Study' (2005) 23 *Windsor Yearbook of Access to Justice* 375, 382–5.

[6] Law Commission, 'Renting Homes' (Law Com No 284, 2003); Law Commission, 'Renting Homes: The Final Report', vols 1 and 2 (Law Com No 297, 2006) <http://www.lawcom.gov.uk/renting_homes.htm> accessed 24 October 2006.

For many Law Commission projects, this would represent the end of the project rather than 'the most advanced stage' mentioned above. But use of this phrase is deliberate. While the final report and Bill are now in the public domain, in this case the Commission is undertaking a considerable amount of 'after-sales service' to brief key actors in the rented housing world on the implications and opportunities for their work that the report's recommendations represent.

The reason why the Commission is undertaking this additional work is quite simple. Right from the start of the project, when the then Minister of Housing Nick Raynsford MP commissioned the work, it has been clear that however obvious the need for reform of the law may be to lawyers, the world beyond them is likely to have little interest in taking reform proposals forward unless they also deliver added policy benefits as well. What Raynsford was interested in was a legal framework that, while robust, was sufficiently flexible to assist in housing policy-making and delivery. Although he has now left the government, the issue remains: how can recommendations for reform of the law assist in the delivery of housing policy?[7]

It was made clear that in undertaking its work, the Law Commission should assume that the broad distribution of rights and obligations, especially those that had arisen from the three major Housing Acts of the Thatcher era (1980–85, 1988 and 1996), should not be disturbed.[8] Thus the market principles introduced into the private rented sector would stand. Rent regulation would not be re-introduced; there would be no significant change to the rules on security of tenure.

But the Law Commission was equally clear that reform could not be achieved without making some adjustments to the status quo. The Commission's consultation process was designed to identify and, where possible, build consensus around the changes required to bring greater rationality and flexibility to the law. The Commission determined that there should be a very proactive consultation with all sides of the renting industry. Members of the team addressed meetings up and down the country and also received written submissions.[9] In the light of this very

---

[7] This is not a party political point; the Law Commission is briefing not only the government but the principal opposition parties as well. Separate arrangements are in place for discussion of the recommendations in Wales. Indications of ways in which policy on renting homes may be developing are contained in two sets of essays: T Dwelly and J Cowans (eds), *Rethinking Social Housing* (London, Smith Institute, 2006); and P Bill (ed), *More Homes for Rent: Stimulating Supply to Match Growing Demand* (London, Smith Institute, 2006)< http://www.smith-institute.org.uk/publications.htm> (accessed 5 January 2007).

[8] Had the New Labour Government thought otherwise, the project would not have been suitable for the Commission. The fact that, to a large extent, party politics had been removed from this area of policy making made the project appropriate for the Law Commission.

[9] See M Partington, 'The Relationship between Law Reform and Access to Justice: A Case Study' (2005) 23 *Windsor Yearbook of Access to Justice* 375, 382–5.

intensive consultation period, the Commission made its judgments about the changes needed to achieve a simpler and more flexible legal framework.

The basic recommendations were initially set out in the report 'Renting Homes', published late in 2003. A preliminary report of this sort is unusual for the Commission, but it knew that the process of drafting instructions for Parliamentary Counsel, who would draft the Bill, would be long and complex. The Commission thought that, having engaged in such a wide consultation, many would want to know what it had concluded. The final report and draft Rented Homes Bill were then published in May 2006.

I do not intend here to offer a detailed account of the content of the reports but rather to highlight some of the key issues and principles.

Landlord Neutrality

Central to the final report is the principle of landlord neutrality. The purpose of adopting this principle is to uncouple the link between the identity of the landlord and the legal rights that attach to those who rent from different landlords. At present only local authorities can offer secure tenancies; registered social landlords (RSLs) can only offer assured tenancies. Though the difference between the two is not all that great in practice, there is a clear perception that the tenants of RSLs are, by comparison with local authority tenants, second-class citizens. And those in social need who are provided with housing in the private rented sector are at a serious disadvantage. Landlord neutrality enables local authorities, RSLs and those private landlords who wish to let in the social rented sector to do so on exactly the same legal basis. It allows for the creation of the single social tenure that a number of organisations have long been urging.[10]

The policy advantages of landlord neutrality are clear. First, management of the social housing stock is made much more flexible. Local authorities required to deliver their local housing strategies will be able to use local authority, RSL and (where appropriate) the private rented sector on an equal footing. Current distinctions, which often inhibit the delivery of policy, become irrelevant.

Second, in relation to the provision of new build-to-let accommodation, a single social tenure facilitates the creation of new partnerships between local authorities, RSLs and private developers. It enables arm's-length management organisations (ALMOs), who currently only manage local

---

[10]   M Hood, *One for All: A Single Tenancy for Social Housing, A Discussion Paper for the Chartered Institute of Housing* (Coventry, Chartered Insititute of Housing, 1998). It is worth observing that this is not actually a wholly new idea; the Housing Act (1980) put housing associations and local authorities on the same footing, certainly as regards security of tenure. The Housing Act (1988) moved away from that position.

authority stock, to engage in the provision of new stock, lettable on the same terms as other social landlords. It therefore offers enormous scope for innovation in the provision of social housing.

Consumer Protection

A second key principle of the Law Commission's recommendations is consumer protection. The purpose of the consumer protection approach is to ensure that both landlords and occupiers have written copies of their contract (as happens with the provision of an employment contract), which provide a clear statement of the parties' rights and obligations. The Commission knew that, particularly in the private rented sector, rental agreements often failed to reflect the legal position as between landlords and tenants that Parliament, in successive Rent and Housing Acts, had sought to regulate. The Commission also knew that relatively few people—landlords as well as occupiers—have the ability to find out their legal rights and obligations. The Commission concluded that the current legislative practice of enacting rules and hoping that landlords and tenants would become aware of them simply did not work.

The Commission thus recommends the creation of occupation contracts, the terms of which are underpinned by statutory provisions. The most important provisions appear in the Bill; other provisions will be set out in delegated legislation. The 'Final Report' contains two draft model agreements that are written in plain language and indicate how these ideas can be put into practice. In 24 pages, landlords and occupiers will have as full a statement as practicable of their mutual rights and obligations under the contract.[11] To minimise the burden of landlords providing these documents, they will be freely downloadable from the web. They can be completed simply by filling in one page, giving the names of the parties, the rent, the address of the property and other key information.

One of the key policy advantages of such an approach is that, so long as landlords use the prescribed agreements, they will be immune from challenge to the Office of Fair Trading as being contrary to the provisions

---

[11] Some may argue that a document of 24 pages is too long, but this is simply a reflection of the numbers of rights and obligations enacted by Parliament, which supplement common law contractual principles. When the Scots drew up a model agreement following enactment of the Housing (Scotland) Act (2001), it ran to 80 pages. The Commission envisages that the contract will need supplementation with an explanatory booklet, such as many social landlords already provide and which, for the private rented sector, the Government publishes. These are currently available on the website of the Department for Communities and Local Government <http://www.communities.gov.uk/index.asp?id=1151894> accessed 25 May 2006.

of the Unfair Terms in Consumer Contracts Regulations[12]—an issue raised by many landlords in the consultation.

A second advantage is that the Law Commission's recommendations in effect create a direct line of communication between government, landlords and renters. For example, the Housing Act (2004) envisages changes to the statutory definition of 'overcrowding'; by simple amendment to the provisions of the Rented Homes Bill, the new definition can be incorporated in the contract for all to see and understand. The same applies to proposals for new energy efficiency certificates.

Probably the most important initial use of the scheme will be to make the rules relating to the protection of tenancy deposits more effective. It is well known that officials in the (then) Office of the Deputy Prime Minister were resistant to the inclusion of provisions on tenancy deposits in what became the Housing Act (2004); they wanted to use the Law Commission's Bill for that purpose. Back-bench pressure led to Ministers including a scheme in the Act. But the result is another example of provisions that will be far less effective than they should be because there is no efficient mechanism for making information about the scheme available to landlords and occupiers. There is every likelihood that the Law Commission's recommendations, if enacted, would facilitate this.

The Law Commission's recommendations also have a wider significance. For many, the private rented sector still has a very negative 'image'. While Rachman may be long dead, there are still those who think that the private rented sector is comprised solely of greedy rentiers, with little if any social conscience. There is no doubt that instances of bad landlordism still arise; but to tar the whole sector with the same brush is absurd. Nonetheless, the fact is that, unlike other countries, serious institutional investment in 'build-to-let' schemes is almost wholly absent in England and Wales.[13] It appears that, at least in part, institutional investors see the negative image of private landlordism as a significant factor in their reluctance to invest in new rental development.[14] The Law Commission model contracts would be a welcome step in enhancing the professionalism of the sector, thereby encouraging new investment.

---

[12]   Unfair Terms in Consumer Contracts Regulations (1999) (SI 1999 No 2083); Office of Fair Trading, 'Guidance on Unfair Terms in Tenancy Agreements' (September 2005).

[13]   This is of course distinct from the quite separate and very substantial investment in 'buy-to-let' schemes.

[14]   P Bill (ed), *More Homes for Rent: Stimulating Supply to Match Growing Demand* (London, Smith Institute, 2006) < http://www.smith-institute.org.uk/publications.htm> (accessed 5 January 2007).

Occupation Contracts

The reports and Bill contemplate two classes of occupation contract: 'secure contracts' (initially called 'type 1 agreements') modelled on the current secure tenancy; and 'standard contracts' (initially called 'type 2 agreements') modelled on the assured shorthold tenancy. Social landlords will be required to use the former save in prescribed exceptional circumstances; it is anticipated that private landlords will usually use the latter.

The Commission's intention is that, in addition to applying to new contracts, all existing residential tenancies should also be 'mapped' onto the proposed scheme. This would avoid one of the great problems of the past, namely that each legislative reform added to legal complexity rather than reduced it. It has not included those still protected by the Rent Acts, largely because of the very negative response to the idea given by Rent Act-protected tenants in the consultation. Even so, the Secretary of State is given power to bring this group into the scope of the scheme, which might well happen once this group of tenants realises that they would be as well or even better protected under the new scheme than they are at present.

Although certain classes of agreement are excluded from the scheme, either because they are covered by other legislation[15] or for social policy reasons,[16] the intention is for the scheme to be as comprehensive as possible. Thus no distinction is drawn between leases and licenses; so long as there is a contract, both are in the scheme. And many of the detailed qualifying rules that apply to trigger Housing Act protections are abandoned—for example, the requirement in the private rented sector that rents must be above or below predetermined levels.

Better Regulation

The overall effect of the Law Commission's recommendation will be better regulation. The provision of housing has long been subject to regulation. Initially done by the common law, over the last 100 years regulation has been increasingly statute driven. Most, if not all, advanced countries have housing legislation. The question is not whether there should be regulatory intervention but rather how it can be done well.

In this country, there is widespread agreement that the current law regulating rented housing is too complicated. This has significant drawbacks. A legal framework that is inflexible cannot achieve its policy

---

[15] For example long leases and business leases. See the Law Commission 'Final Report' [2.58].

[16] For example holiday lets or lettings with resident landlords (defined much more narrowly than in the current law). See the Law Commission 'Final Report' [2.59].

objectives. Those whom the law is designed to protect cannot use its protection. Those whose behaviour should be regulated are not influenced by what they cannot understand.

Some may ask whether a Bill with more than 200 clauses achieves simplification. The Commission's answer is that there is an important distinction between simplicity and simplification. Making law simple will not produce a legal framework that is sufficiently nuanced to meet the varied ways in which people actually live. But there is considerable room for simplification, in which the end results are simpler for people to understand.

The Better Regulation Task Force[17] argues that simplification includes three elements:

1. Deregulation—removing regulations from the statute book, leading to greater liberalisation of previously regulated regimes;
2. Consolidation—bringing together different regulations into a more manageable form and restating the law more clearly. By improving transparency and understanding, it should reduce compliance costs;
3. Rationalisation—using 'horizontal' legislation to replace a variety of sector-specific 'vertical' regulations.

The Rented Homes Bill achieves all these objectives. Although the draft Bill does not include schedules of repeals, when it reaches the statute book, the final version will repeal a great deal of existing legislation. The Bill offers a fundamental restatement of the law that significantly improves transparency and understanding, particularly through the use of model contracts. It rationalises sector-specific rules (for example current legal distinctions between local authorities and housing associations, and between the public sector and private sector) to eliminate unnecessary differences between them. This enables both the social and private sectors of the rental housing market to operate with greater freedom.

Supported Housing

A more specific achievement of the Law Commission's work is the set of recommendations relating to supported housing—accommodation provided for the most vulnerable people living in hostels, foyer schemes and the like. Initially the Commission suggested that these should fall wholly outside the legal regime it was developing, but representatives of those who

---

[17] Better Regulation Task Force, 'Regulation—Less is More: Reducing Burdens, Improving Outcomes' (March 2005). The Better Regulation Task Force became the Better Regulation Commission in 2005; work on better regulation is undertaken by the Better Regulation Executive. See <http://www.cabinetoffice.gov.uk/regulation/index.asp> accessed 31 July 2006.

provide such accommodation were very critical of this approach. The Commission therefore established a specialist group, which produced proposals that, while giving scheme managers powers to manage their accommodation effectively and without unnecessary legal inhibition, provided the most vulnerable with a ladder of opportunity to move from emergency provision to full rental protection. This will remedy the current situation whereby scheme managers often work in legally dubious ways, relying on the lack of legal advice available to those people with whom they deal and the low probability of legal challenge.

Legal Implications

Although the emphasis in the previous paragraphs has been on the policy implications of the Report, lawyers will find much of interest in the recommendations. These include: abolition of the 'tolerated trespasser';[18] new rules to deal with the termination of joint tenancies by notice to quit;[19] new rules on 'dealing' with the premises, which replace the common law rules on assignment;[20] new rules on the effect of death on the transfer of an occupation agreement;[21] and a new procedure to deal with the abandonment of premises, which should avoid the complexities and pitfalls of the common law on surrender.[22] The final report recommends that judicial discretion in determining discretionary possession proceedings should be structured so as to achieve greater consistency of outcome.[23] And the opportunity is taken, consistent with the consumer protection approach, to recommend implementation of the proposal made by the Law Commission in 1996 that accommodation should be fit for human habitation at the start of the letting.[24] Given the replacement of the old fitness rules by the new housing health and safety rating system contained in the Housing Act (2004), the precise recommendation is that, at the time of letting, the property should at least be free of any 'category 1 hazard'.

---

[18] An issue recently considered in detail by the Court of Appeal in *Bristol City Council v Hassan* [2006] EWCA Civ 656.

[19] This effectively alters the rule in *Greenwich London Borough Council v McGrady* (1982) 46 P&CR 223.

[20] See the Law Commission Draft Bill, cls 120–40.

[21] *Ibid*, cls 133, 136 and 141–51.

[22] *Ibid*, cls 160–3. This reflects changes already adopted in Scotland: see Housing (Scotland) Act (2001) ss 17–19.

[23] Law Commission Draft Bill, cls 199, 200 and sch 7.

[24] Law Commission, 'Landlord and Tenant: Responsibility for State and Condition of Property' (Law Com No 238, 1996).

The Position in Wales

One intriguing prospect that emerged towards the end of the Law Commission's work was the publication of the Government of Wales Bill.[25] It makes provision (among other things) for a form of primary legislative competence to be extended to the National Assembly for Wales on a case-by-case basis. Schedule 5 to the Bill sets out a series of 'fields' that cover the areas of policy devolved to the Assembly. Housing is one of those fields. It is envisaged that under each field, 'matters' will be added. Once a matter is added, the Assembly will be empowered to make primary legislation (in the form of 'Assembly Measures') in relation to the matter. The Bill itself only adds matters to the field entitled 'National Assembly for Wales'; they concern issues that are internal or incidental to the functioning of the Assembly. Matters related to substantive policy areas will be added in the future. Matters can be added by primary legislation or by a special form of order in council. Before such an order can be made, a draft of it must be approved by, first, the Assembly, and then both Houses of Parliament.

Housing is a devolved field, and housing tenure policy sits at the centre of that field. The Law Commission never saw the rented homes project as providing a once-and-for-all solution to all problems. Rather, it is designed to give policy makers the appropriate tools with which to implement policy changes that have an impact on tenure law, without each time having to interfere with the underlying legal structures involved. That in the future housing policy makers in Wales may take different paths from those in England is inherent in the idea of devolution.[26]

Next Steps

With the final report and Bill published, any decision about implementation is ultimately a matter for government. At the time of writing, no announcement has been made. There are some indications that the timing of the report may be quite opportune. Recent government announcements indicate that rented housing is higher on the political agenda than it has been for some time. The Select Committee for the Department for Communities and Rural Government is on the verge of announcing an inquiry into rented housing. The shortfall in housing provision, identified

---

[25] This became the Government of Wales Act (2006) on 25 July 2006.
[26] Government of Wales Act (2006) s 94 and Sched 5.

in Kate Barker's report on housing,[27] is receiving political attention. The key question is whether Ministers will share the Law Commission's view that the investment of the time and resources needed to bring the draft Bill to the statute book will be repaid through the added flexibility and potential for policy delivery that the recommendations will bring.[28]

THE HOUSING DISPUTES PROJECT

This second Law Commission housing law reform project arose out of *Renting Homes*. The Commission heard many complaints about the ways in which housing disputes are currently resolved. It also received information about the different ways housing disputes are dealt with in other jurisdictions, especially in Australia, Canada and New Zealand. In 2003, the Commission recommended that more work be done, in particular on whether there should be a specialist housing court or tribunal.

Discussions with officials in the Department for Constitutional Affairs led to the conclusion that this would be too narrow an approach. The DCA was developing more general ideas for 'proportionate dispute resolution' and thought that housing disputes could provide a case study in how these ideas might be translated into reality. At the same time, the Legal Services Commission was developing ideas for a new strategy for the Community Legal Service. Central to these ideas was the proposition that fewer resources should be devoted to funding litigation in court, more to funding advice and assistance prior to court proceedings. In addition, the Housing Act (2004) gave the Residential Property Tribunal Service a significant increase in the scope of its jurisdiction, adding a whole raft of appeal issues that in the past would undoubtedly have been given to county courts.

With these background issues in mind, the Law Commission was asked to undertake a much broader inquiry into how housing problems are currently solved, how current procedures might be adapted or reformed, what the relationship is between housing problems and dispute-resolution, how disputes arise, and what social processes are involved in shaping and resolving them. In April 2006, the Commission published an issues paper

---

[27] K Barker, *Review of Housing Supply, Delivering Stability: Securing our Future Housing Needs—Final Report* (London, The Stationery Office, March 2004). A review of social housing by Professor John Hills has also been announced.

[28] The time and resources are not a trivial matter; the Law Commission has not sought to deal with all the consequential changes to the law that implementation of its scheme would require, for example, the rights to buy and acquire.

setting out its initial views on what may be wrong with the current system and thus what the objectives of reform should be.[29]

Historically, and with the possible exception of its work on criminal evidence, the Law Commission has not considered questions of practice and procedure. Its focus has been on reform of the substantive law. But a failure to think how law will work in practice, particularly in an area such as housing law where many, perhaps most, do not seek the advice of lawyers or other professional advisers, may well undermine the effectiveness of substantive law reform. For this project, the Commission has gone well beyond its usual sources of information, drawing on an extensive socio-legal literature on disputing and dispute-resolution.

The Issues

The principal issues identified by the Commission are: the provision of information and advice; choosing the right option; dealing with the underlying problem; feedback; and efficiency/cost.

The Provision of Information and Advice

All relevant research shows that the key to getting problems solved and disputes resolved proportionately is getting good information and advice to those with problems or in dispute as early as possible. The same research also reveals two perennial problems. Too often information and advice is sought too late, by which time a problem or dispute has reached crisis point; and many groups might benefit from information and advice but are extremely hard to reach, for example, members of minority ethnic groups, those with below average levels of educational achievement and many young people. In the housing context, many landlords are equally uninformed about their rights and obligations.

While a great deal of imaginative work is undertaken by, for example, Citizens Advice, Shelter and bodies representing landlords and their managing agents, there are many others whose work is less well known.[30] The Commission wants to find out about this work.

---

[29] Law Commission, 'Housing: Proportionate Dispute Resolution, Further Analysis' (Law Commission Issues Paper, 2006).

[30] The variety of advice providers is revealed in P Pleasence, N Balmer and A Buck, *Causes of Action: Civil Law and Social Justice*, 2nd edn (London, The Stationery Office, 2006).

Choosing the Right Option

A large range of options, both sources of advice and dispute resolution mechanisms, are available to people with housing problems. The Commission's working assumption is that not all clients are provided with information about the full range of available options for solving their problems or resolving their dispute. The Commission clearly needs to know whether this working assumption is correct. If it is not, the Commission also needs to know how agencies that are able to offer a full range of options to their clients achieve this in practice.

Dealing with the Underlying Problem

The process of transforming problems into disputes can mean that the issue facing the adviser, court or other dispute resolution mechanism may not address the underlying problem. One example is possession proceedings being taken for rent arrears. Often the underlying problem is failure of housing benefit administration, rather than default on the part of the tenant. So far as possible, a problem-solving system should be able to deal with the real problem, rather than a problem devised to fit a particular jurisdictional requirement.

Feedback

One of the major problems with the current system is that those who deal with housing problems or disputes do not always provide feedback to the bodies or individuals who have caused them. Some agencies do, but practice is by no means universal. This reduces the impact of the current system to prevent similar problems arising in the future.

Efficiency/Cost

The relationship between the problem or the dispute and the cost of dealing with it must be looked at closely. It is important that the costs of following a particular procedure do not get out of balance with what is at stake. There will be continuing pressure to identify potential cost savings. The Law Commission issues paper asks those with knowledge of the current system to identify ways in which expenditure might be redirected. The Commission is also interested in whether there are other sources of funding that could contribute to meeting the cost of proportionate housing dispute resolution. For example, in some jurisdictions, the interest on tenancy deposits is used to pay for dispute resolution services; would this be possible in the UK? Could an extension of legal expenses insurance policies cover the costs of legal advice for mediation and other non-court dispute resolution?

A Blueprint for Reform?

To achieve a more proportionate system of housing dispute resolution, the Commission's preliminary view is that it should be based around three principal components: triage plus; non-court procedures; and court/ tribunal procedures.

Triage Plus

Central to the Commission's ideas is 'triage plus', which is envisaged as a service that provides signposting, oversight and intelligence. Signposting aims to bring greater discipline to the provision of housing advice and the direction of disputes to appropriate methods of resolution. (This could include advising that there is no solution to a particular problem other than acceptance of it; or enabling people to solve problems themselves.) Through oversight, triage plus would enable different parts of the system to learn from each other, which would help to prevent problems recurring. Intelligence gathering would enable triage plus providers to pass on concerns about systemic problems (for example, widespread disrepair, housing benefit administrative delays) that become apparent from the matters about which advice is sought, with a view to altering practice.

While the Law Commission conceived triage plus as something that would build on existing advice service provision, others believe that it may operate in other contexts as well. For example, the Council on Tribunals is exploring the extent to which triage might be offered directly by tribunals. The Financial Ombudsman Service also provides a form of triage; its processes assist those who contact it to articulate their problems and put inquirers directly in touch with the bodies who might be expected to deal with those problems. It is becoming clear that the concept is applicable in a wide range of contexts where people with problems go, not just in advice agencies.

Non-court Procedures

The Law Commission issues paper identifies three classes of non-court procedure that might be relevant in a reformed housing dispute resolution system: management responses; ombudsmen; and mediation.

Management responses include complaints handling mechanisms and internal or external review of decision making. They are relatively cheap to users, and they should ensure that decisions are right the first time or that wrong decisions are quickly rectified. In the specific context of housing problems, a focus on management responses could lead to better co-ordination of possession proceedings and decisions on homelessness. It could also lead to more appropriate use of possession proceedings, which would not be taken unless prior issues such as housing benefit problems had been sorted out.

A number of ombudsmen—some statutory (for example, the Local Government Ombudsmen) and some privately established (for example, the Estate Agents Ombudsmen)—investigate housing disputes. Not all apply the same criteria for determining cases or adopt the same working practices. The interface between ombudsmen and the courts can cause problems. The fact that ombudsmen's decisions are not at present generally enforceable in the courts raises questions about the extension of their role into the private sector. The Law Commission issues paper asks: what is the role of ombudsmen in a proportionate system for resolving housing disputes? And what is the potential for developing their current roles? Should they be brought together into a single organisation? Or should they remain separate?

Mediation involves an agreement between parties to a dispute to settle the dispute with the help of a neutral third party (a mediator). This may result in solutions that a court could not have ordered. The parties may be more likely to comply with an agreement they reached themselves than a decision imposed on them. Mediation may also maintain or restore ongoing relationships (for example, between neighbours). However, if parties feel coerced, the role of the courts in encouraging mediation can be controversial. Some commentators have concerns about the use of mediation in cases where there is an imbalance of power between the parties. The Commission is seeking to find out more about the potential use of mediation in the context of housing disputes.

Adjudicating Housing Disputes: Court or Tribunal?

A variety of courts (civil and criminal) and tribunals currently hear housing cases. There is a need for such bodies to provide, for example, authoritative interpretations of the law, hear appeals and comply with European Convention on Human Rights requirements for an independent and impartial tribunal. Their strengths include: independence, procedures based on transparency and fairness, and the delivery of authoritative, accurate outcomes. But they also involve what some regard as weaknesses: cost, delay, inequality of arms and failure to consider underlying issues. There have been calls for a specialist housing court or tribunal.

The Commission is seeking views on these matters, including whether the current sharp division between criminal and civil courts should remain sacrosanct in the context of housing disputes. For example, should there be separate civil and criminal proceedings for serious cases of harassment by landlords or of anti-social behaviour by tenants?

Next Steps

In the light of responses to the issues paper, the Law Commission will be developing more detailed proposals for reform, which are likely to be the subject of a further round of consultation in early 2007. The challenge for the Commission is to propose things that will make a difference but that can be afforded, at a time of severe constraint on the availability of public funding. It is likely that a number of specific proposals will need to be piloted and evaluated to see whether they produce better services at reduced cost. Then a business case can be made for their more widespread introduction.

THE RESPONSIBLE RENTING PROJECT

The third project being taken forward by the Law Commission arose out of the first two. The purpose of this project is to explore the mechanisms that might be used to ensure that parties to occupation contracts actually stick to their agreements. Many respondents to the Law Commission's initial consultation paper wondered how the rhetoric of the consumer protection approach could be realised in practice. They asked to what extent it can be expected that landlords (particularly private landlords) and contract-holders adhere to the terms of their agreements. It often does not happen now; why should it in the future? Getting an effective and appropriate regulatory framework is a key element to improving the image of the private rented sector.

As with the Housing Disputes project, this project is taking the Law Commission into new territory, this time into the very considerable academic literature on regulation. Research has looked at the different mechanisms that have been developed to regulate large-scale commercial activity such as environmental issues or health and safety at work. Applying this research to the very different context of the regulation of the landlord–occupier relationship will be wholly novel.[31]

At the time of writing, the project is still in its early stages, but the Commission anticipates that it will consider the role of law not just in

---

[31] For a first analysis of the approach that might be adopted, see M Partington (et al) (eds), 'Ensuring Compliance: The Case of the Private Rented Sector' (University of Bristol CMPO Working Paper No 06/148, 2006) <http://www.bris.ac.uk/Depts/CMPO/workingpapers/workingpapers.htm> (accessed 5 January 2007).

providing sanctions when things go wrong, but also in creating positive incentives to engage in good and sensible practice. It is often suggested that economic incentives are more effective than legal ones in altering behaviour. However, while financial incentives may be effective, they often need legislation to give effect to them. Thus, though novel, the project remains one of law reform, albeit not one that will necessarily lead to the drafting of a detailed Bill.

For example, if Government wanted to use housing benefit to promote good landlord behaviour, eg, by providing that landlords who undertake an accreditation course will receive preferential treatment in the provision of housing benefit, legislative change would be necessary. If the government wanted to create a national accreditation scheme for landlords or tenants (to replace the current plethora of local initiatives), legislation would likewise be required.

The Commission anticipates that many of its proposals are likely to build on initiatives that are already operating. These include: local authority landlord accreditation schemes, which reward landlords who demonstrate a commitment to accepting and abiding by defined standards of behaviour; tenant accreditation schemes, which also give tangible rewards to those, for example, who pay their rent promptly and regularly; landlord association schemes designed to promote good landlord practice; and agency schemes that are designed to promote good practice amongst letting agents. There will be clear links between these issues and the new landlord licensing schemes that have arisen following the passing of the Housing Act (2004).

The Commission will be examining who it is who currently act as regulators in the private rented market, including central government, local authorities and self-regulatory bodies. It may consider whether there is a need for a more overarching regulatory institution, for example an Office of Fair Housing. It will explore the extent to which self-regulation by the industry itself is possible, and how those large numbers of landlords and agents who are not currently part of any regulatory scheme may be encouraged to join.

The Law Commission will also be studying the impact of external bodies such as the Audit Commission on landlord behaviour, especially in the social rented sector. It will also consider the effect of policies such as those relating to Beacon Councils.[32] It will consider the role of the Council of Mortgage Lenders in relation to the policies it is seeking to develop in the context of the 'buy-to-let' market. It will be looking at any potential incentives that landlords' insurers may be able to offer.

---

[32] See information about the Beacon Scheme <http://www.idea-knowledge.gov.uk///.do?pageId=71697> accessed 1 June 2006.

It is likely that the Commission will want to examine how regulation works in other parts of the consumer market—for example the provision of consumer credit and financial services—and ask whether there are any lessons from those schemes that might apply to regulation of private landlords. The Commission will also look at developments in other countries. For example, in Scotland, a new National Landlord Registration scheme has recently been introduced. What are the lessons this initiative might have for regulation in England and Wales? By contrast, in Ireland substantial institutional investment in the provision of rented housing generally, including provision for those in social housing need, has not only resulted in the provision of new accommodation at affordable rents, but also put pressure on small landlords already in the market to improve the quality of the accommodation they let.

A Law Commission consultation paper on these issues is planned for early 2007.

CONCLUSIONS

As emphasised at the outset of this chapter, this is an account of work in progress. There are, perhaps, two particular lessons to which attention may be drawn here. First, in terms of its methodology, the Law Commission has tried within the limits of its resources to be far more proactive in its consultation methods in its housing reform projects than has usually been the case in the past. The Commission has received considerable praise for this. It is likely that there will be other projects in which it will be similarly proactively engaged. Its current work on the reform of the law on murder and its project on co-habitation are two cases in point.

Second, the housing reform project has expanded the scope of the work undertaken by the Law Commission. In particular, the disputes project and the regulation project are quite removed from the Commission's usual 'comfort zone' in black-letter law. There may be some who regard law reform as essentially about getting the substantive law as good as possible. The housing programme challenges that view, arguing that effective law reform should also consider how problems and disputes can be best resolved, and—even more fundamentally—how problems and disputes can be avoided.

However, as stressed throughout this chapter, implementation of the Commission's recommendations is not a foregone conclusion. Ministers and their officials must be convinced of the wider political value of the recommendations. The Commission has sought to argue for this as strongly as for the details of the recommendations it has made. Only time will tell whether others in government agree with those arguments.

II

Law and Equity

2

Equitable Co-ownership: Proprietary Rights in Name Only?

MARTIN DIXON

IN 1970–71, the law reports contained two House of Lords judgments
that were to have far-reaching legal, social and economic consequences.
As is well known, in both *Pettitt v Pettitt*[1] and *Gissing v Gissing*,[2] the
claimants were unsuccessful in their attempts to establish an equitable
interest in the property they once jointly occupied with the legal owner.
However, it is no exaggeration to say that the House of Lords analysis
generated a flood of litigation concerning implied co-ownership of family
homes, whereas previously there had been only a trickle.[3] Indeed, once the
dam had burst, the flow was irresistible, and even an attempt by their
Lordships in 1990 to limit successful claims did little to choke off the
litigation.[4]

The dramatic rise in owner-occupation from 1970[5]—and hence the
increased opportunity to make a claim—has undoubtedly fed the waters.
In fact, the litigation continues to this day, with *Oxley v Hiscock*[6]
reminding us that the judiciary are still searching for a definitive rationale
for the *Pettitt* principles, and *Crossley* v *Crossley*[7] illustrating how the
contest over home ownership is no longer confined to fights between lovers
but can embrace all members of a family, particularly if a parent has
appeared to favour one child to the exclusion of others,[8] or if the property

---

[1] [1970] AC 777.
[2] [1971] AC 88.
[3] Before these cases, claims were based largely on a strict 'purchase money' resulting trust,
and few involved land. For a rare example, see *Diwell v Farnes* [1959] 2 All ER 379.
[4] See *Lloyds Bank v Rosset* [1990] 1 All ER 1111.
[5] Surveys of English Housing, 1993–present, Office of the Deputy Prime Minister.
[6] [2004] 3 All ER 703.
[7] (2006) 1 FCR 655, [2005] EWCA Civ 1581.
[8] In *Crossely*, the dispute was between mother and son, and in *Day v Day*, Chancery
Division 23 June 2005 HC 04C00445, the entire family were involved.

is occupied by an extended family.[9] It is also apparent that these inter-family disputes—which for well-known reasons now rarely involve married couples per se[10]—represent merely the tip of the litigation iceberg.

The realisation that the implied creation of co-ownership could have very serious consequences for third parties generated consequential litigation on a massive scale as third parties (often mortgagees) and co-owners fought for priority over land—land that was, for mortgagees, security for money long spent and not repaid, but for co-owners was home and their principal if not sole economic asset. This litigation encompasses such seminal cases as *William and Glyn's Bank v Boland*,[11] *City of London Building Society v Flegg*,[12] *Abbey National Building Society v Cann*,[13] *Barclays Bank v O'Brien*[14] and *Royal Bank of Scotland v Etridge (No 2)*.[15] Such litigation seems almost as moves on a chess board, with first the co-owners and then the third party out-manoeuvring the other, only to find a new argument or a new approach wiping out the advantage.

At the same time as this jurisprudence was evolving, it also came to be accepted that the statutory machinery regulating co-ownership was itself outdated and simply failed to reflect the social and economic realities of the late twentieth century.[16] The concept of the trust for sale of land, with its necessary emphasis on disposal rather than retention, completely misrepresents the way in which co-owners think about their land and the way they use it. The original trust for sale of the 1925 property legislation was premised on the assumption that co-owned land is an investment to be liquidated as required by uninvolved trustees who are expressly appointed and are at least two in number. The further assumption was that the beneficiaries have no permanent need for possession and would be happy to take their interest in whatever financial investment the trustee chooses.

Although this most certainly did not represent either the reality of trusteeship or the needs of the beneficiaries within (at least) the 30 years before 1996, the statutory trusts still required a sale on relationship breakdown, just when at least one of the co-owners might very well have

---

[9] For example, *Birmingham Midshires Mortgage Services Ltd v Sabherwal* (2000) 80 P&CR 256.

[10] See the property adjustment jurisdiction on divorce, judicial separation or on dissolution of a Civil Partnership. Where a third party, such as mortgagee, is in issue, the claimant may well be the partner of the mortgagor, but it is often the third party that disputes the existence of the equitable interest: *Lloyds Bank v Rosset* [1990] 1 All ER 1111.

[11] [1981] AC 487.

[12] [1987] 3 All ER 435.

[13] [1990] 1 All ER 1085.

[14] [1993] 4 All ER 417.

[15] [2001] 4 All ER 449.

[16] The use of the settlement under the Settled Land Act (1925) was also reminiscent of a different age and created its own set of problems, especially when land accidentally came within its ambit: *Ungurian v Lesnoff* [1990] Ch 206.

needed residential stability. Sale at that point might have been avoidable if the court had had unfettered powers to make subsidiary orders regarding such matters as the payment of rent or equitable compensation.[17] Moreover, the implied creation of co-ownership in *Pettitt* and *Gissing*, which generatied a trust with only a single trustee for sale, fitted awkwardly within the legislative framework,[18] to say nothing of the apparent denial of proprietary status of equitable co-ownership because of the doctrine of conversion.[19] Arguably, it was justifiable in 1925 to utilise the trust for sale to force equitable interests to take effect in purchase money, but there was precious little that could be said in its favour in 1996.[20] Even overreaching, the cousin of the doctrine of conversion, which in 1925 was so urgently needed to restore the alienability of land, had lost some of its justification by the time of the Trusts of Land and Appointment of Trustees Act (TOLATA) (1996), even to the point that the Law Commission contemplated its emasculation.[21]

Of course, before the entry into force of the TOLATA on 1 January 1996, judicial inventiveness had tempered the practical application of the trust as a device requiring sale and had given limited proprietary effect to equitable co-ownership interests in the sense of recognising their ability in some circumstances to keep third parties out of possession. For example, the courts had adopted a 'secondary purpose' doctrine justifying retention of co-owned land in limited circumstances[22] and had assumed a closely

---

[17] Sale was the default solution *whenever* the trustees could not agree unanimously to postpone sale, although cases of forced sale at the behest of a trustee when there is no relationship breakdown are elusive.

[18] See Law of Property Act (1925) s 34, which appears not to contemplate implied trusts at all.

[19] *Irani Finance Ltd v Singh* [1971] Ch 59.

[20] When moving what became the Trusts of Land and Appointment of Trustees Act (TOLATA) (1996), Lord Mackay of Drumadoon noted:

> The trust for sale mechanism is not appropriate to the conditions of modern home ownership, which represents the majority of jointly-owned real property, since it is based on an assumption that property which is not subjected to a strict settlement is intended as an investment rather than as a home, to be bought and sold as market conditions demand, with the beneficiaries being interested in the proceeds of sale rather than the property for its own sake.

Hansard, 1 March 1996, col 1717.

[21] Law Commission, 'Overreaching: Beneficiaries in Occupation' (Law Comm No 188, 1989). These proposals were abandoned, and the Land Registration Act (2002) assumes that overreaching should always be encouraged. The Form A restriction requires money to be paid to at least two trustees, although it can be used by a beneficiary with a sole trustee to alert a purchaser that equitable co-ownership exists: Land Registration Act (2002) s 43(1)(c) and Land Registration Rules (2003) Rule 93(a). It is arguable that an equitable owner also is able to enter a restriction requiring her consent before a disposition is made (see Standard Form N), but the preliminary and untested view of the Land Registry, not currently shared by the present author, is that this would not be permitted because its effect would be to destroy overreaching. That of course would be the point.

[22] *Jones v Challenger* [1961] 1 QB 176.

defined power to order the payment of 'compensation' to non-occupying co-owners as an adjunct to exercising some control over the enjoyment of possession.[23] Moreover, in *Boland*, the House of Lords had accepted the proprietary status of equitable co-ownership for the purpose of establishing an overriding interest within (then) section 70(1)(g) of the Land Registration Act (1925).

Nevertheless, the underlying theory remained that these rights were merely personalty, and not only did this encourage the idea that sale was always the best option—even assuming a judicial discretion to refuse sale under (now defunct) section 30 of the Law of Property Act (1925)—but the 'truth' could surface and have practical consequences.[24] This legislative framework fundamentally misrepresented the reality of how ordinary people use their land and had to be tweaked by the judiciary in order to fit modern circumstances. This not only required the judiciary to usurp the legislative function but also did little to generate respect or understanding of the law among landowners themselves.

It is easy to appreciate how co-owners in such a system might well regard the law with scepticism after being told that their real interest is not in land but in money and that they are under a duty to sell the land (after having just purchased it), which they could be compelled to do by the other co-owners, largely irrespective of their needs at the time. To explain further (although doubtless no conveyancer ever did) that the owners were also trustees of the legal title, usually holding on trust for themselves but possibly later also for others,[25] might well convince our co-owners that they were living in a parallel universe.[26]

In essence then, although the enactment of the TOLATA (1996) regularised the developments already wrought by case law, the overall intention of the legislation was to re-tune the way we think about and deal with co-owned land. This is the central theme of the Law Commission Report on which the TOLATA (1996) is based.[27] That Report makes very clear not only that the TOLATA (1996) was intended to place the powers and duties of the trustees in relation to the land and the equitable owners on a statutory footing and to broaden the discretionary powers of the court, but also that it was designed to assert the essentially proprietary nature of equitable co-ownership.

---

[23]   *Dennis v McDonald* [1982] 1 All ER 590.
[24]   See *Perry v Phoenix Assurance* [1988] 1 WLR 940.
[25]   As in *Flegg* (note 12 above).
[26]   In 'Trusts of Land' (Law Comm No 181, HC 391, 1989), the Law Commission commented: 'the point here is not simply that it should be easier for practitioners to explain the law to their clients, but also that co-ownership should take a form which non-lawyers can make sense of for themselves' [3.5]. See also [3.1–3.4].
[27]   *Ibid.* See also, in part, Law Commission, 'Overreaching: Beneficiaries in Occupation' (Report No 188, HC 61, 1989).

This was the natural counterpart to the reformulation of the trust for sale as a trust of land, and to make sure, section 3 of the TOLATA (1996) abolished the doctrine of conversion in relation to any express trust for sale. This was enough to ensure that equitable interests assumed a proprietary status in theory and hopefully in fact. Further, this status was (and is) unaffected by the ability of a purchaser to continue to overreach equitable interests in appropriate circumstances. Overreaching was never the reason why, pre-TOLATA (1996), equitable interests were in theory personalty. That was caused by the duty of sale, consequent on the existence of the trust *for* sale, with equity assuming that 'what ought to be done' was done. In contrast, overreaching is designed to give the purchaser priority over equitable interests, but it does not affect the status of those interests as 'land' until overreached—and never did so.[28]

This is a matter of some importance. It is clear that the possibility of overreaching per se does not affect the proprietary status of equitable co-ownership, and neither should it influence the courts when determining matters of priority between third parties and co-owners, whether this arises in relation to the court's discretionary powers under section 14 of the TOLATA (1996) or otherwise.[29] The fact that an equitable owner *could have* been overreached, had conditions permitted, should not be taken to imply that preference should be given to a third party in dispute with an innocent co-owner[30] when the third party has not been able to overreach, especially if this would destroy the possessory priority of the co-owners. That would be to misunderstand the nature of overreaching.

Yet despite the assertion of the proprietary character of equitable co-ownership by the TOLATA (1996)—indeed, despite the fact that this was the point of the Act—it is not at all clear that full proprietary effect, in terms of both possession as well as first call on the proceeds of sale, is being given to these interests when disputes arise, even when a dispute is with a third party who has not overreached. It is the purpose of this chapter to analyse whether equitable co-ownership truly is proprietary in the sense of protecting the possession of the co-owner or whether, despite much case law and the TOLATA (1996) itself, these interests are still treated as the temporary physical manifestation of an essentially liquid investment—as cash, not land. To this end, I will analyse the case law since *Pettitt* and *Gissing* at those points where the interest of one of the co-owners clashed with the interest of a third party. This provides the true

---

[28] See Law Commission, 'Trusts of Land' (Law Comm No 181, HC 391, 1989) [3.4] for a full analysis.

[29] Examples of when the issue arises outside of section 14 are the implied consent cases, see text accompanying note 84 below.

[30] Innocent in the sense of not being responsible for the circumstances that led to the dispute about priority and possession.

test of whether such interests are proprietary. As Lord Wilberforce said in *National Provincial Bank v Ainsworth*,

> Before a right or interest can be admitted into the character of property, or of a right affecting property, it must be definable, identifiable by third parties, capable in its nature of assumption by third parties and have some degree of permanence or stability.[31]

Is this true of equitable co-ownership rights?

A MOVE AWAY FROM THE PROPERTY RIGHT?

The trail of litigation leading from *Pettitt* and *Gissing* is quite remarkable. It had, of course, always been possible for a sole owner to grant an equitable interest to, for example, his lover by the simple expedient of declaring a trust in writing within section 53(1) of the Law of Property Act (1925). That is, it was *possible* but rarely done, unless the parties were responding to some social or economic imperative, such as the need to minimise tax, plan retirement or regularise affairs between themselves prior to some expected change in their circumstances. Consequently, when these two House of Lords decisions made it plain that equitable shares could be acquired informally, based around specific types of conduct, the litigation stream began to flow.

At first, a claim would usually be made on the occasion of a breakdown in the parties' relationship, particularly if the disputants were not married or otherwise did not want to rely on the court's property adjustment powers on divorce or judicial separation.[32] Naturally enough, the large volume of cases in the years immediately after *Pettitt* resulted in doctrinal uncertainty and much vagueness about the precise factual circumstances in which a resulting or constructive trust could arise—a vagueness not quite expelled by Lord Bridge's re-examination of the principles in *Lloyds Bank v Rosset*.[33] This relative lack of certainty would not have been too serious if the only persons interested were the potential co-owners themselves. The *Pettitt* principles could and did operate to re-distribute the capital value of the land *inter partes*. However, once this 'simple' re-distribution of personalty was recognised as also encompassing the reallocation of proprietary rights that could affect third parties (even before this status was regularised by the TOLATA (1996)), the cycle of litigation gathered more

---

[31] [1965] AC 1175, 1247–8. This description of the nature of a proprietary right comes with well-known caveats, but it serves for present purposes.

[32] The cases also came at a time when owner-occupation began to boom as a consequence of, inter alia, changing social aspirations, heavy regulation of the private rented sector and more readily available mortgage finance.

[33] [1990] 1 All ER 1111. See MP Thompson, 'Establishing an Interest in the Home' [1990] *Conveyancer and Property Lawyer* 314.

pace. Thus began a trail of litigation that sought to define precisely the circumstances in which an equitable interest could have practical proprietary effect against a third party (usually a mortgagee) and, in turn, how this affects a lender's ability to recover money lent on what might well be a defective security.

ROUND 1: THE CO-OWNERS AND THEIR PROPRIETARY CLAIM

Some 25 plus years after the event, it is easy to forget the furore that greeted the decision in *William & Glyn's Bank v Boland*.[34] The recognition of de facto proprietary status for equitable co-ownership was perhaps overdue, but the realisation that an interest generated under *Pettitt* could not be overreached by a sole trustee and might therefore constitute an overriding interest so as to take priority over a later mortgage, was thought by some to herald disaster. Much money had been lent on the security of apparently solely owned residential property, but a *Pettitt* interest could arise informally—perhaps even in a way that the *claimant* did not realise at the time—and lenders had no consistent practice of seeking to discover before mortgage whether anyone was in actual occupation.[35] It thus became relatively common for lenders to find their proprietary security eroded by a *Boland* claim,[36] a claim that they had not considered when the money was lent and that they had taken no steps to neutralise.

Such was the concern at *Boland* that the Law Commission considered its reversal by statute.[37] Moreover, there is no doubt that many co-owners saw the combination of the *Pettitt* and *Boland* rules as an opportunity to escape from what turned out to be imprudent mortgages. The words of Fox LJ in *Midland Bank v Dobson* in 1986 that 'assertions made by a husband and wife as to a common intention formed 30 years ago regarding joint ownership, of which there is no contemporary evidence and which happens to accommodate their current need to defeat the claims of a creditor, must be received by the courts with caution'[38] are as true now as they were then. Nevertheless, despite these words of caution and the uncertainties over the reach of the *Pettitt* rules,[39] the period immediately following *Boland* saw full proprietary effect being given to equitable co-ownership.

---

[34] [1981] AC 487.

[35] Consent letters were in use by some prudent lenders. See *Midland Bank v Dobson* [1986] 1 FLR 171, 173.

[36] Of course, the personal liability of the borrower to repay remained and in later years this was used to circumvent the proprietary block of *Boland*; see below.

[37] Law Commission, 'The Implications of *William & Glyn's Bank Ltd v Boland*' (Report No 115 Cmnd 8636, 1982).

[38] [1986] 1 FLR 171, 174.

[39] See for example, *Burns v Burns* [1984] FLR 216.

ROUND 2: OVERREACHING WHEN THE TIME IS RIGHT

The determinedly proprietary status of informally created co-ownership rights after *Boland* was a revelation—but was it a miracle? Did the decision mean that equitable rights would *always* have proprietary effect so that a purchaser-lender could be bound in any circumstance where it did not seek the agreement of the non-legal owner to a transaction?[40] Such was argued in *City of London Building Society v Flegg*[41] and accepted by the Court of Appeal, before its rejection by the House of Lords. Although today the limitations placed by *Flegg* on *Boland* seem axiomatic, the general wave of relief in the conveyancing and wider academic community at their Lordships' decision to preserve 'two-trustee' overreaching was real enough.[42]

Significantly, however, the judgments in *Flegg*, particularly those of Lord Templeman and Lord Oliver, do not deny the proprietary nature of the equitable interest. They concentrate instead on the statutory scheme of overreaching and the provisions of the Law of Property Act (1925) in an attempt to marry section 14 of the Law of Property Act (1925) with the overreaching machinery. In this respect, Lord Templeman made it quite plain that the effect of overreaching is to remove the equitable owner's right to possession in virtue of his or her interest and to substitute instead a right enforceable against the trustees for a share of the proceeds of sale or mortgage. In essence, the interest becomes a right in the equity of redemption, and overreaching is seen as a way to alter the priority of interests—*not* the nature of those interests.[43]

For his part, Lord Oliver went on to spell out the fundamental distinction between this and *Boland*, both in terms of legal principle and economic fact. He stated:

> If it be the case, as the Court of Appeal held, that the payment by the appellants in the instant case to two properly constituted trustees for sale, holding upon the statutory trusts, provides no sensible distinction from the ratio of the decision of this House in Boland's case, the legislative policy of the 1925 legislation of

---

[40]   By definition, a legal co-owner would be a party to the mortgage, or else the charge could not take effect as a legal mortgage. Thus, in those cases where consent to the mortgage has been forged, no legal mortgage exists and the lender must rely on an equitable charge of the forge's beneficial interest in the property. This leads usually to a section 14 TOLATA application for sale. See, for example, *National Westminster Bank v Achampong* [2003] EWCA Civ 487, [2003] 2 P & CR DG 11.

[41]   [1987] 3 All ER 435.

[42]   WJ Swadling, 'The Conveyancer's Revenge' [1987] *Conveyancer and Property Lawyer* 451; RJ Smith, 'Trusts for Sale and Registered Land: Orthodoxy Returns' (1987) 103 *Law Quarterly Review* 520; and S Gardner, '"Bleak House" Latest: Law Lords Dispel Fog?' (1998) 51 *Modern Law Review* 365. Note also that in *Flegg*, the overreaching mortgage was not in fact registered within the priority period.

[43]   [1988] AC 54 at 74.

keeping the interests of beneficiaries behind the curtain and confining the investigation of title to the devolution of the legal estate will have been substantially reversed by judicial decision and financial institutions advancing money on the security of land will face hitherto unsuspected hazards, whether they are dealing with registered or unregistered land.[44]

The decision in *Flegg* is not compromised by the enactment of the TOLATA (1996)[45] or the Land Registration Act (2002), despite the earlier knee-jerk and contradictory reaction of the Law Commission's suggestion that *Flegg* should be reversed (or at least modified) by statute.[46] Indeed, we might say that the principle has been extended judicially by the decision in *State Bank of India v Sood*[47] that overreaching may occur on execution of a mortgage by two trustees even if no capital money is immediately payable under that mortgage.[48] Without wishing to draw general conclusions from *Sood* alone, that decision does suggest a willingness to interpret the legislation against giving full *priority effect* to the proprietary nature of equitable co-ownership if this is justified on wider public interest grounds—such as the stability of the domestic lending market. After all, *Sood* could easily have decided that overreaching did not occur unless capital money was actually paid to two trustees, but that would have compromised many existing, standard drawdown mortgages.[49]

Be that as it may, neither *Flegg* nor *Sood* challenge the theory that these equitable rights are proprietary in substance; rather they make it plain that the practical effect of this status can be avoided by appropriate use of the statutory machinery. This is significant not only because it reminds us that commercial lenders really should not, some 25-odd years after *Boland*, find themselves caught by an unregistered interest that overrides through the discoverable actual occupation of a 'mere' equitable owner,[50] but also because in the absence of overreaching we might expect the dormant proprietary status of equitable interests to bite back. After all, if overreaching reverses priorities without altering status, the effect of proprietary status should be felt when overreaching is denied.

---

[44] *Ibid*, 77.

[45] M Dixon, 'Overreaching and the Trusts of Land and Appointment of Trustees Act (1996)' [2000] *Conveyancer and Property Lawyer* 267; G Battersby and G Ferris, 'Overreaching and the Trusts of Land and Appointment of Trustees Act (1996): A Reply to Mr Dixon' [2001] *Conveyancer and Property Lawyer* 221.

[46] Law Commission, 'Overreaching: Beneficiaries in Occupation' (Report No 188, HC 61, 1989). The Commission had earlier considered the reversal of *Boland*.

[47] [1997] Ch 276.

[48] This implies that if money is payable on a transaction but is not paid, then overreaching does not occur.

[49] That is, as in *Sood*, where the mortgage secures a fluctuating overdraft that may never be used but which has a pre-set limit.

[50] Land Registration Act (2002), Schedule 3, para 2.

Finally though, a word of caution and a re-calibration of perspective: it remains relatively unusual for residential property to be held on trust by two trustees for *different* equitable owners, even if one or both of the trustees also has an equitable share. *Flegg* and *Sood* represent an uncommon factual scenario. The norm for residential property is either two legal owners holding on trust for themselves absolutely, or a sole owner holding for others (as well as himself), as in *Boland*. Of course, the chance of another equitable owner emerging in a 'two-trustee' situation will increase if more single dwellings are occupied by extended families, and we have already seen how such equitable owners effectively have little to show for their proprietary interests, as in *Birmingham Midshires Mortgage Services Ltd v Sabherwal*[51] *National Westminster Bank v Malhan*.[52] Nevertheless, we should be wary of shaping our property law to meet situations that do not arise commonly, especially if this is at the expense of certainty in those situations that arise much more frequently.[53]

ROUND 3: DEALING WITH THE CAUSE, NOT THE SYMPTOM—*LLOYDS BANK V ROSSET*[54]

Even though *Flegg* revealed the limitations of *Boland*, the impact of *Flegg* on everyday mortgage lending should not be overstated. Reported examples of sole trustees rushing out to find a co-trustee in order to be able to overreach are non-existent, and it is rare for two trustees to hold on trust for anyone but themselves. Thus, it still remained true post-*Flegg* that the proprietary quality of informally acquired equitable co-ownership could wreak havoc with a mortgagee's security. Given that it was now clear that this was not a situation likely to be altered by statute, and given the potential impact on mortgage lending, one way for a lender to deal with 'the problem' was to treat the cause and not the symptom by challenging the existence of an interest in the first place.

In such a climate, and even discounting the benefit of hindsight, it was inevitable that the House of Lords would be called on to revisit the *Pettitt* and *Gissing* principles. The very fact of the existence of *Boland* would propel an unfortunate—or incompetent[55]—mortgagee to challenge the

---

[51]   (2000) 80 P & CR 256.

[52]   [2004] EWHC 847, [2004] 2 P & CR DG 9. In the event, the claimant failed to establish an equitable interest.

[53]   Although no reason has been given for the quiet abandonment of the suggestion in Law Commission Report No 188 that there should be a statutory reversal of *Flegg* (see note 21 above), perhaps a recognition of the reality of how co-owned land usually is held played a part.

[54]   [1991] 1 AC 107.

[55]   Mortgagees would be *unfortunate* if they could not have predicted the interest nor been alerted by actual occupation; but they would be *incompetent* mortgagees if they had not

basis on which equitable interests were being awarded with some generosity in county courts across the jurisdiction. Indeed, not only did the decision in *Lloyds Bank v Rosset* come at a time when Parliament was tightening up the general formality rules concerning the grant of interests in land,[56] it was also preceded by a number of decisions that pushed the boundaries laid down in *Pettitt*.[57] The result was uncertainty, not only the manageable uncertainty suffered by co-occupiers in dispute with each other, but the rather more disruptive uncertainty affecting lenders who could not predict with any real conviction when an interest would arise.

It is not the purpose of this essay to explore the extent to which *Rosset* narrowed the previous law or merely returned it to orthodoxy after a period of creativity in the Court of Appeal. That is for others,[58] as is the question of the significance of the fact that the judgment was given in a case between a third party and a claimant, rather than in a dispute between co-owners themselves. What is important for present purposes is that Lord Bridge set out with some firmness the circumstances in which a claim to an interest by reason of constructive trust will succeed.[59] It is a judgment that is meant to circumscribe and confine the law within *relatively* certain limits. Indeed, the fact that Mrs Rossett herself was unsuccessful, despite much that *could* have supported an interest if seen through different glasses, illustrates how the trail of litigation from *Pettitt* has now meandered a little further in favour of the third party lender. If it is just that little bit more difficult for the claimant to establish a proprietary interest, lenders will escape the effects of an overriding interest just that little bit more often.

ROUND 4: THE 'PURCHASE MORTGAGEE' PRESERVES PRIORITY

At first blush, the *Boland* principle appears destructive of at least part of the lender's secured interest over the property, and many did indeed find

considered the possibility of an adverse equitable interest or had failed to take proper steps to neutralise it. The cases suggest that the majority of lenders fell into the second category. See M Dixon, 'The Reform of Property Law and the Land Registration Act 2002: A Risk Assessment' in A Hudson (ed), *New Perspectives on Property Law: Obligations and Restitution* (London, Cavendish Publishing, 2004) 129.

[56] See the Law of Property Act (1989) from which, of course, constructive trusts are exempt: section 2(5).

[57] See, for example, M Dixon, 'Co-ownership Trusts: The Denning Legacy' (1988) 5 *Denning Law Journal* 27.

[58] See, inter alia, C Rotherham, 'The Property Rights of Unmarried Couples' [2004] *Conveyancer and Property Lawyer* 268; MP Thompson, 'The Obscurity of Common Intention' [2003] *Conveyancer and Property Lawyer* 411; N Glover and P Todd, 'The Myth of Common Intention' (1996) 16 *Legal Studies* 325.

[59] Resulting trusts were not an issue in the case, although these are more or less confined to circumstances where payments are made to the acquisition at the time of the acquisition: *Curley v Parks* [2005] 1 P & CR DG15.

that they had taken mortgages secured over significantly less of the equity than they calculated when the money was lent. Just how much of the debt the mortgagee was likely to recover of course depended on the extent of the interest established by the occupying partner (and *Rosset* had a hand in reining in the claims) and, crucially, on the mortgagee's ability to force a sale by reversing the possessory priorities in the land.[60] In addition, however, it soon became clear that *Boland* necessarily was limited by normal rules concerning the priority of property interests. Claimants who sought to assert an overriding interest against a lender were naturally defeated if their interest arose after the valid creation of the security, or if they had consented to the priority of a later security before it was executed.[61] What is more interesting for present purposes, however, is the gloss placed on these fundamentals by the judgment in *Abbey National Building Society v Cann*,[62] which was decided at the same time as *Rosset* and followed in part *Paddington Building Society v Mendelsohn*.[63] The judgment in *Cann* illustrates, even more than *Rosset* and *Flegg*, that the House of Lords was willing, even determined, to minimise the proprietary impact of equitable co-ownership in favour of a preference for stability in the domestic lending market.[64]

First, the House of Lords in *Cann* established not only that the relevant time for 'actual occupation' necessary to trigger an overriding interest is the time of completion or transfer of the legal estate (rather than its registration[65]) but also that as a *matter of law*, a mortgage used for the purchase of property must occur simultaneously with that purchase. This closed the *scintilla temporis* and made it impossible for a claimant to establish an overriding interest by virtue of actual occupation against a mortgagee providing the purchase money for the house.[66]

---

[60] See text accompanying note 84 below.

[61] See now ss 28 and 29 of the Land Registration Act (2002), which explicitly embraces the principle of priority of property interests rather than voidness.

[62] [1991] 1 AC 56.

[63] (1985) 50 P & CR 244.

[64] [1991] AC 56 at 76. Lord Oliver's judgment begins: 'My Lords, this appeal raises yet again what has become a familiar hazard for banks and building societies advancing money on the security of real property.'

[65] This is likely to be the position under the Land Registration Act (2002), despite the emphasis in ss 25–7 and Schedule 2 on completion of a disposition by registration. However, given that the interest overrides at registration, albeit triggered by actual occupation at completion, what then would happen if the mortgage failed to register their charge at all? The answer might be that, of the two equities (the now equitable mortgage and the equitable interest), the 'first in time prevails', and this will be the mortgage because there is no *scintilla temporis*.

[66] *Church of England Building Society v Piskor* [1954] Ch 553 is overruled. It is not clear how close in time the mortgage must be to the purchase to gain this legal priority. Is it enough that the mortgage was intended to finance the purchase? Or is it also necessary for it to be executed close in point of time—which, of course, is a prerequisite of domestic lending unless there is some error in the transactions?

Both of these interpretations can, of course, be justified as necessary for the fair and efficient functioning of the land registration system. Closing the 'registration gap' represents a judicial response to an unavoidable administrative defect in the system—the lag between completion and registration[67]; and the close of the *scintilla temporis* recognises the economic reality that a purchase of land often simply is not possible without a mortgage and that a mortgage should not be compromised by an adverse interest that could not have been discovered by inspection of the property. Indeed, we should remember that (assuming all the facts lay with Mrs Cann) closing the registration gap would not have been enough to protect the Abbey National had it not also been for their Lordships' conclusion in respect of the *scintilla temporis*.

Nevertheless, and without wishing to challenge the economic sense of the decision in *Cann*, there is no doubt that it treats equitable co-ownership as interests which, *if at all possible,* should be subservient to third-party claims against the land itself, particularly those of lenders. It would have been perfectly possible to have concluded that the legislation (the old Land Registration Act (1925)) meant literally what it said and that registration of a dealing was the appropriate time for assessing all aspects of priority, albeit that Mrs Cann was doomed after the *scintilla temporis* argument. That this was not beyond the realms of possibility nor without potential effects, is illustrated by the later case of *Barclays Bank v Zaroovabli* where a lease arsing after a mortgage took priority over the charge as an overriding interest under section 70(1)(k) of the Land Registration Act (1925) by reason of the latter's failure to register.[68]

Secondly, although technically obiter, the House of Lords in *Cann* went on to confirm the principle established by *Paddington* that there are circumstances when an equitable co-owner will be taken to have impliedly consented to the priority of a mortgage. Although, as in *Cann* itself,[69] it is clear that consent flows from the equitable owner's implied authority to seek a mortgage and thus their acceptance that the relevant land could only be purchased with the aid of the mortgage,[70] it is not clear in what other circumstances consent can be implied. Does an equitable owner consent to the mortgage simply because she knows of it and does not object? Or is it necessary for the equitable owner to participate in some way in the acquisition of the mortgage or even in the decision about how to spend the funds released by the mortgage before consent will be implied?

---

[67] A lag that will be removed only under e-conveyancing.

[68] [1997] Ch 321.

[69] See the discussion in the Court of Appeal in [1989] 2 FLR 265 and Lord Oliver's approval of the judgment of Dillon LJ on this point in [1991] 1 AC 56, 94.

[70] Even if, as it appears in *Cann*, the amount actually borrowed was more than the equitable owner believed was required.

This issue has not be fully resolved in the case law, probably because of the practice of seeking the express consent of *all* persons who might possibly have an interest in the property. But there is no doubt that the ready finding of implied consent is designed to minimise the proprietary impact of equitable interests. Once again, it allows a lender to avoid the binding effect of an equitable interest not because of steps taken by the lender, but by reason of a sympathetic analysis of the law and a close look at the conduct of the equitable owner

ROUND 5: SAVING THE INCOMPETENT RE-MORTGAGEE

It is clear that there are powerful legal and economic arguments in favour of protecting the position of a lender who provides finance for the purchase of the very property in which a claimant later attempts to establishing a priority proprietary interest. What, however, of the lender who is willing to provide the same or greater finance by way of re-mortgage? In such a case, if the equitable co-owner has established a proprietary interest prior to the re-mortgage and is in discoverable actual occupation within Schedule 3, paragraph 2 of the Land Registration Act (2002),[71] the ordinary principles of registered conveyancing require that the re-mortgagee either overreaches or seeks consent in order to ensure the priority of its charge. This is because the re-mortgagee that properly registers its charge is a disponee for value within section 29 of the Land Registration Act (2002) and takes the charge subject only to registered protected interests and unregistered interests that override.

For the competent lender, this will cause no difficulty at all. The absence of two trustees signals the inability to overreach, and the possibility of an equitable interest adverse to the mortgagee will either be revealed through an inspection of the land[72] or be immaterial—after all, the actual occupation must be 'discoverable' within paragraph 2, Schedule 3 of the Land Registration Act (1925) to trigger an overriding interest. Thus, a re-mortgaging lender can takes steps to preserve its priority or simply not lend. It is submitted that such a solution, had it been adopted in re-mortgage cases, would have given due weight to the proprietary nature of the equitable owner's interest without burdening the competent lender.

---

[71] It makes no difference to the analysis that actual occupation under section 70(1)(g) of the Land Registration Act (1925) need not have been discoverable, save only that the lender is even more protected under the 2002 Act and thus, for this author, deserves even less sympathy if they lose priority.

[72] Or through an answer to enquiries. We should not forget that at the time the mortgage is executed, most people do not anticipate problems and answer freely. Of course, the legal owner may wish to hide the truth from both lender and co-owner, as in *Prestidge* itself. See discussion of the case below.

However, this was not the path chosen, and the cases reveal a much more timid response that again fails to recognise the fundamental proprietary nature of the rights of equitable owners. As the earlier case of *Equity & Law Home Loans Ltd v Prestidge*[73] made clear, a re-mortgagee who fails to secure priority for its charge by the (relatively straightforward) means available to it may nevertheless succeed to the priority enjoyed by the original mortgagee despite its own risky lending practices. The lender is rescued because, luckily, it has offered a re-mortgage. *Prestidge* itself seeks to explain this on the basis of imputed or 'transferred' consent whereby the equitable owner's consent to the original mortgage is somehow made available to the re-mortgagee. However, a better explanation—assuming we are content to accept the premise at all—is based on subrogation, and this is found in the later cases,[74] with the re-mortgagee stepping into the shoes, and hence the priority, of the original mortgagee because the former's funds were used to redeem the latter's debt.[75] This would mean that come default, the property would be available to the re-mortgagee, and it would not matter whether the re-mortgagee has succeeded to the original mortgagee's priority through express or implied consent or simply because the original mortgage was 'first in time' under the law as interpreted in *Cann*.

The ability of a re-mortgagee to triumph over the proprietary interest of the co-owner by use of subrogation (or worse, by some notion of transferred consent), even though the re-mortgagee had every opportunity to secure priority by conventional means, illustrates clearly that when it comes to the crunch, courts are not prepared to follow through the logic that equitable co-ownership interests are truly proprietary. No doubt courts are influenced by the argument that to decide otherwise would be to give a 'windfall' to the equitable owner who was bound by the original mortgage but might not now be bound by the interest of the re-mortgagee who paid off the original debt. Yet why should the re-mortgagee enjoy the 'windfall' of priority when its own lending practices have led it into the problem? It is lenders in these cases who can preserve the priority of their mortgages by adopting good lending practices. Would such consideration be shown to an inattentive purchaser if another type of property right was in issue—perhaps an inconvenient easement or restrictive covenant? Surely, the whole point about proprietary rights is that they can give an advantage to the right holder simply because they *exist* as rights in the land. A third party takes the risk of losing priority to a proprietary right if the third

---

[73] [1992] 1 WLR 137.

[74] For example, *Locabail (UK) Ltd v Bayfield Properties Ltd (No.1)* [2000] QB 451.

[75] See M Dixon, 'Consenting Away Proprietary Rights' in E Cooke (ed), *Modern Studies in Property Law, Volume 1* (Oxford, Hart Publishing, 2001).

party fails to use a recognised method of protecting itself—except it seems if the offending right exists behind a trust of land.

ROUND 6: EXPRESS CONSENT—SIN AND REDEMPTION

In essence, the effect of this series of decisions was, first, to limit the practical effect of *Boland* to cases of post-acquisition mortgages where the equitable owner's interest had arisen before the mortgage was executed,[76] and then to deny its effect further in those cases where the equitable owner had consented either through conduct or expressly when asked to do so by the mortgagee as a condition of providing the money. Not surprisingly, competent lenders would prefer not to rely on implied consent, nor hope that the claimant falls foul of the stricter acquisition rules of *Rosset*, but instead seek blanket express consent from all persons occupying the land without enquiring too closely into their status.

As a matter of principle, this practice should have been perfectly adequate to protect lenders, premised as it was on the assumption that an owner of a proprietary interest can effectively waive its priority (although not its proprietary status) *inter partes*. As is well known, however, the effectiveness of the practice of taking express consent as a matter of routine was challenged with considerable success on the grounds of undue influence. It is not necessary here to rehearse the decision in *Barclays Bank v O'Brien*,[77] save to say that it resulted in a torrent of litigation as equitable owners sought to deprive lenders of priority by seeking first to establish that no real consent was given and, secondly, to assert as a consequence the existence of an overriding interest in virtue of their proprietary interest. Here then, writ large, we see the effect of the decisions in *Pettitt* and *Gissing*. The informal acquisition of a proprietary interest, albeit one whose possessory priority had been cut down by case law, could be used to compromise the security of a lender who had neither overreached nor appreciated that the consent would be valid only if it had been obtained in a manner approved of by the court. *Pettitt* leads directly to *O'Brien*, and *O'Brien* leads to a litigation industry.

It is difficult to assess the true state of affairs revealed by *O'Brien*. For sure, mortgagees found themselves in difficulty despite having done all that they believed was necessary to obtain consent, and this author has more sympathy for lenders caught out, *post hoc* the loan, by the *O'Brien* guidelines than for those relying on the lifeboat of subrogation. However, does the volume of litigation tell the true story? It seems unlikely that *so*

---

[76] For example, with mortgages for property improvements or to finance a business venture of one or both of the co-owners.

[77] [1994] 1 AC 180.

many equitable owners as the number of post *O'Brien* cases suggest really had been pressured by their domestic partners into giving consent. More likely, perhaps, the formulation of the *O'Brien* principles made it easy for a claim of undue influence to succeed whatever the truth of the allegations.

In essence, their Lordships in *O'Brien* had held that once the claim of undue influence is raised, the lender must show either that there was no such influence (an almost impossible task unless the lender is familiar with the details of the parties' private lives) or that steps were taken to avert the risk. Given that when many of these mortgages were executed, lenders simply were not aware of the need to ensure that the other co-owner received a *certain type* of advice, it was not surprising that *O'Brien* came to be regarded as the most convenient way for an equitable owner to assert possessory priority over the lender and thereby to protect at least part of the family's asset.[78] It is impossible to determine how many of these claims were manufactured by colluding parties in a deliberate attempt to isolate some of the property from the security of the mortgagee, but it must have been a great temptation.

For a while, this swing of the pendulum back in favour of equitable owners had the effect of degrading the value of many mortgages, and it also reminds us that the law does not always assume that property rights can be surrendered lightly. More than anything then, it was perhaps recognition of the damage being caused to the mortgage market by the decision in *O'Brien* that led the House of Lords to re-configure the law in *Royal Bank of Scotland v Etridge*.[79] In fact, *Etridge* did more than clarify the law by stipulating that a lender need only seek a letter of confirmation from a qualified adviser to protect themselves from a claim of undue influence. It also sought to re-assert the primacy of the real security of the proprietary mortgage over the dormant proprietary interest of the equitable co-owner. Thus, it was not the point of the judgment in *Etridge* to ensure that no undue influence occurred, although this could be a happy side effect of the process required by *Etridge*. Rather, the point was that if undue influence did occur, the lender could be isolated from its consequences by the administrative procedures it had put in place. The risk would pass to the consenting co-owner's legal adviser. Consequently, since *Etridge*, the number of successful undue influence claims has fallen dramatically, and a lender must be seriously incompetent if it does not secure its priority by obtaining a properly vetted consent from all persons occupying the property.[80]

---

[78] Especially since there are precious few other ways to stave off a mortgagee bent on possession and sale.

[79] [2001] 4 All ER 449.

[80] See *National Westminster Bank v Amin* [2002] 1 FLR 735 for a lender getting it wrong.

ROUND 7: THE IRONY OF THE TOLATA (1996)

It might be thought that the pendulum could swing no further after *Etridge*. The application of the *Pettitt* principles at large had triggered consequential litigation across a range of circumstances as mortgagees in particular sought to define and delimit the proprietary effect of impliedly created interests. As the case law shows, that proprietary effect was indeed limited. The clarification of the circumstances in which a mortgagee retains its possessory priority despite the proprietary status of equitable co-ownership no doubt contributed to the development of sensible lending practices by most institutional mortgagees, but sensible lending practices were not a prerequisite for a sympathetic hearing in the courts. Even so, there remained cases—largely where express consent to a non-purchase mortgage was held void due to undue influence or forgery—in which lenders lost their possessory priority, and the dormant proprietary status of equitable co-ownership awoke.

The acceptance of the equitable owner's possessory priority in this rump of cases could have been the end of the matter—the last station on the railroad of litigation from *Pettitt*. After all, if the equitable owner had managed to navigate this far, what else could conspire against her? The answer is section 14 of the TOLATA (1996). It is now clear that simple proprietary status, even if it appears to translate into possessory priority as a matter of general land law, does not actually mean that the co-owner is always entitled to remain in her home. For sure, where *Boland* still operates, the equitable owner's proprietary interest is not subject to the mortgage, but the effect of a successful application under section 14 of the TOLATA is to sweep aside classical notions of what priority proprietary status actually means. The end result is that proprietary priority may be converted forcibly into money priority.

A mortgagee *with* possessory priority has no need to resort to section 14 of the TOLATA (1996) to secure sale of the property. It may take possession and sell in the normal exercise of its rights as mortgagee, subject only to the limited powers of the court to intervene to defer possession or regulate sale.[81] equitable owner's interest enjoys proprietary status, but this is dormant because of either overreaching or *inter partes* consent. Consequently, a mortgagee seeking an order for sale from the court under section 14 is by definition subject to a proprietary right that is not dormant and that *does* translate into priority possession, usually because it amounts to a *Boland* overriding interest.

---

[81]   S 36 of the Administration of Justice Act (1970) and s 91 of the Law of Property Act (1925). For the duties of a selling mortgage, see *Meretz Investments NV v ACP Limited* [2006] EWHC 74 (Ch).

Under the old section 30 of the Law of Property Act (1925), there were few instances of non-priority mortgagees making an application for sale, let alone doing so successfully,[82] but this has become more common under the TOLATA (1996). One response to the increase in frequency of such applications would be to deny sale outright in all but the most exceptional circumstances. After all, if the equitable owners' interest is actively proprietary, it might be thought entirely proper that the lender should have to show exceptional hardship in order to obtain sale and thereby reverse the possessory priority enjoyed by the equitable owner. Indeed, it is not as if mortgagees have no means of securing possessory priority,[83] and one reason for the enactment of the TOLATA (1996) was to remove the obligation on trustees to sell (and thus the court's duty to enforce sale) in cases of dispute.

Of course, if a sale *is* ordered on the ground that this would be (apparently) fairer to both the 'innocent' mortgagee and the equitable co-owner, there will be concerns on both sides. For its part, the mortgagee must be confident that a sale would generate enough funds to meet (at least) a substantial part of the debt. Yet this is nothing when compared to the concerns of the co-owner who would be forced off the land in which they have an active proprietary interest with possessory priority under the general law, in return for priority in the proceeds of sale to the value of their interest. For most equitable owners, taking priority in cash is not the same as taking priority in land. Most equitable owners would no doubt prefer to see their equitable interest given hard form as a priority property right that prevents possession *and* sale by a lender, rather than in soft form as a mortgage-free pot of money with which they might well find it difficult to secure even roughly equivalent accommodation.

As things stand, there is no real pattern to the case law on section 14 applications by non-priority mortgagees (or other non-priority chargees[84]), save that it is obvious that courts do not appear concerned that ordering a sale effectively reverses active proprietary priority in favour of money priority. *Mortgage Corporation v Shaire*,[85] *Edwards v Lloyds TSB*[86] and *Alliance & Leicester plc v Slayford*[87] suggest that sale will not be granted, or not granted immediately, if this serves the immediate needs of the co-owner with priority, with *Shaire* explicitly finding that the TOLATA

---

[82] For an example, see *Bank of Baroda v Dhillon* (1998) 30 HLR 845. Sale was refused in *Abbey National plc v Moss* [1994] 1 FLR 307.

[83] Lenders could insist on overreaching or obtain effective consent. They might even refuse to lend!

[84] For example, a claimant with a charging order over a co-owner's share in the property.

[85] [2001] Ch 743.

[86] [2004] EWHC 1745 (Ch).

[87] (2001) 81 P & CR DG10.

(1996) had altered the balance in favour of retention.[88] However, even then (with the possible exception of *Slayford*), there is no permanence to the arrangement, as the courts accept that sale *must* take place at some point; and in *Shaire*, the ultimate course of action depended on the parties' ability to agree to a workable arrangement that gave some benefit to the mortgagee if a sale was refused.[89]

It is indeed this last point that seems to cause real difficulty for the courts, for if sale is put off indefinitely, the mortgage debt will continue to rise, and the lender (or chargee) will be kept out of its money until the co-owner is ready to sell or dies in possession. Thus in *Bank of Ireland Home Mortgages v Bell*,[90] *First National Bank v Achampong*[91] *Pritchard Englefield v Steinberg*,[92] sale was ordered despite the existence of a prior binding right specifically in order to salvage something for the creditor from the financial wreckage.[93]

Perhaps we should no longer be surprised that courts are prepared in at least some cases to treat non-priority mortgagees as if they really did have priority *over the land* (at least in respect of their ability to secure a sale), for this is merely the latest example of the courts' determined efforts to denude equitable co-ownership of any effective proprietary status despite *Pettitt*, *Boland* and the TOLATA (1996) itself. Of course, we must recognise that some mortgagees can find themselves caught by overriding interests that, in all fairness, they could not have been expected to discover. (Void consent because of undue influence pre-*Etridge* (*Slayford*, *Bell*) and void mortgage because of forgery by one of the legal owners (*Achampong*) are good examples, especially if (and who knows) the co-owners have colluded in order to manufacture a defence against a mortgagee seeking possession.)

However, mortgage lending should not be risk free. Lenders do not lend out of the goodness of their hearts, and their business models are based on calculations that anticipate that a percentage of loans will be unrecoverable. Mortgagees balance the risk of being caught out against the cost of

---

[88]   In *Banker's Trust v Namdar* [1997] EGCS 20, decided just before the entry into force of TOLATA (1996), Nourse LJ suggested that its enactment must necessarily apply a brake to the court's natural instinct to order sale.

[89]   In *Slayford*, the mortgagee pursued a different route to its money (see below). In *Edwards*, sale was postponed for five years while children continued to be educated.

[90]   [2001] 2 FLR 809.

[91]   [2003] 2 P & CR DG 11.

[92]   [2005] 1 P & CR DG 2. The case involved a long lease, and there is suspicion that the judge ordered sale in order that the equitable co-owner should receive a share of the proceeds rather than risk forfeiture by the landlord (because of the conduct of the legal owner) and receive nothing.

[93]   *TSB Bank Plc v Marshall* [1998] 2 FLR 769 is often thought as a similar case, but in fact it appears that the mortgagee did have priority over the beneficial owner due to the latter's consent to the failed legal mortgage, which, under s 63 of the Law of Property Act (1925), then took effect as a mortgage of her equitable interest.

watertight and time-consuming lending practices. It is perfectly reasonable that courts should be aware of this when balancing the interests of lenders and co-owners, especially co-owners whose interests have, as a matter of property law, a hard-won proprietary priority.

ROUND 8: TWO FINAL TWISTS

Even though we have reached the end of the trail of litigation, this is not the end of the story. There are two further developments that shine a light on the nature of equitable co-ownership in the modern law. First, it is clear that even if a lender should fail in its attempts to secure proprietary priority and then fail in its attempts to secure a forced sale under the TOLATA (1996), it may nevertheless resort to personal remedies against the borrower. This in turn may lead to bankruptcy and a sale of the land by the trustee in bankruptcy. Such was the lot of the equitable owner in *Slayford*, and the Court of Appeal decided that it was not an abuse of the process for the lender to achieve through bankruptcy what they could not achieve through their non-priority secured interest.[94]

There are risks for the lender pursuing this course of action: it must release its security in order to make the borrower bankrupt, and there is always the chance that the borrower has other undisclosed creditors who will share in the distribution of the assets. The Enterprise Act (2000) places some (albeit limited) controls on the trustee in bankruptcy, and it may be that *Barca v Mears* heralds a different approach to disputed sales under section 355A.[95] Nevertheless, for a lender seeking some return or simply wishing to close the account and take a loss, this route will serve the purpose. It will also convert the equitable owner's proprietary right into its cash value—again.

The second development arises from the decision in *Oxley v Hiscock*[96] which establishes how a court should quantify a successful claim to an equitable interest. Although the generality of Chadwick LJ's judgment has been circumscribed by a differently constituted Court of Appeal in *Crossley v Crossley*,[97] *Oxley* is a clear example of the asset sharing function of the *Pettitt* principles. Of further interest is Chadwick LJ's belief that we

---

[94] Of course, sale by the trustee in bankruptcy under s 14 of the TOLATA (1996) and s 335A of the Insolvency Act (1986) is possible irrespective of how the bankruptcy occurred.

[95] [2005] 2 FLR 1; [2005] Conv 161. See, however, *Nicholls v Lan* [2006] EWHC 1255 (Ch) where sale was ordered in favour of a trustee in bankruptcy despite the concerns raised by *Barca*.

[96] [2004] 3 WLR 715. See M Dixon, 'Resulting and Constructive Trusts of Land: The Mist Descends and Rises' [2005] *Conveyancer and Property Lawyer* 79; and MP Thompson, 'Constructive Trusts, Estoppel and the Family Home' [2004] *Conveyancer and Property Lawyer* 496.

[97] [2005] EWCA Civ 1581, 21 December 2005.

might do better to think of these claims to an interest as arising under proprietary estoppel rather than constructive trust. Of course, this is not the first time this has been heard—see Lord Bridge in *Rosset* itself—but if we adopt his suggestion, there are consequences. Successful claims in constructive trust invariably give rise to an equitable share of ownership. Successful claims in estoppel give rise to whatever remedy the court thinks is necessary to relieve the unconscionability,[98] and this may be a time limited proprietary right[99] or not even take the form of an interest in the land at all.[100]

No doubt, it was not the intention in *Oxley* to open the door to 'non-property' solutions by re-casting the claim as one of estoppel (eg, by awarding a compensatory payment in lieu), but given that this is already possible in cases not involving romantically linked couples, it takes no imagination to see that this solution might well be attractive to judges already unhappy with the proprietary status of equitable co-ownership. It would give the remaining owner a choice about how to satisfy the compensatory award (re-mortgage, sale or savings); it would remove the successful claimant from the category of persons entitled to apply under section 14 of the TOLATA (1996); it would remove any lingering danger of a third party being compromised by the equitable interest; and it could bring about a clean break without necessarily obliging one party to surrender possession. The attractions are apparent.

CONCLUSIONS

The simple fact that owner-occupation has now reached 70 per cent of all residential properties means that litigation over shared homes is unlikely ever to recede to the trickle of pre-*Pettitt* days. The Law Commission's long-awaited proposals on shared property may remove some of the impetus for litigation.[101] The now regular conveyancing practice of advising house purchasers to have the property conveyed into joint names, when combined with Land Registry practice that the nature of the beneficial interests should be declared on the application for registration,[102] does

---

[98] *Jennings v Rice* [2002] EWCA 159
[99] *Clark v Clarke* [2006] EWHC 275 (Ch), 24 February 2006.
[100] As in *Jennings*; see also *Campbell v Griffin* [2001] EWCA Civ 990.
[101] It is expected sometime in 2007, following the consultation paper 'Cohabitation: The Financial Consequences of Relationship Breakdown' (Law Comm No 179, 2006).
[102] These do not appear on the title but allow the Registry to decide whether to enter Form A restriction requiring any capital monies to be paid to two trustees. There is no need to enter such a restriction when the co-owners hold the land legally *and* equitably as joint-tenants. See note 21 above.

mean that fewer disputes about ownership arise.[103] Nevertheless, litigation will continue, especially between unmarried partners[104] and when a mortgagee seeks enforcement of a security some time after the property has been purchased.

In most cases, the purpose of making a claim will be to acquire an equitable interest so as to remain in possession either against the other legal owner or against a mortgagee. As to the former, the nature of the claimant's interest should he or she be successful is not a matter of great moment. He or she may continue to occupy and own the property, or their relationship may deteriorate to the point that they either agree to or require a sale. Even if a sale is sought by means of an application under section 14 of the TOLATA, the court is faced with a dispute between two legal equals—both with property rights and neither being superior to the other. There is no question of priority per se, and the court must do the best it can to reach a solution on the facts before it.[105]

By contrast, when a third party is involved, the nature of the claimants' interest is of considerable importance. Fundamentally proprietary, confirmed in that status by statute and capable of being an overriding interest they might be, but in practice, a succession of cases have effectively reduced the proprietary effect to a mere shadow of other more robust interests in land. Equitable interests as property rights easily become dormant, and at times it seems as if the doctrine of conversion has not been abolished. Even when the claimant's interest survives with an actively proprietary status—itself no mean achievement—equitable owners may find themselves forced to take that interest in cash, if not immediately, then later.

No one can doubt that *Pettitt v Pettitt* represents a milestone in the jurisprudence of real property. It has a good claim to be the most influential property law decision since 1925. Its asset sharing potential has been realised to the full, and it may even have pushed a conservative society into accepting that express co-ownership between co-habitants should be the norm. That may well be enough, but we cannot ignore what is now writ large. Equitable co-ownership without legal title is, for all

---

[103] We should note, however, that in a number of recent cases, one legal owner has contested that the other legal owner has no equitable interest—that is, that their legal title is a mere shell. A simple approach to these cases is to insist that the claimant prove why they should have all of the interest, rather than the legal owner having to prove that they have some. Equity should follow the law. However, *Crossley v Crossley* [2005] All ER (D), *McKenzie v McKenzie* [2003] 2 P & CR DG6 and *Carlton v Goodman* [2002] 2 FLR 259 place a burden on the legal owner to establish an interest by way of resulting or constructive trust. To this author, this seems back-to-front and a recipe for more litigation.

[104] Including those *not* in a civil partnership.

[105] *Holman v Howes* [2005] EWHC 2824 (Ch).

practical intents and purposes, a claim on a pot of money, not a claim to an interest in land. Does an equitable owner own their house? It depends on who is asking.

What then is the future? Is the loss of active proprietary status for equitable co-ownership interests—in terms of their ability to secure possessory priority over third parties—to be accepted, despite the history of the TOLATA (1996) and the general dictates of basic property principles? It is not the view of the present author that anything should be done to modify the effectiveness of overreaching or the ability of an equitable owner to give effective consent to an anticipated but non-overreaching mortgage. These methods of eliminating the possessory priority of proprietary equitable interests are sanctioned by statute and the general law respectively. Overreaching serves the public interest, and equitable owners should be free to waive voluntarily the active proprietary status of their interests. Similarly, for this author, there is little merit in introducing, via an imaginative (and unwarranted) interpretation of the TOLATA (1996), a requirement that the trustees should seek the consent of equitable owners before executing a sale or mortgage. The duty to consult the equitable owners does not imply a duty to seek their consent.

However, it is submitted that the analysis presented above demonstrates that the courts have gone beyond necessity in reducing the proprietary impact of equitable co-ownership. There is of course a need to ensure alienability of land and to protect the domestic lending market by providing security for lenders. Effective mortgage remedies mean risk-free lending and low interest rates. But there are other imperatives that counterbalance the interests of third parties. To this end, and to redress the balance by restoring active proprietary effect to equitable interests in limited circumstances, a number of changes and clarifications might be beneficial.

First, when trustees are subject to an *express* consent requirement before dealing with the land—either as a result of a stipulation in the trust instrument[106] or as the outcome of an application by the beneficiaries under section 14 of the TOLATA—then it should be possible to register this by means of a restriction against dealings.[107] This would ensure the effectiveness of the consent requirement. A consent requirement in the trust instrument deserves enforcement because it reflects the will of the settler and the merits of a consent requirement imposed by the court after a TOLATA application have, by definition, been argued fully.

Secondly, principles of subrogation should not rescue re-mortgagees from the folly of their own incompetent lending practices. Instead, the

---

[106] Which is, of course, unlikely with residential property.
[107] A standard Form N would fit.

provisions of the Law of Property Act (1925) and Land Registration Act (2002) should be effective to protect the proprietary interest of equitable co-owners. Those owners might, some would argue, gain a windfall, but it would encourage more secure mortgage lending. Likewise, a finding of implied consent should continue to be available, but only when it is established that the equitable owner actively participated in securing the mortgage advance, as opposed to merely being aware of it.[108]

Thirdly, a mortgagee without proprietary priority should not be able to secure a sale under section 14 of the TOLATA and thus should not be able to translate forcibly the equitable owner's proprietary priority into cash priority. After all, sale is not the purpose of a trust of land. There might be a case for a sale in truly exceptional circumstances but not simply because the lender would otherwise be kept out of its money. Indeed it would—and might consequently take more care next time.

Finally, as a necessary counterpart, sale by a trustee in bankruptcy against the wishes of an innocent equitable owner should be more difficult to achieve, to discourage the lender would from simply suing on the personal covenant and making the borrower bankrupt. Admittedly, this is a more controversial proposal, given the public interest in liberating bankrupt estates, but it may be that *Barca v Mears* points the way to a more sympathetic balance of interests.[109]

---

[108] This may currently be the position, but the precise scope of implied consent has never been settled.

[109] In addition, as noted above, there are disadvantages in a secured creditor forcing the bankruptcy of the debtor.

3

Why is the Law of Undue Influence so Hard to Understand and Apply?

GRAHAM FERRIS[*]

INTRODUCTION

THIS CHAPTER PROPOSES an analysis of the law of undue influence that concedes creative influence to policy. Such an analysis is not in direct contradiction of conventional analysis; rather, it is different in focus. At present, conventional analysis focuses attention upon one aspect of the law, which I will describe as 'will theory'. This single viewpoint is a distortion, as it fails to give appropriate regard to analysis that is not predicated upon will theory. To fully apprehend the law, attention should be focussed on what I will call 'policy'. Undoubtedly, any complete account of the law of undue influence involves both elements of will theory and elements of policy, and one reason for the difficulty in this area is that the relationship between these elements is not stable, with preponderance shifting both over time and between different areas of application.

To illustrate the impact of the proposed analytical structure, one central proposition is advanced: that there are two species of undue influence operating in the law today, traditionally known as actual undue influence and presumed undue influence; and further, that the different species, while both part of the law of undue influence, are different in ways that transcend the presence of an irrebuttable presumption of influence in cases of presumed undue influence.

This proposition is controversial because it seems to ignore dicta in *Royal Bank of Scotland v Etridge (No 2)*[1] to the effect that the nature of

---

* I would like to acknowledge and express gratitude for the constructive criticism and comments offered by the editor and the referee. They deserve credit for whatever of merit is contained here; the remaining weaknesses are my own.
[1] [2001] UKHL 44.

undue influence is unitary.[2] The plainest statement of this position was made by Lord Scott, who asserted that it made no sense to find there was no actual undue influence on the facts of a case and yet to find there was presumed undue influence on the same facts.[3] Either there was undue influence, or there was not. Prima facie, this entails contradiction of the proposition that actual and presumed undue influence are substantively different. However, the finding of undue influence is not the finding of a simple fact. A finding of undue influence could indicate: an assent facilitated by the presence of a habit of submission generated by a relationship of brutal domination;[4] an assent freely given but undermined by the lack of fully informed advice received by the property owner;[5] proof of exploitative actions, such as emotional blackmail used to extort assent from a vulnerable person;[6] or a morally innocent failure to realise that there was a need to ensure that a property owner had adequate and independent advice before effecting a disposition.[7] Finally, and essentially to the argument advanced here, a finding of undue influence is sometimes the result of what has been described as the imposition of a 'duty' on the recipient of a benefit,[8] to ensure that the benefit was given as the result of 'the free exercise of independent will'.[9]

For the purposes of this chapter, it does not matter whether undue influence is always analysable as concerned with wrongdoing[10] or whether it contains cases better analysed as impaired capacity.[11] It is immaterial whether one prefers to view duress as the common law equivalent of undue influence,[12] or if one views undue influence as an aspect of unconscionable bargains.[13] The argument is that whatever the doctrinal expression of the law preferred in analysis, the shape and efficacy of the law is determined by policy. If one regards undue influence as a juristic unity, then this

---

[2] *Ibid*, paras 16, 93, 219 and 281.

[3] *Ibid*, paras 219 and 281.

[4] *Farmers Co-operative Executors & Trustees Ltd v Perks* (1989) 52 SASR 399.

[5] *Allcard v Skinner* (1887) 36 Ch D 145; *Barclays Bank plc v Coleman* [2001] UKHL 44, para 291; *Niersmans v Pesticcio* [2004] EWCA Civ 372.

[6] *Bank of Scotland v Bennett* [1997] 3 FCR 193.

[7] *Allcard v Skinner* (1887) 36 Ch D 145; *Niersmans v Pesticcio* [2004] EWCA Civ 372.

[8] *Allcard v Skinner* (1887) 36 Ch D 145, 190; *Lloyds Bank plc v Bundy* [1975] 1 QB 326, 342H–343B; [2001] UKHL 44, para 104.

[9] *Inche Noriah v Shaik Allie Bin Omar* [1929] AC 127, 135.

[10] R Bigwood, 'Undue Influence: "Impaired Consent" or "Wicked Exploitation"?' (1996) 16 *OJLS* 503; and to similar effect, see (2002) 65 *MLR* 435.

[11] P Birks and CN Yin, 'On the Nature of Undue Influence' in J Beatson and D Friedmann (eds), *Good Faith and Fault in Contract Law* (Oxford, Clarendon, 1995); and to the same effect, see P Birks, 'Undue Influence as Wrongful Exploitation' (2004) 120 *LQR* 34.

[12] N Enonchong, *Duress, Undue Influence and Unconscionable Dealing* (London, Sweet & Maxwell, 2006).

[13] S Waddams, 'Unconscionability in Contracts' (1976) 39 *MLR* 369; M Chen-Wishart, 'The *O'Brien* Principle and Substantive Unfairness' [1997] *CLJ* 60; D Capper, 'Undue Influence and Unconscionability: A Rationalisation' (1998) 114 *LQR* 479.

indicates that the category is useful and should be retained, as it encompasses cases that have a principled connection. Presumably, such a position views undue influence as concerned with a particular type of wrongdoing, albeit a form of wrongdoing that defies definitional constraint.[14] Such an analysis implies that undue influence should retain its analytical separation from duress, unconscionable bargains, want of capacity and the duty of fair dealing. Such a position is perfectly compatible with the analysis advanced in this chapter. Alternatively, undue influence can be analysed as an area of law with divergent principles operating. This is also not in contradiction to the argument advanced. What is important is that the policies held in dynamic tension by the law of undue influence are not thrown out of balance by arguments that regard undue influence as the working out of will theory or any other doctrinally centred theory.

The conventional analysis of undue influence in terms of will theory can obscure the powerful influences on the law from policy concerns. Policy has plainly been extremely influential in recent legal developments. The House of Lords has explicitly emphasised the importance of reasonable expectations of protection from the law on the one side and of practical market concerns on the other side, in the shaping of the law.[15] A casual glance at the structure of the leading speeches in *Barclays Bank plc v O'Brien*[16] and *Etridge* confirms that the House was pushing the bounds of the judicial function as traditionally understood, in an attempt to address practical problems of institutional action.[17] However, these powerful forces that shape the law are often treated as if they were mere obstacles to the logical exposition of will theory in this area. A brief analysis of the influential essay on undue influence by Peter Birks and Chin Nyuk Yin, 'On the Nature of Undue Influence',[18] illustrates the point.

Birks and Yin were not unaware of the pressure of policy upon the law of undue influence. Four policies were expressly identified in the text: prophylaxis against wrongdoing;[19] preventing the unsettling of too many transactions;[20] the danger of infantilising adults; and the danger of post-disposition fraudulent claims.[21] However, prophylaxis was seen as a

---

[14] A position adopted following the decision in *Barclays Bank plc v O'Brien* [1994] 1 AC 180 by M Dixon, 'The Special Tenderness of Equity: Undue Influence and the Family Home' [1994] *CLJ* 21; and much strengthened by the dicta in *Etridge* (see note 1 above and accompanying text).

[15] [1994] 1 AC 180, 188; [2001] UKHL 44, paras 2, 34–7, 98 and 140–1.

[16] [1994] 1 AC 180.

[17] The cases set out 'guidance' for the future conduct of lenders. Indeed, at times the speeches have the texture of legislation. See *National Westminster Bank plc v Spectrum Plus Ltd* [2005] UKHL 41, paras 15–16.

[18] Note 11 above, 57–97.

[19] Birks and Yin, note 11 above, 63 and 79–80.

[20] *Ibid*, 82.

[21] *Ibid*, 91.

'remoter justification' than the analysis advanced and therefore literally subject to a safety warning: 'handle with [great] care'.[22] Unsettling too many transactions was also referred to as the result of 'anxiety', a response to the 'fear of too much restitution', which led to a search for 'defensible cut-off points'.[23] Such policy-generated cut-off points resulted in 'inhibitions' upon the 'natural scope of the relief'.[24] The authors argued that jurists should respect the 'rationality of the law', which could not tolerate abbreviations.[25] Finally, according to Birks and Yin, any analysis that views undue influence as closely related to breach of fiduciary duty is 'dangerous' and can lead only to confusion.[26]

The tenor of the argument advanced by Briks and Yin is that the sole subject matter for analysis should be found in will theory, the overbearing of will through pressure or the absence of capacity through 'morbid dependence'.[27] The law of undue influence was concerned with 'reduced autonomy'[28]—reduced from the 'standard common law capacity',[29] the nature of which standard was unexamined, beyond recognition that it was not related to the individual qualities of the parties to actions.

That analysis denies policy any creative part in the shaping of the law and consigns it to a series of roles that can be characterised as impediments to the operation of will theory: remote cause, product of fear, obstruction to natural development, inhibition on relief, source of confusion. The same analytical assumptions appear in an article by Rick Bigwood in rebuttal of the thesis advanced by Birks and Yin.[30] In a similar vein is a recent book directed at practitioners by Professor Enonchong, which will be considered in more detail below.[31]

METHOD OF PROCEEDING

The first priority, if a policy-determined interpretation of undue influence is to be advanced, is to identify and articulate the relevant policy. Therefore, the first substantive matters addressed are the policy issues. It is argued that the interplay between a policy supporting freedom of contract (and of disposition in particular) and a policy of protection from victimisation (or from the risk of victimisation) creates the central structural

---

[22]   *Ibid*, 63.
[23]   *Ibid*, 81.
[24]   *Ibid*, 81, 89–90 and 91.
[25]   *Ibid*, 95.
[26]   *Ibid*, 91.
[27]   *Ibid*, 72
[28]   *Ibid*, 86.
[29]   *Ibid*, 87.
[30]   *Inche Noriah v Shaik Allie Bin Omar* [1929] AC 127, 135. Bigwood, note 10 above.
[31]   Enonchong, note 12 above.

features of the law of undue influence. However, these are not the sole policies playing an important role in the formation of the law, and the importance of home ownership in modern British society is also noted.

The treatment of policy is followed by preparation for recognising significant differences between actual and presumed undue influence post-*Etridge*. The viability of a reading of *Etridge* that preserves a significant difference between the law of actual and presumed undue influence is established. The chapter proceeds to a critical examination of Professor Enongchong's adoption of a unified tort thesis in response to *Etridge*. An alternative interpretation of the law post *Etridge* is proposed. A comparison is made of the law of presumed undue influence and the law of constructive notice. Nobody argues that the substantive law of constructive notice was concerned with the identification of any mental state of purchasers (despite being known as 'notice'); in a similar way, it is a distraction when considering presumed undue influence to try and identify the actions affecting the conscience of the party subject to an action for rescission. Rather than being explicable in terms of will theory, presumed undue influence is an important 'prophylactic' jurisdiction, closely related to the law regulating the conduct of fiduciaries.[32]

THE POLICY CONFLICTS AT THE HEART OF THE LAW OF UNDUE INFLUENCE

The law of undue influence and its close relations fall across three broad areas of policy.[33] It is the balance between these three areas, and in particular the tension between the first two, that shapes the law more effectively than any principle of free will in undertaking an obligation or in making a disposition.

Freedom of Contract and Disposition

The primary aim of policies that prioritise freedom of contract and disposition is the security of duly executed transactions. In the words of Lord Scarman:

---

[32] Thus, the argument is close to aspects of the analyses of: D Tiplady, 'The Judicial Control of Unfairness' (1983) 46 *MLR* 601; D Tiplady, 'The Limits of Undue Influence' (1985) 48 *MLR* 579; and PJ Millett, 'Equity's Place in the Law of Commerce' (1998) 114 *LQR* 214. However, is not concerned with arguments centred on judicial control of substantive fairness in contract, nor with attempts to rationalise undue influence as a part of the law of unconscionable bargain, unlike: Waddams, note 13 above; D Tiplady, 'The Judicial Control of Unfairness' (1983) 46 *MLR* 601; Chen-Wishart, note 13 above; and D Capper, note 13 above.

[33] Undue influence is clearly a close relation of want of capacity, abuse of confidence and unconscionable bargains. It also clearly shares features with misrepresentation, duress and 'reasonableness' in contracts.

The courts of equity have developed a body of learning enabling relief to be granted where the law has to treat the transaction as unimpeachable unless it can be held to have been procured by undue influence.[34]

Undue influence operates to invalidate formally executed agreements and dispositions of property. Therefore, if undue influence is held to operate too liberally, it will undermine the benefits derived from compliance with formalities and multiply transaction cost astronomically. The law of undue influence must not undermine the validity of duly executed transactions generally; otherwise the jurisdiction will become more burdensome than useful.

Undue influence can undermine freedom of contract. Freedom of contract is an aspect of legal ideology that has been explored by Professor Atiyah at considerable length,[35] and we need add little. Freedom of contract has historically been associated with the politics of 'laissez faire', known nowadays as 'efficient market theory'. In either guise the crucial point is the belief that allowing individuals to act in what they perceive to be their own best interests is more economically efficient than interfering with their ability to so act. There are other important interests protected by the doctrine that freedom of contract is associated with: 'stability, certainty, and predictability'.[36] Finally, as has been emphasised by Rick Bigwood (although in terms of 'binding contract'), freedom of contract 'emphasises the more fundamental values of freedom and autonomy... [A]t the heart of contract is a deep respect for the individual's liberty".[37]

Undue influence can also undermine freedom of disposition. Undue influence does not threaten the validity of contracts only; it also threatens the validity of gratuitous dispositions. There is an obvious overlap between freedom of contract and freedom of disposition; indeed the classic dicta vindicating freedom of contract were delivered with reference to gratuitous dispositions.[38] However, the two principles are not identical. Indeed, in *National Westminster Bank plc v Morgan*[39] Lord Scarman held that the difficulty of bringing gratuitous dispositions within the analytical framework of contract law precluded a rationalisation of the law in terms of a general principle of inequality of bargaining power. Freedom of disposition is limited in a manner that freedom of contract is not, because dispositions create property interests that can bind third parties.[40]

---

[34]   *National Westminster Bank v Morgan* [1985] AC 686, 709.
[35]   PS Atiyah, *The Rise and Fall of Freedom of Contract* (Oxford, Clarendon Press, 1979).
[36]   Waddams, note 13 above, 369.
[37]   Bigwood, note 10 above, 505.
[38]   *Egerton v Brownlow* (1853) 4 HLC 1; 10 ER 359.
[39]   *National Westminster Bank v Morgan* [1985] AC 686, 708B.
[40]   Hence the limitations to freedom of contract illustrated by *Street v Mountford* [1985] AC 809; *Agnew v Commissioners of Inland Revenue* [2001] 2 AC 710; and *National Westminster Bank plc v Spectrum Plus Ltd* [2005] UKHL 41.

Three further distinguishing features of freedom of disposition are of more practical importance for the law of undue influence. First, gratuitous dispositions are often undertaken for emotional reasons that have no obvious link to economic rationality—a link that contracts are assumed to have.[41] Second, the context of dispositions is often within the sphere of 'private' life,[42] a fact that generates policy issues of intrusiveness[43] and appropriate social mores.[44] Third, there is no recourse to equality of exchange value in assessing the reasonableness of gratuitous dispositions.

Finally, there are costs associated with the erosion of freedom of contract and disposition, and these costs of protection from undue influence will ultimately be carried by the group that the law intends to shield from abuse. If a husband and wife must employ a solicitor to validate the execution of a document by the wife, then the cost of the transaction to the husband and wife will be higher than otherwise. The assumption of autonomy, and consequently of the validity of formally executed documents, underpins low transaction costs. Therefore, any group that is not assumed to act autonomously will face higher transaction costs.

Regulation of Protected Relationships

The second policy area operating on the law of undue influence is the protective function of the law. The general nature of the jurisdiction (and kindred jurisdictions) was indicated by Denning J: 'There is the vigilance of the common law which, while allowing freedom of contract, watches to see it is not abused.'[45] The jurisdiction operates as an exception to the rule (freedom of contract and disposition, and enforcement of validly executed agreements and dispositions) to prevent certain forms of improper conduct that a mechanistic regard to the rules would make possible. It is not possible to define simply the factors that call the jurisdiction into operation. In a classic description of undue influence, Lindley LJ referred to 'unfair and improper conduct, some coercion from outside, some overreaching, some form of cheating' in 'actual' undue influence; or to some

---

[41]   *Re Brocklehurst* [1978] Ch 14, 48–9.

[42]   B Fehlberg, 'The Husband, the Bank and Her Signature' (1994) 57 *MLR* 467, 467; and to similar effect, see (1996) 59 *MLR* 675. The classic example of contract law denying legal effect to a private agreement between spouses is *Balfour v Balfour* [1919] 2 KB 571.

[43]   An intrusion into an area protected by Article 8 of the European Convention on Human Rights.

[44]   See: [1994] 1 AC 180, 188C–F; *Zamet v Hyman* [1961] 1 WLR 1442; and *Barclays Bank plc v Coleman* [2001] QB 20; [2001] UKHL 44.

[45]   *John Lee & Son (Grantham) Ltd v Railway Executive* [1949] 2 All ER 584. Used by Waddams, note 13 above, as the epigraph to his article.

'duty to advise the donor, or even to manage his property' requiring proof that undue influence had not been used in 'presumed' undue influence.[46]

Professor Waddams attempted to particularise those factors that justified disregarding the terms of a contract when he stated that the law recognised 'the value of protecting the weak, the foolish, and the thoughtless from imposition and oppression'.[47] He argued for recognition that 'unfairness, or inequality of exchange' could support the invalidating of a contractual term. However, he recognised 'the difficulty of developing ... guidelines' to determine when a contract should be subject to the jurisdiction and suggested that 'a large inequality of exchange combined with inequality of bargaining power' could be a starting point.[48]

However, this is not a suitable starting point for a jurisdiction that encompasses gratuitous dispositions as well as contracts. Furthermore, the qualities identified by Professor Waddams suggest some inherent weakness of the claimant. The law of undue influence has traditionally been far more concerned with a contingent weakness, a weakness that arises from a relationship of dependence. One is not 'weak, foolish or thoughtless' when one relies upon a solicitor to advise. It is in connection with this relationship based undue influence that reference to 'policy' is usually made. The law responds to vulnerability to abuse; in the words of Lord Scarman, the law guards against 'the victimisation of one party by another'.[49]

It is important to notice how analyses of undue influence fit into this policy arena. Professor Birks and Chin Nyuk Yin suggested that the crucial factor in presumed undue influence is 'loss of autonomy' in the claimant, thus explaining with logical precision the ousting of the normal assumption of autonomy that forms part of the doctrine of freedom of disposition.[50] Rick Bigwood preferred to rest upon 'exploitation' as the key feature of undue influence, whether it be actual (and active) or presumed (and passive).[51] Generally the law takes no interest in the actual existence of 'autonomy' when considering the validity of a transaction. Autonomy is assumed to exist. Generally the law places no duty upon one party to a contract to inform or protect the other party; the law does not protect people from their own folly,[52] and it is no exploitation to allow a person to make a bad decision. The writers are identifying the absence of the normal assumptions that form part of the doctrines of freedom of contract and disposition.

---

[46]   *Allcard v Skinner* (1887) 36 Ch D, 181.
[47]   Waddams, note 13 above.
[48]   *Ibid*, 391–2.
[49]   *National Westminster Bank v Morgan* [1985] AC 686, 705A.
[50]   Birks and Yin, note 11 above.
[51]   Bigwood, note 10 above.
[52]   *Allcard v Skinner* (1887) 36 Ch D 145, 182.

The assumption of autonomy forms a necessary part of the core concepts of will theory in the field of contract law. As such, it is part of what Duncan Kennedy has described as the rhetoric of the formalist jurist.[53] One problem with formalist analysis is that it is prone to confuse doctrine, informed and shaped in part by economic theory, with a description of the legal and social world. The formal nature of the classic doctrine of freedom of contract has been long recognised.[54] The starting point of the law of undue influence is the policy of upholding transactions, and in particular upholding the validity of formally executed dispositions. However, this is the reflection of policy considerations supporting the doctrines of freedom of contract and disposition, and not the working out of abstract theories about consensual dealings. This can be demonstrated by a consideration of the relationships affected by presumed undue influence. These relationships are not identifiable by any analysis of mental states. If we seek to understand the law, we will have to view it from a perspective of practical judicial policy.

The relationship of banker and customer is an arms-length relationship in the absence of exceptional circumstances.[55] The courts have shown no interest in whether customers actually repose trust and confidence in their banks; the issue was effectively settled by *Foley v Hill* in 1848.[56] Even the intimate relationship of husband and wife is not a relationship that produces any presumption of reliance (or dependence or vulnerability) that gives rise to a presumption of influence. The law was not concerned with the mental state of most wives when it decided that the relationship was not one that gave rise to presumed undue influence.[57] Despite the fact that Lord Scott 'would assume in every case in which a husband and wife are living together that there is a reciprocal trust and confidence between them',[58] there is no presumption of influence as between husband and wife.

The dominant policy in this area is surely (and rightly) a policy to deny a presumption of influence to many relationships in which it could realistically be applied, in order to safeguard freedom of contract and disposition. However, in most discussion it is the abnormal suspension of the policy supporting freedom of disposition that is referred to as 'policy'. This alleged disparity between 'principles' that support will theory and 'policy' that threatens these principles, is part of the rhetoric of formalistic legal argument. What is novel is that this rhetoric is being used to support a

---

[53] D Kennedy, 'Form and Substance in Private Law Adjudication' (1976) 89 *HLR* 1685.
[54] *Ibid.*
[55] *National Westminster Bank v Morgan* [1985] AC 686.
[56] (1848) 2 HLC 28; 9 ER 1002.
[57] *Bank of Montreal v Stuart* [1911] AC 120.
[58] [2001] UKHL 44, para 159.

jurisdiction that threatens to undermine the policy imperatives protected by freedom of contract and disposition.

The classic resort to policy as the underlying rationale of presumed undue influence was made in *Allcard v Skinner* by Cotton LJ, who stated that the policy was 'to prevent the relations which existed between the parties and the influence arising therefrom being abused'.[59] The effect of this policy was to reverse the normal presumption of due execution and place an onus on a defendant to prove affirmatively not that she had acted correctly but that 'the gift was the spontaneous act of the donor acting under circumstances which enabled him to exercise an independent will'.[60] This usage made perfect sense, as it reflected the terms of the discussion over the impact of policy on dispositions in *Egerton v Brownlow*.[61] The problem, as was also recognised by Lindley LJ and Bowen LJ, was to protect freedom of disposition whilst safeguarding a vulnerable donee.[62]

The policy of avoiding victimisation of the vulnerable party in a relationship and encouraging integrity in relationships is not necessarily antagonistic to a free-market economy. The policy conflict is not between economic 'efficiency' and protection of the weak. No market can be effective over the long term without laws safeguarding the rewards of honest endeavour and dispossessing the abusive of the gains of improper endeavour. This regulative impact of general law has been recognised by economists as essential to the successful functioning of market systems.[63] Indeed, it has been argued that the absence of such a legal regulative foundation can lead to a self-perpetuating system of illegitimate and inefficient economic action.[64] Rather, the issue is one of balance. Too much emphasis on freedom of contract and disposition can lead to a damaging erosion of trust and undermine the very legitimacy of the law. Over extension of undue influence can lead to the denial to the protected class of access to markets and threatens to make them in practice incompetent to make dispositions.

The law of actual undue influence is focused on the redress of wrongs. Therefore, any regulative effect that flows from this law is of the same kind as occurs in tort law. The imposition of a general duty of 'fair conduct' (that is, conduct not involving duress, misrepresentation or undue influence) is important in defining the area of freedom available to parties to

---

[59]   (1887) 36 Ch D 145, 171; echoed by Bowen LJ at 190.
[60]   *Ibid*, 171.
[61]   (1853) 4 HLC 1; 10 ER 359.
[62]   (1887) Ch D 145, 182–3 and 189–90.
[63]   DC North, *Institutions, Institutional Change and Economic Performance* (Cambridge, Cambridge University Press, 1990) .
[64]   JE Stiglitz and K Hoff, 'The Creation of the Rule of Law and the Legitimacy of Property Rights: The Political and Economic Consequences of a Corrupt Privatization' (NBER Working Paper No 11772, 2005).

transactions. Actual undue influence is not concerned with asymmetrical relationships, except to the extent that such a relationship may provide an opportunity for wrongdoing.

For presumed undue influence, the regulative function of the law provides organising principles that shape doctrine. The purpose of presumed undue influence is not primarily to redress the results of the victimisation of the vulnerable within asymmetric relationships. The law is an attempt to prevent the occurrence of such victimisation, by removing the incentive for the potentially exploitative party to the relationship to take advantage of the asymmetrical nature of the relationship. In this respect the law of undue influence shares characteristics with the law regulating the conduct of fiduciaries and the law of constructive notice.

House Ownership as Home Ownership and Investment Asset

The third area of policy that has had influence on the developing law of undue influence in modern times has been the protection of the family home. As was noted by Stephen Cretney, the engine driving litigation, and therefore legal development, has been concern with protection of the interests of spouses or co-habitees in the home.[65] Brenda Fehlberg based her accounts of the law on the conflict between vulnerable wives and creditors seeking repossession of the home, and found the law to be an inadequate shield for the wife.[66] A similar negative assessment of the law was expressed extra-judicially by Millett LJ, who felt that the law was 'manifestly failing to give adequate protection to the wife or cohabitant who acts as surety'.[67] The House of Lords in both *O'Brien* and *Etridge* gave express attention to the conflicting pulls on the family house as home and the sole utilisable capital asset available to fund family business.[68] Finally, in an extension of this area of policy, Mummery LJ in *Niersmans v Pesticcio* commented:

> The *O'Brien* and *Etridge* jurisprudence is an outcrop of joint ownership of the matrimonial home ... social trends are already leading to a renewed interest in the law governing the validity of life time dispositions of houses, both in and outside the family circle, by the elderly and infirm.[69]

In short the influence of this policy area has been recognised and has clearly played an important independent role in the law of undue influence; and it can be anticipated that it will continue to do so.

---

[65] 'Monied Might and the Entrapped Wife' (1989) 105 *LQR* 169.
[66] Fehlberg, note 42 above.
[67] PJ Millett, 'Equity's Place in the Law of Commerce' (1998) 114 *LQR* 214, 215.
[68] [1994] 1 AC 180, 188; [2001] UKHL 44, paras 2, 34–7, 98 and 140–1.
[69] [2004] EWCA Civ 372, para 4.

THE SIGNIFICANT DIFFERENCE BETWEEN ACTUAL AND PRESUMED UNDUE INFLUENCE

In *Etridge*, Lord Clyde made comments that could be interpreted as rejecting the traditional division of undue influence into two types.[70] Lords Hobhouse and Scott also made comments that were critical of analytical divisions of undue influence.[71] Lord Scott's attack upon the incoherence of finding that undue influence was both present (presumed) and not present (actual) on the facts of a case has been noted and discussed above. Therefore, if the argument advanced by this chapter is to be supported, it must be established that it is viable to read *Etridge* as preserving the distinction between actual and presumed undue influence.

Four arguments support such a reading of *Etridge*. First, *Etridge* was not concerned with presumed undue influence, because the relationship between husband and wife does not generate any presumption of influence. Second, the division of cases of undue influence into actual and presumed was established over a century ago by *Allcard v Skinner*,[72] a case cited with approval in *Etridge*.[73] Third, their Lordships took care to reaffirm the importance of the traditional classification of presumed undue influence relationships.[74] Finally, the attacks on classifications within the law of undue influence were directed at the sub-category of presumed undue influence known as 'class 2B' undue influence in *Bank of Credit and Commerce International SA v Aboody*.[75] In the light of these arguments it is submitted that *Etridge* is compatible with the recognition of an important distinction between actual and presumed undue influence.

Rather than seeking to undermine the distinction between cases involving presumed undue influence and cases involving actual undue influence, the tendency of the analysis in *Etridge* was to emphasise the distinction between cases involving those relationships that led to a presumption of undue influence (classified by *Aboody* as class 2A cases) and those relationships that did not generate such a presumption (classified by *Aboody* as class 1 and class 2B cases). Lord Scott in his application of the law of undue influence to the cases under appeal in *Etridge* emphasised that a presumption of undue influence was exceptional in cases of husband and wife, despite the existence of trust and confidence in marriage.[76] Such

---

[70]   [2001] UKHL 44, para 92.
[71]   *Ibid*, paras 107 and 161.
[72]   (1887) 36 Ch D 115, 181; see also 171.
[73]   [2001] UKHL 44, paras 8–9.
[74]   *Ibid*, paras 18, 98, 104–7 and 157–61.
[75]   *Ibid*, paras 98, 104–7 and 157–61; [1990] 1 QB 923.
[76]   *Ibid*, paras 9, 22 and 29.

emphasis was entirely consonant with the importance of maintaining the distinction between presumed undue influence cases and other relational undue influence cases.

The Unified Tort Theory Advanced by Professor Enonchong

As argued above, analysis of presumed undue influence should begin with identifying the policy conflicts that shape the law. The law of presumed undue influence operates as a check on unrestrained selfishness in certain circumstances. It denies legitimacy, in the context of a restricted class of relationships, to the generally tolerated pursuit of self-interest, which is protected by the doctrines of freedom of contract and freedom of disposition.

Professor Enonchong advances a more conventional alternative view. He accepts that the distinction between actual and presumed undue influence was preserved by *Etridge* and subsequent case law but sees the distinction as merely forensic in nature.[77] Professor Enonchong presents the topic of his book *Duress, Undue Influence and Unconscionable Dealing* as the law that is 'concerned to protect the freedom of contracting parties'.[78] Consequently, the book 'deals with the circumstances when an otherwise valid and enforceable transaction may be avoided on the ground that the consent of the party seeking avoidance was procured by duress, undue influence or unconscionable dealing'.[79] Moreover, '[d]uress is the weapon with which the common law protects the victim of improper pressure', and "undue influence is the equitable version of common law duress'.[80]

There is one aspect of undue influence that extends beyond the confines of this analogue, as 'it extends to cases where there is no specific act of pressure':[81]

> Undue influence is improper or unacceptable use of influence to procure consent to a transaction... [T]he conduct of the defendant must be capable of being stigmatised as unconscionable.[82]

For Professor Enonchong the only distinctions between different types of undue influence relate to the means by which the wrong is committed, being either overt or insidious. Following from this, the rules for proving the wrongdoing, which in insidious cases lack overt acts of pressure that could be proved, allow for presumptions to operate. The sole difference

---

[77] Enonchong, note 12 above, 7-008.
[78] *Ibid*, vii.
[79] *Ibid*, 1-001.
[80] *Ibid*, 1-002 and 1-003.
[81] *Ibid*, 1-003.
[82] *Ibid*, 7-003.

between actual and presumed undue influence is the absence or presence of an irrebuttable presumption of influence.

Thus, for Professor Enongchong, actual undue influence is 'undue influence proved by affirmative evidence', and presumed undue influence 'requires proof of a pre-existing relationship'.[83] Professor Enonchong considers it an error to view presumed undue influence 'within a wider framework of fiduciary obligations'[84]. 'In English law the conceptual basis of the doctrine [of presumed undue influence] is evidential.'[85] The sole distinction between cases of presumed undue influence and other relational undue influence cases is that in presumed undue influence cases it is not necessary to prove that the relationship gave rise to influence.[86]

Two things should be noted. First, in the arrangement of his book, Professor Enonchong has not stopped dealing with all relational undue influence cases as essentially similar. Following *Etridge*, he has assimilated those relationships that do not give rise to a presumption of influence with actual undue influence. However, he has treated those relationships that have traditionally been classified as presumed undue influence in the same way, to create one unified tort of undue influence. This organisation of the material is not responsive to the criticism of *Aboody* classifications in *Etridge* and suggests the implicit retention of the *Aboody* analysis.

Second, Professor Enonchong considered and rejected the possibility that the law of undue influence has another aspect, a similarity or relationship with the law governing the conduct of fiduciaries. The argument for rejecting this possibility seems to be that either the law of undue influence would have to cover the same relationships as the law governing the conduct of fiduciaries or it must be a tort analogue.[87]

Criticism of the Unified Tort Theory of Undue Influence

Rejection of Professor Enonchong's unified tort theory is not rejection (or acceptance) of the theory that actual undue influence can best be viewed as an extension of the common law tort of duress. It is rejection of the thesis that all undue influence cases are properly analysed as such. The argument is that presumed undue influence survived *Etridge* as a category that describes a collection of cases that have more in common than an

---

[83] *Ibid*, 8-001 and 10-001.
[84] *Ibid*, 10-001.
[85] *Ibid*, 10-001.
[86] *Ibid*, 10-001.
[87] *Ibid*. His authority is Lord Nicholls in *Etridge* [2001] UKHL 44, para 11: 'The principle is not confined to cases of abuse of trust and confidence.' The significance for Enonchong of presumed undue influence cases involving relationships not generally recognised as fiduciary is confirmed at 14-054.

irrebuttable presumption of influence. There are two aspects of the authorities that suggest the unified tort theory is inadequate as a description of the law of undue influence.

First, the Court of Appeal has not endorsed the claim that the essential feature of undue influence is 'wrongdoing' or 'unconscionable conduct'.[88] Since *Etridge* the Court of Appeal has twice emphasised the survival in the law of the innocent undue influencer.[89] Professor Enonchong recognises this is incompatible with the unified tort thesis, and he ascribes it to repeated error by the Court of Appeal.[90]

Second, the unified tort theory demands the ascription of a further error to the courts over a very long period of time and continuing to this date. Professor Enonchong is unafraid to so ascribe error. He says that the courts have (over more than a century) continued mistakenly to conflate presumed undue influence with abuse of confidence, and sadly they continue to fall into error to this day: 'The confusion ... was not dissipated by that decision [in *Etridge*].'[91] Indeed in *Etridge*, Lord Hobhouse fell into error,[92] although Lord Scott managed to keep abuse of confidence and undue influence separate.[93] Professor Enonchong seems to consider it inconceivable that there might be a type of undue influence that is not the same as abuse of confidence and yet operates in a similar manner for similar reasons.

It seems Professor Enonchong has fallen into the trap of assuming that the ascription of the term 'fiduciary' to an aspect of a relationship involves the imposition of a standard set of duties. The error was identified and exploded in *Coomber v Coomber* by Fletcher Moulton LJ, as noted extra-judicially by Millett LJ.[94] Millett LJ specified a minimum of three categories of fiduciary relationships: the relationship of trust and confidence, with its duty of loyalty; the relationship of influence, founded in ascendancy and dependency, with the purpose of preventing the exploitation of the vulnerable; and the relationship of confidentiality, with its duty to respect confidentiality.[95] This analysis placed the relationship of influence at the centre of the law of undue influence. The assertion that such

---

[88] Enonchong, note 12 above, 9-005 (wrongdoing) and 7-003, 7-006 (unconscionable conduct).

[89] *Hammond v Osborn* [2002] EWCA Civ 885; *Niersmans v Presticcio* [2004] EWCA Civ 372.

[90] Enonchong, note 12 above, 9-006.

[91] *Ibid*, 14-050.

[92] *Ibid*, 14-051.

[93] *Ibid*, 14-052.

[94] [1911] 1 Ch 723, 728–9; P J Millett, 'Equity's Place in the Law of Commerce' (1998) 114 *LQR* 214.

[95] P J Millett, 'Equity's Place in the Law of Commerce' (1998) 114 *LQR* 214, 219. See also PD Finn, 'The Fiduciary Principle' in TG Youdan (ed), *Equity, Fiduciaries and Trusts* (Toronto, Carswell, 1989) 1–56, 41–9.

analysis is founded upon confusion is not argued by Professor Enon-chong.[96] Neither, does he recognise the connection between such an analysis and the continued 'errors' by the Court of Appeal noted above.

It is submitted that in advancing the unified tort theory Professor Enonchong is being prescriptive in his analysis, advancing beyond the decided cases. It is further submitted that we should reject the theory that the law of undue influence is solely concerned with an equitable tort analogous to duress. There are two species of undue influence. Actual undue influence is based upon wrongdoing and has similarities to duress. The House of Lords in *Etridge* was very clear that many cases assimilated to presumed undue influence by *Aboody* should be analysed in the same way as cases of actual undue influence had been analysed traditionally. However, the House was careful to preserve the separate treatment of presumed undue influence cases.

AN ALTERNATIVE INTERPRETATION OF PRESUMED UNDUE INFLUENCE

Actual undue influence can be explained as a legal response to wrongdo-ing. Presumed undue influence can be explained partially as a response to wrongdoing. However, any explanation limited to this aspect of the jurisdiction will be a distortion of the law.

The starting point for analysis is the 'policy' referred to by Cotton LJ in *Allcard v Skinner*.[97] Lord Scarman inveighed against appeals to 'vague public policy' and described the relevant policy as protection of the vulnerable from victimisation in *Morgan*.[98] However, in the context of the law of undue influence, the prevention of victimisation is the same policy as the imposition of ethical standards upon parties to relationships. Presumed undue influence operates to regulate certain relationships.

The courts have had a clear appreciation of the regulative effect the law of undue influence has upon parties to transactions. The leading speeches in *O'Brien* and *Etridge* emphasised the potential impact of the decisions for access to the capital market for small businesses.[99] In each case, the House of Lords essentially laid down a code of conduct for banks to follow. It has been recognised judicially by Lord Nicholls that his speech in *Etridge* was a peculiar use of the power of judicial declaration of the law, because it was crafted with a primary purpose of being useful for the future guidance of banks and solicitors.[100]

---

[96] Enonchong, note 12 above, 10-001 and 14-048–14-056.
[97] (1887) 36 Ch D 145.
[98] [1985] AC 686, 705A.
[99] [1994] 1 AC 180, 188H; [2001] UKHL 44, paras 34–7.
[100] [2005] UKHL 41, paras 15–16.

Undue Influence and Fiduciary Duties

Presumed undue influence clearly demonstrates a concern with relationships that are fiduciary. In *Etridge* Lord Nicholls gave as examples of relationships subject to an irrebuttable presumption of influence: 'parent and child, guardian and ward, trustee and beneficiary, solicitor and client, medical advisor and patient'.[101] The list contains very familiar examples of relationships generally treated as fiduciary in nature. The less clearly fiduciary relationships listed are relationships in which typically one would not expect the property of the vulnerable party (child and patient) to be under the control of the dominant party (parent and medical advisor).

In *CIBC Mortgages Plc v Pitt*,[102] Lord Browne-Wilkinson recognised an unexplored relationship between the principle that informed the doctrine of undue influence and the 'principle laid down in the abuse of confidence cases viz. the law', which 'requires those in a fiduciary position who enter into transactions with those to whom they owe fiduciary duties to establish affirmatively that the transaction was a fair one.'[103]

The puzzle was why presumed undue influence operated only when there was an actual and apparent conflict of interest between the parties to the protected relationship (ie, 'manifest disadvantage'). Hence the requirement that the 'wrongfulness of the transaction, must, therefore be shown'[104] or that 'something that calls for an explanation'[105] must be present to activate presumed undue influence. If there is no transaction that suggests the action of improper influence, then presumed undue influence does not come into operation. If the actions of the claimant are apparently against her own best interests and serve the interests of the defendant, then, and only then, does undue influence become operative.[106]

This demand for an actual disadvantage to be demonstrated differs from the approach of the law to the regulation of fiduciaries elsewhere. Fiduciaries are prevented from acting whenever the potential for a conflict of interest arises, unless they have authority to act in such circumstances. In the context of presumed undue influence it is actually executed advantage to the dominant party in the relationship that brings the law into operation.

---

[101] [2001] UKHL 44, para 18. See also paras 104 and 158. Similar lists were given in *Lloyds Bank v Bundy* [1975] 1 QB 326, 338B and *Re Brocklehurst* [1978] Ch 14, 42.
[102] [1994] 1 AC 200.
[103] *Ibid*, 209E-H.
[104] [1985] 1 AC 686, 707C.
[105] [2001] UKHL 44, para 24.
[106] See: *National Westminster Bank v Morgan* [1985] 1 AC 686; *Barclays Bank Plc v O'Brien* [1994] 1 AC 180; *CIBC Mortgages Plc v Pitt* [1994] 1 AC 200; *Royal Bank of Scotland v Etridge (No 2)* [2001] UKHL 44.

The link between the two areas of law is obvious. In each case the nature of a relationship gives rise to a risk of abuse, and the law operates to counteract that risk of abuse. The difference in the approach taken to conflict of interests is explicable by differences in the risks to be counteracted. In the classic fiduciary relationship the fiduciary has control over the property of the person owed fiduciary duties, and it is the action of the fiduciary that the law seeks to restrain. In undue influence it is the action of the victimised that the law is concerned with. The remedy for undue influence is release of the claimant from the consequences of his own past actions.[107] Therefore, the argument that the two doctrines are aspects of a single protective principle is supported, but the extension—that the two doctrines should be harmonised by treating presumed undue influence as merely an example of the regulation of fiduciaries—is rejected.

One feature in particular points towards a common organising principle operating in both areas, namely the rejection of defences based upon the innocence of the defendant. In both presumed undue influence and the law of fiduciary relationships, the defence of honest action is not available. This refusal to recognise a defence of innocent action in the context of fiduciary duties was most famously affirmed in *Regal (Hastings) Ltd v Gulliver*[108] and *Boardman v Phipps*.[109] A similar position has been consistently maintained in the field of presumed undue influence.[110]

This approach is supportable because presumed undue influence is directed towards the removal of temptation rather than the punishment of transgression. In this it shares, with such rules as the barring of a trustee from acquiring trust property, a disinterest in the moral quality of the individual defendant. This common feature is generated in each area by the operation of the same regulative principle.[111]

The importance of the correct identification of the policy concerns for the law can now be appreciated. If the law seeks to safeguard the freedom of disposition of vulnerable property owners, whilst at the same time minimising the risk of exploitation of their vulnerability, two conflicting policies must be balanced. First, to provide effective protection there must be some effective means to restrain the potential exploiter, as *ex hypothesi* the vulnerable property owners cannot protect themselves. Second, to support freedom of disposition there must be a relatively simple means to achieve an unchallengeable disposition.

---

[107] Where third-party rights have been acquired in the property disposed of then a restitutionary personal remedy may be substituted for the now unavailable primary remedy. See *Niersmans v Pesticcio* [2004] EWCA Civ 372.

[108] [1967] 2 AC 134n.

[109] [1967] 2 AC 46.

[110] *Allcard v Skinner* (1887) 36 Ch D 145, 172 and 184–5; *Lloyds Bank plc v Bundy* [1975] 1 QB 326, 340C and 346E; *Niersmans v Pesticcio* [2004] EWCA Civ 372, para 20.

[111] See [2001] UKHL 44, paras 2–3, 34–7, 42–3, 53–5 and 98.

It is with respect to this second end that accounts founded upon will theory distract analysis. The law needs a readily verifiable process that can be resorted to for safeguarding the validity of transactions. If concern with the autonomous nature of the claimant's actions is a vital issue then litigation directed towards that issue will almost always be possible. However, the very possibility of such litigation is destructive of the policy ends served by freedom of disposition. The potential for the 'cleansing' of a disposition from any taint of suspicion is a vital aspect of any successful law of presumed undue influence. Achieving the correct balance between protection of the vulnerable and allowing for the cleansing of a transaction is the crux of the law. In the context of the pre-*Etridge* law, Millett LJ regretted what he saw as the failure to correctly establish this balance:

> We have substituted an inappropriate bright line rule for a proper investigation of the facts and have failed the vulnerable in the process.[112]

It is submitted that the demand for a 'proper investigation of the facts', if intended to apply generally, was the unfortunate product of the over-extension of the influence of will theory to the law of undue influence. A bright-line rule is demanded by the need to protect freedom of disposition. However, the degeneration of the protective operation of the law into 'a ritual reliance on the provision of legal advice' was a failure to find the correct point of balance.[113] The centrality of readdressing this balance for the House of Lords in *Etridge* is obvious.[114]

Undue Influence and Constructive Notice

The development of constructive notice was of course part of the development of the defence of the bona fide purchaser of the legal estate for value without notice. The courts developed a concept of 'should have had notice', or constructive notice, to prevent the destruction of equitable interests through a deliberate omission to make inquiries. The courts did not insist upon inquiries being made; it was always possible for a purchaser to decide not to inquire, and there was no breach of duty involved. Failure to make inquiries shifted risk from the equitable owner to the purchaser. If an equitable interest existed, and inquiries would have revealed its existence, then the purchaser with constructive notice took subject to the equitable interest. The risk that a bona fide purchaser would destroy an equitable interest was inherent in equitable interests. Therefore, the holder

---

[112] (1998) 114 LQR 215, 220.

[113] *Ibid*, 220, quoting Sir Anthony Mason.

[114] [2001] UKHL 44, paras 3, 37, 44–68, 75–80, 82–9, 108–22, 148, 163, 183–4 and 189–91.

of an equitable interest had an incentive to make the existence of the interest known. The problem was to provide an incentive to purchasers to seek out notice, despite the fact that the receipt of notice was likely to thwart the objectives of a purchaser. Constructive notice was the solution. In the absence of investigation it was the purchaser, and not the equitable owner, who was at risk. Constructive notice imposed prudential conduct on the purchaser, in order to protect holders of equitable interests.

Presumed undue influence has a similar effect. As with the purchaser and the equitable owner, there is a risk. The risk arises from the power imbalance in the relationship. The risk is on the weaker party to the relationship, and the problem is to provide an incentive for the stronger party to act in a manner that minimises the risk. However, as with the purchaser, the minimising of the risk is likely to thwart the objectives of the stronger party to the relationship. The courts require prudential conduct from the stronger party to the relationship, by threatening with rescission any transaction under which the stronger party benefits to the disadvantage of the weaker party. The stronger party can avoid this risk by taking steps to ensure the weaker party has an opportunity to make an independent decision, generally by ensuring that adequate independent advice is available. The courts will uphold a transaction when the weaker party has had the opportunity to exercise independent judgment, even though it is disadvantageous to the weaker party (as it must be, *ex hypothesi*, if presumed undue influence is in operation). The purchaser who had made all the usual inquiries and not received notice of an equitable interest destroyed the interest. The stronger party to an asymmetrical relationship of trust and confidence who ensures the weaker party has opportunity to make an independent decision takes the benefit conferred by the transaction.

The similarity between the two doctrines points towards a similarity of purpose. The purpose of the doctrine of constructive notice was not to destroy equitable interests, nor to make land inalienable. The purpose of constructive notice was to create a legal environment in which it made sense to follow the current best practice for investigation of title. Constructive notice regulated the land market, by shifting a risk from one party (the equitable owner) onto another (the purchaser), unless the normal investigations were made. Essentially, the extent of constructive notice balanced the interest of the market in security of transactions (purchasers) with the interest of owners in security of property rights (holders of equitable interests). The purpose of presumed undue influence is to regulate certain relationships, relationships that carry an inherent risk of abuse. The doctrine seeks to encourage good conduct by those in the position to abuse, by placing upon them the risk of abuse, unless they follow a course of action designed to protect the vulnerable from abuse. Essentially, the availability of rescission balances the policy imperatives advanced by freedom of contract and disposition with the policy imperatives advanced by the protective policy towards those who are unusually vulnerable to abuse.[115]

The effect of constructive notice has been described as creating a 'duty' upon purchasers. Presumed undue influence has been described as imposing a 'duty' on the dominant party in a relationship to ensure that the vulnerable party in the relationship has an opportunity to make an independent decision. In both cases 'duty' should be understood as acting at one's own risk if the 'duty' is not complied with. Duty should not be understood as a duty owed to another party who has a correlative right. The requirement of prudential conduct by the donee is almost always expressed as the need for independent advice to the vulnerable party. For example, Lindley LJ, in *Allcard v Skinner*, stated:

> In this class of cases it has been considered necessary to shew that the donor had independent advice, and was removed from the influence of the donee when the gift to him was made.[116]

Bowen LJ expressed it in terms of a duty:

> Passing next to the duties of the donee, it seems to me that, although this power of perfect disposition remains in the donor under circumstances like the present, it is plain that equity will not allow a person who exercises or enjoys a dominant religious influence over another to benefit directly or indirectly by the gifts which the donor makes under or in consequence of such influence, unless it is shewn that the donor, at the time of making the gift, was allowed full and free opportunity for counsel and advice outside—the means of considering his or her worldly position and exercising an independent will about it.[117]

The 'duty' imposed upon the dominant party to a protected relationship is an important part of the law. Although pregnant with the potential for misunderstanding, references to a 'duty' have an advantage over the alternative terms deployed; which refer to the nature of the evidence required to rebut a presumption of undue influence once it has arisen. At least the references to a duty on the dominant party draw attention to the reality of the situation, which is the law requires the dominant party to facilitate the provision of adequate and independent advice to the vulnerable party if she is to be safe from the risk of rescission. The 'duty' is not a forensic detail but a point at which the courts can balance the tension between freedom of contact and disposition and the protective policy of the law.

---

[115] *Ibid*, paras 2–3, 34–7, 42–3, 53–5 and 98.
[116] (1887) 36 Ch D 145, 181. See also 184–5.
[117] *Ibid*, 190. Cotton LJ was implicitly to like effect at 172–3.

Whichever way the issue is framed, the key factor for liability is: 'For what act or omission can the defendant fairly be criticised?'[118] Failure to ensure that independent advice and counsel have been obtained by the weaker party to the transaction is an omission solely because presumed undue influence has imposed a prudential duty to ensure the same. A policy analysis of presumed undue influence suggests that what is usually discussed under the rubric 'evidence capable of rebutting the presumption' should be a main focus of analysis for jurists.

CONCLUSIONS

An attempt has been made to restrict the analysis above to a descriptive exercise. However, if the analysis is correct, it carries a prescriptive importance. The position both of solicitors in advising their clients and of banks relying upon legal advice to avoid constructive notice has been greatly clarified and rationalised by *Etridge*.[119] The position of donees in presumed undue influence cases and relational undue influence has received far less attention. *Etridge* itself contains dicta that suggest there may be hypothetical cases in which regardless of the availability of informed independent advice, there might be transactions that cannot be freed from the taint of undue influence.[120] The standard and extent of the legal advice required to rebut a presumption of undue influence in one recent case suggests a fancifully high standard for legal advice is being set.[121] Once a presumption of undue influence has arisen, the tension between protection of the vulnerable and freedom of disposition must ultimately be resolved in the details of the nature of rebutting evidence. It is hoped that articulation of the policy issues that bear upon this issue will illuminate the academic and judicial approach to the subject.

It has been argued that the law of presumed undue influence has an important protective role to play. *Etridge* has assimilated cases of relational undue influence to actual undue influence. Such assimilation emphasises the exceptional quality of the facts giving rise to a presumption of undue influence outside of the confines of presumed undue influence cases and the particularity of the facts in disposing of such cases. Of more importance for the future of the law is the possibility that cases of actual undue influence involving relationships of influence might be capable of being recognised by judicial decision as cases of presumed undue influence. This issue cannot be articulated unless two species of undue influence are

---

[118] *Re Brocklehurst* [1978] Ch 14, 48.
[119] [2001] UKHL 44, paras 58–68 and 79; also paras 169–70 and 181–2.
[120] *Ibid*, paras 20 and 62.
[121] *Wright v Hodgkinson* [2004] EWCA 3091 Ch, paras 142–6.

recognised.[122] Further, the decision to allow such a transformation must be informed by the policy constraints discussed above.

Finally, one reason that the two types of undue influence must be kept apart is that the imposition of a prudential duty is justifiable only in cases of presumed undue influence. In cases of actual undue influence there is no justification for the imposition of a prudential duty. In cases of relational undue influence there is no justification for requiring action from the defendant to ensure the claimant had the opportunity to make an independent decision unless the particular and exceptional facts that generated the presumption also warrant such a further step.[123] The presence or absence of independent advice in actual undue influence is a relevant fact for deciding the issue of whether undue influence was exercised. The failure to provide for the provision of such advice is not an independent ground for the finding of wrongdoing.

---

[122] This process is not a remote theoretical possibility; it seems likely that such is taking place today in the courts, as evidenced by *Hammond v Osborn* [2002] EWCA Civ 885; and *Niersmans v Prestico* [2004] EWCA Civ 372.

[123] In the words of Sir Eric Sachs LJ in *Lloyds Bank Ltd v Bundy* [1975] 1 QB 326, 345D: 'The situation was thus one which to any reasonably sensible person, who gave it but a moment's thought, cried aloud Mr Bundy's need for careful independent advice.'

4

The Lie of the Land: Mortgage Law as Legal Fiction

INTRODUCTION

T
HE ENGLISH MORTGAGE is a work of fiction. It is a lie. This
was most apparent in the days of the classic mortgage by conveyance and reconveyance of the fee simple, for then the mortgage deed
was 'one long *suppressio veri* and *suggestio falsi*'.[1] Maitland attributed the
falsehood to the 'action of equity', but the mortgage deed was inherently
dishonest, for it pretended to convey title when the parties merely intended
to create security. Equity tried to give effect to the true substance of the
arrangement and was forced to resort to the fiction of giving back to the
mortgagor a beneficial interest in the land, the so-called 'equity of
redemption', when in fact equity considered the mortgagor to continue to
be the true owner of the land despite the mortgage. Equity did not make a
liar of the legal deed; it was the other way round.

The Law of Property Act 1925 abolished the mortgage by conveyance
and reconveyance of the fee simple, but even then the lie refused to die. We
will see that the dishonesty inherent in the classic form of mortgage is
perpetuated in the very words by which the statute describes the modern
charge by way of legal mortgage. The truth is that 'mortgages have always
pretended to a greater or less degree to be something which they are not'.[2]
The task of this chapter is to identify the nature of the pretence and to
uncover the underlying truth of the English mortgage— which is that the
mortgage is today, and was in the days of the classic mortgage by
conveyance and reconveyance, a hypothec. We will see that the most

* The author is grateful to Professor George Gretton and an anonymous referee for
their insightful comments on an earlier draft.
[1] F Maitland, *Equity* (1909), revised 2nd edn (edited by Brunyate) (Cambridge, CUP,
1936) 182.
[2] A W B Simpson, *An Introduction to the History of the Land Law* (Oxford, OUP, 1961)
225.

persistent fictions are the notion that the mortgagee has a legal estate in the mortgaged land (fee simple or lease, as the case may be) and that the mortgagor's interest in the mortgaged land is merely an 'equity of redemption'.

This chapter agrees with F H Lawson that '[n]othing would be lost if the notion that the mortgagee has an interest in the mortgaged property were entirely given up and the existence of the equity of redemption entirely disregarded'.[3] Others have argued that the doctrine that prevents 'clogs on the equity of redemption' is essential to protect mortgagors,[4] but nowadays mortgagors are protected by common law[5] and statutory[6] rules in ways they were not when the fiction of the equity of redemption was invented. This is not to pretend that property law can operate without fictions, only that fictions should be abandoned when their efforts to create harmony in the law can be shown to produce the opposite effect. This chapter will demonstrate that the fictions entrenched within our mortgage law have not only rendered it internally discordant, but have also created barriers to harmony with other legal systems, including Civilian, Islamic and Torrens systems.

A broader but no less significant aim of this chapter is to examine the storytelling processes by which fictions in property law at times inform and at other times obscure the science of the law. Property law, like all law, is a work of science fiction, and as we seek to comprehend the science, we will do well to appreciate the fiction. Admittedly, the term 'legal fiction' was traditionally applied in a narrow way to describe facts which the courts knew or believed to be false but deemed to be real—such as the fiction of 'lost modern grant'. Here, fiction is used in a wider sense, to include judicial rhetoric which deliberately or conveniently disguises the truth.

An appreciation of judicial storytelling may be particularly useful in elucidating equity's contribution to the story of the English mortgage, for, as Professor Thompson has noted, it is a subject that 'prompts rhetorical flourishes'.[7] Jeremy Bentham, the pre-eminent legal scientist of the English Enlightenment, understood well the conflict between stories and science. Ogden identifies Bentham's fearful reaction to ghost stories, which he never outgrew, as one motive for Bentham's drive to banish fictions in favour of

---

[3] F H Lawson, *Introduction to the Law of Property* (Oxford, Clarendon Press, 1958) 182; F H Lawson and B Rudden, *The Law of Property* (Oxford, Clarendon Press, 2002) 199.

[4] M G Shanker, 'Will Mortgage Law Survive? A Commentary and Critique on Mortgage Law's Birth, Long Life, and Current Proposals for Its Demise' (2003) 54 *Case W Res L Rev* 69.

[5] Such as the rules against restraint of trade (*Esso Petroleum Co Ltd v Harper's Garage (Stourport) Ltd* [1968] AC 269' HL).

[6] For example, Consumer Credit Act (1974) ss 137–9; Administration of Justice Act (1970) s 36; Administration of Justice Act (1973) s 8(3).

[7] M P Thompson, 'Do We Really Need Clogs?' [2001] *Conv* 502, 515.

science.[8] Nowadays we might be more fearful of a world of science devoid of stories, but Bentham's call to abandon unreasonable prejudices against usury applies as well to the present call to abandon the peculiar fiction of the equity of redemption:

> 'If our ancestors have been all along under a mistake, how came they to have fallen into it?' is a question that naturally presents itself... in matters of law more especially, such is the dominion of authority over our minds, and such the prejudice it creates in favour of whatever institution it has taken under its wing, that, after all manner of reasons that can be thought of, in favour of the institution, have been shown to be insufficient, we still cannot forbear looking to some unassignable and latent reason for its efficient cause. But if, instead of any such reason, we can find a cause for it in some notion, of the erroneousness of which we are already satisfied, then at last we are content to give it up without further struggle; and then, and not till then, our satisfaction is complete.[9]

PROPERTY LAW AS FICTION

Property is a construct. Things may be real enough, but the idea of property rights in and over things is necessarily distinct from material fact—realty is not the same thing as reality. This is nowhere more evident than in the property law system of England and Wales, where, despite popular perception, it is theoretically impossible for any citizen to be an absolute owner of real property. The best that can be hoped for is to be what Maitland called an 'unqualified tenant in fee simple'.[10] The land register adds another layer of abstraction. Even if it were a true mirror of title, it would only reflect a constructed reality; but we know that in England and Wales the mirror is distorted or cracked by 'overriding interests'.[11]

The fact that property law is an artificial construct usually lies submerged within legal language, but occasionally it rises to the surface. Concepts such as 'constructive notice' and 'constructive trust' play a crucial role in working out the most fundamental dilemma of land allocation, the choice between the innocent residential occupier and the innocent third-party purchaser, but the word 'constructive' concedes that the dilemma cannot, as a matter of fact, be resolved by bright-line rules. Sir Robert Megarry identified the storytelling process intrinsic to the word:

---

[8]   C K Ogden, *Bentham's Theory of Fictions* (London, Kegan Paul, 1932).
[9]   J Bentham, *Defence of Usury* (1787) Letter X.
[10]   Maitland, note 1 above, 182.
[11]   Land Registration Act (2002) Schedule 3, para 2.

'Constructive' is, of course, an unhappy word in the law… 'Constructive' seems to mean 'It isn't, but has to be treated as if it were', and the less of this there is in the law, the better.[12]

No doubt the best system of property law would be the one that most closely reflected factual reality, but it would be a naïve and hopeless (not to mention soulless) project to seek to dispel all abstractions from property law. What may be attempted is to identify the points at which coherent constructs of property law, what we might call the science of property law, give way to less coherent, even intuitive, fictions. It must then be determined on a case-by-case, or story-by-story, basis whether the fiction serves any useful purpose. We might retain an apparently useless fiction if, in a harmless way, it adds to the elegance of the law, but a fiction should be removed if it obstructs the harmonious development of the law. 'Have nothing in your houses that you do not know to be useful, or believe to be beautiful' was William Morris' 'golden rule',[13] and it applies as well to the house of law. Unchecked, fictions tend to breed fictions, and legal science is then in danger of being overrun by illegitimate progeny. 'Legal fictions have their place, but this would be legal fairyland'.[14]

The idea of the 'constructive trustee' provides an example of how one fiction may produce another. If an express trustee is a true trustee, a constructive trustee is one step removed from the truth. Yet despite the fiction already inherent in the notion of the 'constructive' trustee, strangers wrongfully interfering with trusts have been held personally liability in equity 'as if' they are constructive trustees;[15] thus the fiction of the constructive trust is overlaid with a further layer of make-believe. In the following section we will see that mortgage law supplies striking illustrations of the same phenomenon.

THE MORTGAGE FICTION

Lord Macnaghten alleged that 'no one, I am sure, by the light of nature ever understood an English mortgage of real estate'.[16] He was right. To understand the English mortgage by conveyance and reconveyance of the fee simple, one has to appreciate that it is unnatural. Like a sphinx, it is a *mischwesen*; a confusion of things. At one level the confusion is caused by the discrepancy between the mortgage at law and the mortgage in equity,

---

[12]   *Fiduciary Duties (Special Lectures of the Law Society of Upper Canada 1990)* (Ontario, De Boo, 1991) 1, 5.
[13]   William Morris, *Hopes and Fears for Art* (1882).
[14]   *Tower Hamlets v Barrett* [2005] EWCA Civ 923, [68] (Neuberger J).
[15]   *Selangor United Rubber Estates Ltd v Cradock (a Bankrupt) (No 3)* [1968] 1 WLR 1555, 1582.
[16]   *Samuel v Jarrah Timber and Wood Paving* [1904] AC 323, 326.

but the confusion goes deeper than this. Whereas a *mischwesen* is a confusion of natural things, the classic English mortgage was a confusion of unnatural things, for it was unnatural in both legal form and equitable substance. The legal form pretended to be a conveyance to the mortgagee of the mortgagor's fee simple estate, and the equitable substance pretended to effect an immediate reconveyance to the mortgagor of an interest or estate known as the 'equity of redemption'. The reality, as we will see in the next section, is that the classic English mortgage was a transaction under which the borrower retained ownership with possession, and the lender obtained mere security. In short, the English mortgage pretended to be a pledge or gage of land when in truth it was a hypothecary arrangement.

It is informative to consider how the story began. It is no easy task, for the story of English mortgage law is like many an old book: its first few pages have come loose and gone missing. G Wood Hill once observed:

> [I]n the course of time, and no one seems to know exactly how it came about, or when it came about exactly, but it did come about ... a Court of Equity interfered and exercised its jurisdiction to relieve the mortgagor, from the consequences of his not having tendered the money on the prescribed day... Notwithstanding that he had lost his right, at law, to redeem the property, it was held that he had, in equity, the right so to do, and that was called his 'equity of redemption'.[17]

Our search for the earliest origins of the English idea of mortgage takes us to the Old Testament. John Joseph Powell noted in *A Treatise on the Law of Mortgages* that 'notions of mortgaging and redemption are, by some, thought to have originated with the Jews'.[18] The law of the ancient Israelites required debts and mortgages to be cancelled on the seventh year,[19] and the Levitical law enlarged this obligation by requiring all alienated land to be restored to its original owner in the year following seven times seven years (the 'year of Jubilee').[20]

However, whereas it is plausible that the Christian doctrine of redemption, derived from the Judaic concept, might have created an image with great appeal to the clerical mind of the mediaeval Chancellor, it is doubtful that the Israelite model would have appealed directly. In any case, there is no doctrinal correspondence between the classic English mortgage and the mortgage of the ancient Israelite, for the latter was a species of *vivum*

---

[17] G Wood Hill, *Lectures on the Law of Real Property in England*, (London, C&E Layton, 1898) 86.

[18] J J Powell, *A Treatise on the Law of Mortgages* (1785) 1.

[19] Deuteronomy 15:7–18.

[20] Leviticus 25:8–55. See, generally, R Westbrook, *Property and the Family in Biblical Law* (Sheffield, Journal for the Study of the Old Testament, Supplemental Series No113, 1991).

vadium under which the borrower remained in possession of the land and 'instead of signing a mortgage on his property, farmed the property himself to gradually work off the indebtedness',[21] whereas the form of English mortgage, when Powell was writing, was closer in nature to a *mortuum vadium* under which, in the eyes of the law, the land could only be redeemed by repayment of the entire debt at the due date.

Powell, perhaps sensible to this discrepancy, identified Roman law as the more likely inspiration for the classic form of English mortgage.[22] Roman law is a natural candidate, given Chancery's general openness to the Romano-Christian jurisprudence of mainland Europe. Thus Chancery's refusal to recognise irremediable mortgages appears to echo the Emperor Constantine's statute against *pactum commissorium* in the context of pledge, *pactum commissorium* being any contractual agreement by which the pledgee would keep the security in the event of the pledgor's default. The statutory prohibition, which was subsequently incorporated in Justinian's Code and is still retained in some form in every modern Civilian legal system, can be translated thus:

> Since amongst other harmful practices the severity of the *lex commissorium* in pledges is on the increase, it has been decided to invalidate it and abolish all memory of it for the future. If therefore anyone is oppressed by such a contract, he shall find relief by this decree, which annuls such provisions past and present and proscribes them in future. For we decree that creditors shall give up the thing pledged and recover what they have given.[23]

There is also some correspondence between the English mortgage by conveyance and reconveyance of Powell's day—and in particular the liability of a mortgagee in possession to account on the basis of wilful default—and a species of *actio praescriptis verbis* described in Justinian's Code:

> If your parents sold a tract of land under the condition that if they themselves, or their heirs, should indefinitely, or within a designated time, tender to the purchaser the price of the property he would restore it; and if you are ready to comply with the above-mentioned condition, and the heir of the purchaser refuses to fulfill the contract, the *Actio praescriptis verbis*, or the action on sale, shall be granted you; and an account shall be rendered you of the amount of the crops taken from the land which have come into the hands of your adversary, after the price was tendered in compliance with the terms of the agreement.[24]

---

[21] R North, *Sociology of the Biblical Jubilee* (Rome, Pontifical Biblical Institute, 1954).
[22] Powell, note 18 above, 2.
[23] Just Cod lib 8 tit 34.3 AD 326. This translation is taken from *Graf v Buechel* 2000 (4) SA 378 (Supreme Court of Appeal of South Africa) [9]. I am grateful to Professor Gretton for bringing this provision of the *Codex* to my attention.
[24] Just Cod lib 4 tit 54 s 2.

So much for possible biblical or classical inspiration for the idea of the equity of redemption; the next challenge is to identify English equity's doctrinal explanation for the idea. It is no straightforward task. Lord Bramwell observed that 'one knows in a general, if not in a critical way, what is an equity of redemption'.[25] In a similar vein, it has been observed that '[a]n equity of redemption can be more appropriately illustrated than defined or described'.[26] Our task of understanding the equity of redemption 'in a critical way' is not made easier by the scant historical record. The exact period when courts of equity first established the 'incontrovertible right to redeem... cannot... be traced with precision',[27] but it is clear that the English mortgage of a fee simple has been through at least four significant incarnations.

In its first incarnation, broadly contemporary with the reign of Henry II, there was no mortgage as such, but a creditor could take possession of his debtor's land by way of pledge.[28] Under a 'living pledge' (*vivum vadium*), the lender took rents and profits in reduction of the debt, whereas under a 'dead pledge' (*mortuum vadium*), he did not.[29] The second incarnation, which appears to have occurred sometime in the thirteenth century and to have survived at least until the late fifteenth century, involved a conveyance to the lender of the fee simple estate in the borrower's land, with the borrower retaining a formal right to re-enter upon repayment of the debt at the appointed date. By this stage, the 'mortgage' label did not refer to the old *mortuum vadium* but to the fact that the land conveyed became dead to the debtor if he failed to repay his debt at the appointed time.[30] The third incarnation, which might have occurred as early as the late fifteenth century and was well-established by the early seventeenth century, is the classic English mortgage under which the mortgagor made a formal conveyance of his land to the mortgagee, and the mortgagee covenanted to reconvey the land to the mortgagor upon repayment of the debt by the mortgagor at the appointed time. At first, the charging of interest was prohibited by usury laws, and the mortgagee went into possession to disguise interest as profits, but the reform of usury laws during the reign of Henry VIII[31] allowed interest to be charged; and thereafter it became rare

---

[25] *Salt v Marquess of Northampton* [1892] AC 1 HL, 18.
[26] JJ Powell, *A Treatise on the Law of Mortgages*, 6th edn (edited by T Coventry) (1826) vol I, 205, note A.
[27] *Ibid*, 108, note B.
[28] Said to derive from the 'customary law of Normandy' (*ibid*, 3).
[29] Glanvill, *Tractatus de legibus* (1187–9) Book X c 6.
[30] Sir Thomas Littleton, *Tenures* (1481); *Sir Edward Coke's Commentarie on Littleton* (1628–9) sec 332.
[31] 37 Henry VIII c 9 (1545).

for the mortgagee to go into possession during the mortgage term.[32] The fourth incarnation is the modern charge by way of legal mortgage, which is discussed later in this chapter.

In his seminal treatise, *The Equity of Redemption*, R W Turner argued that it was not until after Chancery's supremacy over Common Law had been established in 1616 by King James' intervention in *The Earl of Oxford's case*[33]—in fact not until Lord Bacon became Chancellor in 1618—that recognition of the equity of redemption became routine.[34] But Turner's conclusion may have been based on an assumption that the Common Law judges were more hostile to the equity of redemption than in fact they were.[35] It is true that the Court of Chancery was in competition with the Common Law courts at the beginning of the seventeenth century, but for much of the time it was a more healthy competition than is sometimes imagined.[36] It seems somewhat doubtful that the notion of an 'equity of redemption' could have gained the secure grip it had undoubtedly achieved by 1625[37] if Common Lawyers had resisted it as lately as 1618. It is plausible, however counter-intuitive it may appear, that the radical nature of the equity of redemption is evidence that it was introduced before *The Earl of Oxford's case* established the supremacy of equity. After *The Earl of Oxford's case*, Chancery tended to act with a degree of responsibility appropriate to its superior status, so that by the end of that century, under the guidance of Lord Chancellor Nottingham, it had more or less become just another system of precedent-based law.

The equity of redemption does not bear the hallmarks of a restrained, considered Chancery. It is the product of a radical policy-driven Chancery. It does not 'soften and mollify the extremitie of the law' as the equitable function is described in the *Earl of Oxford's case*;[38] it simply ignores the legal deed by which the mortgaged land is conveyed to the lender. Chancery's recognition and protection of the equity of redemption is a barefaced disavowal of the legal form. That Chancery was permitted to 'get away' with this, and apparently without serious objection from the

---

[32] B Rudden and H Moseley, *An Outline of the Law of Mortgages* (London, Estates Gazette, 1967) 4. See also A M Burkhart, 'Freeing Mortgages of Merger' (1987) 40 *Vand L Rev* 283, 317.

[33] (1615) 1 Ch Rep 1; *His Maiesties Speach in the Starre-Chamber* (20 June 1616) STC 14397 (London, Robert Barker [etc], 1616).

[34] R W Turner, *Equity of Redemption: Its Nature, History and Connection with Equitable Estates Generally* (Cambridge, CUP, 1931) 26 and 27–8.

[35] C M Gray, *The Writ of Prohibition: Jurisdiction in Early Modern English Law* (New York, Oceana Publications, 2004).

[36] W J Jones, *The Elizabethan Court of Chancery* (Oxford, Clarendon Press, 1967) 278, 481–4.

[37] *Emmanuel College v Evans* (1625) 1 Ch Rep 18.

[38] (1615) 1 Ch Rep 1, 6–7.

Common Lawyers, indicates that by the time Chancery recognised the 'equity of redemption', there was already a tradition, accepted by lawyers on both sides of the jurisdictional divide, of ignoring the strict terms of the legal mortgage. Why was there such broad acceptance of the equity of redemption? And why has it survived so long when it is clearly a falsehood devised by Chancery in response to a Common Law lie? Some have attributed its success to a 'morality' inherent in the concept:

> [T]he doctrine of the clog on the equity of redemption seems one of the striking examples of the great truth that the ethical standard of our law is often higher than the average morality of the commercial community.[39]

Whether it was purely morality, or that blend of morality and political pragmatism that nowadays passes under the name of consumer protection, is open to question; but doubtless there was a real concern to prevent a mortgagee from taking unconscionable advantage of a debtor's vulnerability. Of course this does not explain why so complex a fiction was required, and neither does it explain why the fiction has lasted so long. More cynically, and perhaps mischievously, Lord Bramwell identified the Chancery lawyers themselves to be the true reason for the success of the mortgage fiction:

> We should have been spared the double condition of things, legal rights and equitable rights, and a system of documents which do not mean what they say. But the piety or love of fees of those who administered equity has thought otherwise. And probably to undo this would be more costly and troublesome than to continue it.[40]

Whatever motivated the Chancery lawyers to develop the equity of redemption, develop it they did. The next challenge is to identify the doctrines by which it was developed, for this will determine whether it is realistic to remove the fiction. There are two main candidates for the doctrinal source of equity's refusal to follow the law in the mortgage context. On the one hand, there is equity's doctrinal commitment to relieve against penalties and, closely related to it, the equitable doctrine of relief against forfeitures.[41] On the other hand, there is equity's willingness to issue injunctions (decrees) requiring specific performance of the mortgagee's covenant to reconvey the mortgaged land to the mortgagor.[42] The two

---

[39] B Wyman, 'The Clog on the Equity of Redemption' (1908) 21 *Harvard Law Review* 457, 475.

[40] *Salt v Marquess of Northampton* [1892] AC 1, 19.

[41] '[T]he relief afforded to mortgagors who had failed to perform the condition and suffered forfeiture to take place in consequence followed upon the same lines as the relief given in the case of bonds' (Turner, note 34 above, 26).

[42] *Ibid*, 21. See also R Wooddeson, *A Systematic View of the Laws of England* (Dublin, Private subscription, 1794) vol III, Lect LVI, sec 409, citing the *Practical Register in Chancery* (1714) 211.

bases are compatible, but distinct. The former is concerned to set aside the conveyance to the mortgagee, whereas the latter is concerned to enforce the reconveyance to the mortgagor. Both bases were united in permitting the mortgagor to bring a bill to redeem even though this was considered at law to be a breach of the mortgagor's covenant to grant the mortgagee quiet enjoyment of the estate 'conveyed'.[43]

Of the two bases of equitable intervention, the latter basis (specific performance of the covenant to reconvey) provides the better doctrinal justification for the 'equity of redemption'. For one thing, there is a chronological coincidence between the invention of the 'equity of redemption'[44] and the advent of specific performance of the covenant to reconvey. As Professor Simpson has noted, the equity of redemption 'seems to have come into prominence in the sixteenth century, when the Chancellor became ready to enforce the covenant specifically'.[45] The precise connection, if indeed there was one, between the equity of redemption and specific performance of the covenant to reconvey is hard to discern. It is tempting to say that in the spirit of the maxim 'equity sees as done that which ought to be done', the covenant to reconvey might have been deemed performed before it was in fact performed, so as to vest the 'equity of redemption', in the nature of beneficial ownership, in the mortgagor. The difficulty with this analysis is that the mortgagee had no legal obligation to reconvey before the debt was paid, so technically beneficial ownership could be deemed to vest in the mortgagor only from the moment the debt was paid, whereas the 'equity of redemption' was assumed to exist from the moment the mortgage was made.

Ultimately, the search for a satisfactory scientific explanation for the equity of redemption seems a futile one. It appears that when it invented the equity of redemption, equity did not see as done merely that which ought to have been done *to fulfil the law*, as the maxim would have it,[46] but that it also saw as done that which ought to be done as a matter of policy and morality *in spite of the law*. Whatever doctrinal light one attempts to shine on the problem succeeds only in producing a new doctrinal shadow. This dilemma was encapsulated by Powell:

> The truth seems to be, that the interest of the mortgagee before foreclosure is contemplated in a Court of Equity rather as a right than as an estate, while the equity of redemption is considered as having rather the quality of an estate than a right. But it is next to impossible to give a definite denomination to the

---

[43] Wooddeson, *ibid*.

[44] The word 'invention' is used advisedly, for whereas Common Law rules are 'supposed to have been established from time immemorial', it is accepted that the rules of equity 'were invented' (*Re Hallett's Estate* (1880) 13 Ch D 696, per Sir George Jessel MR, 710).

[45] A W B Simpson, *An Introduction to the History of the Land Law* (Oxford, OUP, 1961) 225.

[46] G Watt, *Trusts and Equity*, 2nd edn (Oxford, OUP, 2003) 25.

interests either of the mortgagor or mortgagee, when they vary so much according to the light in which they are viewed.[47]

Even though he does not identify the doctrinal *source* of the equity of redemption, it was reasonably clear to Powell that the doctrinal *result* of the mortgage transaction was to confer on the mortgagee a mere right or interest against the mortgaged land whilst conferring on the mortgagor a substantial estate by the name of 'equity of redemption'. With this discovery he comes close to revealing the true nature of the English mortgage, namely that it is a hypothecary transaction under which the borrower retains a beneficial estate in the land, with factual possession, and the lender receives a mere security right enforceable against the land.

THE TRUE NATURE OF THE ENGLISH MORTGAGE

Before the hypothecary analysis of the English mortgage can reign in peace, it is first necessary to dispose of a pretender to its throne: the trust. The argument runs that if the mortgage transaction confers formal title to the fee simple on the mortgagee, whilst leaving an equitable estate in the mortgagor, the mortgage transaction must necessarily create a trust by operation of law.

Trust

The US edition of White & Tudor's *Leading Cases in Equity* asserts that the classic mortgage by conveyance and reconveyance is really a trust:

> A mortgage is in fact a conditional conveyance of the legal title, first, in trust to secure the payment of the mortgage debt, and next for the benefit of the mortgagor, who holds the equitable estate in the land, subject only to a lien for the debt.[48]

That assertion was based on a number of American cases, but it finds scant support in the English reports.[49] Orthodoxy asserts that an equity of redemption is 'in many respects most materially different' to a trust.[50] Lord Browne-Wilkinson purported to identify one respect in which they differ:

---

[47] J J Powell, *A Treatise on the Law of Mortgages*, 6th edn (Thomas Coventry, ed) (1826) vol I.

[48] F T White & O D Tudor, *Leading Cases in Equity*, vol II, part II with notes on the American cases by J I Clark Hare and H B Wallace (Philadelphia, T & J W Johnson, 1852) 450, citing the American cases *Fenwick v Morey* 1 Dana 200; and *Glass v Ellison* 9 New Hampshire 69.

[49] Lord Nottingham was clear that '[a]n equity of redemption charges the land, not a trust' (cited in *Burgess* v *Wheate* (1759) 1 Eden 177 at 206).

[50] *Tucker v Thurstan* 17 Ves 131, 133 (Lord Chancellor Eldon).

that the mortgagor's action to recover the mortgaged property takes the form of an action for redemption and not an action for breach of trust.[51] However, that fact should, with respect, cast doubt on the nature of the remedy before it casts doubt on the nature of the right. Sir Matthew Hale went deeper when he observed that the power of redemption (by which it is supposed his lordship meant the equity of redemption and not merely the legal right to redeem) is inherent in the land, whereas beneficial interests under a trust are collateral to the land and have their origin in agreement of the parties:[52]

> I conceive, that a mortgage is not merely a trust; but a title in equity . . . There is a diversity betwixt a trust and a power of redemption; for a trust is created by the contract of the party . . . But a power of redemption is an equitable right inherent in the land, and binds all persons in the post or otherwise; because it is an ancient right which the party is entitled to in equity.[53]

This also fails to inflict a fatal blow on the pretender. It is true that beneficial interests under trusts are enforced in accordance with the terms of the trust, whereas beneficial interests under mortgages may be enforced despite the terms of the mortgage; but the suggestion that the equity of redemption is somehow inherent in the land so as to exist independently of the parties' agreement does not stand up. The equity of redemption is defined by its relationship to the mortgage terms. Before the mortgage, there is no equity of redemption; there is no equitable right to redeem. There is no equity at all—there is only absolute ownership. It is no answer to say that the equity of redemption is inherent in absolute ownership, for equitable ownership is subsumed within absolute ownership, or to put it another way, absolute ownership defines equitable ownership out of existence.

The pretender claims that if the mortgage transaction divides ownership of the fee simple between the mortgagee as legal owner and the mortgagor as equitable owner, there is a trust as a matter of property law. The fact that the trust does not operate as such in terms of remedy does not mean that it is not a trust, just as there is a trust of property underlying an estate contract even though the parties' remedies are framed according to the terms of the contract – there is no less a trust of property underlying a mortgage than a trust of property underlying an estate contract,[54] so the argument runs. Doctrinally speaking there is some merit in the pretender's claim, but the authorities have not sought to kill it off with fine doctrinal points; rather they have been content to avoid the issue. Thus in one case

---

[51] *Westdeutsche Landesbank Girozentrale v Islington London Borough Council* [1996] AC 669, 707.
[52] *Pawlet v Attorney General* (1667) Hard 465.
[53] *Ibid*, 467, 469.
[54] *Lysaght v Edwards* (1876) 2 Ch D 499, 506 (Jessel MR).

when the question arose whether a real security in the form of a trust for sale of land was or was not a mortgage, the judge held:

> It is not for a Court of Equity to be making distinctions between forms instead of attending to the real substance and essence of the transaction. Whatever form the matter took, I am of the opinion that this was solely a mortgage transaction.[55]

So, like Mortimer in the tower, the pretender still has life in it, but has been stripped of all its power.[56] Even if the mortgage by conveyance and reconveyance was a trust as a matter of property law, equity would refuse to recognise it as such. Equity is committed to attach the 'mortgage' label to *any* real security for a debt, whatever doctrinal form it takes, because equity is committed to protect the vulnerable mortgagor from the power of the mortgagee. However that may be, we should not forget that the trust analysis only has life to the extent that it is true to say that the mortgagor under a mortgage by conveyance and reconveyance had an estate in the nature of an 'equity of redemption'. As a matter of legal doctrine he was said to have had such, but as a matter of fact he did not. Equity regarded the substantial reality of the transaction as one in which the mortgagor's ownership remained undisturbed and the mortgagee acquired a mere security interest. Add to this the observation that, from around the reign of Henry VIII,[57] the mortgagee did not in fact take possession during the currency of the mortgage, and we can say that the English mortgage has been in fact and function a hypothec since that time.

Hypothec

The distinguished historian of land law, A W B Simpson, observed:

> The medieval mortgage had been both in form and in fact a pledge; the land was actually handed over to the creditor. In form the mortgage continued a pledge; thus in the classical form of mortgage the fee simple was conveyed to the mortgagee. In substance, however, the nature of the transaction changed; it became a hypothecary transaction, in which the entry into possession of the mortgagee was an unusual step.[58]

---

[55] *Locking v Parker* (1873) 8 LR Ch App 30, 39.

[56] As depicted in Shakespeare's *The First Part of King Henry the Sixth*, Act 2, scene 5.

[57] B Rudden and H Moseley, *An Outline of the Law of Mortgages* (London, Estates Gazette, 1967) 4. See also A M Burkhart, 'Freeing Mortgages of Merger' (1987) 40 *Vand L Rev* 283, 317.

[58] A W B Simpson, *An Introduction to the History of the Land Law* (Oxford, OUP, 1961) 229, heading 'Pledge and Hypothec'.

In fact, by 1620 it was prohibited to disturb the mortgagor's possession of the premises except in the event of default of payment,[59] and by 1756 the mortgagor's right to remain in quiet possession had become so well established that one anonymous author was emboldened to assert:

> A Mortgage is the same thing as the Hypotheca of the Civilians, and may be defined a Pledging of Lands, or other immoveable thing, for money lent in such manner, that the profit or Usufructus of the thing pledged remains with the debtor till such time as default is made in payment of the money at the time appointed.[60]

Given the early date of this insight, it is a testament to the power and appeal of mortgage law fictions that they have submerged the truth for so long.

THE CHARGE BY WAY OF LEGAL MORTGAGE

Since 1 January 1926 it has not been possible to create a mortgage by conveyance and reconveyance of the fee simple. It was replaced by the so-called 'charge by way of legal mortgage'.[61] It is also possible to create a mortgage by granting a 3000-year lease, determinable upon repayment of the debt,[62] but this method is not popular and will become even less so as a consequence of section 23(1) of the Land Registration Act 2002, which prohibits the creation of any new mortgage by demise or sub-demise of a registered estate.

Could it be that the charge by way of legal mortgage introduced by the Law of Property Act 1925 is a long-hoped-for *suggestio veri* in the English law of mortgage—a natural creature at last? A W B Simpson welcomed this new form of mortgage as the first 'realistic' form of English mortgage,[63] since it recognises the reality that the borrower remains the 'true' owner throughout. B Rudden and H Moseley agree that the charge by way of legal mortgage 'most nearly approximates to the true position of the parties without recourse to cumbersome fictions'.[64] In an earlier volume of

---

[59]   *Powsley v Blackman* (1620) Cro Jac 659.
[60]   A Gentleman of the Middle Temple, *General Abridgement of Equity* (London, Henry Lintot, 1756) 310.
[61]   Law of Property Act s 85(1).
[62]   *Ibid.*
[63]   A W B Simpson, *An Introduction to the History of the Land Law* (Oxford, OUP, 1961) 229.
[64]   B Rudden and H Moseley, *An Outline of the Law of Mortgages* (London, Estates Gazette, 1967) 32.

Modern Studies in Property Law, Sarah Nield hit the nail on the head when she observed that the charge by way of legal mortgage 'is by nature a hypothecation'.[65]

However, despite the improvement that the new charge represents over the traditional form of mortgage by conveyance and reconveyance, it is clear that the charge 'by way of' legal mortgage still operates in the world of make-believe. In legal form it is a quite fabulous creature: nothing less than a *charge* that professes to be a *mortgage* but which confers a right to possession on the mortgagee 'as if' he had a *lease* and (in favour of a first mortgagee) confers a right to possess title documents 'as if' the security were in fact a *fee simple*. The relevant sections have to be seen to be believed:

> A mortgage of an estate in fee simple shall . . . be capable of being effected at law . . . by a charge by deed *expressed to be by way of* legal mortgage: Provided that a first mortgagee shall have the same right to the possession of documents *as if* his security included the fee simple.[66]

> Where a legal mortgage of land is created by a charge by deed *expressed to be by way of* legal mortgage, the mortgagee shall have the same protection, powers and remedies (including the right to take proceedings to obtain possession from the occupiers and the persons in receipt of rents and profits, or any of them) *as if*. . . where the mortgage is a mortgage of an estate in fee simple, a mortgage term for three thousand years without impeachment of waste had been thereby created in favour of the mortgagee.[67]

THE DOCTRINE OF CLOGS ON THE EQUITY OF REDEMPTION

The statutory description of the charge by way of legal mortgage is confusing, but one thing is abundantly clear: this form of mortgage contains no covenant to reconvey the mortgaged land. It follows from this that even if specific performance of the covenant to reconvey might once have supplied a doctrinal explanation for the 'estate status' of the equity of redemption from the date the debt was repaid (and probably, given equity's zealous commitment to see as done that which ought to be done where mortgages are concerned, from the date of the mortgage itself),[68] that doctrinal explanation can no longer hold good.

Parliament has killed off the mortgage by conveyance and reconveyance of a fee simple, yet the courts have so far failed to acknowledge that the

---

[65] S Nield, 'A Reappraisal of s 87(1) Law of Property Act 1925' in E Cooke (ed), *Modern Studies in Property Law*, vol 3 (Oxford, Hart Publishing, 2005) 155, 157.

[66] Law of Property Act (1925) s 85(1), emphasis added.

[67] *Ibid*, s 87(1) and (1)(a), emphasis added.

[68] 'A mortgage is an assignment on condition. The condition being performed, the conveyance is void *ab initio*. Equity dispenses with the time.' *Burgess* v *Wheate* (1759) 1 Eden 177 at 256.

notion of the equity of redemption should have died with it. They have failed to acknowledge that land subject to a registered charge is not 'redeemed' as was land conveyed under the classic form of mortgage; rather the charge is simply discharged from the land upon repayment of the debt.[69] The result is that the doctrine preventing clogs on the equity for redemption continues to haunt mortgage law and is prone to 'wander into places where it ought not to be'.[70] It is precisely the sort of fiction that would have horrified Jeremy Bentham.

Giving up the Ghost

There have been calls to exorcise (or to excise)[71] the doctrine of the clogs on the equity of redemption, but until judges accept that the equity of redemption is dead, they are unlikely to acknowledge that the doctrine of clogs on the equity of redemption is only a ghost. None of this would matter if the ghost performed some useful function—perhaps to instil fear into mortgagees who might wish to oppress mortgagors—but the doctrine of clogs has become 'a technical doctrine, in no way connected with oppression in fact'.[72] This is most apparent in the case of a mortgagee taking an option to purchase as a condition of the mortgage. In *Samuel v Jarrah Timber and Wood Paving*,[73] where the doctrine of clogs was applied to set aside the mortgagee's perfectly fair contractual option to re-purchase the mortgaged land, the Lord Chancellor the Earl of Halsbury confessed that he was unable to see the 'sense or reason' of the equitable principle.[74] The rule against purchase by the mortgagee would make sense if the mortgagee was in truth a trustee of the power of sale, since a trustee cannot sell to himself,[75] but, as we have seen, the courts have always insisted that the mortgagee is not a trustee and that the power of sale is not held in trust. It is therefore hard to fathom any doctrinal justification for the rule. The rule does not survive because it is part of a coherent doctrinal analysis, but because it is assumed to effect a policy of protecting oppressed borrowers.

---

[69] S Nield, note 65 above, 160: 'a charge is not redeemed, it is discharged'.

[70] *Kreglinger v New Patagonia Meat and Cold Storage Company Ltd* [1914] AC 25, 46 (Lord Mersey).

[71] '[T]he doctrine of a clog on the equity of redemption is, so it seems to me, an appendix to our law which no longer serves a useful purpose and would be better excised.' *Jones v Morgan* [2001] EWCA Civ 995; [2001] Lloyd's Rep Bank 323 CA Civ Div, para 86 (Lord Phillips MR).

[72] P B Fairest, *Mortgages* (London, Sweet & Maxwell, 1980) 25.

[73] [1904] AC 323 HL.

[74] *Ibid*, 325.

[75] *Tito v Waddell (No 2)* [1977] Ch 106; Hon Mr Justice B H McPherson CBE, 'Self-dealing Trustees' in A J Oakley (ed), *Trends in Contemporary Trust Law* (Oxford, Clarendon Press, 1996) 135.

Peter Devonshire has criticised the doctrine of clogs on the equity of redemption, especially as it operates to set aside a perfectly sound contractual agreement to repurchase, but he concluded that the doctrine is not completely redundant.[76] Other commentators on the Australian cases have reached a different conclusion:

> The need to protect necessitous borrowers against unscrupulous lenders is as relevant today as ever before. However, it is submitted that the application of the doctrine against clogging the equity of redemption is not the appropriate vehicle through which to safeguard the interests of those in need of protection.[77]

This writer agrees that current mortgage law supplies safeguards of a piecemeal and inadequate type. What is required is to give up the ghost of the equity of redemption and replace it with a comprehensive and coherent statutory scheme of mortgagor protection.[78]

When Chancery judges have sought to explain the doctrine of clogs on the equity, they have normally done so by reference to broad ideas of mortgagor protection. The following statement of Lord Henley, Lord Chancellor, is typical:

> This court, as a court of conscience, is very jealous of persons taking securities for a loan, and converting such securities into purchases. And therefore I take it to be an established rule that a mortgagee can never provide at the time of making the loan for any event or condition on which the equity of redemption shall be discharged, and the conveyance absolute. And there is great reason and justice in this rule, for necessitous men are not, truly speaking, free men, but, to answer a present exigency, will submit to any terms the craft may impose on them.[79]

The learned judge portrays a world in which mortgagees are the Big Bad Wolf and mortgagors are Little Red Riding Hood, but a microscopic examination of the cases reveals something scientific lurking within the rhetoric by which mortgagees are prohibited from turning a mortgage into a sale.

The underlying, 'scientific' aim of the rule is to achieve a fair balance of risk between mortgagor and mortgagee. A vendor may convey land to a purchaser and the conveyance may contain a proviso for reconveyance to the vendor at the original price. This transaction is a conveyance and reconveyance, but it is not, without more, a mortgage. The additional factor that will turn the arrangement into a mortgage is if the purchaser

---

[76] 'The Modern Application of the Rule Against Clogs on the Equity of Redemption' (1997) 5 *Australian Property Law Journal* 1, 10.

[77] W B Duncan and L Willmott, 'Clogging the Equity of Redemption: An Outmoded Concept?' (2002) 2 *QUT Law and Justice Journal* 35, 49.

[78] J Houghton and L Liversey, *Mortgage Conditions: Old Law for a New Century, Volume I: Property 2000* (Hart Publishing, Oxford, 2001) 163, 180.

[79] *Vernon v Bethell* (1761) 2 Eden 110, 113.

takes security on the land for the recovery of the principal purchase monies. The relevance of this factor is that it turns a sale into a mortgage, and once this has occurred, the mortgage cannot be turned back into a sale. If a single transaction were permitted to take effect as both a mortgage and a sale at the option of the mortgagee at a fixed price, the effect would be to throw all the risk upon the mortgagor. For if the value of the land were to fall below the fixed price, the mortgagee would be able to recover his debt up to the value of the land and to recover any shortfall by a personal action on the contractual bond, whereas if the land value were to increase above the pre-agreed price, the mortgagee would have the advantage of purchase. As between the parties it is not fair that the mortgagee should reap the rewards of any increases in the land value while the mortgagor is left to bear the risk of any decrease. The mortgagee is not permitted to have his cake and eat it. Lord Redesdale put the point in more sophisticated language:

> [A] proviso for re-purchase will not, of itself, be sufficient to turn a *bona fide* purchase into a mortgage, though it be limited to be exercised within a certain time, and at an advanced price . . . If, however, the purchaser, instead of taking the risk of the contract upon himself, takes a security for the repayment of the principal money . . . such circumstances will vitiate the sale.[80]

If the fundamental concern is to achieve a fair allocation of risk between the parties, why did Chancery adopt the strict rule that 'a mortgage must not be converted into something else'?[81] Surely it would have been better to allow a closer examination of the particular transaction and to allow a mortgage to be rendered irredeemable if the parties fairly reached an agreement to that effect. That the rule is so strict can probably be attributed to the very limited judicial resources in Chancery in the seventeenth and eighteenth centuries. It was not until 1729 that the Master of the Rolls (the chief Chancery Master) was appointed to sit as a second judge in certain cases, and even that reform did little to reduce the burden on the Chancellor, because any decision of the Master of the Rolls could still be appealed to the Chancellor. It was not until 1833 that the Master of the Rolls achieved a genuinely concurrent jurisdiction, and it was not until 1813 that a Vice Chancellor was appointed to assist the Chancellor and the Master of the Rolls. When, in 1816, Sir Launcelot Shadwell V-C was asked by a Commission of Inquiry whether the three judges could cope, he is said to have replied 'No; not three angels'.[82] The straightened resources of the Court of Chancery must have encouraged the Lord Chancellor to prefer

---

[80]   *Verner v Winstanley* (1805) 2 Sch & Lef 393.
[81]   *Noakes & Co Ltd v Rice* [1902] AC 24 HL, 33–4 (Lord Davey).
[82]   Cited in Radcliffe and Cross, *The English Legal System*, 3rd edn (London, Butterworth, 1954) 153 n 1.

strict rules (albeit explained and justified in terms of conscience) in preference to case-by-case examination of the individual consciences of the parties to each cause.

In the seminal case of *Newcomb v Bonham*,[83] an absolute conveyance was made on a certain day, and, by another deed made between the same parties on the same day, the land was made redeemable upon repayment of £1000 during the lifetime of a named person. The Lord Chancellor laid down the general rule 'once a mortgage always a mortgage' and held that since the mortgage was redeemable during the lifetime of the named person, it must be redeemable thereafter. It is significant that Counsel for the disappointed mortgagee had argued that the mortgagee had 'run hazard enough' (that is, had borne sufficient risk), since although it turned out to be a good bargain 'it might have been a bad one'.[84]

If that plea had been accepted, the strict rule prohibiting a mortgage from being converted into a sale might have been replaced by a more flexible attempt to achieve a fair allocation of risk between the mortgagor and mortgagee on a case-by-case basis, but one can only imagine the delays in the Court of Chancery if every mortgage transaction—and every transaction involving a mortgage—had been examined to determine whether the mortgagee had run a fair risk of loss when he entered the transaction. Since then, greater resources have been placed at the disposal of the courts. This might explain why the rule began to thaw with the *Kreglinger* case,[85] in which Viscount Haldane LC attributed the clogs doctrine to Chancery's 'general power to relieve against penalties and to mould them into mere securities'.[86] The thaw was possible precisely because his Lordship chose to define the protection of the mortgagor in terms of a flexible *remedy*. It is less likely that there would have been a thawing of the doctrine if he had traced it back to the fiction of the mortgagor's incontrovertible right to the equity of redemption. According to his Lordship, the purpose of the equitable jurisdiction:

> has always been to ascertain, by parol evidence if need be, the real nature and substance of the transaction, and if it turned out to be in truth one of mortgage simply, to place it on that footing. It was, in ordinary cases, only where there was conduct which the Court of Chancery regarded as unconscientious that it interfered with freedom of contract...The equity judges looked, not at what was technically the form, but at what was really the substance of transactions, and confined the application of their rules to cases in which they thought that in its substance the transaction was oppressive.[87]

---

[83] (1681) 1 Vern 7.
[84] *Ibid*, 8.
[85] *Kreglinger v New Patagonia Meat and Cold Storage Company Ltd* [1914] AC 25 HL.
[86] *Ibid*, 35.
[87] *Ibid*.

It is possible to discern a further thawing of the doctrine today. It is still the case that a mortgage cannot be turned into a sale, but the courts have demonstrated a willingness to examine the particular facts in greater depth to determine whether a transaction ought to be defined as a mortgage or a sale. In one recent case, Parker LJ even went so far as to state (without laying down any general rule) that where an option to purchase is granted 'for a price which was to be left outstanding on mortgage', there is a 'very strong likelihood that, on an examination of all the circumstances, the court would conclude that the substance of the transaction was one of sale and purchase and not one of mortgage'.[88] That case was referred back to the Chancery Division of the High Court, where it was held on the particular facts that the substance of the transaction was indeed a sale and purchase,[89] with the result that there could be no finding of a clog on the equity of redemption.[90]

If the transaction had been defined as a mortgage, the sale would probably have been held to be a clog and on that basis set aside. It is a shame that the opportunity did not arise (or was not taken) to construe the transaction to be a mortgage and to attempt a relaxation of the rule against clogs. If the allocation of risk had been acknowledged to be the substantial question, the court could have relied on the fact that the price for exercising the option had not been fixed as a ground for holding the transaction to be a fair one. It is noteworthy that the parties themselves conceived the transaction to be a commercial investment designed to provide a fair return for the taking of risk.[91]

THE STORIES 'OTHERS' TELL

In the introduction to this chapter, two reasons were advanced for removing the fictions from the mortgage law of England and Wales. The first was that the fictions create disharmony within our domestic law. This has now been proved. The second reason is that our domestic mortgage stories create barriers to harmony with the stories of other legal systems; including Civilian, Torrens and Islamic systems. We will now briefly consider each of those systems.

---

[88] *Warnborough Ltd v Garmite Ltd* [2003] Civ 1544 CA [76].
[89] *Warnborough Ltd v Garmite Ltd* [2006] EWHC 10 Ch (Transcript) [34].
[90] *Ibid*, [35].
[91] *Ibid*, [10].

Civilian

In many Civilian jurisdictions, and in many European legal systems that do not have exclusively Civilian origins, the preferred device for securing loans against land is a hypothecary charge. We have seen that when the fictions are stripped away from the English mortgage, it is also revealed to be hypothecary in nature. This revelation suggests great potential for the reception into England and Wales of Civilian ideas of mortgage. This will be especially conducive to the introduction of a pan-European form of mortgage.[92] In June 2005, the European Commission confirmed that it is giving serious consideration to 'the feasibility and desirability' of a 'Euromortgage' of this sort.[93]

Torrens

It is testament to the seductive appeal of the mortgage story that it survived the wholesale and radical reform of land registration introduced to Australia through the efforts of Sir Robert Richard Torrens,[94] which has since also been adopted elsewhere. In contrast to the system in England and Wales, the Torrens system is 'not a system of registration of title but a system of title by registration'.[95] The Torrens register does not validate documentary title; it *is* title—and the state guarantees it as such.

Surely there is no place in such a robustly realistic system for the notion that the mortgagor has a spectral off-register title in the nature of an 'equity for redemption'. Surely it is a truism that 'the Torrens title mortgagor remains the registered proprietor of the land—the owner, not only in equity but also at law'.[96] The High Court of Australia acknowledged the reality of the situation,[97] but only a few months later it reverted to the fiction when it suggested that 'a mortgage in the old common law form . . . differs in law from a mortgage under the Torrens System, although not substantially in equity'.[98] Despite that setback, it is clear from

---

[92]   G Watt, 'The Eurohypothec and the English Mortgage' (2006) 13(2) *Maastricht Journal of European and Comparative Law* 173; S Nasarre-Aznar, 'The Eurohypothec: A Common Mortgage for Europe' (2005) 69 *Conv* 32.

[93]   Commission of the European Communities, 'Mortgage Credit in the EU' (Green Paper, COM (2005) 327 final) para 48.

[94]   Real Property Act (Act 15 of 1857–58).

[95]   *Breskvar v Wall* (1971) 126 CLR 376, per Barwick CJ, 385–6.

[96]   P Butt, *Land Law*, 3rd edn (Sydney, LBC Information Services, 1996) 536.

[97]   *Latec Investments Ltd. v Hotel Terrigal Pty Ltd (in Liquidation)* (1965) 113 CLR 265, 275.

[98]   *Haque v Haque (No 2)* (1965) 114 CLR 98 High Court of Australia.

more recent decisions that the Australian courts no longer believe the fiction.[99] The courts in England and Wales would do well to follow their lead.[100]

Islamic

Islam does not prohibit the use of land as security for a loan, but it forbids the charging of interest, for this is *Riba* (usury). The 'problem of interest'[101] is not easily overcome. Francis Bacon argued that 'all states have ever had it' and suggested that the argument against usury ought to be 'sent to Utopia'.[102] According to Bacon, the great attraction of the 'trade of usury' is that it provides the usurer with 'certain gains', whereas merchant trade can only promise 'gains of hazard'.[103] Islam accepts that 'Trade is like usury'[104] but makes this crucial distinction: 'Allah hath permitted trade and forbidden usury.'[105] The very factor that made usury attractive to Bacon—the reduction of risk—is the very factor that renders it abhorrent to Islamic scholars. In Islam usury is prohibited because the charging of interest represents an unjust allocation of risk as between lender and borrower; merchant trade, on the other hand, is permitted because a commercial bargain is an honourable transaction in which both parties share the risk:

> [J]ustice in transactions is achieved by approaching equality . . . For things which are not measured by weight and volume, justice can be determined by means of proportionality.[106]

It might appear that there is no potential for the harmonious coexistence of the English mortgage and Islamic principles. The potential is limited, but in the course of this chapter we have at least discovered something that both systems have in common, and which has until now been covered by layers of fiction. Namely, that the fundamental concern of equity's radical

---

[99] For example, *Figgins Holdings v SEAA Enterprises* [1999] 196 CLR 245 High Court of Australia; *Gutwenger v Commissioner of Taxation* (1995) 55 FCR 95 Federal Court of Australia, 108–9: 'The land is under Torrens title so that it is not correct to speak of there being an equity of redemption.'

[100] See generally Nield, note 65 above.

[101] T El Diwany, *The Problem with Interest*, 2nd edn (London, Kreatoc, 2003)

[102] Essay XLI: *Of Usury*, 1612 (London, Dent: Everyman's Library, 1906) 124.

[103] *Ibid*, 126.

[104] The Qur'an, 2:275.

[105] *Ibid*.

[106] M 'Ibn Rushd, *Bidayat Al Mujtahid wa Nihayat Al Muqtasid*, verified by Abd Al Majid Tu'mat Halabi (Beirut, Dar Ai Ma'rifat, 1997) vol 3, 184 (translated by M A El-Gamal in 'An Economic Explication of the Prohibition of *Riba* in Classical Islamic Jurisprudence', *Proceedings of the Third Harvard University Forum on Islamic Finance* (2000) http:// www.ruf.rice.edu/~elgamal//.pdf accessed 1 December 2006. See also *Muwatta' of Imam Malik*, Muhammed Rahimuddin (trans), paras 1353–5.

intervention in the mortgage context has been to effect a more just allocation of risk as between mortgagor and mortgagee.

There is, however, a twist in the tale. For the Islamic principle of risk-sharing is said to be exemplified by the traditional legal maxim *Al-Kharaj bid Daman* (return must be justified by risk), but like so much of English mortgage law, reliance on this maxim may be rhetorical. One leading scholar of Islamic finance admits that he has 'yet to read a single satisfactory explanation of what it means'.[107] He goes on to observe:

> In theory, there may be some differences in risk allocation between Islamic instruments and their conventional counterparts. However, until a few cases are brought to court to test possible discrepancies between the juristic and the regulatory understandings of Islamic finance instruments, it is difficult to say whether or not those differences are substantive.[108]

It may be that the concern for fair allocation of risk that underlies equitable intervention in the English mortgage is not far removed from the concern underlying the Islamic prohibition on usury. However, even if the two systems do not share this common root concern it is at least clear that both systems struggle with the same task of unearthing fact from fiction.

CONCLUSION

In the preface to his *Treatise on the Law of Mortgages*, John Joseph Powell suggested that 'of all the branches of learning which the science of the law embraces, none appears to be more interesting' than the law governing the English mortgage.[109] This writer would agree with the sentiment but not with the expression. The very thing that makes the English mortgage so interesting is that a functional or factual analysis of the mortgage, which would analyse the mortgage scientifically according to what it actually does, has consistently given way to a fictional analysis of the mortgage, which explains the mortgage according to what judges say it does. In function and fact the English mortgage is hypothecary, which is to say that the mortgagor remains in possession of the land as owner, and the mortgagee remains out of possession with a mere security to recover the debt. In the fictional account, the mortgagee is imagined to have a legal estate in the mortgaged land (a fee simple or lease, as the case may be), and the mortgagor's interest in the mortgaged land is said to be a mere 'equity of redemption'.

---

[107] M A El-Gamal, '"Interest" and the Paradox of Contemporary Islamic Law and Finance' (2004) *Fordham International Law Review* 108, n 48. (Professor El-Gamal holds the Chair of Islamic Economics, Finance and Management at Rice University, Houston.)
[108] *Ibid*, n 53.
[109] 1785, Preface, v.

The mendacity of the classic English mortgage by conveyance and reconveyance goaded an exasperated F F Pollock to declare that '[i]t must be difficult for any one but a lawyer to believe that so clumsy an operation is to this day the regular means of securing a debt on land in England'.[110] We may not agree with Sir Henry Maine that all legal fictions 'have had their day',[111] but this chapter has sought to show that, with the advent of the simple registered charge, the day has surely come to rid English law of the fictional nature of the lender's 'mortgage' and the notion of the borrower's 'equity of redemption'.

---

[110]   *The Land Laws*, 3rd edn (London, Macmillan, 1896) 134.
[111]   H Maine, *Ancient Law*, Everyman's Library edn, 1861 (London, Dent, 1917) 16.

5

Curbing the Enthusiasm of Finders

ROBIN HICKEY

RECENTLY I WAS watching an episode of *Curb your Enthusiasm*, the sardonic US situation comedy series starring *Seinfeld* creator Larry David. Larry found an expensive watch belonging to his colleague David Schwimmer. He recognised the watch, so he picked it up and put it in his coat pocket for safekeeping, intending to return it to Schwimmer later that day. When they met, Larry placed his hand inside his coat pocket to retrieve the watch and discovered that it was not there. Schwimmer said to Larry, 'Well now you owe me a watch.' Larry told him not to be ridiculous. And so an argument ensued as to Larry's liability as a finder for losing the watch.

Of course this all makes for good comedic television, but the facts of such disputes do not lend themselves as readily to legal resolution. English law would struggle to answer the question 'Does Larry David owe David Schwimmer a watch?' In the first place, it has not chosen to regulate the position of finders with general legislation, as has been the fashion in some jurisdictions, notably Scotland.[1] In England the resolution of finding disputes depends on the common law.[2] Here it is tolerably clear that a

---

[1] See Pt VI of the Civic Government (Scotland) Act (1982), s 67 of which provides that a person who finds property is under a duty to take care of it and to deliver it or report the matter to one of several people, including the police. Section 68 empowers the chief constable to take various steps, including offering the property to the finder after two months. These provisions are derived from the common law. For an explanation, see KGC Reid, *The Law of Property in Scotland* (Edinburgh, Law Society of Scotland, 1996) para 547.

[2] *Parker v British Airways Board* [1982] QB 1004, 1008 (Donaldson LJ). There are a few exceptions. For example, s 8(1) of the Treasure Act (1996) requires a finder to report to the coroner within 14 days any item that he has reasonable grounds for believing to be treasure; s 4 of the Dogs Act (1906) requires any person who finds a stray dog either to return it to its owner or to hand it over to the police: *Ramish Kumar Sharma & Another v Plumridge* (Court of Appeal (Civil Division), 22 May 1991, unreported). But such exceptions are discrete and incremental and do not represent anything like a comprehensive legislative position on finders duties.

finder of goods[3] acquires some property rights in the object of his find;[4] but less (indeed, virtually nothing at all) has been said about the obligations (if any) that a finder of goods owes to the person who lost those goods in the first place. Plainly the property rights of the loser will withstand the loss of the chattel,[5] for even if divesting abandonment of goods is possible at common law,[6] such divesting certainly will require a positive intention to be rid of an item and not merely an accidental loss.[7] It follows that a finder is subject to those general duties of the law of obligations that serve to protect proprietary interests.[8] But aside from the ability of the loser as a result of his continuing rights to hold accountable the finder in this way, does our law impose on the finder any positive obligation(s) to deal with the goods found in a way beneficial to or mindful of the loser?

In *Parker v British Airways Board*,[9] the Court of Appeal answered this question in the affirmative. When a person by finding acquires a property right in an object, then that person:

> has an obligation to take such measures as in all the circumstances are reasonable to acquaint the true owner of the finding and present whereabouts of the chattel and to care for it meanwhile.[10]

---

[3] Or of any other tangible personalty. In particular, it seems clear that the rights and obligations of a finder apply also to money: see *Bridges v Hawkesworth* (1851) 21 LJQB 75; and *Moffatt v Kazana* [1969] 2 QB 152. This admits of qualification only to the extent that the general liabilities of a finder are affected where the find is money. For example, it is easier perhaps to argue that a finder is unjustly enriched by finding money than by finding a chattel: below pp 26-7.

[4] So it was held in *Armory v Delamirie* (1722) 1 Stra 505, where a chimney sweep's boy found a jewel and was deemed to have property in the jewel sufficient to maintain an action for wrongful interference against a goldsmith who took it away from him. This 'finders keepers' principle is well embedded in our personal property law, and *Armory* has been approved or applied in every finding case to come before a court in the 300 or so years since its decision.

[5] 'A man who loses anything does not thereby lose his property in it': *R v Reed* Car & M 306, 308 (Coleridge J).

[6] It might not be possible. Or at least it remains unclear whether putative acts of abandonment have any divesting effect at common law. The authors in *English Private Law* suggest that the stronger view is that divesting abandonment of chattels is not possible: PBH Birks (ed), *English Private Law* (Oxford, OUP, 2000) 4.567–4.569. For a fuller discussion with an argument to the contrary, see AH Hudson, 'Abandonment' in Palmer and McKendrick (eds), *Interests in Goods*, 2nd edn (London, Lloyds of London Press, 1998) and compare the view of M Bridge, *Personal Property Law*, 3rd edn (Oxford, Clarendon Press, 2003) 22–3.

[7] *Williams v Phillips* (1957) 41 Cr App Rep 5; *R v Edwards and Stacey* (1877) Cox CC 384.

[8] Principally the torts of conversion and negligence, which are discussed further below. Of a course, a dishonest finder may also occasion criminal liability as a thief: Theft Act (1968), especially s 2(1)(c), which contemplates expressly the case of finding. See generally D Ormerod (ed), *Smith and Hogan Criminal Law*, 11th edn (Oxford, OUP, 2005) 694.

[9] [1982] QB 1004.

[10] *Ibid*, 1017 (Donaldson LJ).

If this is right, then two positive obligations are imposed on the acquisitive finder.[11] First is the obligation to take care of the goods. Since it is an obligation for *reasonable* care, it is safe to assume that it aims at the ordinary standards of the tort of negligence, though possibly the finder bears the burden of showing that is satisfied. In other words, it is for the finder to prove that he took care of the goods, not for the loser to establish that the finder has been negligent in damaging or losing them.[12] Second is the obligation to acquaint the loser with what has happened. This has as its aim only that the loser learns of the discovery of his goods and their location. It does not expressly contemplate that the finder will return the goods to the loser. So the finder might discharge his obligation by delivering the goods to the police or to the occupier of the place where they were found.[13]

In this chapter I argue it is doubtful that English law requires such conduct of finders, for three reasons. First, despite the clear assertion in *Parker*, there is very little authority to suggest that our law imposes specific duties on finders, and as the law stands, the better view is that the act of finding goods and taking control of them generates no duty owed to the loser of the goods. Sometimes this problem has been avoided by suggesting that a finder acts as a bailee for the loser, such that he owes equivalent obligations in virtue of that status. But here too there are difficulties, both authoritative and doctrinal, and so the chapter argues secondly that finders should not be treated as bailees of the loser. A third way is equally unfruitful. In the likely absence of positive obligations on a finder, there is no sense that their putative content is being compelled by general civil liabilities in tort or unjust enrichment, such that their existence would in any event be rendered unnecessary. On the contrary, it seems that the common law is well aware of the necessity of finder-obligations, despite having no firm authoritative base on which to ground them.

AUTHORITY FOR FINDER OBLIGATIONS

The judgment of Donaldson LJ in *Parker v British Airways Board*[14] contains by far the most unequivocal statement of a finder's obligations.

---

[11] It is important to note that no rights or obligations arise simply by the act of finding, that is, by mere discovery of an item: 'If a man comes upon an object, he has no duty to pick it up. He may leave it where he finds it. For not intermeddling, he has no liability to the owner of the chattel and acquires no rights with respect to it' (Sullivan JA in *Kowal v Ellis* (1977) 76 DLR (3d) 546). It follows that for the generation of these rights and duties, the finder must at least reduce the item into his physical control: see Donaldson LJ in *Parker* [1982] QB 1004, 1009.

[12] *Morris v CW Martins & Sons Ltd* [1966] 1 QB 716 (CA), below p 18.

[13] [1982] QB 1004, 1017–18 (Donaldson LJ).

[14] [1982] QB 1004 (CA).

Mr Parker was an outbound passenger lawfully present in an airport departure lounge operated and occupied by the defendant board. He found a gold bracelet in the lounge and handed it to the defendants' employees with a note of his name and address, asking that it be returned to him if it be claimed by no one. When it was not claimed, the defendants sold it for £850 and kept the proceeds. Mr Parker brought an action for conversion in the county court. The defendants counter-claimed for a declaration that, as occupiers of the premises on which the find was made, they had a better title to the bracelet than the claimant.

At first instance, judgment was entered for Mr Parker. A unanimous Court of Appeal upheld this decision, finding that he had a title to the bracelet based on 'the ancient common law rule' in *Armory v Delamirie*.[15] This claim could only be defeated by the defendants if they had antecedent rights to the bracelet.[16] Reviewing the authorities, Donaldson LJ found a rule covering this situation:

> An occupier of a building has rights superior to those of a finder over chattels upon or in, but not attached to, that building if, but only if, before the chattel is found, he has manifested an intention to exercise control over the building and the things which may be upon it or in it.[17]

The defendants' claim failed because they had not met this requirement of manifesting an intention to control lost chattels. Although the court stopped short of listing express criteria for satisfying the requirement, we are told that in the instant case the kind of control the defendants were asserting over the premises (such as retaining the right to exclude certain classes of passenger and certain kinds of specific chattels, like guns and bombs) bore 'no real relevance to a manifest intention to assert custody and control over lost articles'.[18] In these circumstances the court thought it impossible for the defendants to assert a right to the bracelet in priority to that of Mr Parker, and so Mr Parker was entitled to the value of the bracelet.[19]

From this it is clear that the contest in *Parker* turned on the relative rights of the parties to the bracelet discovered by the claimant. The conduct

---

[15] [1982] QB 1004, 1008, above p 2.
[16] *Ibid* (Donaldson LJ), 1019 (Eveleigh LJ), 1021 (Sir David Cairns).
[17] *Ibid*, 1018.
[18] The court noted, with apparent disapproval, that there was no evidence that the defendants regularly searched the premises for lost property and that the staff policy on dealing with items found on the premises had not been published or otherwise communicated to patrons of the lounge: *ibid*, 1018–19. Most probably the 'found on land' rule seeks to invoke the general common law of possession, where establishing a clear intention to possess an item has always been necessary in asserting any possessory right. See generally F Pollock and RS Wright, *An Essay on Possession in the Common Law* (Oxford, Clarendon Press, 1888) 41.
[19] [1982] QB 1004, 1019.

of the claimant was not at issue, and the appeal entailed no comment from the court on the obligations (if any) owed by a finder to a loser of goods. Indeed, only Donaldson LJ turned his mind to this question, dealing with it shortly in the quotation reproduced above.[20] His Lordship did not cite any authority for the propositions offered, though he was much impressed with the Canadian case of *Kowal v Ellis*,[21] which seems to hold that a finder owes obligations as bailee of the loser. But beyond lengthy citations from that case, there was no attempt at any discussion or synthesis of the existing law such as would lead to a coherent position on the obligations of a finder.[22] Although it is abundantly clear that Donaldson LJ supposed the existence of two specific finder-obligations at common law (viz the duty to take care of the goods and the duty to acquaint the loser with what has happened), this proposition must rank as the barest statement of principle, and there is little within *Parker* to support it.

Donaldson LJ's treatment of this issue accords with four more general deficiencies in the existing law on finder-obligations. First, there are very few direct authorities on the matter, and no case that holds unequivocally that a finder owes the kind of obligations contemplated in *Parker*. Secondly, the vast majority of litigated finding disputes are cases between finders and non-owning possessors, to which the obligations of a finder to a loser are not immediately relevant. Thirdly, in most of the reported finding disputes, finders have behaved reasonably or honestly and have not needed to have their conduct curtailed by positive obligations. And fourthly, in the absence of any more direct authorities, English courts have tended to rely rather uncritically on the idea that a finder is a bailee to justify the supposition that he owes obligations, without really subjecting that idea to proper scrutiny. In order to be clear about the lack of authority at common law, we will turn briefly to consider each of these deficiencies.

Absence of Direct Authority

There seems to be only one reported decision in English law in which a loser of goods has relied on finder-obligations in framing his action,[23] and

---

[20] See note 10 above and accompanying text.

[21] (1977) 76 DLR (3d) 546.

[22] Simon Roberts, highlighting the judgment's reliance on lengthy citation, suggests that it contains 'rather little that could pass for conventional legal analysis': S Roberts, 'More Lost than Found' [1982] 45 *MLR* 683, 686.

[23] NE Palmer, *Bailment*, 2nd edn (London, Sweet & Maxwell, 1991) 1467, suggests that there are 'few' cases of this nature, but does not identify any. Palmer discusses at this point only the New Zealand decision of *Helson v McKenzies* [1950] NZLR 878 but sets it aside as not raising the issue.

even this is equivocal. In *Newman v Bourne and Hollingsworth*,[24] the claimant accidentally left her diamond brooch in the defendants' shop. It was handed to the shopkeeper by another of the defendants' employees, and the shopkeeper put it in his desk for safekeeping. When the claimant returned to claim the brooch, it was not in the desk, and a further search did not yield its discovery. At the trial, the judge held that the defendants 'had not exercised that degree of care which was due from one who had found an article and assumed possession of it'.[25] However, this holding and the remainder of the judgment are consistent with the view that the claimant's action lay for breach of a general tortious duty of negligence and not for breach of any obligation owed in virtue of the defendants' status as finders. The Divisional Court upheld the decision at first instance, but the judgments are confined to a consideration of the meaning of 'gross negligence', with some further remarks on vicarious liability, and they do not discuss expressly the nature of the obligation in question.[26]

Beyond this, there is no sign of the actionabilty of deficient conduct on the part of the finder, let alone authority to suggest that the common law imposes specific obligations on a finder. Undoubtedly part of the problem is the relative paucity of litigated disputes between finders and losers of goods,[27] but occasionally the courts have missed useful opportunities to comment on or clarify the position. For example, in *Moffatt v Kazana*[28] the defendant found a biscuit tin containing about £2000 in £1 notes hidden in the chimney flue of a bungalow conveyed to him by the claimant. The court was satisfied that the claimant had hidden the notes and had forgotten about them. Having done nothing to divest himself of the property in them, he remained their owner and could recover their value in an action for money had and received. In that sense the case was straightforward and could be disposed of shortly. Nonetheless, there was a chance for the court to comment on the obligations owed to the claimant in the interim. Counsel for the defence argued that the sale of the moneys to the defendant should be implied in the conveyance of the bungalow.[29] If such a conveyance were not implied, he suggested, an impasse might be

---

[24]   (1915) TLR 209.

[25]   *Ibid.*

[26]   *Ibid*, 210.

[27]   Generally it is conceded that the case law on finding and other possessory concepts is scarce (see eg, D Riesman, 'Possession and the Law of Finders' (1939) *Harv LR* 1105). On the question of finder-specific obligations the matter is compounded by the fact that, when they do arise, the vast majority of litigated disputes occur between a finder and a non-owning third party: below pp 10-12.

[28]   [1969] 2 QB 152.

[29]   And he did so notwithstanding s 62 of the Law of Property Act (1925), which provides 'in effect that a conveyance of land does not include a conveyance of chattels': [1969] 2 QB 152, 156 (Wrangham J).

reached between claimants and defendants in the situation where the defendant refused to redeliver a chattel to the claimant:

> Suppose that [the defendant] had said to [the claimant], 'I do not claim this tin box at all, it is not mine; I dare say it is yours, but in no circumstances am I going to allow you upon my land. Still less am I going to allow you to burrow about in the false flue of the bungalow, possibly damaging the flue, and in those circumstances the tin box remains where it is'.[30]

This argument was aimed squarely at the conduct required of a finder who discovers lost property in his custody. Wrangham J thought it raised 'difficulties which [counsel for the claimant] was never able wholly satisfactorily to answer'. Conceivably it could have been answered in a number of ways. It could have been answered by arguing that the common law imposed on a finder a specific obligation to redeliver lost goods to an identified owner. It could have been answered by arguing that a refusal to deliver goods in such circumstances amounted to a conversion. It could even have been answered by arguing that the finder by notifying the loser had done all that was required of him,[31] such that there was a genuine impasse between loser and finder and a gap in the finder's obligations. But beyond the flat assertion of its difficulty, the court did not engage with the argument of counsel, missing a rare opportunity to comment on the obligations of a finder in a case where these were sensibly pertinent to the outcome.

On the authorities then, it seems doubtful that the common law imposes on a finder specific obligations of the kind envisaged in *Parker*. There is no case in English law that decides unequivocally the existence of these obligations, and evidence of some uncertainty where they are concerned.

The Loser of Goods is a Background Consideration

The vast majority of finding cases adjudicate the position between non-owning possessors and finders,[32] and in almost all of these cases there is no express discussion of the finder or possessor's obligations. Included here is the Court of Appeal decision in *Waverly Borough Council v Fletcher*,[33] which now is taken as the leading case on the law of finds. The contest was between the owner-occupier of a public park and a metal detecting enthusiast who found a medieval gold brooch buried nine inches below the

---

[30] [1969] 2 QB 152, 156–7. The quotation is Wrangham J's rehearsal of the argument of counsel.

[31] The conduct suggested by counsel does seem to satisfy a literal reading of the acquaintance obligation as proposed in *Parker*.

[32] Palmer, n 23 above, 1419.

[33] [1996] QB 334.

surface of the park. Each of the protagonists claimed to be entitled to the brooch,[34] and the decision turned on which of them had the better claim. Auld LJ stated:

> [The appeal] raises two questions. (1) Who, as between an owner or lawful possessor of land and a finder of an article in or attached to the land, is entitled to the article? (2) How is the answer to (1) affected by, or applied, when the land is public open space?[35]

Framed thus, the answer to this appeal entails no decision on the obligations, if any, that a finder or an occupier-of-land owes to a loser of goods. The case can be (and was) dealt with by applying the rules of title that determine the relative priority of claimant and defendant.[36] And this of course is the reason why most of the finding decisions are silent on the obligations on a finder. The relativity of title disputes allows (indeed, requires) a court to treat the loser of goods as a background considera-tion.[37] The court must adjudicate the competing claims of the parties to the dispute, and as such, unless the loser is one of those parties,[38] his interest in the goods is not a proper matter for the court's consideration.

This was very clearly illustrated in the judgment of the High Court of Ontario in *Bird v Fort Frances*.[39] A young boy found a quantity of banknotes underneath a pool room on private property, and he claimed their value from the municipality of Fort Frances, with whom the notes had been deposited following their seizure by the police. Again the contest turned on the relative titles of the boy and the police (and particularly on the extent to which the title of the former would be limited by any wrongdoing or felonious activity on his part), but additionally the munici-pality sought to resist the boy's claim on the basis that it had received a demand for return of the monies from the owner of the premises on which they were found. At the trial McRuer CJHC refused to consider this element of the defence, unless the owner of the premises was prepared to make his claim formally and at the consequent risk of costs. With that, the

---

[34] The proceedings were begun by Waverly Borough Council, which issued a writ claiming: (1) the brooch was its property; and (2) delivery up of the brooch or, alternatively, damages ([1996] QB 334, 336). The defendant denied this claim on the ground that he was entitled to retain the brooch as its finder. Although not formally a counterclaim to entitlement, the success of the defence entails a conclusion on whether the defendant's assertion is correct at law, and so in substance it seems acceptable to render the case a contest on competing claims to entitlement.

[35] *Ibid*, 338

[36] Which in this case led to an award in favour of the owner-occupier, inasmuch as such a person will always have a better title to goods buried in his land than a subsequent finder. For Auld LJ's statement of the applicable principles of title see *ibid*, 346.

[37] S Roberts, 'More Lost than Found' [1982] 45 *MLR* 683, 686.

[38] Whether directly, or as a result of being joined as a defendant under the *ius tertii* provisions of s 8 of the Torts (Interference with Goods) Act (1977).

[39] (1949) 2 DLR 791.

matter was dropped, and the judgment reveals clearly the disjunctive and relative approach to dispute resolution that has always governed title disputes to personal property:

> Whatever the rights of the [owner of the premises] may be, they cannot be considered or disposed of in this action as framed.[40]

Precisely the same core principle is at work in the English finding cases. Unless the loser of goods is a party to the proceedings, then the merits of any claim he might have should not be considered by the court. Necessarily this forces the loser to the background of the claim and offers a reason why our courts have been slow to consider the obligations that might be owed to him. Put very simply, many of these disputes can be decided without reference to the loser of goods, who should be left to pursue any claim in later proceedings.

The Honesty of Litigants

Perhaps a further reason for the lack of judicial authority in this area is that a great many of the litigated finding disputes concern finders who were considered by the courts to have behaved commendably or honestly. In other words, the reported disputes concern finders who did not need to have their conduct curtailed by positive obligations. In *Waverly*,[41] Mr Fletcher reported his find to the coroner in the belief that it might be treasure, satisfying the reporting duty required of him by the Treasure Act (1996). In *Hannah v Peel*,[42] a soldier on duty reported the find of a brooch to his commanding officer and to the police as soon as he believed the brooch to be of value. In *Bridges v Hawkesworth*,[43] the finder of a packet of banknotes caused them to be stored by the owner of the shop in which they were found and caused their find to be advertised, only claiming them himself on the expiry of three years after the date of their find and offering an indemnity for expenses to the shopkeeper. And in *Parker* itself, Donaldson LJ thought that the claimant finder 'acted as one would have hoped and expected [him] to act'.[44]

Perhaps in circumstances such as these the courts have been so confident that the finder has done all that his duty requires of him that they have not needed to express formally the existence of that duty or its content. Of course we would then expect the contrary to be true in cases where the finder's behaviour has been unmeritorious or dishonest, but here such

---

[40] *Ibid*, 793.
[41] [1996] QB 334.
[42] [1945] 1 KB 509.
[43] (1851) 21 LJQB 75.
[44] [1982] QB 1004, 1007.

complaints have largely been made in the different context of theft proceedings,[45] have been considered irrelevant to the issues at hand[46] or have simply been ignored.[47]

Reliance on Bailment Concepts

In *Parker*, Donaldson LJ reproduced lengthy citations from the Canadian case of *Kowal v Ellis*.[48] *Kowal* was decided on facts very similar to *Parker*, and in the absence of any more direct authority, Donaldson LJ seems to have allowed the judgment to influence his comments on a finder's duty. The claimant took possession of a pump lying unattached on land belonging to the defendant. The defendant took the pump from the claimant, but the latter recovered damages in detinue. An appeal against this judgment was dismissed by the Manitoba Court of Appeal. Sullivan JA clearly contemplated that the claimant incurred obligations to the owner of the pump:

> [When] a person finds a chattel and takes possession of it, then he immediately becomes responsible to the owner of the chattel to take reasonable care of it and, in my view, to make reasonable efforts to locate the owner.[49]

It is also clear that the court considered these obligations to have arisen from the creation of a bailment between the owner of the pump and the finder:

> The plaintiff, when he took possession of the pump, acquired a special property in it arising out of his relationship to the unknown owner. The relationship was one of bailment and, like any other bailee, the plaintiff has become entitled to sue in trover or, as here, detinue anyone who has interfered with his right of possession, save only the true owner or someone claiming through or on behalf of the true owner.[50]

The proposition that finders (or anyone claiming goods without the best title) are bailees was used by the courts to do all the work in this case. Sullivan JA considered that for the defendant to succeed, he would have needed to show that he was a 'prior bailee' of the chattel, with all the

---

[45] *Hibbert v McKiernan* [1948] 2 KB 142; *Rostron* [2003] EWCA Crim 2206; [2003] All ER (D) 269.

[46] *Bird v Fort Frances* (1949) 2 DLR 791.

[47] For a famous example, often overlooked, see *Armory v Delamirie* (1722) 1 Stra 505. There is a good chance the chimney sweep's boy was a thief intending to keep the jewel for himself, but in the half-page report the matter is not discussed, and the boy is awarded damages to the value of the most expensive jewel that could have been set in the socket.

[48] (1977) 76 DLR (3d) 546.

[49] *Ibid*, 548.

[50] *Ibid*, reproduced in *Parker* [1982} QB 1004, 1015.

rights and obligations of a bailee.[51] But he thought that the defendant would have been surprised if, prior to the finding by the claimant, the true owner had come along and asserted that the defendant owed him any duty either to take care of the pump or to seek out its owner. The reality was:

> [T]he defendant, not even being aware of the existence of the pump, owed no duty with respect to it to its true owner. He was not a bailee of the pump and consequently ha[d] no claim to possession which [could] prevail over the special property which the plaintiff ha[d] by virtue of his having become a bailee by finding.[52]

The problem here is that Sullivan JA used a duty concept to do the work of a rights concept. Nothing is achieved by 'bailment' that cannot be achieved through the use of possessory rights simpliciter. In *Bridges v Hawkesworth*, on which Sullivan JA relied, the dispute between shopkeeper and finder was said to turn on the existence of a relatively better possessory right in the shopkeeper, which was antecedent to that created in the finder at the time of the finding.[53] The single point in the case was 'whether the circumstance of the notes being found inside the defendant's shop gives him, the defendant, the right to have them as against the plaintiff'.[54] The answer to his question was negative, and so the plaintiff-finder was successful on the basis of his better title. It was the same in *Parker*. Moreover, there are signs in the *Kowal* judgment that Sullivan JA realised that the dispute before him could have been settled on consideration of the rights (as opposed to the duties) of the respective parties. The second line of the judgment characterised the case as a dispute over 'the right to possession of a chattel';[55] Sullivan JA thought the principle of *Armory v Delamirie* encapsulated 'in a nutshell' the law applicable to the facts before him;[56] and citing *Bridges v Hawkesworth* and *Hannah v Peel*, he stated the conclusion in the case thus:

> It follows that the plaintiff is entitled to possession of the pump, unless the defendant asserts and proves a title to the pump superior to that of the plaintiff.[57]

Clearly the bailment concept is only operative here to the extent that Sullivan JA thought that a bailment is required to generate the necessary possessory right in a successful claimant. But on the basis of the cases cited in his judgment, possession itself is enough to generate that right. For our

---

[51] *Ibid*, 549.
[52] *Ibid*.
[53] (1851) 21 LJQB 75.
[54] *Ibid*.
[55] (1977) 76 DLR (3d) 546, 547.
[56] *Ibid*, 548.
[57] *Ibid*.

present purposes, it comes to this. The existence of finder-obligations in this case is parasitic on the concept of bailment and on the characterisation of the finder as a bailee. But it is not necessary for the decision to characterise the finder as a bailee. So *Kowal* can only be used as an authority for the existence of finder-obligations to the extent that it is more generally true that a finder of lost goods is a bailee of the same for their loser.

It follows that, without more, the rehearsal of *Kowal v Ellis* does little to support Donaldson LJ's statement of a finder's obligations. The quotations reproduced are not valuable in the absence of a more general holding that finders are bailees, which is nowhere discussed in *Parker*. We will turn next to consider this more general question, but thus far it ought to be clear that at common law there is very little authority to suggest that a finder owes to a loser of goods the kind of obligations contemplated by Donaldson LJ. Certainly there is no direct authority that settles the matter and very little else in the case law that could be taken as providing support for the existence of such obligations.

THE FINDER AS BAILEE

Palmer describes the equation of bailee and finder as 'partial and imperfect'.[58] His great work on bailment has a chapter devoted to 'finders and other unrequested keepers', which begins by suggesting that finding 'represents one of the more questionable forms of bailment'.[59] It is questionable because the fact scenario of finding does not neatly align to that of bailment, such that there are a number of identifiable difficulties. In the first place, there is no contract, agreement or delivery between loser and finder, as there would be normally between bailor and bailee. This is not a critical objection, especially as (we shall see shortly) modern authorities have preferred to define bailment as depending only on the voluntary assumption of possession of the goods of another, and not on that transfer of possession from bailor to bailee contemplated by the literal case.[60]

However, there are difficulties yet. A finder has no bailor in the literal sense, and perhaps no means of identifying his bailor. There is no relation that informs the content of the finder's bailment, and some of the terms that the courts would require of the finder seem difficult to reproduce in a

---

[58] Palmer, note 23 above, 1418.
[59] *Ibid*, 1418.
[60] *Morris v CW Martin & Sons Ltd* [1966] 1 QB 716 (CA); *Gilchrist Watt and Sanderson Pty Ltd v York Products Pty Ltd* [1970] 3 All ER 825 (PC).

conventional bailment scenario.[61] Moreover, an ordinary bailee is at common law estopped from denying his bailor's title.[62] A finder, by contrast, is permitted time to investigate the claims of putative losers and can require those claims to be substantiated.[63]

Despite these kinds of evident difficulty, Palmer does think that there is 'strong modern authority' for the equation of finder and bailee.[64] His principal argument in this regard suggests that finders are bailees because and insofar as they owe obligations to the loser:

> [T]he absence of any relation, either direct or indirect, to identify the terms on which the finder assumes possession . . . suggests that finders are bailees only to the limited extent that the custodial rights and obligations of both classes of possessor are . . . in substance the same.[65]

In the context of our discussion in the previous section, this argument is difficult: it makes for circular reasoning. In *Kowal*, Sullivan JA thought that the finder owed obligations because he was a bailee. But according to Palmer, the finder is a bailee because he owes obligations. The problem is exacerbated inasmuch as two of the 'strong authorities' used by Palmer to support his contention are *Parker* and *Kowal*,[66] neither of which, as we have seen, will do as an authority for this argument. The other suggested authorities are *Morris v CW Martin & Sons Ltd*[67] and *Gilchrist Watt and Sanderson Pty Ltd v York Products Pty Ltd*.[68] Each of these was a case of sub-bailment, and the judgments concerned the liabilities incurred by a sub-bailee to his principal.

In *Morris*, the claimant owned a mink stole and wanted to have it cleaned. She took it to a furrier. He did not offer cleaning services, but with the claimant's permission he sent the stole to the defendants, a large and well-known cleaning company. While the fur was in the defendants' care, it was stolen by one of their employees, though without any negligence on the part of the defendants. The question in the appeal concerned any liability of the defendants to the claimant for this loss. Lord Denning MR identified it even more precisely as 'the important question of how far a master is liable for theft or dishonesty by one of his servants'.[69] Relying on

---

[61] Palmer (note 23 above, 1421), commenting on *Parker*, notes that it would be difficult to imagine any situation in which it would be necessary (or doctrinally legitimate) to impose upon a conventional bailee the positive obligation to take steps to reunite bailed goods with their true owner.

[62] *Ibid*, 265ff.

[63] *Isaac v Clark* (1615) 2 Bulstr 306.

[64] Palmer, note 23 above, 1467.

[65] *Ibid*, 1420; and see also 32–6 and 1418.

[66] *Ibid*, 1465, fn 64 and accompanying text.

[67] [1966] 1 QB 716 (CA).

[68] [1970] 3 All ER 825 (PC).

[69] [1966] 1 QB 716, 723.

a passage from Pollock and Wright, his Lordship held that a sub-bailee for reward owed to the principal all the duties of a bailee of reward, and hence in the instant case the defendants were answerable to the claimant unless they could show that the loss occurred without fault on the part of the defendants or their servants.[70]

Plainly, a finder is not a bailee for reward. *Morris* was not a case about finding, nor one in which the circumstances of finding were immediately relevant. Nonetheless, Diplock LJ is credited as providing an authoritative view on the idea that finders might be bailees.[71] But he mentioned finding only very briefly (indeed, in only three words) and assumed rather than proved that finders provide an example of a bailment arising otherwise than by contract or agreement:

> While most cases of bailment today are accompanied by a contractual relation-ship between bailee and bailor which may modify or extend the common law duties of the parties that would otherwise arise from the mere fact of bailment, this is not necessarily so—as witness gratuitous bailment or bailment by finding.

Diplock LJ's real mission here is to characterise bailment generally as a set of obligations voluntarily assumed by lawfully taking into one's custody goods belonging to another. The obligations of a finder are only relevant to the extent that they arise because of a bailment relationship existing between finder and loser, the existence of which is assumed rather than argued or evidenced. Neither Lord Denning MR nor Salmon LJ mentioned the case of the finder at all, and this being so, it seems better to discount *Morris* as authority for the proposition that finders are bailees.

Gilchrist Watt follows the same course. The defendants were ships agents and stevedores and had in their custody two cases of clocks for delivery to the claimants. One of the cases was lost by the defendants' failure to exercise reasonable care. Lord Pearson, relying on *Morris*, held that defendants as sub-bailees were given and took possession of the goods for the purpose of looking after them and delivering them to the claim-ants.[72] In so doing they assumed an obligation to the claimants 'to exercise due care for the safety of the goods, although there was no contractual relation or attornment' between them.[73]

In the course of this judgment, Lord Pearson referred to some of the early finding cases, including *Newman v Bourne & Hollingsworth*,[74] which his Lordship took as an unequivocal authority for the existence of finder-obligations. Even allowing for the deficiency in that supposition, it is clear the existence of such obligations is relevant only as analogical

---

[70]   *Ibid*, 725.
[71]   Palmer, note 23 above, 33.
[72]   [1970] 3 All ER 825, 829.
[73]   *Ibid*.
[74]   (1915) TLR 209.

support to the argument at stake, which is to overcome the absence of a contract between claimants and defendants by characterising bailment as a set of duties voluntarily assumed by taking possession of the goods of another. To argue, as his Lordship did, that taking possession following a finding 'involves an assumption of responsibility for the safe keeping of the goods'[75] plainly supports the more general conclusion on bailment. The problem is that there is no authority at common law to support the premise that finders of goods assume a responsibility for their care.

As things stand, this circle is unbroken. More recent cases on sub-bailment continue to use the finding cases as exemplary of a general principle that an assumption of possession also involves an assumption of responsibility, which grounds the existence of obligations.[76] Meanwhile, in the finding cases, judges use bailment literature to assume (hypothetically) that finders are kept in check by bailment obligations. These arguments are as weak as each other. Moreover, they are dealt a blow inasmuch as there was a case as recently as 1965 in which a finder was held not to be a bailee. In *Thompson v Nixon*,[77] the defendant found a bag of rabbit feeding pellets and took them in the belief that he could find their owner by taking reasonable steps. Several hours later, the appellant formed the dishonest intention of keeping the pellets for himself. Since the initial taking was not trespassory, larceny would not lie,[78] unless it could be shown that the defendant was a bailee.[79] The Court of Appeal rejected any argument to this effect, quashing the defendant's conviction. Authoritatively, a finder was not a bailee.

We need not make too much of *Thompson v Nixon*. It is clear that the Court of Appeal reached the decision in the case with some reluctance and felt constrained by earlier authority on the definition of larceny.[80] Nonetheless, the decision hints at longstanding doubt over the status of finders as bailees.[81] Taken together with the difficulty in aligning their obligations,

---

[75] This passage is cited by Palmer, note 23 above, 34.

[76] *East West Corpn v DKBS* [2003] 2 All ER 700; *The Pioneer Container* [1994] 2 AC 324 (PC).

[77] [1965] 2 All ER 741; Hadden [1965] CLJ 173.

[78] At common law and under the provisions of the Larceny Act (1916), for larceny to lie the initial taking must have been wrongful. A direct trespassory interference with goods was the essence of the offence: see generally JP McCutcheon, *The Larceny Act 1916* (Dublin, Round Hall Press, 1989) 25; J Edwards, 'Possession and Larceny' [1950] 3 *Current Legal Problems* 127.

[79] S 1(1) of the Larceny Act 1916 offers a general exception to the requirement of wrongful taking and expressly provides that a bailee may be guilty of stealing if he converts goods to his own use. See generally McCutcheon, *ibid*, 35–6

[80] Particularly *Matthews* (1873) 28 LT 646; 12 Cox CC 491. Given that it was dealing with a matter involving the liberty of the subject, the court preferred to leave questions as to the justification of the larceny rules to Parliament: see [1965] 2 All ER 741, 742–3 (Sachs J).

[81] Indeed, ATH Smith suggests their non-equivalence when he observes that the creation of the offence 'larceny by finding' in the Larceny Act (1916), s 1(2)(i)(d) was needed to close a

and the analogously circular reasoning offered by the sub-bailment cases, there is little to suggest that the equation of finder and bailee is permissible at common law, and there is thus little to suggest that the concept of bailment can be used to justify the existence of finder-obligations.

LIABILITY UNDER GENERAL DUTIES

Whilst there is only weak evidence to support the proposition that English law imposes positive obligations on finders of goods, whether as bailees or otherwise, it is certain that a finder will be subject to those general duties of the law of obligations that serve to protect interests in property. It might be that the content of these general duties compels a finder to act in the manner required of him by Donaldson LJ in *Parker*.

An exhaustive review of the obligations that protect interests in property is well beyond the scope of this chapter. At least the torts of conversion and negligence, and probably the law of unjust enrichment, have something to say about the legal position of finders. To offer a coherent account of each of these and then to expose their specific implications for the finder would take us far from our immediate objective. To meet that, I intend only to show that by carelessly losing David Schwimmer's watch, Larry David does not necessarily incur any civil liability in English law. That he does not is enough to reject the view that the conduct required by Donaldson LJ's putative finder-obligations is provided for in general liabilities.

CONVERSION

Despite for centuries doing most of the non-criminal work in theft scenarios, the tort of conversion long evaded satisfactory definition.[82] Bramwell LJ once observed that he never understood with precision what counted as a conversion,[83] and textbooks approached discussion by listing and expounding discrete examples.[84] But increasingly it is accepted that, in

loophole in the law after general recognition that bailees could be prosecuted for larceny: *Property Offences* (London, Sweet & Maxwell, 1994) 9.

[82] The role of finding in the development of the tort is evident. Conversion is the modern successor of a specialised action on the case known as trover, which counted that the claimant casually had lost, and the defendant subsequently had found, the goods which were in dispute. On trover and conversion generally see: JB Ames, 'The History of Trover' (1897) XI *Harvard Law Review* 276; AWB Simpson, 'The Introduction of the Action on the Case for Conversion' [1959] 75 *LQR* 364.

[83] *Hiort v L & NWR* (1879) 4 Ex D 188, 194.

[84] Even in the most recent edition of *Clerk & Lindsell* there is a long discussion devoted to 'Forms of conversion': A Dugdale and M Jones (eds), *Clerk & Lindsell on Torts*, 19th edn (London, Sweet & Maxwell, 2006) 17.07–17.32.

its essence, the tort seeks to compensate a claimant for positive acts, done in relation to certain goods, which amount to a denial of his title in them. As it is put in *Clerk & Lindsell*, 'conversion is an act of deliberate dealing with a chattel in a manner inconsistent with another's right whereby that other is deprived of the use and possession of it.'[85]

This formulation recently was approved by the House of Lords in the *Kuwait Airways* case,[86] in which, for conflict of laws purposes, their Lordships were afforded the opportunity to discuss conversion in English law. Lord Nicholls, concurring that the variety of circumstances in which a conversion could occur made framing a general definition nigh on impossible, nonetheless identified three general features of the tort.[87] First, the defendant's conduct must be inconsistent with the rights of the owner (or of some other person entitled to possession). Second, the defendant's conduct must be deliberate, not accidental. And third, the defendant's conduct must be so extensive an encroachment on the rights of the owner as to exclude him from use and possession of the goods.[88] Lord Steyn concurred that the essential feature of conversion was the denial of the claimant's title but put the matter more shortly: whenever a defendant manifests 'an assertion of rights or dominion over the goods which is inconsistent with the rights of the plaintiff', he converts the goods to his own use.[89]

It is extremely unlikely that Larry David converts David Schwimmer's watch. In the first place, casual loss of goods is no conversion. Their Lordships in *Kuwait Airways* clearly contemplate that conversion consists of a deliberate and voluntary act, which by definition an accidental loss is not. The only exception to this is contained in section 2 of the Torts (Interference with Goods) Act (1977), which imposes a liability on a bailee for loss or destruction caused in breach of duty to his bailor. This section will only affect Larry's liability to the extent that finders are bailees, which at best is doubtful. So it seems that the tort of conversion imposes no duty on Larry to take care of the watch such that he is liable for its loss.

Neither does conversion compel Larry to acquaint Schwimmer of the find. Of course, like any other non-owning possessor, a finder who chooses deliberately to keep and use a found item for himself commits a conversion, as does a finder who manifests any assertion of rights inconsistent

---

[85] *Ibid*, 17.07.
[86] *Kuwait Airways Corp'n v Iraqi Airways Co (Nos 4 & 5)* [2002] 2 AC 883.
[87] *Ibid*, 1084.
[88] The contrast here is with lesser acts of interference in which a defendant, say, damages goods without excluding the claimant from their possession. Such claims can give rise to claims for trespass or negligence, but they are not conversion. This preserves distinctions between the scope of the 'property torts' at common law and prevents conversion from being used as an all-purpose tort for the compensation of interference with goods.
[89] [2002] 2 AC 883, 1104.

with the title of the loser, for example, by selling the chattel.[90] Very often this kind of wrongful conduct has been set in contrast to the conduct of an honest finder, who, 'laying-up' lost goods for their owner, has been said to commit no tort.[91] Such polarisation might create the impression that honest finding is a general defence to conversion proceedings, which in turn might go some way towards suggesting that Donaldson LJ's acquaintance obligation is required of a finder, viz that he must show an attempt to lay up the goods to their owner if he is to avoid liability in conversion. The difficulty is that there is some middle ground. Specifically, it does not seem to be a conversion merely to store goods belonging to another.[92] In other words, if Larry on finding the watch picks it up and puts it in a safe place and does nothing else, he does no wrong.[93] He does not acquaint the loser of the find, but yet he commits no conversion.

Negligence

Newman v Bourne and Hollingsworth[94] will do as authority for the proposition that a finder will be liable for loss of a chattel if that loss was caused by his negligence. This will go some way to meeting Donaldson LJ's assertion that finders are under an obligation to take care of lost items, yet the duties are not symmetrical. A general duty in negligence of course places the burden of proving breach of that duty on the claimant, in this case the loser. On the other hand, if the finder owes a specific duty to the loser to take care of lost items, it seems that the burden is on the finder to show that he was *not negligent* in causing any loss. So Larry is answerable to Schwimmer for negligence, but Schwimmer's case is more difficult to make if he must rely only on the general law of negligence.

UNJUST ENRICHMENT

A more difficult question is whether Larry owes Schwimmer a restitutionary obligation arising from unjust enrichment.[95] Here there are two doubts. The first is whether Larry is unjustly enriched by taking possession

---

[90]   Though it seems an offer to sell, without more, is not enough: *Marcq v Christie Manson & Woods Ltd* [2004] QB 286.

[91]   *Isaac v Clark* (1615) 2 Bulstr 306.

[92]   *Hollins v Fowler* (1875) LR 7 HL 757, 767 (Blackburn J). See generally *English Private Law*, note 6 above, 14.315.

[93]   This is implicit in *Newman v Bourne and Hollingsworth* (1915) TLR 209, where the liability was for negligence in the choice of storage location, rather than for storage itself.

[94]   *Ibid.*

[95]   There is very little authority on these kind of bi-partite claims in unjust enrichment, one reason being that 'a claimant in this situation will normally choose to sue for a wrong seeking

of lost goods. Clearly there is no basis for any enrichment: it is not difficult to argue that a loser of goods has no intent to transfer possession of them to a finder. But there must at least be a doubt over whether there is an enrichment in a case where the finder does not also convert the goods. If the find had been money, it is likely that Larry would have been enriched simply by taking it.[96] But since it is a chattel, the matter is more difficult, though there are options. One is that Larry is enriched inasmuch as a watch is easily realisable in monetary terms through its sale.[97] Another is that simply by keeping the watch Larry in effect precludes himself from denying that he was enriched, the keeping of a chattel being inconsistent with any assertion of its worthlessness.[98] A third school of thought would deny completely the possibility of any enrichment on these facts, inasmuch as there has been no transfer of title between Schwimmer and Larry.

Even if a finder is unjustly enriched by the simple act of taking and keeping, it is not clear that the resultant restitutionary obligation would compel the kind of conduct envisaged in *Parker*. Donaldson LJ is aiming at a form of specific restitution. The finder is supposed to care for the goods and take steps to acquaint the loser with their whereabouts. The goal is that losers and lost items are reunited.[99] But the unjust enrichment of a finder in these circumstances would raise only an obligation to make restitution of the value he received. Since the property rights of the loser withstand the loss of the goods, unjust enrichment has got nothing to say about the allocation of property in the asset received: it requires of the finder the payment of debt, rather than the return of specific goods.[100] If anything this serves as a disincentive to finders who are thinking about locating a loser. The finder who locates the loser will in any case be bound to deliver up the goods if the loser asks for them: it would be a conversion not to do so. The finder who does nothing does not convert the goods. He will be answerable for any enrichment he has received if the loser ever identifies him, but that is much less likely to happen if he says nothing.

---

compensation, or, less commonly, restitution for the wrong': A Burrows, *The Law of Restitution* (London, LexisNexis UK, 2002) 185. Thanks to Paul Mac Mahon for drawing this to my attention.

[96] 'It is nearly always impossible to deny that a receipt of money is enriching': *English Private Law*, note 6 above, 15.36. But compare 15.37, specifically on the case of the finder, and *cf* generally G Virgo, *The Principles of the Law of Restitution* (Oxford, OUP, 1999) 593–5.

[97] Goff & Jones, *The Law of Restitution*, 6th edn (London, Sweet & Maxwell, 2002). It is the fact of potentially realisable value that constitutes the enrichment rather than the actual realisation of that value through sale, which would of course be a conversion.

[98] *English Private Law*, note 6 above, 15.43.

[99] [1982] QB 1004, 1017.

[100] Contrast the position in tortious proceedings, where orders for specific delivery are available: Torts (Interference with Goods) Act (1977), s 3.

CONCLUSION

Taken together, the previous sections should do little to curb the enthusi-asm of finders. In the first place, the imposition of positive obligations looks authoritatively doubtful. There is no case that decides directly for the existence or content of a finder's duty, and no real authority for the proposition that the finder is a bailee, owing obligations in virtue of that status. Nor is there any sense that English law is fully replicating the function of these putative obligations through general tortious or unjust enrichment liabilities, such that their existence would in any event be rendered unnecessary. So, whilst it looks certain that at common law a finder acquires some property rights in the object of his find, it seems at least very doubtful that he incurs obligations.

The previous sections *should* suffice to curb the enthusiasm of common lawyers. It is disappointing enough that a sophisticated legal system with a millennium of experience should still struggle to resolve a personal property dispute better suited to a playground than a court of law, but there is a greater difficulty. We have seen that, almost certainly, a loser's property interest in goods survives their loss.[101] The loser is entitled to have that interest protected by the legal system. In English law, this means protection through the law of obligations, inasmuch as we never offer direct vindication of property rights in our courts.[102] To the extent that the absence of finder-obligations amounts to a gap in this protection system of the law of obligations, it amounts to a failure to protect the private property rights of the loser. In a society where the protection of possessions is considered a basic human right,[103] this could be a critical failing.

Possibly it was Donaldson LJ's recognition of this difficulty that led him to assert the finder-obligations in *Parker*. Certainly his Lordship accepted the need to have common law rules that 'facilitate rather than hinder the ascertainment of the true owner of a lost chattel and a reunion between the two'.[104] As things stand, however, the common law does not fully meet this objective. The issue needs to be addressed, though quite how to do so is still a matter for discussion. There are at least a number of competing alternatives. One is to recommend a thorough legislative review of the position of finders; another is to extend the scope of the tort of conversion and have even more strict liability for dealing with the property of another; and still a third is to posit expressly the kind of finder-obligations we have been discussing, which as yet are missing from the common law. But

---

[101] *R v Reed* Car & M 306.
[102] *English Private Law*, note 6 above, 14.308–14.311.
[103] European Convention on Human Rights, First Protocol, Article 1.
[104] [1982] QB 1004, 1017

whatever we do, it will be a matter of some novelty. We will be imposing a new civil liability on finders like Larry. We can only hope that they greet it enthusiastically.

6

Leases: Rethinking Possession against Vulnerable Groups

WARREN BARR

INTRODUCTION

T
HE PURPOSE OF this chapter is not simply to examine the property rights and regimes that govern possession actions by landlords against vulnerable tenants.[1] Nor is it to consider the different models of social housing provision that exist and to assess their quality in practice.[2] Instead, it aims to demonstrate that the right to possession, inherent in all forms of letting agreement, is not the only or best remedy available to social landlords in managing lettings, and that alternatives exist in rethinking approaches to housing problems rather than simply relying as a matter of property law on rights and obligations. This will involve sketching out the housing framework for housing and providing services to the vulnerable, as well as examining the common triggers of repossession and the legal and practical problems faced in seeking repossession. With that achieved, a consideration of the many alternatives to possession can be explored and considered against the repossession action, and some conclusions can be drawn.

OVERVIEW OF SOCIAL HOUSING PROVISION FOR THE VULNERABLE

First, some definitions. There are many individuals who may be regarded as 'vulnerable', for example through infirmity, youth, ethnic background or status. The focus of this chapter will be on adults suffering from mental disorders or learning disabilities, in this context described as the 'mentally

---

[1] For a good general treatment of leasehold property rights, see K Gray & S Gray, *Elements of Land Law*, 4th edn (Oxford, OUP, 2005) ch 14.

[2] There is considerable literature on these issues—see, as a good starting point, D Cowan and A Marsh, 'From Need to Choice, Welfarism to Advanced Liberalism? Problematics of Social Housing Allocation' (2005) 25(1) *Legal Studies* 22.

vulnerable',[3] although the issues raised should be of wider interest to those dealing with other vulnerable groups. Similarly, this chapter will talk about social landlords in the widest possible context and not tied to any legal landlord condition.

The total number of mentally vulnerable people in the UK is unknown, although it is recognised as being an increasing population.[4] Part of the difficulty lies in the fact that many may be 'hidden' statistics[5] due to the policy of care in the community.[6] However, research demonstrates that, whatever the total number of individuals, the mentally vulnerable are one and half times more likely to be living in rented accommodation,[7] which is mainly provided by the social housing sector.[8]

Social Housing: The Statutory Framework

It is recognised that the social housing sector itself is increasingly being viewed as a 'sector of last resort'.[9] There are now more than one million fewer homes in local authority or housing association homes than in 1977.[10] There are also evident problems with care and housing of the mentally vulnerable as a group.[11] Quite apart from the expense of providing quality services and support through either supported housing

---

[3] This is a large and diverse group, covering those who may be able to live independently with little or no support to those with enduring, chronic mental health needs. Relevant distinctions will be made, where appropriate, in the treatment that follows.

[4] See, generally, Social Exclusion Unit (SEU), *Mental Health and Social Exclusion: The SEU Report* (London, Office of the Deputy Prime Minister, 2004).

[5] Individuals with mental disorders may be cared for within family homes, or in bed and breakfast accommodation, so that they are part of the 'hidden homeless' problem. See 'Sustainable Communities: Settled Homes, Changing Lives' (London, Office of the Deputy Prime Minister, 2005). Research undertaken in 1997 demonstrated that the mentally disordered made up 9% of those accepted by local housing authorities on the grounds of priority need under the homeless legislation, a figure that was already on the rise. See A Murie, 'The Social Rented Sector, Housing and the Welfare State in the UK' (1997) 12 *Housing Studies* 437.

[6] For a contextual overview, see N Glover-Thomas, *Reconstructing Mental Health Law and Policy* (London, Butterworths, 2002).

[7] The *SEU Report*, note 4 above. See also H Meltzer, *The Social and Economic Circumstances of Adults with Mental Disorders* (National Statistics Office, HMSO, 2002): people with mental disorders are more likely to be living in rented accommodation (38% compared to 24% non-disordered). If the disorder is psychotic the figure rises to 62%, with just under half living in housing association or local authority accommodation.

[8] SEU, note 4 above.

[9] C Kiddle, 'The Impact of the Large Scale Voluntary Transfer of Local Authority Housing Stock on the HA Sector', Housing Corporation Sector Study 17 (London, 2002) 8.

[10] 'More than a Roof: A Report into Tackling Homelessness' (London, Office of the Deputy Prime Minister, 2003). The alternative, which has been in political favour since the early 1980s, is owner occupation. See generally J Alder & A Handy, *Housing Associations: The Law of Social Landlords*, 4th edn (London, Sweet and Maxwell, 2001).

[11] See generally S Richards & R Smith, *Community Care: Policy and Practice* (Bristol, Palgrave Macmillan, 2003).

projects[12] or more mainstream housing, a number of factors have increased the complexity of provision: a paucity of suitable housing stock;[13] inadequate funding of housing and support services;[14] and major difficulties in achieving effective inter-agency cooperation between the various bodies involved in providing services to the mentally disordered.[15] Moreover, social housing services have moved away from direct local authority involvement, with most functions being discharged by Registered Social Landlords (RSLs)[16] or non-registered housing associations. Many large- to medium-sized organisations are general providers, due to increasing competition and the adoption of a 'business' ethos within social housing to maximise funding and services.[17]

Provision for the disordered has therefore fallen to smaller, more specialist providers and, in particular, to the charity sector.[18] Research demonstrates that 90% of services to the mentally disordered are through housing associations or charities, with only 10% direct involvement by local authorities themselves.[19] Studies have illustrated that charities have played a wider and more complex role than was anticipated, with some organisations providing housing management services or direct housing provision from owned stock, although they predominantly act as housing mangers and/or service providers to housing associations.[20] Where housing is provided or managed, there is a broad range of provision from permanent homes to emergency overnight accommodation.[21]

---

[12] For an excellent discussion of the problems and opportunities in successful provision, see H Carr, '"Someone to Watch over Me": Making Supporting Housing Work' (2005) 14(3) *Social and Legal Studies* 387.

[13] A major factor in this is that the shift from hospital to community based care was not accompanied initially with any recognition that housing had a significant role to play in achieving good care. See N Glover-Thomas & W Barr, 'Housing an Individual: Property Problems with the Mentally Vulnerable' in Hudson (ed), *New Perspectives on Property Law, Human Rights and the Home* (London, Cavendish, 2003).

[14] See W Barr and N Glover-Thomas, *Housing the Mentally Vulnerable: The Role of Charities* (Charity Law Unit, 2005, ESRC Award Ref: RES-000-22-0286) < http://www.liv.ac.uk////HousingMVReport05.pdf > accessed 1 December 2006 (hereinafter referred to as the *ESRC Report*) ch 4.

[15] See the *ESRC Report*, 47–9 for a list of the bodies involved in housing the vulnerable, and also some of the problems, explored in detail at note 115 below.

[16] These bodies, created under the Housing Act (1996), are regulated by the Housing Corporation.

[17] The *ESRC Report*, note 14 above.

[18] *Ibid.*

[19] ODPM, 'Local Authority Supporting People Returns for England on Supply of Housing and Support Services' (London, The Stationery Office, 2002).

[20] The *ESRC Report*, 24–7. The *Report* was designed to fill a recognised gap in the research literature about the extent and nature of services provided by charities. The research aims and process are detailed in chs 1 and 2.

[21] The extent and nature of this provision is discussed in full in chapter 3 of the *ESRC Report*, which considers the types of housing provided (the physical stock, the mode in which it is occupied and its geographical location), as well as the nature and range of support services offered by the data sample.

The legal framework of occupation agreements is also complex.[22] The most common form of arrangement is assured tenancies under the Housing Act (1988), which offer security of tenure because they can only be brought to an end on defined statutory grounds. Local authority tenants may also be secure tenants under the Housing Act (1985),[23] and charities or other providers might be managers of these tenants. A more recent innovation that is available directly only to local authority landlords or RSLs are introductory tenancies under the Housing Act (1996), which are effectively assured shorthold tenancies for a one-year term.[24] Assured shorthold tenancies,[25] which differ from assured tenancies in that they offer no real security of tenure beyond their initial six-month terms, are also available where charities or housing associations let directly to occupiers.[26] Finally, for charities and housing association providers, a contractual licence may also be used, which confers no security of tenure and will occur where the nature of the letting means that only exclusive occupation rather than possession has been granted.[27]

Repossession: Common Triggers

For most social landlords, possession is an emotive topic, and there is a real tension between their social housing function and the need to regain possession in certain circumstances.[28] Sometimes eviction is sought to move someone on to a new, more suitable scheme, which is in the objective best interests of both the vulnerable individual and the provider.[29] Even when this is the case, given that many specialist providers for the vulnerable only manage housing stock or provide services to owned stock, the decision to initiate proceedings to evict a tenant may be outside their control and part of a wider stock management strategy.

---

[22] For a discussion of the development and application of the current statutory regulation, see Law Commission, 'Renting Homes 1: Status and Security', Consultation Paper No 162 (April 2002) Part II.

[23] While no new secure tenancies may be created after the Housing Act (1988), existing secure tenancies were not converted into assured tenancies.

[24] These tenancies can be extended by a further six months (Housing Act (1996) ss 125A–125B), and powers now exist to allow the demotion of assured tenancies to introductory tenancies in certain circumstances (Housing Act (1985) s 82A; Housing Act (1988) s 6A).

[25] Housing Act (1988) s 19A and Schedule 2A. This complexity has led the Law Commission to consider a root-and-branch reform of this area of the law and the introduction of a twofold system of consumer contracts. See chapter 1 of this volume.

[26] Assured shorthold tenancies are also technically possible for property owned or managed by a local authority or RSL, although they are discouraged, as Housing Corporation regulations provide that secure tenure is to be preferred.

[27] Problems with licenses will be discussed below.

[28] This is demonstrated in the context of the mentally vulnerable in the *ESRC Report*, 64.

[29] The *ESRC Report*, 70.

Even considering these factors, there is clear evidence that court actions by social landlords have doubled between 1994 and 2003.[30] 550,000 notices seeking possession are issued each year, which amounts to actions issued for 13% of stock.[31] In 2002–03, 26,000 social tenants were evicted, which amounts to one in every 20 tenants.[32] There are no exact figures on how many of these were vulnerable tenants or what that vulnerability might be,[33] but such figures are an obvious cause for concern within the sector.

Rent Arrears

It is unsurprising that the foremost cause of all possession actions by social landlords is rent arrears. In 2002-2003, rent arrears totalled some £231 million in housing associations generally.[34] More significantly, rent arrears make up 90% of actions for mentally disordered tenants.[35] There is no consistent level of arrears that prompts action; research defined a period of between four and sixty-eight weeks in actions analysed.[36]

For many social tenants, and particularly for those vulnerable tenants who may not be able to hold down full- or part-time employment, the payment of Housing Benefit is the single greatest reason for rent arrears. 60% of tenants of social landlords were claiming Housing Benefit in 2002-3,[37] and over 95% of housing associations[38] initiated possession proceedings with Housing Benefit claims outstanding.[39] It is now a matter of accepted fact that the administration of Housing Benefit is both slow and unreliable. The average delay in processing claims is 49 days,[40] but in many cases it exceeds 100 days. The complexity of the process means that

---

[30] H Pawson, J Flint, S Scott, R Atkinson, J Bannister, C McKenzie and C Mills, *The Use of Possession Actions and Evictions by Social Landlords* (London, Office of the Deputy Prime Minister, 2005).

[31] *Ibid.*

[32] *Ibid.*

[33] That this may be significant is explored below in relation to the effectiveness of possession actions and the Disability Discrimination Act (1995).

[34] Audit Commission, *Housing Association Rent Income: Rent Collection and Arrears Management by Housing Associations in England* (Essex, CW Print Group, 2003).

[35] A Warnes, M Crane, A Whitehead and R Fu, *Homelessness Factfile* (London, Crisis, 2003).

[36] *Ibid.*

[37] *Survey of English Housing 2002/03* (London, Office of the Deputy Prime Minister, 2004).

[38] In the broadest sense, including all social housing providers, absent almshouses and provident societies.

[39] Pawson et al, note 30 above. One explanation for such figures is the fact that the Housing Corporation requires bodies under its control to 'operate viable businesses, with adequate recourse to financial resources to meet their current and future business and financial commitments'.

[40] HC Deb, vol 423, col 876W, 12 July 2004.

incorrect levels may be set at the outset,[41] from which appeals are difficult,[42] and there is clear evidence of regional variations in the efficiency and levels of benefit obtainable.[43] Nor is the position better when a possession action comes to court.[44] Such is the inconsistency that one County Court judge is on record as saying that he is more likely to trust a defendant who claims that a benefits claim has been lost than a Housing Benefit officer who claims otherwise.[45] Indeed, in the words of Dyson LJ:

> [A] housing benefits department cannot now be relied upon to rectify matters before a possession claim is heard.[46]

The impact of arrears will be felt particularly by smaller and specialist providers, who may not have the financial reserves to absorb the costs of delay[47] and may depend upon rental payments directly to fund front-line services.[48] It is therefore to be expected that many of the possession orders issued are strategic attempts by social landlords to 'frighten' tenants into paying arrears[49] or to seek to minimise arrears at the date of court action,[50] or they are often vain attempts to get housing benefit claims prioritised.[51]

Anti-social Behaviour

In spite of significant media coverage of anti-social behaviour,[52] it is not a major trigger for possession. Indeed, evidence suggests that anti-social

---

[41] C Hunter, S Blandy, D Cowan, J Nixon, E Hitchings, C Pantazis and S Parr, 'The Exercise of Judicial Discretion in Rent Arrears Cases' (DCA Research Series 6/05, October 2005). The authors assert that County Court judges struggle with the complexity of benefits forms (80).

[42] The *ESRC Report*, 49–51.

[43] *Ibid.*

[44] Tenants are not blameless in problems over housing benefit, but even when they are engaged and properly advised, general delays can still occur.

[45] Hunter et al, note 41 above, 81.

[46] *North British Housing Association Ltd v Matthews* [2005] 1 WLR 3133, 3157.

[47] This is particularly true when the majority of tenant rent payments come from or are supported by housing benefit, as any delay in the system will mean that reserves can not be built up and the level of housing benefit is strictly set and allows no cushioning effect.

[48] The *ESRC Report*, 49–51. Note that funding for support services will come from the Supporting People regime <http://www.spkweb.org.uk/> accessed 1 December 2006. In the case of charities, funding for support services will also come through donation.

[49] Interestingly, this tactic is explicitly condemned by Pawson et al (note 30 above) and the Housing Corporation, yet there is evidence, at least in a general context, that judges understand and appreciate the impact of such 'frightening' orders: 'Well it actually makes them understand that the house has to be the first priority and not the children's Christmas present or whatever it might be' (Hunter et al, note 41 above, 45, quoting District Judge T).

[50] The effectiveness and importance of this measure are discussed below.

[51] Hunter et al, note 41 above, 13–14.

[52] There is no all-pervasive definition of anti-social behaviour, but see generally Social Exclusion Unit, National Strategy for Neighbourhood Renewal, 'Report of the Policy Action Team 8: Anti-social Behaviour' (London, SEU, 2000). Most definitions include noise

behaviour only relates to around 3% of overall possession orders.[53] That this may be due to other methods used to seek to control such behaviour, such as Anti-social Behaviour Orders (ASBOs) is considered further below.

Other Triggers

There is a multiplicity of other factors that trigger possession, such as public nuisance or any of the listed statutory grounds for possession. The factors are too multifarious to list here,[54] especially as they contribute collectively to only 7% of possession claims. Benign motivations, such as the wish to move someone from one particular service that they have outgrown to another, perhaps from another provider, also fall within this category.

ASSESSING THE DIFFICULTIES IN REGAINING POSSESSION AGAINST VULNERABLE ADULTS

Much has been said about the incidence and cause of possession actions by social landlords, so it is now important to consider what legal or practical difficulties they may face in actually achieving possession.

Legal Difficulties

The legal difficulties of regaining possession depend upon the scheme under which the occupier holds,[55] and these have been explored in detail elsewhere in the context of the vulnerable.[56] Briefly, introductory tenancies and assured shorthold tenancies may be easily terminated once the initial fixed period has expired;[57] licences must simply be terminated by court

---

nuisance, and in this respect, the nuisance grounds under an assured tenancy have been extended recently. See Housing Act (1996) ss 144 and 148.

[53] Warnes, note 35 above.

[54] For a summary and pictorial representation of the types of disputes that can arise, see Law Commission, 'Housing—Proportionate Dispute Resolution: Further Analysis' (April 2006) 25, Figure 1.

[55] For a good, general discussion of the rules relating to repossession with 'social' housing, see Hughes & Lowe, *Public Sector Housing Law*, 3rd edn (London, Butterworths, 2000) ch 3.

[56] See W Barr & N Glover-Thomas, 'Charitable Housing Providers and the Mentally Vulnerable: Housing Problems' [2005] 8 *JHL* 81; and W Barr, 'Charitable Lettings and their Legal Pitfalls' in E Cooke (ed), *Modern Studies in Property Law, Volume 1* (Oxford, Hart Publishing, 2001).

[57] It is this flexibility of the assured shorthold that makes it so attractive. See J Morgan, 'The Casualisation of Housing' (1996) 18 *JSWFL* 445.

order;[58] and assured or secure tenancies can be terminated only on the statutory grounds set out in the respective schemes.[59] The focus of what follows is on recovery under Ground 8 in the assured tenancy regime in the light of recent developments, and the potential impact of the Disability Discrimination Act (1995) on all possession actions against mentally disordered individuals.

Assured Tenancies: Ground 8 and Article 8

Interestingly, this first legal problem is one that might seem to operate in favour of social landlords, but it remains a problem nonetheless. Under Schedule 2, Part 1, Ground 8 of the Housing Act (1988) a landlord may recover possession if at least two months' rent arrears are due.[60] This differs from Ground 11 of the same Act in that it is a mandatory action;[61] if the arrears are proved at the time of court action, the court has no option but to make a possession order, unless there are exceptional circumstances on the facts to allow an adjournment. This is significant, since if the arrears arose through maladministration in housing benefit through no fault of the tenant, it is 'not an exceptional circumstance' according to the legislation.[62]

Social landlords are strongly advised not to use this ground,[63] but research demonstrates that possession cases are actually increasing in number, due to a combination of changes in the benefit system and the eight-week arrear period.[64] It is also ill-favoured by the judiciary, and DCA-commissioned research has found that Ground 8 cases have been

---

[58]   Protection From Eviction Act (1977) s 3(2B).

[59]   Barr & Glover-Thomas, note 56 above, 83, which considers the efficacy of Grounds 14 & 15 of the Housing Act (1988) for charity landlords, which is also applicable to specialists dealing with the vulnerable.

[60]   As amended by the Housing Act (1996).

[61]   Ground 11, which is a discretionary action for 'some rent lawfully due' also does not have a time period.

[62]   See *North British Housing Association v Matthews*, note 46 above, 3148. Dyson LJ gave examples of exceptional circumstances, such as ill health stopping the arrears being paid on the due date or because a cheque had not cleared, which present a defence at the date of trial to the action.

[63]   See J Neuberger, 'Consultation Response: Housing Corporation Proposals in Improving Best Practice in Exclusions and Evictions' (London, Shelter, 2003). When housing bodies are created through large-scale voluntary stock transfer, as happened in the 1990s (see note 9 above), they enter into a covenant not to use ground 8. Many of the properties managed by specialist providers might fall within this group.

[64]   Pawson et al, note 30 above, 26–9 and 70–1. *Cf* Hunter et al, note 41 above, 91, who found that very few of the Housing Associations observed used Ground 8, which may be explained by the fact that this research only considered local authority landlords and RSLs, and not other social landlords.

operating in a very non-mandatory manner; judges have used minor technical defects to adjourn claims so that levels fall below the eight-week level.[65]

Ground 8 has attracted sharp academic criticism. Morgan has argued vehemently that the possession ground is unnecessary and draconian,[66] especially given the nature of delays in housing benefit claims,[67] and suggests that it should neither be used by social landlord nor survive the Law Commission law reform process.[68] One particular contention made is that the mandatory ground may be in contravention of Article 8(1) of the Human Right Act (1998).[69] This deserves further consideration, given the recent decision of the House of Lords in the consolidated appeal of *Kay v London Borough of Lambeth*[70] on the application of human rights to possession claims.

Basically stated, Article 8(1) provides everyone with 'the right to respect for his private and family life, his home',[71] but interference with those rights can be justified under Article 8(2), where it is 'necessary in a democratic society . . . for the protection of the rights and freedoms of others'. This justification operates within a wide margin of appreciation.[72] The leading decision in English law was *Harrow LBC v Quazi*,[73] in which a bare majority of the House of Lords said that where domestic property law gives a landlord an unqualified right to possession, interference would always be justified in exercising that right. Their Lordships, sitting in an appellate jurisdiction of seven, were invited in *Kay v Lambeth*[74] to revisit

---

[65] Hunter et al, note 41 above, 91. It is unlikely that such practices will survive post-*Matthews* and the clear statement of exceptional circumstances listed therein.

[66] J Morgan, 'Rent Arrears: The Disproportionate Effect of Administrative Delay' [2005] *Conv* 524.

[67] Morgan makes the point that the average 49 days for processing claims for Housing Benefit, paid in arrears, is 'perilously close' (534) to the Ground 8 time periods.

[68] The Law Commission have suggested abolishing this ground and substituting general grounds with structured discretion. See 'Renting Homes', note 22 above, paras 9.26–9.29.

[69] Further argument is made on the basis on Article 14 and on the First Protocol of the European Convention on Human Rights, which are not considered further here.

[70] [2006] 2 WLR 570.

[71] To be able to bring an action under this ground, the housing must be provided by a body that is a 'public authority' for the purposes of the Human Rights Act (1998). This does not apply to all social landlords as yet beyond local authorities, although as Morgan has noted (note 66 above, 528), it is 'surely only a matter of time before the same recognition is accorded to housing associations in general.'

[72] See Morgan (note 66 above, 528–34) for full details, including all relevant case law.

[73] [2004] 1 AC 983.

[74] [2006] 2 WLR 570.

this reasoning, following two cases at the European Court of Human Rights in Strasbourg[75] that seemed to cast doubt on the correctness of *Quazi*.

Their Lordships held by a majority that *Quazi* still stands,[76] but they saw a need for further explanation. Domestic property law rights will *usually* provide a justification under Article 8(2) unless there is a 'seriously arguable case'[77] that the law itself is discriminatory and incompatible with the Convention.[78] Translated to Ground 8, provided the necessary arrears are owed at the date of action, no challenge based on the individual circumstances of the defendant would be permissible:[79] the action would be justified, and so no challenge could be mounted. The only possibility would be to argue that Ground 8 itself is discriminatory, as it is only available for assured tenants. This, it is suggested, is unlikely to succeed, as comparator tenures either provide an unqualified right to possession without grounds (assured shorthold and introductory tenancies) or are no longer capable of creation (secure tenancies).

In other words, currently Ground 8 remains a possibility, albeit a loaded one, for landlords seeking action for rent arrears. It is important not to overstate the problems caused in using it, as it may provide an efficient method to allow a social landlord to recover possession when it is necessary to do so effectively and efficiently,[80] but it is suggested that it only be used in this context, given the problems noted above and the guidance of the social sector regulators.

The Impact of the Disability Discrimination Act (1995)

A very real legal barrier to a successful possession action against a mentally disordered tenant may be provided by the interface of the Disability Discrimination Act (1995) and housing law in *Manchester City Council v*

---

[75] *Connors v UK* (2004) 40 EHRR 189 (concerning the right of gypsies to occupy land: action was upheld); and *Blecic v Croatia* (2004) 41 EHHR 185 (concerning the rights of a national ousted by war; the action was declined, as relevant procedural safeguards has been operated by the Member State).

[76] Lord Bingham, Lord Nicholls and Lord Walker dissenting.

[77] [2006] 2 WLR 570, 588–9 (Lord Bingham, who was not in dissent on this issue). Their Lordships also made it clear that a justification to Article 8 does not need to be pleased in every possession case, as this would be an abuse of process. See p 599 per Lord Hope.

[78] In such cases, leave should be given to appeal the decision to the High Court. It was on this basis that the decision in *Connors* was distinguished, as, inter alia, the law had been discriminatory in not providing a right to gypsies that would have been available to other occupiers under the Mobile Homes Act (1983).

[79] *Kay*, note 70 above, 627 (per Lord Scott). Morgan's detailed arguments (note 66 above) that the means used are more than what is 'necessary' will therefore be inapplicable.

[80] See further W Barr and N Glover Thomas, 'Housing Reform: A Better Deal for the Mentally Vulnerable?' [2005] 69 *Conv* 207, 215.

Romano and Samari.[81] The effect of this decision is that eviction from social housing for a reason relating to mental health[82] is discriminatory[83] unless it is justified as necessary to safeguard the health of others.[84] In contrast to other anti-discrimination legislation,[85] it is not necessary to show that the disabled person has been treated differently from a non-disabled person—the order seeking possession is enough.[86] There is nothing objectionable about anti-discrimination legislation in itself, but the form that the current duties take has been subject to considerable criticism and calls for reform.[87] A recent commentator argues that by preventing landlords from taking action against the mentally disordered, the Disability Discrimination Act (1995) patronises the mentally disordered by denying them the opportunity to take moral or other responsibility for their actions.[88]

The application of the discrimination provisions was raised in the context of anti-social behaviour in *Romano*, but it is arguably applicable to any other ground of possession, provided the necessary nexus between the reason for a possession order and the occupier's mental impairment can be demonstrated (for example, rent arrears have arisen because of the failure of the occupier to do something to facilitate housing benefit due to a lack of understanding caused by learning disabilities).[89] On this understanding, a social landlord who wishes to recover the premises in the best interests either of an individual occupier who needs to be moved on to another service or of the housing project as whole, will be prevented from getting possession unless the landlord can show a reasonable interference

---

[81] [2004] EWCA Civ 834. For a summary of the decision and its application see The *ESRC Report*, 66–9.

[82] Under section 1(1) of the Disability Discrimination Act (1995), a disabled person includes someone who 'has a physical or mental impairment which has a substantial and long term adverse effect on his ability to carry out normal day to day activities'.

[83] See s 22(3). The definition of discrimination includes 'evicting the disabled person, or subjecting him to other detriment'.

[84] See ss 24(2) and 24(3)(a). The list of other justification in s 24(3) is not relevant in the housing context. Normal possession proceedings are effectively superseded by the requirements of the Act.

[85] See, for example, the Race Relations Act (1976), which requires that the effect of the treatment complained of should be compared with that of a person without the particular status of the complainant.

[86] Disability Discrimination Act s 24.

[87] See, for example, B Doyle, 'Enabling Legislation or Dissembling Law?' (1997) 60 *MLR* 64. Many of these calls for reform centre around the definition of discrimination within the Act. One suggestion is to issue regulations under powers conferred in the Act under s 24(5) to clarify the meaning of discrimination: The *ESRC Report*, 76–7.

[88] N Cobb, 'Patronising the Mentally Disordered? Social Landlords and the Control of "Anti-social Behaviour" under the Disability Discrimination Act 1995' [2006] 26 *Legal Studies* 238.

[89] As noted by Cobb (257), this argument has succeeded in at least one case, *Liverpool City Council v Slavin*, 29 April 2005, *Legal Action* (July 2005).

with the health and safety of other occupiers.[90] That the threshold of interference with health and safety may be low is cold comfort, and Cobb argues that any reform of the Disability Discrimination Act (1995) might have to include an exception of social housing projects.[91]

It is also likely that the impact of the Disability Discrimination Act (1995) is not limited to assured tenancies but will apply to all lettings to disabled tenants, whatever the legal structure adopted;[92] the legislation itself is landlord-neutral, as it focuses on the rights of the individual tenant. What is not settled, as has been suggested elsewhere,[93] is whether the relevant sections of the Act are applicable to possession proceedings where there is an unqualified right to possession,[94] such as under Ground 8 of the Housing Act (1998) in assured tenancies, or rights to possession by notice to quit under a licence, assured shorthold or introductory tenancy. In these situations, the role of the court is reduced to considering whether the necessary procedural steps have been upheld, and nothing more; there is no discretion to entertain a consideration of whether the action has been discriminatory. If this is so, then ironically it might give the Ground 8 action a greater role than has been ascribed to it. If this argument were to fail, then, absent any reform, all social landlords will have to adapt to couching possession cases in terms of the impact on the health and safety of others when they deal with a 'disabled' person.

Practical Difficulties

Even when the legal issues of repossession can be overcome, there are significant practical problems that suggest that repossession is not an ideal solution to problems with vulnerable clients.

Possession Outcomes: Difficulties in Achieving Desires

The nature of proceedings at the County Court has a significant impact on the outcome of possession hearings. Listing practices means that 'on average judges have fewer than five minutes to arrive at a decision'[95], and this may in practice be as little as two minutes for a particular session. The time given to each hearing seriously compresses the issues, so that if information is not properly recorded or signposted, then it is unlikely that

---

[90] The *ESRC Report*, 67.
[91] Cobb, note 88 above, 266.
[92] *Ibid*, 257.
[93] The *ESRC Report*, 69.
[94] *Romano* was concerned with the discretionary nuisance ground of possession (Ground 2) under the Housing Act (1988).
[95] Hunter et al, note 41 above, 106.

any particular issues of fact, such as any vulnerability of the tenant or the individual case history, will be discovered from the evidence. When the case is factually complicated, judges may employ a strategy of using adjournments to obtain further evidence.[96]

Similarly, research demonstrates that unresolved housing benefit issues often lead to adjournments, which casts serious doubt on the sense of bringing such actions when benefit arrears are outstanding. Of the 540 cases observed by Hunter et al in their research, 55% were adjourned, leading them to conclude that this was the standard order in rent arrears cases,[97] though of course not the only order.[98] The factors that influence the form of order include the level of arrears,[99] although there was no evidence of a clear correlation between arrears levels and orders granted, and the payment history.[100] It is important to note that there was considerable variation between the decisions of individual judge's, so much so that it was felt 'likely that even the introduction of some form of structured discretion . . . [would] still lead to different outcomes for similar cases'.[101]

Nevertheless, there was very clear consistency evidenced in the treatment of individuals with known mental health problems. In response to a scenario concerning a single man with a poor payment history and £2,700 arrears owing at the date of action, all judges interviewed suggested that they would adjourn proceedings.[102] This is particularly significant as the majority would have given an outright order on the same facts, minus the mental health problems. While this does not provide a definite answer to what the likely chance of an action will be, it does suggest that judges are interested in ensuring that mental health issues are given a fair hearing, despite the limitations of the listings,[103] and that there may be very real time and cost implications for social landlords bringing possession actions if there are to be adjournments.

[96] *Ibid*.

[97] *Ibid*, 18.

[98] *Ibid*, 106. This research also demonstrates that adjournment on terms is more likely than a suspended possession order, because of the legal and costs implications of the suspended order.

[99] *Ibid*, 61.

[100] *Ibid*. There was evidence of some of the judges drawing a clear distinction between worthy ('can't pay') and unworthy ('won't pay') tenants.

[101] *Ibid*, 88, the point on which the research was commissioned to conclude.

[102] *Ibid*, 68.

[103] There is further evidence that the judiciary are aware that when granting a possession order, they are depriving someone of their home, not just creating an eviction statistic. See Hunter et al, note 41 above, 74 and 101.

EXAMINING THE ALTERNATIVES

It should now be evident that repossession is not a clear or predictable solution to problems caused by lettings to vulnerable tenants. The purpose of this section is to consider the legal and practical alternatives to possession that exist to deal with the trigger events.

Alternative Legal Remedies

Distraint and Attachment of Earnings

Distraint, which involves impounding a tenant's possessions in lieu of debt repayment, is one potential alternative to possession for rent arrears. In social housing, there may well be nothing of particular value to impound, and the action is explicitly discouraged by the Housing Corporation.[104] Attachment of earnings as a remedy is similarly weakened, as vulnerable occupants may not be in regular employment or have sufficient earnings to make the action worthwhile.[105]

Injunctions and Codes of Conduct

Social landlords may seek to control anti-social behaviour rather than seek possession,[106] which might help explain the small percentage of possession actions on this ground.[107] This can be done through seeking an injunction to restrain damaging behaviour in the property. Injunctions have been overtaken in this context by ASBOs, which are the most common form of action against anti-social behaviour, even if they are not universally welcome or effective.[108] Noise Abatement Orders (NAOs), Acceptable Behaviour Contracts (ABCs) and mediation have all been identified as potentially effective.[109] In addition, the new powers under the Anti-social Behaviour Act (2003) and the proposed powers to be given to landlords

---

[104] Housing Corporation, 'Tenancy Management Eligibility and Evictions' (Circular 07/04, London, 2004). This may help explain the findings of Pawson et al (note 30 above, 68) that only 13 of 325 landlords surveyed reported using distraint.

[105] Pawson et al, note 30 above, 69. They nevertheless suggest that there may be scope for more frequent deployment.

[106] See Cobb note 88 above, 254–6 and 266,who argues that one of the benefits of the problems caused by the Disability Discrimination Act (1995) is that it will force social landlords to make use of preventative strategies such as those listed.

[107] See note 53 above and accompanying text.

[108] See, for example, S Campbell, *A Review of Anti-Social Behaviour Orders* (Home Office, 2002).

[109] For details, see Pawson et al, note 30 above, 81–8. There is also limited evidence of support and rehabilitation schemes, which set out to tackle the root causes and change

under the Law Commission reforms[110] give further alternatives to social landlords, so that possession should really only be sought when the other remedies have been exhausted.

Preventative Strategies

Robust Rent Arrears Policies

Given that the major trigger of possession is rent arrears, there is a wealth of guidance on preventative and management steps to minimise and deal with the impact of arrears. The most recent of these, published by the ODPM, stresses that '[r]ent arrears strategies must emphasise proactive, preventative approaches rather than being focused mainly on reactive enforcement procedures.'[111] Amongst many matters, it emphasises the importance of a robust IT infrastructure, incentive schemes and flexible payment methods to prevent arrears building up. The central idea is to prevent actions coming to court by tackling the root causes of arrears build-up and by engaging with tenants and other agencies. One example of how this might work is to provide regular reviews of the circumstances of vulnerable individuals or those with previous arrears.[112] There is little doubt that if most of the suggestions contained in this publication alone were implemented by all social landlords, then a number of possession actions could be prevented.

Good Communication

The importance of good communication with tenants as part of an effective rent arrears strategy is clear, and, for the vulnerable, the use of advocates to explain concepts has been recommended elsewhere.[113] It is equally important that effective communication also occurs between landlords and the different agencies that provide help and support to vulnerable tenants in property. This ranges from local Housing Benefit officers to medical support teams, and real 'efforts should be made to overcome communication problems as such problems will have a negative impact

---

tenant's anti-social behaviour, although it is noted that the financial costs of such projects may put them outside the reach of social landlords.

[110] For an analysis of both sets of powers, see Barr and Glover Thomas, 'Housing Reform: A Better Deal for the Mentally Vulnerable?' [2005] 69 *Conv* 207, 219–33.

[111] S Scott, 'Improving the Effectiveness of Rent Arrears Management: Good Practice Guidance' (London, Office of the Deputy Prime Minister, 2005).

[112] *Ibid*, 38.

[113] The *ESRC Report*, 70–1.

upon the effectiveness of housing projects.'[114] This is, of course, an aim and may not be readily achievable in practice.[115]

REPOSSESSION: THE LAST RESORT

In spite of guidance that possession proceedings should be brought against a social tenant for rent arrears caused by housing benefit only as a last resort,[116] it is clear that many social landlords continue to take this route. Indeed, as already stated, some landlords issue proceedings in the hope that it will speed up benefits claims, although the discussion of the housing benefit system above has proved how futile a step this is in the majority of cases. A consideration of the costs of unsuccessful actions might further discourage such action on the part of landlords.

These costs can be broken down into three categories.[117] The direct financial costs of a failed action are estimated at between £1,913–3,190, or £6,500–9,500 for ASB-related possession claims.[118] On top of this, indirect costs, such as opportunity costs in diversion of staff time, and societal costs, such as costs to other departments who may be under a duty to re-house the evictee, must be added.[119] Such figures led Pawson et al to conclude:

> The under-estimation of the full costs of eviction may make some of the alternatives look expensive. In fact, the majority of alternatives to possession action appear to offer real cost effective alternatives to at least some of the cases who currently go through the legal process.[120]

In spite of all that has been discussed above, there are times when all alternatives have been exhausted—the so-called 'hard' cases in which there is no alternative but to seek possession. Initiating proceedings to evict is particularly unpalatable for specialist providers to the vulnerable; for many people, they represent the last stop in the social housing process in their particular area. For others, the reason for eviction may have little to do with the common triggers identified but is instead to remove someone from

---

[114] *Ibid.*

[115] Good multi-agency working is difficult to achieve in practice, which has been explicitly recognised. See National Audit Office, 'Delivering Efficiency: Strengthening the Links in Public Service Delivery Chains' (London, NAO, 2006). For a discussion of the contributing factors in the context of the mentally vulnerable, see the *ESRC Report*, 47–9. These include problems with communication, trust and confidentiality, different organisational agendas and local variations in national services.

[116] See Housing Corporation Regulatory Circular 07/04.

[117] Pawson et al, note 30 above, 102, Tables 8.1 and 8.2.

[118] *Ibid*, 117.

[119] Complete cost figures are not possible, because of the gaps in current accounting procedures—see above.

[120] *Ibid* note 118.

a service that they have outgrown and to move them to another type of tenancy or service, either within the current organisation or with a working partner organisation. In these circumstances, it is clear that eviction is not the end of the process for the specialist provider:

> One mantra that the organisation has is that evictions shouldn't be forever. If somebody goes out onto the street you want them back again at some point or to give them the option of coming back at some point.[121]

This objective is really the key for social landlords involved in either type of possession case, and it has been recognised in some of the sector guidance, particularly in relation to dealing with rent arrears:

> Post eviction procedures should be incorporated within rent arrears and home-lessness strategies. These should include, for example, notification of Social Services and homelessness departments, as well as information sharing with other social landlords in the locality.[122]

NECESSARY REPOSSESSION: IMPROVING SUCCESS

Where there is simply no alternative to a repossession action, how can a social landlord seek to maximise their chances of the action being successful?

Specialisation: The Impact of Dedicated Housing Officers

Evidence suggests that the repetition of a dedicated housing officer appearing in court for repossession cases has a bearing on the outcome, not least because familiarity means that both the judge and the claimant officer get to know each other and start asking for what might be granted.[123] This can be particularly important given the time pressures of most actions, as judges may well rely on representatives to give them the full story.[124] Similarly, evidence shows that judges favour local authorities over housing associations, as they see them as more reliable and less amateurish[125]—a factor that may be countered by the employment of dedicated specialists.

---

[121] The *ESRC Report*, 64.
[122] Scott, note 111 above, 58.
[123] Hunter et al, note 41 above, 48.
[124] *Ibid*, 50: 'Confidence can play a crucial role . . . [T]he judge feels that that they do not necessarily have to press the landlord for further information or, even, feel that they are being excluded from some information...It does not change the decision, but it makes it easier to make...'
[125] *Ibid*, 57—though the evidence is slight.

Clear Paper Trails

It has already been suggested that, given the constraints of time at many possession actions, if information is not properly recorded, it may not be heard. This is made more difficult by the fact that County Court information forms are standard for a particular court, not across the country.[126] Social landlords should take particular effort in the information they record and how they record it, so that it should be comprehensive, succinct, well presented and easy to read. Indeed, if social landlords do use possession as a last resort, keeping appropriate paperwork might explain what otherwise look like very high rent arrears levels at first hearing,[127] as there is evidence to suggest judges look unfavourably at this.[128] Similarly, if they are to be troubled by the requirements of the Disability Discrimination Act (1995), social landlords must be sure to record information that relates to the health and safety risks posed to others.

Improving Tenant Attendance: Best Interests

Tenant attendance at proceedings should be encouraged for two reasons. First, it is considered an important factor by the judiciary in exercising their discretion in favour of a tenant, although it may not necessarily result in a more favourable outcome.[129] Second, Hunter et al observed:

> Much greater consistency in approach and outcomes was noted in relation to the impact of the personal circumstances of tenants, for example, dependant children, problems caused by age, mental health problems or an inability to understand the proceedings. This suggests that while participation per se is not a key influence on outcomes, unless tenants attend hearings judges may not be made aware of factors which could have a significant impact on their decision-making process.[130]

Legal Self-help: The Importance of Tenure

Specialist providers who house vulnerable individuals can greatly assist themselves by making sure that they offer a form of arrangement that is appropriate to the needs and requirements both of the individual being

---

[126]   *Ibid*, 30. Interestingly, Pawson et al (note 30 above, 84) highlight some good practice in facilitating robust witness evidence at ASB-related repossession hearings, further underlining the importance of a clear structure for possession proceedings.

[127]   *Ibid* (per District Judge N): '[Where arrears are high], why? . . .You know . . . it's just not black and white.'

[128]   Hunter et al, note 41 above, 74.

[129]   *Ibid*, 71.

[130]   *Ibid*, 103.

housed *and* of the specialist provider's obligations and responsibilities as a whole.[131] This does not mean that occupiers must be provided with the least security of tenure possible in all circumstances[132] but that providers should simply consider that the nature of the services being carried out by the relevant body, which might be intended to be temporary in nature, are in fact matched by a legal arrangement which allows this.[133] This requires a degree of honest self-analysis by specialist providers as to their capabilities on the one hand and aspirations or mission statements on the other hand, which might differ considerably. Such considerations are only relevant where the specialist provider provides both accommodation and services.

The utility of introductory tenancies as a mechanism to help settle potentially difficult tenants has been recognised: while they are 'not an "easy option" for social landlords, [they] may help to provide additional means for promoting a positive culture of behaviour and regular rent payments.'[134] Research has demonstrated that there is some misunderstanding within parts of the sector about their use,[135] and it must be remembered that introductory tenancies are currently not available to general housing associations or charities, who instead may use assured shorthold tenancies, which mainly differ in that the period of security of tenure is only six months.

There may be occasions, such as in homelessness projects or emergency accommodation offered by providers, that licences rather than any form of tenure are preferable. It is clear that creating a licence is now much more than a simple matter of expressed intent,[136] and the position has been greatly complicated by the creation of a new right, the contractual or '*Bruton*' tenancy.[137] However, collectively two decisions of the Court of

---

[131] Barr and Glover-Thomas, note 56 above. *Cf* R Turney, 'Housing Law and the Mentally Vulnerable: A Response' [2006] 9 *JHL* 13, who argues that it is in the best interests of all mentally disordered occupiers that they be given more security of tenure in a stable living environment.

[132] This would be in breach of Housing Corporation guidance for RSLs. See Housing Corporation, 'The Way Forward: Our Approach to Regulation' (London, Housing Corporation, 2002) para 3.5.2, which requires providers to give the greatest tenure possible, given the purpose of housing and sustainability of community.

[133] The *ESRC Report*, 63–5. Many providers do not do this, and instead offer full assured tenancies to known problem clients, and then come unstuck when repossession is sought against them.

[134] Scott, note 111 above, paras 4.27–8.

[135] The *ESRC Report*, 61.

[136] This has been the situation since *Street v Mountford* [1985] AC 809, as applied by the House of Lords in *Bruton v London Quadrant Housing Trust* [2000] 1 AC 406.

[137] This concept has been subject to considerable criticism, regarding both the reasoning that led to it and the effect it has had on lettings. See W Barr, 'Charitable Lettings and their Legal Pitfalls' in E Cooke (ed), *Modern Studies in Property Law, Volume 1* (Oxford, Hart Publishing, 2001). See also M Pawlowski, 'Occupational Rights in Leasehold Law: Time for Rationalisation' [2002] 66 *Conv* 550.

Appeal (*Kay v Lambeth London Borough Council*[138] and *London Borough of Islington v Green and O'Shea*[139]) and the consolidated appeal in *Kay v London Borough of Lambeth*[140] have confirmed the continued existence of this particular species of tenancy, and these decisions have sought to define some of the characteristics of *Bruton* tenancies.

It is now beyond doubt that a *Bruton* tenancy will not bind an estate owner as superior title holder when the licence or other non-estate interest granted by that estate owner is terminated.[141] In this situation, a *Bruton* tenant loses his or her tenancy, which is terminated with the licence or other arrangement from which it was created. In a very real sense, this suggests that Hill was correct in his analysis of *Bruton* tenancies as nothing more than a demonstration of the relativity of rights to possession, rather than a new form of occupation arrangement. Hill argued that 'the fundamental characteristic of a property right is that it is enforceable against strangers,' and he drew an important distinction between 'exclusive possession', in the sense of physical possession of the property, and 'the right to exclusive possession', which is the right to exclude the world at large.[142] On this analysis, the tenancy granted in *Bruton* confers exclusive possession of the property but not the exclusive right to possession, because it did not bind the head lessee.[143] Before adopting this approach, the reasoning behind the extent of the *Bruton* tenancy deserves examination for reasons that will become apparent.

In the Court of Appeal, it was argued that the *Bruton* tenancies bound through agency; although they had been created between the occupiers and the housing provider, this relationship bound the local authority in each case, as the housing provider had been acting as agent for the local authority.[144] This was rejected on the basis that there had never been a properly created agency relationship between the local authority and either provider. This causes no real difficulties and seems to make perfect sense.

---

[138] [2005] QB 352.

[139] [2005] EWCA Civ 56.

[140] [2006] 2 WLR 570. Of the seven Lords sitting, only Lord Scott gave a fully reasoned decision on this domestic law issue, with which their Lordships concurred.

[141] On the facts of the original *Bruton* decision, this is exactly what happened. Following the decision of the House of Lords, the housing trust surrendered the lease and then granted a lease to the housing trust, which was subsequently terminated by notice to quit. *Kay v Lambeth* charts the challenge by one of the *Bruton* tenants against the Council in both the Court of Appeal and House of Lords.

[142] J Hill, 'The Proprietary Character of Possession' in E Cooke (ed), *Modern Studies in Property Law, Volume 1* (Oxford, Hart Publishing, 2001) 39.

[143] See also Hinjosa, 'On Property, Leases, Licences, Horses and Carts: Revisiting *Bruton v London & Quadrant Housing Trust*' [2005] 69 *Conv* 114, who puts forward a similar argument on the basis of property rights as a continuum, as first identified by Professor Gray in Gray, 'Property in Thin Air' (1991) 50 *Cambridge Law Journal* 252.

[144] See M Pawlowski, 'The *Bruton* Tenancy: Clarity or More Confusion?' [2005] 69 *Conv* 262 for a thorough analysis of the reasoning in both cases.

In the House of Lords, however, counsel for the *Bruton* tenants put forward some ingenious but ultimately weak arguments based on the protection of derivate interests on surrender of the licence agreement between the housing trust and the local authority, meaning that the *Bruton* tenancies bound the local authority before a lease was granted to the housing trust, and that these tenancies survived a notice to quit because they predated the creation of the lease being terminated. Lord Scott, in dismissing these arguments, first confirmed that the *Bruton* tenancies could not bind the local authority on surrender of the lease, for though the housing trust could not prejudice the rights of the *Bruton* tenancies against itself, 'these rights never were enforceable against Lambeth [the local authority]. Once the LQHT licence had been terminated the appellants were trespassers as against Lambeth.'[145] On grant of the lease to the housing trust, his Lordship suggested that the trespassers then became estate, or non-*Bruton* tenancies, because the '*Bruton* tenancies were, so to speak, fed by the estate that their landlord . . . had acquired'.[146] It followed, therefore, that when the lease was terminated by the local authority, the tenancies no longer bound the local authority as, in accordance with the established principle in *Barrett v Morgan*,[147] they were 'derived from and could not survive the termination of the . . . lease'.[148]

On a preliminary assessment, the reasoning expressed excites little interest. On closer examination, however, there is something very disturbing about the idea that the *Bruton* tenancies were 'fed' and became full tenancies as against the local authority on the grant of the lease by the local authority to the housing trust. This suggests that a *Bruton* tenancy is some inchoate right, much like a tenancy by estoppel, which waits to be corrected by the grant of a greater right. Following Hill's argument, this could just be a logical consequence of conferring the exclusive right to possession by the grant of the estate. It is difficult to see, however, why such a convoluted argument would have need to be run—but for the creation of the *Bruton* tenancy. If Lord Scott had instead decided, in line with many commentators' views, that the 'non-estate' tenancies did not survive because they were no more than contractual licences, there would have been no need for such judicial ingenuity.[149] Such complications come

---

[145] *Kay*, note 70 above, 618.
[146] *Ibid*, 618–19.
[147] [2000] 2 AC 264.
[148] Note 146 above.
[149] Interestingly, the reasoning of Lord Scott is open to this interpretation. See for example, the following: 'The [*Bruton*] tenancies were not granted by Lambeth and were not carved by LQHT out of any estate that Lambeth had granted to LQHT. They were not derivative estates . . . In these circumstances the . . . point that the intermediate landlord cannot by a consensual surrender give away an interest that belongs to a sub-tenant has no

from the fact that Lord Scott was, with respect, trying to explain the inexplicable and should instead have considered the reasoning in *Bruton* as suspect and reaffirmed the traditional distinction between a lease and a licence. There is a more fundamental reason to be aggrieved that the *Bruton* tenancy has survived scrutiny by the House of Lords, and this comes from considering the position of a specialist provider to the vulnerable who is also a licensee in the same position as the housing trust. It was implicit in *Green v O'Shea*, and not doubted in the House of Lords in *Kay v Lambeth*, that the *Bruton* tenancy attracts the benefit of legislation designed for tenants, which would not apply to mere or contractual licensees, such as 'statutory security of tenure, rent control, succession rights, etc under the housing legislation.'[150] For short-life provision, this could be disastrous, as providers would find themselves with the responsibilities and costs of being landlords. It is also arguably overturning the will of Parliament, given that legislation has granted certain rights to tenants in the proper estate sense of enjoying property rights against their landlords, and not to licensees who enjoy merely personal rights—something Pawlowski sees as 'an inevitable consequence of the *Bruton* line of thinking'.[151]

Neither the recent case law nor the explanations of the *Bruton* tenancy put forward by commentators have done anything to alleviate the difficulty in distinguishing between the grant of tenancies, licences and *Bruton* tenancies, to the evident confusion of all (not least providers who might want to grant licences). If services are being provided to a vulnerable individual, even in this temporary arrangement, such that neither exclusive possession nor a right to exclusive possession are conferred, then the arrangement will most likely be a licence.[152] The problems mostly arise when the accommodation is general and intended to be short-lived. The recently published Housing Bill from the Law Commission[153] might add some clarity in changing the goal posts and removing classic distinctions between different forms of occupation altogether.[154]

---

substance . . . [T]hese rights were never enforceable against Lambeth' (note 141 above, 618). Now, add the words 'because it was a contractual licence' to the end of each sentence, and the reasoning becomes more robust.

[150] Pawlowski, note 145 above, 270.

[151] *Ibid.*

[152] See further Barr, note 138 above.

[153] See Law Commission, 'Renting Homes: Volumes 1 (Report) & 2 (Draft Bill)' (2006) Law Comm No 297.

[154] The previous proposals, as published in November 2003, did not address these concerns completely. See Barr & Glover-Thomas, 'Housing Reform: A Better Deal for the Mentally Vulnerable?' [2005] 69 *Conv* 207, 224–5.

CONCLUSIONS

It should by now be clear that the role played by specialist and other housing and service providers to the vulnerable, and to mentally disordered individuals in particular, is a complex and very difficult one. It should also be evident that there is a significant amount of good practice that might benefit both social landlords and, as importantly, the individuals they house, so that they should rethink their strategies in dealing with the common triggers of possession actions. On the other side of the equation, it is plain that in situations where possession of premises is necessary, either in the best interests of the individual concerned or the housing project as a whole, or simply because all reasonable alternatives have been exhausted, much thought should be given to the process of repossession, even to the extent of deciding whether the tenure offered at the outset of the occupation arrangement matches the requirements of the services being provided.

Such considerations may already be taken into account by the best providers, but there is always room for improvement, and it would be dishonest to assert that all social landlords do everything well, all of the time. They may not be able to afford to do all that they would like within their operating costs and funding regimes. Nevertheless, it is hoped that the issues raised here should at the very least give providers and their advisors, or those just interested in the subject area, something to consider.

Regarding the legal issues discussed in this chapter, it is suggested that the law is more of a hindrance than a help in its current form. The operation of the Disability Discrimination Act (1995), however laudable its intent, is significantly flawed, and if its application is as wide as has been suggested, it effectively replaces the statutory schemes in domestic property law in relation to those groups that fall within the wide definition of 'disabled'. The confusion over granting licences and the contractual tenancy, as well as the considerable issues surrounding the use of the mandatory ground for rent arrears in the assured tenancy regime, requires that social landlords have expert legal knowledge or advice, which, sadly, may not always be the case.

What might not be so apparent from the discussion to date is the very clear distinction made by current law and practice regarding the rights of (vulnerable) social tenants and social housing providers before eviction and after eviction. In the process leading up to eviction, tenants are protected to a degree both by the framework of housing law and the practice of possession proceedings. As Hunter et al conclude in their study,

> The hardest thing is for judges to make the final decision to put people out of their homes.[155]

---

[155] Hunter et al, note 41 above, 108.

That is not to say that such protection as it exists is perfect, merely that some protection does exist. In stark contrast, if an eviction order is made, there are few general legal duties upon the housing provider to deal with the evictee.[156] Indeed, this imbalance is illustrated by *Circle 33 Housing Trust Ltd v Ellis*,[157] where it was made clear that if a tenant is evicted for an unresolved housing benefit issue that is resolved after eviction, there is nothing a court can do:

> It is not open to the court to reinstate a tenant merely because of its sympathy towards his plight... [I]t is not part of the court's function to introduce further safeguards for the protection of tenants which Parliament has not thought it necessary or appropriate to enact.

Vulnerable tenants are often left unprotected at a time when such protection is probably needed the most, as conditions are at their most problematic. While no actual legal duties exist, it is encouraging that many social landlords and advice and regulatory agencies recognise the importance of post-eviction engagement. In rethinking possession against vulnerable adults, providers not only should look well beyond their reactive legal right to possession and have robust strategies to prevent the causes of repossession, but also should have equally robust post-eviction strategies to deal with those situations where eviction is necessary. Eviction should be part of a continuing obligation, not the end of all obligations.

[156] For a discussion of the duties of homelessness and the problems caused by intentional homelessness, see Barr & Glover-Thomas, note 14 above.
[157] [2005] EWCA Civ 1233.

7

Reconciling Property Law and Social Security Law: Same Concepts, Different Meanings?

NICHOLAS HOPKINS AND EMMA LAURIE*

INTRODUCTION

THE AIM OF this chapter is to examine the relationship between property law principles and social security law and policy, focusing on housing benefit, the principal means of state-funded assistance with housing costs for those in rented accommodation. The legislation providing for entitlement to this benefit requires local authority officers, who make decisions on eligibility, to apply a number of property law principles. This chapter focuses on the definition of who is an 'owner' for the purposes of eligibility for housing benefit and examines the relationship of the definition with another of the regulations that determines eligibility.

The chapter considers two matters in particular: it first asks how the notion of owner is dealt with in the legislation and interpreted by the Social Security Commissioners* and the courts when issues arise on appeal; secondly, the chapter considers the extent to which, in determining this point, guidance should be taken from property law. Conceptually, while the same matters arise for determination in property law and social security law, arguably the objectives of each branch of law are different. This raises the question of the extent to which a common interpretation is either necessary or desirable.

The unsuitability of traditional property law principles in giving effect to more welfarist objectives of the law is a common theme in the literature. For example, writing in the context of the family home, Fox has argued for

* The authors would like to thank Professor Nick Wikeley for his helpful comments. Housing benefit was brought into line with the appeal rights in other areas of social security law relatively recently: a statutory right of appeal to an appeal tribunal and then (with leave) to a Commissioner was created by the Child Support, Pensions and Social Security Act (2000) s 68 and Sched 7.

the development of a coherent legal concept of home, as distinct from the current ad hoc protection afforded in a variety of legislative provisions.[1] She contends that a law that reflects the fact that the home is a special type of property would enable the meanings and values associated with 'home' to play a role in informing legal decision-making.[2]

More specifically in the context of social security law, Carney has suggested that the use of common terms in social security and tax systems is inappropriate because the two systems have divergent interests, and consequently social security law requires a unique set of appropriate concepts.[3] He argues that neither system can simply adopt the concepts of the other without diverging from its respective aim.[4] In particular, he has drawn attention to the deficiencies of drawing on property law principles in a social security context, arguing that the concepts on which the social security legislation relies (such as that of a proprietary interest) have proved to be too inflexible:

> They are neither an embodiment of welfare objectives, nor have they yet proved malleable enough to be moulded to a form which would accommodate such goals. Property law does not lend itself to a 'rubbery' approach.[5]

Hudson, too, has highlighted the different priorities of property and social security law—specifically that social security law demonstrates a prioritisation of need, whereas property law is primarily concerned with protecting pre-existing rights to private property.[6] He has emphasised the need for a contextual understanding of property law concepts.[7] While we concur with the importance of such an approach, this chapter will discuss the difficulty in achieving it given the immutable nature of property terms.

This chapter will first outline the broad policy objectives of the housing benefit scheme and the relevant eligibility criteria. This discussion will provide a background for the later detailed analysis of the specific provisions under consideration. It will be argued that because of the terminology used in the legislation, the definition of 'owner' does not necessarily give effect to one of the scheme's objectives: to exclude

---

[1] L Fox, 'Creditors and the Concept of "Family Home": A Functional Analysis' (2005) 25 *LS* 201, 202.

[2] *Ibid*, 202 and 227. See also: L Fox, 'The Meaning of Home: A Chimerical Concept or a Legal Challenge?' (2002) 29 *JLS* 580; A Hudson, 'Equity, Individualisation and Social Justice: Towards a New Law of the Home' in A Hudson (ed), *New Perspectives on Property Law, Human Rights and the Home* (London, Cavendish, 2004) 31; J Miles, 'Property Law v Family Law: Resolving the Problems of Family Property' (2003) 23 *LS* 624.

[3] T Carney, 'Assets Testing: Problems in Reconciling Economic, Welfare and Legal Perspectives when Defining Assets' (1987) 22 *Australian Journal of Social Issues* 498, 503.

[4] *Ibid*, 503.

[5] *Ibid*, 508.

[6] Hudson, note 3 above, 1.

[7] A Hudson, 'Rapporteur's Overview: Differentiation in Property Law' in Hudson, note 3 above, 327.

owner-occupiers from claiming housing benefit. The chapter will then examine the relationship between the attempted exclusion of owner-occupiers and the broader anti-abuse provision. We will show that the definition of 'owner' has failed to keep pace with the amendments to the anti-abuse provision and consequently the current definition arguably excludes otherwise meritorious claimants. Nevertheless, we explore whether the legislative formula adopted can be justified by reference to the broader policy objective of formulating rules that are clear and simple to apply, on the ground of 'administrative convenience'.

HOUSING BENEFIT POLICY AND ELIGIBILITY

Housing benefit has become the largest single housing subsidy.[8] There are some four million housing benefit recipients, the majority of whom are tenants of local authorities or housing associations.[9] Overall, one in seven households in England and Wales depends on this benefit to meet basic housing needs.[10] The principal aim of housing benefit is to help people on low incomes in rented accommodation with their housing costs[11] and as such it acts as a safety net to prevent post-rent incomes from falling below an acceptable level.[12]

The cost of housing benefit has doubled in real terms since 1988–89.[13] Despite convincing evidence that the rise was caused by the shift away from subsidising building to subsidising individual tenants' housing costs,[14] from the mid-1990s governments attempted to contain the cost of the system, even if this conflicted with its underlying safety-net objective.[15] More recent concerns have centred on its alleged adverse impact on moving people from welfare to work, its poor administration and potential for abuse.[16] These two latter points will be returned to in the context of the discussion on administrative convenience. It is important to emphasise at

---

[8] Office of the Deputy Prime Minister (ODPM), 'Evaluation of English Housing Policy 1975–2000, Theme 2: Finance and Affordability' (London, ODPM, January 2005) para 5.1. For the year 2002–03 (the latest figures accessible), the housing benefit bill was £12.3 billion: Department for Work and Pensions (DWP), 'Housing Benefit & Council Tax Benefit Expenditure, 2003–04'.

[9] 48 and 33 per cent respectively: *ibid*, DWP.

[10] Audit Commission, *Housing Benefit: The National Perspective* (London, Audit Commission, 2002) 5.

[11] Housing Benefit Review, 'Report of the Review Team' (HMSO, Cmnd 9520, 1985) para 5.

[12] ODPM, note 9 above, para 5.10.

[13] P Kemp, *'Shopping Incentives' and Housing Benefit Reform* (York and Coventry, Joseph Rowntree Foundation and Chartered Institute of Housing, 2000) 9.

[14] Evidence of the Social Security Advisory Committee, quoted in 'Report of the Review Team', note 12 above, para 1.20.

[15] ODPM, note 9 above, para 5.18.

[16] *Ibid.*

this stage that the various eligibility tests for housing benefit that are discussed below must be viewed in the light of the scheme's policy objectives, as well as concerns about the sizeable bill, poor administration and fears of abuse.[17]

The housing benefit scheme has always focused on the housing costs of tenants. Proposals to bring low-income owner-occupiers within the scheme failed to find favour with the government.[18] Owners may receive assistance with their housing costs through different schemes. Although mortgage interest tax relief has been abolished,[19] owner-occupiers who are eligible for the primary means-tested income maintenance benefits (income support and income-based job seeker's allowance) may still claim certain housing costs.[20]

A person is entitled to housing benefit if he or she is liable to make payments in respect of a dwelling in Great Britain that he or she occupies as his/her home.[21] As discussed above, owner-occupiers are excluded from the scheme,[22] and thus these payments do not include mortgage payments.[23] Secondary legislation spells out in detail the circumstances in which a person is to be treated as liable to pay rent[24] and when a person is to be treated as not liable and therefore ineligible for housing benefit.[25] Thus, claimants can be excluded from receiving housing benefit on three distinct bases. First, within regulation 12 of the Housing Benefit Regulations (2006), they are the owner of the property upon which benefit is sought.[26] 'Owner' is defined in regulation 2(1). Secondly, within regulation 8, they are not legally liable to pay rent. Thirdly, within regulation 9, they are legally obliged to pay rent but are treated as if they were not so liable.

Once these initial eligibility hurdles have been surmounted, a claimant's income and capital assets are then scrutinised. A claimant will only be eligible for housing benefit if he or she has no income, or it does not exceed the prescribed amount,[27] and his or her capital does not exceed the

---

[17] M Stephens, 'An Assessment of the British Housing Benefit System' (2005) 5 *European Journal of Housing Policy* 111. It has been estimated that fraud and error in housing benefit and council tax benefit costs around £850 million per year: P Howarth, 'Dealing with Complexity' (2005) 13 *Benefits* 16, fn 3.

[18] Department of the Environment, 'Assistance with Housing Costs' (London, DOE, 1981) para 7.

[19] Finance Act (1999) s 38.

[20] The principal type of housing cost met under income support is that of mortgage interest payments: Wikeley, Ogus and Barendt, *The Law of Social Security*, 5th edn (London, Butterworths, 2002) 306.

[21] Social Security Contributions and Benefits Act (SSCBA) (1992) s 130(1)(a).

[22] The Housing Benefit Regulations (2006) SI 2006/213 reg 12(2)(c).

[23] SSCBA (1992) s 130(2).

[24] The Housing Benefit Regulations (2006) SI 2006/213 reg 8.

[25] *Ibid*, reg 9.

[26] *Ibid*.

[27] SSCBA (1992) s 123(1)(c).

relevant threshold.[28] This chapter focuses solely on the initial eligibility criteria and not the issue of the valuation of claimants' assets.[29]

To exclude an application for housing benefit on the basis that the claimant is an owner is consistent with the scheme's overall objective of assisting with housing costs solely of tenants. And, as we have seen, owner-occupiers may have recourse to other social security benefits to help with their housing costs. As such, the provisions that exclude owners simply seek to delineate the scope of the scheme. In spite of this apparently straightforward objective, we will show that the specific statutory definition of 'owner' that is adopted by the legislation has led the Commissioners and the courts to rely on traditional property law principles. This approach has, in turn, produced results that appear inconsistent with the overall objectives of the housing benefit scheme.

INTERPRETATION OF 'OWNER'

As explained above, the definition of an owner is contained in regulation 2(1) of the Housing Benefit Regulations (2006):

> In relation to a dwelling in England and Wales, the person who, otherwise than as a mortgagee in possession, is for the time being entitled to dispose of the fee simple, whether or not with the consent of other joint owners.

Initially, regulations 2 and 12 operated as the principal filter to exclude owner-occupiers. The reference to 'entitlement to dispose of the fee simple' pre-empted attempts to disguise (or hide) ownership behind a trust by focusing on one of the powers associated with legal ownership rather than on legal ownership per se.[30] However, to exclude owner-occupiers by virtue of a single, all-embracing definition, is a Herculean task. As will be seen, regulations 2 and 12 have now diminished in significance. At the time of its enactment, regulation 9, which deems certain categories of people who are legally liable to pay rent as not in fact liable, was in its infancy. This regulation has subsequently been amended and expanded and has become the primary means of preventing abuse of the housing benefit scheme.

---

[28] The Housing Benefit Regulations (2006) SI 2006/213 reg 43.

[29] For a discussion of this issue, see N Wikeley, 'The Valuation of Co-owners' Interests in Capital and Means-tested Benefits: Half the Value or the Value of Half?' in Hudson, note 3 above.

[30] Child Poverty Action Group (CPAG), *CPAG's Housing Benefit and Council Tax Benefit Legislation*, 18th edn (London, CPAG, 2005–06) 229. *Cf* Carney, note 4 above, 505–8. He criticises an attempt in Australian social security law to define 'home owner' by reference to whether the claimant's interest in the land is alienable.

Despite this shift in emphasis from regulations 2 and 12 to regulation 9, regulation 2 has remained largely unamended.[31] To interpret regulation 2, the Commissioners and the courts have considered who is entitled to dispose of the fee simple as a matter of property law—an approach that is perhaps inevitable given the terminology used. This has led to an over-inclusive and unnecessarily complex concept of ownership which, following the expansion of regulation 9, is no longer necessary.

An initial point arises as regards the limitation to entitlement to dispose of the 'fee simple'. As a consequence, tenants under a long lease are not generally regarded as owners within this regulation. This is intentional, as payments made under a long tenancy are excluded from housing benefit by regulation 12(2)(a). Through defining ownership by reference to entitlement to dispose of the fee simple, regulation 2 is clearly focused on legal ownership. However it is not, in its terms, confined to legal ownership, and the extent to which entitlement to dispose of a fee simple correlates with legal ownership has remained obscure. A link with legal ownership and the possible reason for this apparently restrictive definition is indicated by Gage LJ:

> Those who have to administer the housing benefit scheme would have an additional burden placed upon them if before deciding whether a person was eligible they had to make enquiries as to what lay behind the title to registered property. By virtue of, what in my view is the correct construction of regulation 2(1), they simply have to examine the register and go no further.[32]

As is discussed below, this is implicitly an argument based on administrative convenience, as it precludes the need to look behind legal title.[33] An examination of the register will, of course, reveal only the holders of the legal title. Hence, Gage LJ's comment makes sense only if ownership is equated with holding legal title. A similar view of the definition as based on legal ownership was taken for different reasons in the decision of the Commissioner in *CH/1278/2002*. He noted that the reference to the fee simple itself indicated that legal ownership was in issue.[34] However, two related issues have arisen as regards the scope of the definition. First, whether there are circumstances in which a person may be a legal owner but not be entitled to dispose of the fee simple. Secondly, and conversely, whether is it possible to be entitled to dispose of the fee simple without being the legal owner.

---

[31] The only amendment to regulation 2 since its enactment has been the addition of the final phrase 'whether or not with the consent of other joint owners'. This is explained at note 56 below.

[32] *Burton v New Forest District Council* [2004] EWCA Civ 1510, 53.

[33] See note 116 below.

[34] *CH/1278/2002*, para 14.

Is a Legal Owner Necessarily Entitled to Dispose of the Fee Simple?

The issue of whether a legal owner is necessarily entitled to dispose of the fee simple lay at the heart of the most authoritative discussion of the definition of 'owner' in *Burton v New Forest District Council*.[35] There, the claimant to housing benefit was severely disabled. At the time of his application he held legal title to the house he occupied as trustee of a trust established to assist with the costs of his physical care. The house had originally been let to third parties but following a change in circumstances the claimant had moved in as a tenant of the trust liable for rent on a commercial basis.

The court accepted the existence and terms of the trust at face value. Notwithstanding, it was held that the claimant was entitled to dispose of the fee simple and therefore precluded from entitlement to housing benefit. The court rejected arguments that ownership related to beneficial ownership and that a distinction should be drawn between entitlement to dispose, as necessarily indicating a right to do so, and ability to dispose. As regards the former argument, an analysis of previous decisions supported the view that ownership within regulation 2 is 'not restricted to beneficial ownership'.[36] As regards the latter argument, reliance was placed on the prevailing provision in section 20(1) of the Land Registration Act (1925). It was considered to 'follow inexorably' from this provision that a third party to whom the claimant transferred the fee simple would take title free from any interest of the trust.[37] The claimant's responsibility as trustee as regards the proceeds of sale and the possibility of sale being a breach of trust would have no effect on the purchaser's title.[38] Hence, by virtue of holding legal title as trustee, and despite the court's acceptance that the claimant had no beneficial interest in the house, the claimant was precluded from obtaining housing benefit. Wall LJ noted that the outcome may be 'harsh', and the claimant may appear to be 'a worthy candidate for housing benefit'.[39] However, he commented that the 'function of this court . . . is limited to a construction of the Act of 1992 and regulations'.[40]

The decision in *Burton* is indicative of the strict approach that has been taken to legal owners. Entitlement to dispose has been interpreted by reference to and consistently with legislation governing powers of sale. That case, as has been seen, establishes that a trustee with no beneficial

---

[35] [2004] EWCA Civ 1510.
[36] *Ibid*, 41 (Wall LJ).
[37] *Ibid*, 35.
[38] *Ibid*. As noted at 17, the deed of trust gave the trustees power to sell and re-invest the proceeds of sale.
[39] *Ibid*, 51.
[40] *Ibid*.

entitlement is still regarded as an owner. An extreme possibility is high-lighted by the Commissioner's decision in *CH/1278/2002*. There the issue was whether the claimant had 'previously owned' a dwelling within regulation 9(1)(h). Like regulation 2, a finding of ownership within that provision operates to exclude entitlement to housing benefit. Therefore, as would be expected, it was accepted by the Commissioner that ownership should be accorded the same definition as in regulation 2.[41] The claim to housing benefit related to rent the claimant paid to her sister, who was now the sole legal owner of the house. The house had previously been owned by the claimant's mother and following the mother's death intestate, legal title had been held by the claimant initially as her mother's personal representative and subsequently as a trustee for herself and her two sisters, who were equally entitled to their mother's estate. The Commissioner noted that in these circumstances the claimant had clearly previously owned the estate.

The Commissioner further considered whether ownership merely as a personal representative would have been sufficient to bring a claimant within regulation 9(1)(h). Once administration of an estate has been completed, the personal representatives may become trustees of the statutory or wills trust. At this stage, *CH/1278/2002* shows that a trustee who is also a beneficiary is within the definition of owner. *Burton* demonstrates that the claimant's trusteeship alone would have been sufficient for her to be classified as an owner and therefore precluded from entitlement, regardless of her beneficial entitlement. As a trustee is caught by the definition by reason of being entitled to dispose of the fee simple, there seems no convincing basis on which a personal representative could be excluded. As the Commissioner noted, during the period of administration the only persons entitled to dispose of the fee simple are the personal representatives. Indeed, they may be required to do so to meet liabilities of the estate. The Commissioner considered that their inclusion could pro-duce 'a very unfair result'. While the point did not arise for decision, he questioned whether this result was required by the regulations or 'whether ownership as a personal representative . . . rather than in a personal capacity' could be removed from the scope of the definition.[42] However, in light of *Burton*, there seems no feasible way to remove personal representa-tives from the scope of the definition on the basis that title is not held in a personal capacity. Such exclusion would seem equally relevant to the position of a trustee who is not also a beneficiary.

Hence, *Burton* and the decision in *CH/1278/2002* both demonstrate that entitlement to dispose, as regards the position of legal owners, has been defined strictly by reference to property legislation. It is suggested that the

---

adoption of this definition means that the exclusion of housing benefit is cast too wide. There seems no reason in policy why a trustee with no beneficial interest or a personal representative should automatically be excluded.

The inclusion of trustees as owners has raised the question whether their entitlement to dispose should take into account limitations on their powers. As with the interpretation of entitlement to dispose itself, this question has been answered by considering the effect of such limitations in their general (property) statutory context. The issue of limitations on powers has arisen principally in relation to consents to sale, a matter that is itself now dealt with by the express words of regulation 2. It has additionally been raised in relation to the powers of a sole trustee.[43] The general position will be discussed first, before consideration of the specific provision that has been made in relation to consents.

General Limitations on Trustees' Powers

The general position as regards limitations on powers can be derived from *Burton*. As has been noted, in that case the court rejected a distinction between a trustee's entitlement to dispose of the fee simple and their ability to do so. The possibility of a sale being in breach of trust and the trustee's responsibility as regards the proceeds of sale did not detract from the trustee's entitlement to dispose for the purposes of regulation 2. The basis of the decision was that by virtue of the prevailing provision in section 20(1) of the Land Registration Act (1925), a purchaser's title would not be affected by these matters. Conversely, it is implicit in this reasoning that a trustee would not be considered entitled to dispose of the fee simple in circumstances in which the purchaser's title *would* be affected.

In the scheme of registration of title, the ability of a trustee as registered proprietor to pass title to a purchaser is dependent on the presence or absence of restrictions on the title. This was assumed to be the case under the Land Registration Act (1925),[44] but the matter has been put beyond doubt (subsequent to the decision in *Burton*) by sections 23–6 of the Land Registration Act (2002).[45] Those provisions are designed to ensure that the register is conclusive as regards the ability of the registered proprietor to exercise 'owner's powers', which include powers of disposition.[46] By virtue of section 26(1), the registered proprietor's ability to dispose of the land is

---

[43] *Fairbank v Lambeth Magistrates' Court* [2002] EWHC 785.

[44] *State Bank of India v Sood* [1997] Ch 276, 284.

[45] The purpose of these provisions is explained by the Law Commission, 'Land Registration for the Twenty-first Century: A Conveyancing Revolution' (Law Comm No 271, 2001) paras 4.01–4.11.

[46] Land Registration Act (2002) s 23.

to be taken to be free from any limitations except, inter alia, those reflected by an entry on the register. Hence, applying *Burton* in light of the Land Registration Act (2002), a trustee is considered entitled to dispose of the fee simple (and is therefore an owner within regulation 2) when title can be passed to a purchaser; it is assumed that there are no limitations on the trustee's entitlement to do so, except those reflected by entry of a restriction.[47] Where a restriction is entered, a trustee is entitled to dispose of the fee simple only through compliance with the restriction.

This analysis is consistent with that adopted by the court as regards consents to sale: the existence of a requirement of consent was considered sufficient to hold that a trustee is not entitled to dispose of the fee simple when consent has not been obtained.[48] It may be questioned whether such a strict interpretation of entitlement to dispose would in fact be taken in a property law context. The general principle of alienability may still be persuasive, save when the power of sale has specifically been removed by virtue of section 8 of the Trusts of Land and Appointment of Trustees Act (1996). Notwithstanding, the consequence of the prevailing interpretation can be illustrated by reference to the position of a sole trustee.

In *Fairbank v Lambeth Magistrates' Court*, in an obiter discussion,[49] the court rejected an argument that a sole trustee is not an owner as the trustee is unable to give a valid receipt for capital moneys.[50] The court noted that it is not concerned with the proceeds of sale but only with the entitlement to sell.[51] This general statement must be qualified. A sole trustee's entitlement to dispose of the fee simple can be presumed unless limited by a restriction on the register precluding dispositions by a single proprietor. If such a restriction has been entered, it cannot be said that the sole trustee is entitled to dispose of the fee simple. The trustee is unable to dispose of the fee simple unless (and until) a second trustee is appointed. Further, a restriction in these terms is now entered in every case of joint ownership in order to limit the powers of a sole surviving trustee.[52]

Hence, following the approach adopted in *Burton*, a trustee's entitlement to dispose must be assessed by reference to restrictions on their title. On the one hand, this does not prejudice the underlying reasoning for defining ownership by reference to legal entitlement. As has been seen, Gage LJ has

---

[47] Although the position is clarified by the Land Registration Act (2002), this argument is consistent with the reliance placed on the Land Registration Act (1925) s 20(1) in *Burton*. That section provided that on the disposition of a registered freehold, the transferee's title was subject to 'incumbrances and other entries, if any, appearing on the register'. This would cover all forms of entries then permitted, including restrictions.

[48] See note 57 below.

[49] [2002] EWHC 785.

[50] *Ibid*, para 18.

[51] *Ibid*.

[52] Land Registration Act (2002) s 44(1).

attributed this to the ease of establishing legal ownership by searching the register.[53] Equally, searching the register will reveal the existence of any restrictions. On the other hand, this illustrates the artificiality and potential for arbitrary results within regulation 2. In *Burton* we have seen that the claimant was precluded from housing benefit because, as a trustee, he was entitled to dispose of the fee simple. Applying the reasoning in *Burton*, it is arguable that on the same facts (at least since the clarification of the position under the Land Registration Act (2002)), a claimant would not be classed as an owner if a restriction prohibiting sale is entered on the register.

The Effect of Consent to Sale Limitations

As regards consent, regulation 2 specifies that a person is an owner if he or she is entitled to dispose of the fee simple, 'whether or not with the consent of other joint owners'.[54] The reference to joint ownership was inserted to overrule the decision in *R v The Housing Benefit Review Board for Sedgemoor District Council ex parte Weaden*.[55] There, the claimant was joint legal and beneficial owner of her home with her (non-resident) parents. She claimed housing benefit in relation to rent she paid to her parents. Schiemann J concluded, 'A person is not entitled to dispose of the fee simple if he needs the consent of others to dispose of it and has not got it.'[56]

Schiemann J's decision was based on the general powers of disposal of trustees. He noted that the other trustees 'had not been asked to agree to join in the disposition of the fee simple, still less had they agreed to do so'.[57] Legal co-owners, as joint tenants, necessarily require each other's consent to a disposal. Hence, Schiemann J's judgment would potentially exclude most co-owners from the definition of ownership in regulation 2.[58] The subsequent decision in *Burton* suggests that Schiemann J's judgment is too broad: a requirement of consent would only affect the ability of a trustee to pass title to a purchaser if reflected in the entry of a restriction. In any event, the amendment to regulation 2 ensures that the necessity for consent does not remove joint owners from the scope of the definition. In *ex parte Weaden* the court was concerned with consent of joint owners of

---

[53] Note 33 above.
[54] In CH/2740/2003 'joint owner' was defined as denoting joint tenants or tenants in common.
[55] (1986) 18 HLR 355.
[56] *Ibid*, 360.
[57] *Ibid*, 359.
[58] He rejected as irrelevant the issue of whether courts would order sale on an application: *ibid*.

a legal title. Subsequent to the amendment to regulation 2, in *Fairbank*, the court considered obiter that a requirement of consent to sale by beneficiaries would equally not preclude a trustee from being categorised as an owner.

If *Burton* applied to the issue of consents, the same position would apply as has been outlined in relation to sole trustees. Hence, a trustee would not be considered entitled to dispose of the fee simple if sale was subject to consent when (but only when) the requirement of consent is entered as a restriction on the register. Applying section 26(1) of the Land Registration Act (2002), the trustee is not entitled to sell the fee simple in such circumstances unless consent has been obtained. Although pre-dating the Land Registration Act (2002), the specific reference to consent in regulation 2 appears sufficient to supersede this reasoning. Hence, even if a requirement of consent is entered as a restriction, the trustee is still to be treated as being entitled to sell. However, as has been seen, in *Weaden* consent had not been sought. While this point is not addressed in *Fairbank*, there is nothing on the facts to suggest that consent had been sought in that case. The question therefore remains open as to whether a trustee is to be considered entitled to dispose of the fee simple if his or her power to dispose is subject to consent entered as a restriction, in circumstances in which consent has been actively withheld.

Can a Beneficiary be Entitled to Dispose of the Fee Simple?

In considering the position of holders of the legal title, entitlement to dispose of the fee simple has been defined consistently with the strict position in property law. As a result, it has been argued that the scope of regulation 2 has been cast too wide. Entitlement to dispose has been held to catch holders of the legal title regardless of the capacity in which title is held but subject to limitations on their ability to pass title to a purchaser recorded as a restriction on the register. However, as has been noted, regulation 2 is not in its terms restricted to legal ownership. This raises the question whether there are any circumstances in which a beneficiary would be considered entitled to dispose of the fee simple.

The relationship between regulation 2 and legal ownership has remained ambiguous. Gage LJ's suggestion in *Burton* that the provision is designed to ensure that those administering the scheme need go no further than an examination of the register makes sense only if the regulation is confined to legal ownership. However, the Commissioners and the courts have not precluded the possibility of a claimant being classified as an owner through beneficial entitlement. Indeed, it has been implicitly acknowledged that a beneficiary may be within the scope of the definition, although circumstances in which this would be the case have not been identified. In *Burton*, as has been noted, Wall LJ suggested that regulation 2 is '*not restricted* to beneficial ownership'.[59] Similarly, in decision *CH/1278/2002*, despite defining fee simple as denoting a legal title, the Commissioner suggested only that the '*primary*' meaning of the regulation was the holder of the legal title.[60]

The absence of a clear statement excluding beneficiaries indicates that the regulation is not necessarily confined to legal ownership. This is inconsistent with Gage LJ's rationale for the provision. Further, as the regulation is confined to entitlement to dispose of the fee simple, it appears that a beneficiary could be included within its scope only if it is shown that the beneficiary is entitled to dispose of the legal title. Applying the same property-based approach that has been adopted in relation to legal owners, it is difficult to identify circumstances in which a beneficiary would be entitled to dispose of the *legal* title.[61] A reluctance expressly to exclude beneficiaries from the scope of the regulation may have been understandable while regulation 9 remained in its infancy. However, since the shift in balance towards regulation 9, there seems no reason not to exclude beneficiaries from regulations 2 and 12.

The significance of this interplay between the provisions in the regulations in this regard is illustrated by *R v Sheffield Housing Benefits Review Board ex parte Smith*.[62] In this case, the position of beneficiaries was considered by the court in an obiter discussion. The case concerned applications for housing benefit made by occupants of a community house who were members of the Jesus Fellowship Community Church. Under the terms of their licence agreement with the Church, each occupant was liable to raise a specified minimum income, and all income was paid into a common purse. Any surplus from the common purse after meeting the reasonable living expenses of occupants was paid into a trust, the beneficiaries of which were the contributing members of the Church. None of the claimants for housing benefit were trustees or holders of the legal title to the house. Notwithstanding, it had been determined by the local authority Review Board that the claimants were entitled to dispose of the fee simple as they were beneficiaries of the trust and would be entitled to share in the surplus of the trust if it was wound up. In fact it emerged that the trust itself held only a long lease of the house.

On this basis, it was clear that the claimants were not owners within regulation 2, which, as has been seen, is concerned only with entitlement to dispose of the fee simple. However, Blackburne J expressed a view on the

---

[59] Note 33 above, 41 (emphasis added).
[60] Para 15.
[61] As discussed at note 65 below, *Saunders v Vautier* (1841) 4 Beav 115 has been held to be irrelevant in this context. An exceptional example may be the existence of a bare trust.
[62] (1996) 28 HLR 36.

arguments raised. Counsel for the parties had forwarded polarised approaches to the interpretation of the provision. The claimants sought to confine the regulation to holders of the legal title or with a 'specific power' of disposal. The Review Board suggested an interpretation whereby beneficiaries capable of bringing the trust to an end under *Saunders v Vautier*[63] would collectively be considered entitled to dispose of the fee simple.

Neither approach was endorsed by Blackburne J. He specifically rejected the relevance of *Saunders v Vautier* to defining ownership on the basis it would equate the provision with beneficial ownership. Equally, he considered that ownership was not confined to those vested with legal title.[64] However, his judgment at least implies that there are circumstances in which a beneficiary is still within the scope of the regulation. Notably, even the argument of the Review Board for the inclusion of the beneficiaries is based solely on disposal of the *legal* title; Counsel relied on the collective ability of the beneficiaries to bring the trust to an end, rather than on their status as beneficiaries per se.

The reluctance of the court to exclude beneficiaries from the definition of owner was understandable at the time *ex parte Smith* was decided. In deciding that beneficiaries should be within the scope of regulation 2 (when the requirements of *Saunders v Vautier* are met), the Review Board had in mind one particular situation:

> We specifically reject the argument that in the case of a dwelling owned by five people who reside in it the four persons in whom the property is vested would not be entitled to claim housing benefit . . . but that the beneficiary who was not so named could do.[65]

At the time of the decision, ensuring that the fifth beneficiary was also an owner appeared to be the only way of preventing such an outcome. As will be seen below, however, following the amendments to regulation 9, this is no longer the case. While none of the five occupants would be entitled to housing benefit, the basis on which they are excluded is different: the trustees are precluded by regulation 2 as owners, while the fifth beneficiary is not an owner, but his or her payments are excluded under regulation 9.

This section of the chapter has highlighted the difficulties that ensue from the specific definition of 'owner' adopted by the legislation and the interpretation, derived from traditional property law principles, that it has been given. It has also demonstrated the relationship between regulations 2 and 12 on the one hand and regulation 9 on the other, and thus the necessity of taking a holistic view of the housing benefit provisions. At the

---

[63] Note 62 above.
[64] *Ibid*, 47.
[65] *Ibid*, 46.

time regulation 2 was drafted, the definition of 'owner' represented the principal filter through which owner-occupiers were to be excluded from housing benefit. The foregoing discussion has shown the definition to be over-inclusive, in catching all legal owners, and to lead to the possibility of arbitrary results through the entry of restrictions. At the same time, unnecessary complexity arises through an on-going reluctance to exclude beneficial owners who do not also hold legal title from the definition. The definition of 'owner' adopted in regulation 2 may have been acceptable, despite these criticisms, while the onus of excluding owner-occupiers rested with regulation 2. However, now the balance has shifted to regulation 9, these criticisms are less readily answered.

The next section of this chapter will consider in more detail the scope of regulation 9 and will show how it now functions as the primary way of protecting the housing benefit scheme from abuse.

REGULATION 9

It has been demonstrated that the purpose of regulation 2 is to define the scope of the housing benefit scheme, and as such it has a relatively straightforward policy objective. By contrast, more complex policy-based arguments arise in connection with regulation 9. As described above, the function of this regulation is to deem those who are in fact legally liable to pay rent as not so liable. It is clear that its purpose is to prevent abuse of the housing benefit scheme,[66] through the use of so-called contrived tenancies. Concern about abuse of social security benefits in general, and housing benefit in particular, has led to the introduction of various initiatives aimed at combating such practices.[67] Regulation 9 raises especially thorny issues, since it is intended to catch arrangements that are not only *actually* abusive but also *potentially* abusive.[68]

While provisions to prevent exploitation have existed since the scheme's inception, they have become increasingly detailed and wide-ranging in response to fears expressed by government and local authorities that the regulations 'provided no clear test and . . . that collusion between the parties often made it difficult to collect evidence to substantiate a belief

---

[66] This overriding aim has been acknowledged by the government (see Waller LJ's summary of the Secretary of State's evidence in *Tucker v Secretary of State for Social Security* [2001] EWCA Civ 1646, 19); by the Commissioners (see CH/716/2002, para 14 (Commissioner Jacobs)); and by the courts (see Waller LJ in *Tucker*, endorsing Kay J's dicta in the Administrative Court [2001] EWHC Admin 260, 42).

[67] For example, the Verification Framework was introduced to complement initiatives already undertaken by local authorities in the detection of fraud: Department for Work and Pensions, 'Housing Benefit Guidance Manual: Amendment 8 September 2005', para 1.40.

[68] CH/716/2002, para 14 (Commissioner Jacobs).

that the tenancy was contrived'.[69] Like other social security benefits, housing benefit legislation is subject to constant change, and the anti-exploitation provisions have received particular attention.[70] Substantial changes to these provisions were introduced in 1999, with the objective of creating a clear and workable test.[71]

Regulation 9 now contains twelve separate categories, which encompass both cases of actual abuse and those in which the arrangement between landlord and tenant gives rise to the potential for abuse. Some of the categories derive from the previous version of the provision, but additional ones were added to spell out more explicitly circumstances that were intended to be caught by the original 'contrived tenancy' provision.[72] The majority of the categories allow no opportunity for a claimant to adduce evidence of the genuine nature of the agreement. Two, however, do provide for such a possibility[73] by reversing the burden of proof and requiring the claimant to satisfy the local authority that the liability was not intended to be a means of taking advantage of the housing benefit scheme.[74] When the 1999 amendments were implemented no formal reference was made to the Social Security Advisory Committee (SSAC),[75] and consequently there is no indication why it was decided that these two categories (and these alone) should provide claimants with an opportunity to rebut the presumption that housing benefit should not be paid.[76] Notwithstanding these two exceptions, because regulation 9 has been designed to identify cases in which there is risk of abuse, it has been acknowledged that it has the potential to produce 'rough justice',[77] a point to which we will return below in the context of administrative convenience.

As explained above, regulations 2 and 9 provide separate and distinct eligibility tests. They also, however, inter-relate to achieve the broader policy purpose of protecting the housing benefit scheme from abuse. The Jesus Fellowship Church cases provide a useful illustration of this point. As

---

[69]   S Rahilly, 'Contrived Tenancies and Housing Benefit: Revising the Rules' (2002) 9 *JSSL* 61, 66.
[70]   The anti-exploitation provisions were originally contained in the Housing Benefit Regulations (1985) SI 1985/677 reg 26. They were subsequently amended by SI 1987/1971 reg 7. Regulation 7 was further amended by the Housing Benefit (General) Amendment (No 2) Regulations (1998) SI 1998/3257. Under the 2006 consolidating Regulations, regulation 7 becomes regulation 9.
[71]   Department for Work and Pensions (Adjudication) Circular A1/1999.
[72]   Reg 7(1)(b) of the pre-1999 regulations.
[73]   Note 23 above, reg 9(1)(e) and (g).
[74]   *Ibid*, reg 9(3).
[75]   Under the procedure set out in the Social Security Administration Act (1992) s 173(1).
[76]   A challenge to the *vires* of regulation 9 because of its lack of referral to the SSAC was rejected by the Court of Appeal: *Campbell & Ors v South Northamptonshire District Council* [2004] EWCA Civ 409, 51–2.
[77]   CH/716/2002, para 14 (Commissioner Jacobs).

we have seen in *ex parte Smith*,[78] the local authority initially denied the claimants' eligibility on the ground that they were owners. By contrast, in *Campbell & Ors v South Northamptonshire District Council*,[79] in which the claimants were also liable for housing costs on the same basis as those in *ex parte Smith*, the case was decided purely on the basis of regulation 9.

The Court of Appeal upheld the Commissioner's decision that the tenancies were not on a commercial basis and thus fell foul of regulation 9. However, it would not have been possible to challenge the claimants' eligibility in *ex parte Smith* on the basis of regulation 9. This is because, as it was then worded, the commercial status of a tenancy was relevant only when the claimant was 'residing with' the person to whom the rent was owed.[80] The abolition of that requirement was made by the amendments introduced in 1999. These changes have also addressed the Review Board's concern that a non-owning beneficiary needed to be classified as an owner in order to be excluded from housing benefit.[81] In the situation anticipated by the Board, the fifth beneficiary would now be disentitled to benefit by virtue of regulation 9.[82]

It is clear that the policy makers have chosen regulation 9 as the primary vehicle to control abuse of the housing benefit scheme. It has been amended on numerous occasions, with the inclusion of ever more wide-ranging categories of relationships that are deemed to fall outside the policy intention of the housing benefit scheme. Consequently, it has been suggested that local authorities may find it more straightforward to deny housing benefit on the basis of regulation 9 than on the basis of whether someone comes within the definition of 'owner':

> It appears that local authorities are having to deal with such unorthodox arrangements for the holding of property with increasing frequency. Rather than grapple with the complexities as to whether the claimant is an 'owner', some are simply finding that the arrangements fall foul of the provisions in [reg 9(1)].[83]

As has been noted, Gage LJ in *Burton* implicitly appealed to administrative convenience as a justification for the definition of 'owner' in regulation 2. In light of the shift in emphasis to regulation 9 as the primary means of preventing abuse, the final section will consider the legitimacy of this rationale. It will be argued that administrative convenience is more readily justified in relation to regulation 9 and does not provide a convincing explanation for maintaining the current definition of 'owner'.

---

[78]   [1994] 28 HLR 36.
[79]   [2004] EWCA Civ 409.
[80]   SI 1987/1971 reg 7(a)(ii).
[81]   Note 66 above.
[82]   Regulation 9(1)(e) excludes payments made by a person whose liability is 'to a . . . trustee of a trust [of] which . . . he . . . is a trustee or beneficiary'.
[83]   CPAG, note 31 above, 194.

ADMINISTRATIVE CONVENIENCE

There will inevitably be tensions in a mass scheme, such as housing benefit, between individualised justice and maintaining operating costs within acceptable limits.[84] In his seminal work, Mashaw identified three broad models of administrative justice:[85] bureaucratic rationality, professional treatment and moral judgment.[86] It is the bureaucratic rationality model that has predominated in social welfare administration in the post-war period.[87] It can be identified by its legitimating values (accuracy and efficiency), its primary goal (policy implementation), its structure (hierarchical) and its technique (information processing).[88] The influence of New Public Management from the 1980s onwards, with its functional values of economy, efficiency and effectiveness,[89] has driven social welfare decision-making further towards the predominance of the bureaucratic model. As Wikeley has observed,

> The administrative and bureaucratic imperative is to devise a streamlined, efficient system which can process large numbers of claimants whilst deploying relatively low grade civil service staff and utilising computers, wherever possible, for routine tasks.[90]

Housing benefit has been identified as the most complex of the income-related social security benefits,[91] and as the Audit Commission has commented, it is 'a service that many councils struggle to deliver well'.[92] The speed (or lack thereof) in processing housing benefit claims has been the subject of constant criticism since the scheme's inception.[93] Decisions therefore have to be made about the trade-off between administrative efficiency and justice.[94] There are clear examples within social security law when priority has been given to administrative efficiency.[95] In the housing benefit context, as we have seen, regulation 9 is a prime example of the

---

[84]   R Sainsbury, 'Social Security Decision Making and Appeals' in N Harris (ed), *Social Security Law in Context* (Oxford, Oxford University Press, 2000) 229.
[85]   That is, the principles that can be used to evaluate the justice inherent in administrative decision-making: M Adler, 'A Socio-legal Approach to Administrative Justice' (2003) 25 *Law & Policy* 323, 323–4.
[86]   J Mashaw, *Bureaucratic Justice* (New Haven, Yale University Press, 1983).
[87]   Adler, note 86 above, 332–3.
[88]   Mashaw, note 87 above, 31.
[89]   C Harlow and R Rawlings, *Law and Administration*, 2nd edn (London, Butterworths, 1997) 131.
[90]   Wikeley, note 30 above, 153.
[91]   Howarth, note 18 above, 17. See also Audit Commission, note 11 above, 7.
[92]   Audit Commission, note 11 above, 3.
[93]   Housing Benefit Review, note 12 above, para 1.11.
[94]   Mashaw's models of administrative justice can coexist, but the more there is of one, the less there will be of the other two: Adler, note 86 above, 330.
[95]   Eg, Wikeley's analysis of the valuation of jointly owned assets: note 30 above.

desire to create rules that can be administered quickly, efficiently and in a routinised way by staff with limited awareness of legal niceties.[96]

The Social Security Commissioners and the courts have been called upon to interpret rules that have apparently been formulated with simplicity of application as their primary objective, and even before the enactment of the Human Rights Act (HRA) (1998), they have weighed the arguments made for administrative convenience. The HRA has brought more sharply into focus the need for such rules to satisfy the requirement of proportionality.[97] We examine below the response of the Commissioners and the courts to the justification of certain provisions on the ground of administrative convenience. While the cases discussed involve a variety of social security benefits, they share in common rules of eligibility that have apparently been drafted with bureaucratic efficiency as the overriding priority.

In the first pair of cases, the Commissioners and subsequently the Court of Appeal were required to interpret the rule common to all means-tested social security benefits (including housing benefit) that determines the valuation of jointly owned capital. This rule has had a particularly chequered history and has been subjected to a number of amendments and a series of challenges.[98] In brief, regulation 51 provides that when capital is jointly held, all joint owners must be treated as if they own an equal share. This construction is intended to provide a straightforward approach for decision-makers in valuing a benefit claimant's capital assets.

In *Chief Adjudication Officer v Palfrey*,[99] the term 'administrative convenience' was not explicitly used, but the Chief Adjudication Officer's argument clearly raised this issue.[100] While accepting the basic proposition that those responsible for making the regulations would have had ease of administration in mind, Hobhouse LJ nevertheless rejected the contention that it was impossible—or even disproportionately difficult—to prefer the

---

[96] Housing benefit has been characterised generally as being highly rule-bound: B Walker and P Niner, 'The Use of Discretion in a Rule-bound Service: Housing Benefit Administration and the Introduction of Discretionary Housing Payments in Great Britain' (2005) 83 *Public Administration* 47, 48.

[97] In the pursuit of legitimate policy aims, states may interfere with certain of the rights set out in the European Convention on Human Rights (including art 8). However, states must ensure that such interference is proportionate to the policy aims that underlie them: P Sales and B Hooper, 'Proportionality and the Form of Law' (2003) 119 *LQR* 426, 426.

[98] See Wikeley, note 30 above, for a detailed analysis.

[99] *R(IS) 26/95*.

[100] Hobhouse LJ summed up the appellants' argument as providing a simple formula whereby potentially complicated investigations and contentious evaluation issues could be avoided: *ibid*, 489.

meaning argued for by the benefit claimants.[101] He thus implicitly rejected the justification of administrative convenience for the CAO's interpretation of the regulation.

In *Hourigan v Secretary of State for Work and Pensions*,[102] the Secretary of State's main argument for the government's interpretation of the same regulation was explicitly that of administrative convenience: staff who administer the scheme do not necessarily have legal acumen and thus administrative convenience demands that there is a statutory code that is reasonably simple to administer.[103] While recognising the policy behind the income support scheme (that people should be expected to dip into their capital rather than be reliant on the state), Brooke LJ could not understand why Parliament should have expected people to utilise capital that they did not in fact possess, and he rejected the Secretary of State's argument that this should be so for the sake of administrative convenience.[104] As Brooke LJ observed somewhat tartly, 'Justice is not always the handmaiden of administrative convenience.'[105]

In the second pair of cases, the issue of proportionality was directly at issue. In *Francis v Secretary of State for Work and Pensions*,[106] a challenge was brought under the Human Rights Act (1998) that the eligibility criteria for the benefit in question contravened articles 8 and 14 of the European Convention on Human Rights.[107] On the question of whether the discrimination was proportionate, emphasis was placed by the Secretary of State on administrative convenience and the need for so-called 'bright-line' eligibility rules.[108] Sir Peter Gibson accepted that such issues are relevant considerations but did not consider either that seriously adverse consequences would ensue from accepting the claimant's argument, or, ultimately, that administrative convenience alone could justify sufficiently the discrimination caused.[109]

The justification for discriminatory treatment was also in issue in *Hockenjos v Secretary of State for Social Security*.[110] While accepting the

---

[101]   *Ibid*, 491.
[102]   [2002] EWCA Civ 1890.
[103]   *Ibid*, 19 (Brooke LJ).
[104]   *Ibid*, 24.
[105]   *Ibid*, 21.
[106]   [2005] EWCA Civ 1303.
[107]   Under art 8(2), a breach of a person's right to respect for his private and family life can only be lawful when it is in accordance with the law and necessary in a democratic society.
[108]   *Francis v Secretary of State for Work and Pensions*, note 107 above, 29. At Commissioner level, the issue of administrative convenience was not argued: *CIS/1965/2003*, para 19.
[109]   *Francis v Secretary of State for Work and Pensions*, note 107 above, 29–30.
[110]   [2004] EWCA Civ 1749. The discrimination complained of in *Hockenjos* was under art 4 of the Council Directive (EEC) 79/7, relating to equal treatment for men and women in matters of social security.

Secretary of State's argument that the system was administratively convenient, cost-effective and provided for consistent decision-making, Scott
Baker LJ nevertheless described it as 'rough and ready'.[111] *Francis* and
Hockenjos both involved the breach of statutory rights that could be
lawful only if objectively justified. The arguments thus reveal the tension
between the efficient administration of a mass benefit scheme and the need
to achieve justice in individual cases. In both cases, the Court rejected the
argument that administrative convenience sufficiently justified the breaches
complained of. This was despite the fact that in *Hockenjos* Scott Baker LJ
explicitly recognised that the current system produced a fair result in the
majority of cases.[112]

Sales and Hooper suggest that often it may be difficult to formulate
simple and clear laws that are capable of satisfying the doctrine of
proportionality.[113] Nevertheless, the authors identify welfare benefit systems as an example of situations in which fact-insensitive laws are required
to ensure an efficient use of limited resources:

> As a matter of policy, it will often be desirable for a benefit system to be
> constructed on the basis of clear and simple rules, which are easy and
> inexpensive to apply, because of the importance of ensuring that the greatest
> proportion of money available to be spent on the benefit system is actually
> transferred into the hands of those in need rather than being expended on
> administration.[114]

Nevertheless, as we have seen, the courts have recognised the principle of
administrative convenience while rejecting it on the specific facts. By
contrast with the approach in the cases discussed above, there appears to
be greater acceptance of the justification of administrative convenience in
relation to housing benefit. It will be recalled that in Gage LJ's short
judgment in *Burton*, he believed there was 'an obvious reason' for
adopting the local authority's restricted meaning of 'owner': those who
have to administer the housing benefit scheme would simply have to
examine the register and go no further, thereby being relieved of the
additional burden of questioning what lies behind the title to the registered
property.[115] Thus, administrative convenience was central to his judgment.
However, Wall LJ, who gave the leading judgment, did not discuss this
aspect at all, and it was apparently not raised in argument before the
Court.

As discussed above, regulation 9 is intended to prevent abuse of the
scheme. It was noted that because the regulation catches not only actual

---

[111]   *Ibid*, 32.
[112]   *Ibid*.
[113]   Sales and Hooper, note 98 above, 426.
[114]   *Ibid*, 443.
[115]   *Burton v New Forest District Council*, note 33 above, 53.

but potential abuse, it may cause rough justice in individual cases. Nevertheless, the anti-abuse justification for this provision has consistently been accepted by the Commissioners and the courts. Despite identifying its potentially harsh effects for certain claimants, Commissioner Jacobs was in no doubt that the formulation of regulation 9 was based on a policy decision to err on the side of protection for the scheme, rather than on fairness in individual cases.[116]

In *Tucker v Secretary of State for Social Security*,[117] it was claimed that it was irrational to bar benefit to everyone in given circumstances, irrespective of whether there had been any abuse and with no regard to their particular circumstances. This argument was dismissed by Kay J, who accepted that it was a legitimate and proportionate response to the problem of abuse.[118] Commissioner Jacobs, too, identified that part of the rationale for regulation 9 was ease of administration. He went on to find that such administrative convenience is an objectively justifiable consideration that is both reasonable and proportionate.[119]

While we have seen that the courts have been prepared to accept the principle that administrative convenience is a legitimate consideration in drafting and construing social security legislation, it is interesting to note that in the cases not concerning housing benefit where it was raised in argument, it was rejected on the facts. By contrast, in *Burton*, where it did not appear as if the argument was raised by the local authority, the justification of administrative convenience was the central plank of one of the judgments. Equally, the Commissioners and the courts have consistently upheld the policy aims behind regulation 9, despite recognising its potential for injustice in individual cases. This approach accords with the argument of Sales and Hooper that while the rules err on the side of 'fact insensitivity' and thus are less likely to be able to satisfy the requirement of proportionality, housing benefit nevertheless falls squarely within the ambit of social policy, where the European Court of Human Rights has consistently acknowledged the state's wide margin of appreciation.[120] In light of the development of regulation 9 as a primary anti-abuse provision,

---

116   *CH/716/2002*, para 14.
117   [2001] EWHC Admin 260.
118   *Ibid*, 29. The Court of Appeal similarly rejected the argument that reg 9 was *Wednesbury* irrational or fell foul of arts 8 and 14 of the European Convention on Human Rights: [2001] EWCA Civ 1646. See also *Painter v Carmarthenshire County Council Housing Benefit Review Board* [2001] EWHC Admin 308.
119   *CH/5125/2002*, para 61. The issue of administrative convenience was not discussed in the Court of Appeal (n 77 above).
120   Sales and Hooper, note 98 above, 436. The domestic courts have also acknowledged the legislature's margin of appreciation in matters of social welfare policy: see, for example, Lightman J in *Painter*, note 119 above, 19.

the consistent acceptance of administrative convenience within this provision appears appropriate. However, we argue that the justification now has no legitimate place in regulation 2, where it has been accepted only in the absence of full argument.

It is possible that the Commissioners and the courts have more readily accepted the argument of administrative convenience in relation to regulation 9 because its objective as an anti-fraud provision is clearly discernable, and the legitimacy of such policy aims is accepted. By contrast, writing in relation to the provision discussed above that determines the valuation of benefit claimants' jointly owned assets, Hobhouse LJ in *Palfrey* observed that the detailed policy of the regulations is in many respects obscure and equivocal, which makes it difficult to discern any clear principles that guide the drafting.[121]

CONCLUSION

It has been argued that the purpose of regulation 2 (in conjunction with regulation 12) of the Housing Benefit Regulations (2006) is to limit the scope of housing benefit to those who rent their homes and to exclude owner-occupiers. These regulations are not *prima facie* or primarily about preventing abuse of the system. By contrast, it has been shown that the purpose of regulation 9 is avowedly anti-abuse. We have seen that the formula adopted for the definition of 'owner' (as entitled to dispose of the fee simple) has been interpreted by reference to property legislation. This is hardly surprising given the terms that are employed. However, it has proved to be over-inclusive, prone to arbitrary outcomes and overly complex. This chapter has explored whether this 'rough and ready' definition of owner can be justified on the ground of administrative convenience. This argument has been rejected because it has been shown that regulation 9 in its amended form now takes the primary role in preventing abuse of the housing benefit scheme. Furthermore, the Commissioners and the courts have accepted the argument of administrative convenience in relation to regulation 9, despite its potential to cause injustice in individual cases.

---

[121] *R(IS) 26/95*, 488–9.

III

Possession of Land

8

The Acquisition of Rights in Property by the Effluxion of Time

AMY GOYMOUR[*]

I. INTRODUCTION

Any legal system must have rules ... which prevent the disturbance of long-established de facto enjoyment.

Lord Hoffmann, *R v Oxfordshire CC, ex p Sunningwell Parish Council*[1]

THIS CHAPTER EXAMINES the types of rules that protect long-established enjoyment of property by the creation of new property rights. Analysis to date has focused largely on distinct long-use doctrines, in isolation from others;[2] it is the aim of this chapter to call into question time's effect across the whole of property law. Because the extent of time's creative effect is rarely appreciated, the rules have escaped proper scrutiny and as a result are messy, inconsistent and capable of doing injustice. This chapter draws attention to the merit in conceiving long use as a cohesive body of law through which property rights are acquired. It does this by first drawing together the various devices through which long use enables rights in property to be acquired. It then considers the types of problems to which this complex collection of rules might give rise. Finally, the chapter suggests how a more coherent and principled approach might be taken.

The time is now ripe for addressing these concerns. Recent case law has called into question whether at least one of these doctrines complies with

[*] I am enormously grateful to Matthew Conaglen, Elizabeth Cooke, David Fox, Angus Johnston and Graham Virgo for their comments on an earlier draft.

[1] [2000] 1 AC 335, 349.
[2] See WW Buckland and AD McNair, *Roman Law and Common Law*, 2nd edn, revised by FH Lawson (Cambridge, CUP, 1965) 414. There are some very useful exceptions: A Clarke, 'Use, Time, and Entitlement' (2004) 57 *CLP* 238; and S Bridge, 'Prescriptive Acquisition of Easements: Abolition or Reform?' in E Cooke (ed), *Modern Studies in Property Law, Volume III* (Oxford, Hart, 2005) ch 1.

the principles of the Human Rights Act 1998.[3] Moreover, the Law Commission has recently examined the law of limitation and is currently investigating possible reforms to the law of prescription of easements. Also, the government has recently given extensive consideration to common land and village greens, including the ways in which they may arise through long use. The resulting Commons Act 2006 will make some significant changes to the law in this area.[4]

II. DOCTRINES THAT ALLOW RIGHTS IN PROPERTY TO BE ACQUIRED THROUGH THE EFFLUXION OF TIME

It is necessary at the outset to set some parameters for the sorts of doctrines which are included within the analysis. First, the chapter is concerned with legal doctrines in which the passage of time is a necessary component in the acquisition of a right, as distinct from being merely incidental to its acquisition. But it will be seen that rights in property do not arise by the passage of time alone: time must be coupled with the use or possession of land or a chattel to have any creative effect. So, for example, the acquisition of prescriptive easements requires two elements: use of the relevant land; and the passage of time.[5] As a second criterion for analysis, this chapter looks only at those doctrines through which rights in property are acquired, as distinct from personal rights. Account is taken of all forms of proprietary entitlement: rights over both real and personal property; private, public and quasi-public rights; and property rights of varying strengths—from ownership through to incorporeal rights, such as easements. Thirdly, a functional approach has been taken as to what constitutes the 'acquisition' of a property right. Naturally included are those doctrines that confer on a person or persons rights to which they were not previously entitled, such as the prescription of an easement. But also included are those rules, hidden in the law of limitation, that improve the strength of an existing property right by extinguishing another's right over the same piece of property. Adverse possession of unregistered land is an example. Finally, this chapter is as much concerned with the effluxion of time as an original means of acquiring property rights as it is with the role of time in derivative acquisition.[6]

---

[3] *Beaulane Properties Ltd v Palmer* [2005] EWHC 817, [2006] Ch 79; *JA Pye (Oxford) v UK* (2006) 43 EHRR 3.

[4] This chapter considers the law in force at the time of writing (January 2007). Account is, however, taken of the changes that will result when the relevant parts of the Commons Act 2006 are brought into force, the date for which has yet to be set.

[5] Coke Co Lit 113b, 114a. Doctrines such as estoppel and common intention constructive trusts of land are excluded from the analysis because reliance, rather than the passage of time, is crucial to their operation.

[6] See B Nicholas, *An Introduction to Roman Law* (Oxford, OUP, 1962) 115–16.

It is also useful at this stage to outline some of the rationales commonly given for time's creative effect. The law has developed in an ad hoc fashion. Consistent with this, there appears to be no single theory behind time's creative effect. Indeed, Buckland and McNair have written:

> [N]either our legislature nor our judges have ever faced squarely the relevant questions of principle, and the result is that any writer who seeks to discover an underlying theory . . . finds himself in difficulty.[7]

This chapter does not attempt to search for such a unifying theory. However, it does draw upon various possible rationales, of which at least six, some of them overlapping, can be gleaned from case law and academic literature. They are the public interest in being able to identify with certainty those who own or have rights over particular property;[8] preventing owners from sitting on their rights indefinitely;[9] the interest in 'cloth[ing] the fact with right';[10] and the benefit of encouraging the greater use of a scarce resource. Alternatively, the rationale behind time's creative effect might be more philosophical—that the law should give effect to 'the bond that grows between a person and thing over time'.[11] Finally, acquiescence on the part of the owner in someone else acquiring a right might explain why time should have a creative effect.[12]

As to the technical rules of long use, the doctrines by which rights arise through the effluxion of time can be divided into three broad types of mechanism. Under the first mechanism, time's creative effect is hidden within rules of limitation. Under the second, long use triggers a fictitious evidential presumption that a property right has already been created in some other way, for example, that it has been expressly granted. Thirdly are those welcome but rare doctrines that openly acknowledge that long use, in itself, is capable of generating rights.

Mechanism 1: Limitation

The mechanism of limitation allows possession, when coupled with the passage of time, to strengthen existing proprietary entitlement. An example will illustrate its operation. Person A has a book. Assuming that he has the

---

[7] Buckland and McNair, note 2 above, 414–16.
[8] See eg, *Dalton v Angus* (1880-81) LR 6 App Cas 740, 818 (Lord Blackburn); and *Moody v Steggles* (1879) 12 ChD 261, 265 (Fry J).
[9] See *JA Pye (Oxford) Ltd v Graham* [2000] Ch 676, 709–10 (Neuberger J).
[10] *Moody v Steggles*, note 8 above, 265 (Fry J).
[11] See Clarke, note 2 above, 274; and M Bridge, *Personal Property Law*, 3rd edn (Oxford, OUP, 2002) 29.
[12] *Sunningwell*, note 1 above, 351–4 (Lord Hoffmann).

best right to possession, he can loosely be termed the owner.[13] Without A's consent, person B takes the book and treats it as her own. As soon as B takes exclusive possession, she positively acquires a possessory title.[14] Her title is proprietary in the sense that it is enforceable against third parties with a weaker title to possession.[15] But the title is defeasible because A has a better right. Through the passage of time, however, the rules on limitation, as found in the Limitation Act 1980, render that title indefeasible, thereby leaving B by default with the best right to possession. In lay terms, B is now in the position of an owner.

To accomplish this, limitation employs two necessary and cumulative steps. As soon as the property is taken, A acquires the right to sue B in conversion.[16] The first step taken by the Limitation Act is to bar A's right to sue B after six years,[17] provided that B's conversion was not related to theft of the property, either by B herself or by another.[18] Secondly, and also after six years, A's own possessory title is extinguished.[19]

The first step is typical of limitation, which generally bars a claim against a particular defendant without destroying the underlying right.[20] If this were the sole effect of the Limitation Act, A would still be the owner. B personally would be safe from A's claims but he would be unable to pass the property to another person without rendering that third party vulnerable to A's persisting superior title. Furthermore, A could take the property back from B were the opportunity to arise. The second step is therefore essential in conferring indefeasible title on B. By destroying the underlying right, this step goes beyond the normal rules of limitation. Once A's title is extinguished, B has by default the best right to possession. Although appearing to act negatively, the substantive effect of long possession through the mechanism of limitation is positive: B positively acquires a title merely by taking possession. Through the passage of time, that title becomes free from prior rights.[21] In other words, through the operation of limitation, defeasible possessory titles are upgraded to indefeasible rights.[22]

---

[13] Bridge, note 11 above, 29.

[14] *Armory v Delamirie* (1772) 93 ER 664.

[15] AP Bell, *Modern Law of Personal Property in England and Ireland* (London, Butterworths, 1989) 81–2.

[16] *Granger v George* (1826) 5 H&C 149.

[17] Limitation Act 1980 s 2.

[18] *Ibid*, s 4.

[19] *Ibid*, s 3(2).

[20] A McGee, *Limitation Periods*, 4th edn (London, Sweet & Maxwell, 2002) 30.

[21] D Fox, 'Relativity of Title in Equity and Personal Property' [2006] *CLJ* 330, n 6; and Buckland and McNair, note 2 above, 415.

[22] It should be noted that a similar doctrine exists in some civil law jurisdictions in relation to personal property. See eg, Art 2279 of the Code Civil (France), which provides that when personal property is lost or stolen, the owner can reclaim it for a period of three years, after which the current possessor will have good title.

Rules of limitation apply both to chattels and to unregistered land, the relevant limitation period for the latter being twelve years rather than six.[23] It should be noted that registered land is now governed by a new statutory regime, which is considered under the third mechanism below.

Limitation, however, has its limits. It would appear to have no application to the acquisition of rights that are not grounded in possession, such as easements.[24] For rights over land, this is made clear by the Limitation Act, which requires there to be 'adverse *possession*' before the limitation period starts to run.[25] Although not expressly stated in the statute, the same is probably true for chattels, for a practical reason: possession confers a title that ripens into ownership upon the extinction of the previous owner's title; by contrast, someone who has not had possession has no such interest that can so ripen. This means that were the owner's title to be extinguished owing to an interference with the property by someone with no possessory title, the property would in effect become ownerless. To avoid this conclusion, it is preferable to interpret the statute as operating only in favour of possessors.

Mechanism 2: Time as Evidence

Under the second mechanism, time has an outwardly evidential function. Long use raises a presumption that a property right is already in existence. Accordingly, long use does not itself trigger the acquisition of a property right but instead constitutes evidence of a different reason for why that right exists. There are two types of presumption. Most commonly, time raises the presumption that a property right had been created expressly, for example, by way of gift, sale, declaration of trust or dedication to the public. Less commonly, long use raises a presumption that customary law recognises the right. Customary law is a separate body of rules that apply to a particular locality. The rules are distinct from but respected by the common law.[26]

Evidential presumptions vary in strength.[27] They range from presumptions of fact, which depend on 'an inference from all the facts, coupled

---

[23] Limitation Act 1980 ss 15 and 17. For the operation of limitation in unregistered land, see the discussions in Law Commission, 'Land Registration for the Twenty-first Century: A Consultative Document' (Law Com No 254, 1998) para 10.6; and Fox, note 21 above, n 6.

[24] *Copeland v Greenhalf* [1952] Ch 488, 498 (Upjohn J).

[25] Limitation Act 1980, s 15(6) and sched 1, para 8.

[26] *Egerton v Harding* [1975] QB 62, 68 (Scarman LJ).

[27] See C Tapper, *Cross and Tapper on Evidence*, 10th edn (London, Butterworths, 2004) 148–51.

with a general statement of probability drawn from general experience'[28] to presumptions of law, which are raised even though general experience would not necessarily lead a reasonable person to believe that the event presumed actually occurred. Inferences of law are either rebuttable or irrebuttable. Those that are irrebuttable are more accurately described as rules of substantive law.

The various presumptions that are raised by long use, and their relative strengths, are outlined below. Inherent in each of them is the notion that time is capable of generating proprietary interests. However, it will be argued in a later section that the fact that the presumptions vary in strength reveals that it is more appropriate for time to have a creative function in some contexts than in others.

(a) Presumption of Express Creation

(i) *Easements and Profits à prendre*   Easements and profits can be acquired through the effluxion of time by prescription.[29] Typically, a prescriptive easement arises from 20 years' continuous use, where that use is *nec vi, nec clam, nec precario* (not secretive, nor violent, nor with the owner's permission).[30] Unhappily, prescription suffers from the 'anomalous and undesirable ... coexistence of three separate methods of prescribing'.[31] Most of these methods involve presuming a grant. There is, however, one part of one of the methods that adheres to the third mechanism instead. The following discussion focuses on easements. The rules on profits à prendre are almost identical, save that different time periods apply.

First is prescription at common law, the oldest of the three methods. Analysed carefully, it involves two separate presumptions. First, after 20 years' use,[32] it is presumed that the right has existed since time immemorial, which has been set at 1189.[33] This involves a presumption of law but is very vulnerable to rebuttal. Proof that at some time since 1189 the right could not or did not exist will defeat the claim.[34] If, exceptionally, the first

---

[28]   S Anderson 'Easement and Prescription: Changing Perspectives in Classification' (1975) 38 *MLR* 641, 642.

[29]   See generally J Gaunt and P Morgan, *Gale on Easements*, 17th edn (London, Sweet & Maxwell, 1997) (hereinafter 'Gale') ch 4.

[30]   The requirements are taken from Roman law (see Cod 3.34.1; Dig.8.5.10) and are now firmly embedded in English law: *Sunningwell*, note 1 above, 350 (Lord Hoffmann).

[31]   *Tehidy Minerals v Norman* [1971] 2 QB 528, 543 (Buckley LJ).

[32]   *Angus v Dalton* (1877) 3 QBD 85, 105. The time of 20 years is believed to have been adopted by analogy with the limitation period within the Limitation Act 1623: TH Carson, *Prescription and Custom: Six Lectures* (London, Sweet & Maxwell, 1907) 24.

[33]   Statute of Westminster the First (1275) c 39. (The year 1189 marks the accession of Richard I to the throne.)

[34]   'First Report of the Real Property Commissioners' (House of Commons Paper No 263, 1829) 51.

presumption holds, the second presumption is triggered. This involves the fiction that a grant had been made before 1189. This presumption is irrebuttable, save by proof that it would have been legally impossible for such a grant to have been made before 1189.[35] Hence, to the extent that it involves an irrebuttable presumption of law, prescription at common law goes beyond a mere rule of evidence: it becomes a rule of law through which long use actually creates property rights.[36]

The second method of prescription is by lost modern grant, through which time has a more powerful creative effect. Here it is presumed after 20 years' use and in the absence of any other explanation, that an easement was once expressly granted but the evidence for that grant has since been lost.[37] This presumption, like the second presumption involved in common law prescription, is an almost irrebuttable presumption of law.[38] It is so strong that it applies even if 'neither judge nor jury, nor any one else, had the shadow of a belief that any such instrument had ever existed'[39] and will hold in the face of direct evidence that there was never any grant made. As before, it is rebutted only by showing that a grant was legally impossible.

The presumed grant necessarily involves a sub-presumption that the servient owner had the capacity to make such a grant. Accordingly, one way of demonstrating that the making of a grant was legally impossible is to lead proof of incapacity. For example, the grantor may have been incompetent to make a grant because he or she lacked either the mental[40] or legal[41] capacity to grant the easement[42] or, insofar as it might differ, did not have sufficient proprietary entitlement to be able to make such a grant. In substance, the doctrine does not depend in any sense on inferring an actual grant. This is widely acknowledged. Indeed, it has been described by certain members of the judiciary as 'a revolting fiction'[43] that amounts to 'judicial legislation'.[44]

---

[35] Bl Comm ii 265. See W Holdsworth, *A History of English Law*, 4th edn (London, Sweet & Maxwell, 1936) vol 3, 166–71 and vol 7, 343. For example, if it would traverse a custom that has already been proven to have existed in 1189, prescription cannot operate: *Perry v Eames* [1891] 1 Ch 658, 667 (Chitty J).

[36] See Holdsworth, *ibid*, vol 9, 140.

[37] *Tehidy Minerals*, note 31 above.

[38] For the history of the development of lost modern grant, see *Bryant v Foot* (1867) LR 2 QB 161, 181; *Earl de la Warr v Miles* (1881) 17 Ch D 535; *Duke of Norfolk v Arbuthnot* (1879–80) LR 5 CPD 390.

[39] *Bryant v Foot*, *ibid*, 181 (Cockburn CJ).

[40] K Gray and SF Gray, *Elements of Land Law*, 4th edn (Oxford, OUP, 2005) 705–6.

[41] *Rochdale Canal Co v Radcliffe* (1852) 18 QB 287, 314–15.

[42] *Tehidy Minerals*, note 31 above, 552. In theory, the same applies to prescription at common law; in practice, proving lack of capacity prior to time immemorial will be prohibitively difficult.

[43] *Angus v Dalton*, note 32 above, 94 (Lush J).

[44] *Bryant v Foot*, note 38 above, 181 (Cockburn CJ).

Thirdly, a prescriptive right might arise by statute. The Prescription Act 1832 provides for two main types of prescription, termed here 'long' and 'short' statutory prescription.[45] Short statutory prescription allows for an easement to arise after 20 years' use.[46] However, as for the other two methods of prescription, a claim can be defeated by proof that the alleged servient owner lacks the capacity, for whatever reason, to grant the easement claimed.[47] It is generally assumed that short statutory prescription also operates on the theory of a presumed a grant.[48] A good, but not necessarily conclusive, indicator of this is the relevance of the grantor's capacity to make a grant.

Long statutory prescription differs from its short counterpart in two main respects. First, it requires 40 rather than 20 years' use. Secondly, after the necessary period has passed, the user's right to an easement is 'deemed absolute and indefeasible'.[49] Although there is conflicting case law on the point, long statutory prescription appears not to depend on any presumed grant.[50] If this position is correct, the doctrine would appear to operate even against an incapable servient owner.[51] Being an open acknowledgement that time might create rights, without resort to presumptions, long statutory prescription falls for further discussion below, under the third mechanism.

(ii) Rights of Common and Common Land   Until the Commons Act 2006 comes into force, long use has two effects with regard to commons, one of which is very far-reaching. First, it can serve to create rights of common. A right of common exists when two or more people have the benefit of identical profits à prendre.[52] For example, two people who both have the right to graze cattle on another's land have a right of common. Because profits are capable of arising through long use, it follows that so too are rights of common.

---

[45] Note that there is a further type of statutory prescription not dealt with here, concerning rights to light. It very broadly follows the rules for long statutory prescription except that it only requires 20 years' use: Prescription Act 1832, s 3; and Rights of Light Act 1959. See further C Harpum, *Megarry & Wade: The Law of Real Property*, 6th edn (London, Sweet & Maxwell, 2000) (hereinafter 'Megarry & Wade') paras 18.163–18.170.

[46] Prescription Act 1832, s 2. The right can only be claimed, however, in litigation.

[47] This mode of rebuttal is confirmed by the Prescription Act 1832, s 7. See further *Hulley v Silversprings Bleaching and Dyeing Co Ltd* [1922] 2 Ch 268, 279.

[48] Gale, note 29 above, 182.

[49] Prescription Act 1832, s 2.

[50] *Wright v Williams* (1836) 150 ER 353. Cf *Staffordshire and Worcester Canal Navigation (Proprietors) v Birmingham Canal Navigation (Proprietors)* (1866) LR 1 HL 254.

[51] Note that s 7 of the Prescription Act expressly provides that long statutory prescription is unaffected by mental incapacity.

[52] See Gale, note 29 above, para 1.129; B Harris and G Ryan, *An Outline of the Law Relating to Common Land and Public Access to the Countryside* (London, Sweet & Maxwell, 1967) paras 2.9 and 2.49.

Secondly, long use might have the consequence of changing the status of land that was once wholly private into a common. This is because a common is defined by statute as including 'land' that is 'subject to rights of common'.[53] Therefore, once rights of common over land are created through long use, that land acquires the status of a common and can be registered as such in the Commons Register. Although the private land-owner remains owner, his rights as owner are curtailed once the land is registered as a common. For example, the public acquires a qualified statutory right of access to the land on foot.[54] The land will have become a quasi-public space.

The Commons Act 2006 abolishes the prescription of rights of common,[55] and consequently the creation of common land through long use. Whether or not this change should be welcomed is examined below.

(iii) Public Rights of Way Public rights of way may also arise through long use. However, whereas prescription relies largely upon a presumed grant to an individual, this is not possible in favour of fluctuating classes, as they are not capable grantees.[56] Public rights of way are therefore not granted but dedicated to and accepted by the public. By statute, after 20 years' use by the public, the way is 'deemed to have been dedicated as a highway'.[57] Being a presumption of law, Lord Hoffmann rightly stated, *obiter*, in *Sunningwell* that it is 'unnecessary to infer an actual dedication'.[58] The doctrine nonetheless adheres to the theory of presumed express creation owing to the possibility that the presumption might be rebutted, rather easily, on proof that the landowner did not intend to dedicate the

---

[53] Commons Registration Act 1965, s 22(1)(a).

[54] Countryside and Rights of Way Act 2000, part I. The 2000 Act only applies to those commons not already providing public access. See P Clayden, *Our Common Land: The Law and History of Common Land and Village Greens*, 5th edn (Henley-on-Thames, Open Spaces Society, 2003) 45. Before the 2000 Act, the public was only entitled to access about 1/5 of all common land: Law of Property Act 1925, s 193. Note that for common land over which rights of common existed prior to 1926, the erection of any building or fence or other work is unlawful without permission from the Secretary of State: Law of Property Act 1925, s 194.

[55] Commons Act 2006, s 6(1). However, the effect of this is subject to a possible ambiguity: the section abolishes only prescription of rights of common; prescription of profits is untouched. It was seen above that rights of common are, according to the common law, merely profits held by two or more people. Arguably, therefore, rights of common might still arise indirectly by prescription. A sensible reading of the statute, however, would be that the Act has by implication abolished the rule that two or more prescribed-for profits equates to a right of common.

[56] *Goodman v Mayor of Saltash* (1882) 7 App Cas 633, 648; *Attorney General v Antrobus* [1905] 2 Ch 188.

[57] Highways Act 1980, s 31(1). Note that a presumption of dedication can also be raised at common law. See further Megarry & Wade, note 45 above, paras 18.067–18.068.

[58] *Sunningwell*, note 1 above, 358.

way to the public.[59] As a result, this presumption is weaker than the presumption of grant of a private easement for which the alleged grantor's actual intention is irrelevant.

(iv) Trusts in Favour of Inhabitants of a Locality   More obscurely, a few isolated cases have presumed a declaration of charitable[60] trust in favour of a locality or, exceptionally, the general public,[61] through long use.[62] In one case, for example, after 200 years' use, a trust was presumed for a locality to enjoy an oyster fishery in spring.[63] There have been so few cases in which a charitable trust has been presumed that rules are hard to extract.[64] The presumption is strong and probably one of law because it involves a 'splendid effort of equitable imagination'.[65] The fictitious conclusion must, however, be 'reasonably possible'.[66] The owner of the servient land may defeat the presumption by clear evidence that a trust had never been declared,[67] although in practice proving this will be difficult.[68]

(v) Crown Grant to a Corporation   Another curious mechanism by which long use allows fluctuating groups to benefit is by allowing a presumption to be raised that the Crown granted certain rights, such as profits, to a group of people and in so doing incorporated that group.[69] Cases in which such claims have been successful are again few in number.[70] This is because the presumption, despite being a fictitious presumption of law,[71] cannot operate if in 'violent antagonism' with the actual state of

---

[59] Highways Act 1980, s 31(1). See also *Godmanchester Town Council v Secretary of State for Environment, Food and Rural Affairs* [2005] EWCA Civ 1597, [2006] 2 WLR 1179, where Auld LJ confirmed in this context that landowners 'should not be credited with giving their land over to public use if they did not intend it': [59]. *Godmanchester* is on appeal to the House of Lords. Note that the presumption of dedication is raised by long use alone; positive intention is not a requirement. Intention assumes relevance only at the rebuttal stage.

[60] See *Goodman*, n 56 above, 642 and 650. Cf *Alfred F Beckett v Lyons* [1967] Ch 449, 484 (Harman LJ).

[61] See *R v Doncaster BC, ex p Braim* (1989) 57 P & CR 1, where McCollough J, in an unreserved judgment, presumed a trust in favour of the general public.

[62] Cases are set out in Megarry & Wade, note 45 above, para 18.089.

[63] *Goodman*, note 56 above.

[64] See J Hill, 'Public Access to Land for the Purposes of Recreation' [1988] *Conv* 369, 373.

[65] *Harris v Chesterfield* [1911] AC 623, 633 (Lord Ashbourne, dissenting).

[66] *Goodman*, note 56 above, 639 (Lord Selborne LC).

[67] In *Antrobus*, note 56 above, no trust was presumed in favour of visitors to Stonehenge because there was clear documentary evidence to the contrary.

[68] *Ibid*, 647; *Braim*, note 61 above, 11.

[69] See Megarry & Wade, note 45 above, para 18.088; Holdsworth, note 35 above, vol 3, 477.

[70] Eg, *Willingdale v Maitland* (1866) LR 3 Eq 103.

[71] See *Lord Rivers v Adams* (1878) 3 ExD 361, 367.

affairs.[72] If, as will quite often be the case, the claimants do not act as though incorporated, the presumption cannot operate. This is a weaker presumption than that of a trust.[73]

(b) Presumption of Existence of Customary Rights

Although it has been suggested that customary rights lie in grant,[74] this analysis is not supported by the case law.[75] The better analysis is that the fact presumed by long use is that the alleged customary rights simply existed in 1189. These types of right benefit a fluctuating class of people rather than the public at large,[76] and they tend to be quintessentially English in content. They include, for example, dancing in a field[77] or around a maypole,[78] playing cricket[79] or holding an annual fair.[80]

The length of use required to raise the presumption is not fixed.[81] Proof of use as far back as living witnesses can remember is enough, but proof of 20 years' use might suffice.[82] The presumption is fragile and can be rebutted by proof that that the right was incapable of existing in 1189. It therefore would not be possible to establish, through the effluxion of time, a custom specifically to skateboard in a town car park. However, it would be possible to establish a general custom to play games (since games as a generic category did exist in 1189), which might, for example, today include skateboarding.[83]

Once established, customary rights bind the land over which they operate. Until 1970, customary rights had further, and potentially severe, consequences for the landowner, for their existence provided a reason for the land to be registered as a town or village green.[84] The creation of a

---

[72] *Mayor of Saltash v Goodman* 5 C.PD 431, 454 (Denman J).

[73] This is evident from the *Goodman* case, note 56 above, in which a trust was presumed but not a grant to an incorporation.

[74] N Ubhi & B Denyer-Green, *Law of Commons and of Town and Village Greens* (Bristol, Jordans, 2004) 120.

[75] *Oxfordshire CC v Oxford City Council* [2005] EWCA Civ 175, [2006] Ch 43, [31].

[76] *Blewett v Tregonning* (1835) 111 ER 524; *Hammerton v Honey* (1876) 24 WL 603. Gray and Gray, note 40 above, state that there is no property right as such and give as authority *Mason v Tritton* (1993) 6 BPR 13639, 13644. However, there are indications in *Wyld v Silver* [1963] Ch 243, 272 (Russell LJ) that 'there is in the inhabitants' in such cases 'a proprietary right of a sort, not shared with the members of the public'.

[77] *Abbot v Weekly* (1665) 1 Lev 176.

[78] *Hall v Nottingham* (1875–76) LR 1 ExD 1.

[79] *Fitch v Rawling* (1795) 126 ER 614.

[80] *Wyld v Silver*, note 76 above.

[81] See *Hammer v Chance* (1865) 46 ER 1061, 1064.

[82] *Brocklebank v Thompson* [1903] 2 Ch 344, 350.

[83] *Fitch v Rawling* (1795) 126 ER 614; *Sunningwell*, note 1 above, 357; and *Oxfordshire CC v Oxford City Council* [2006] UKHL 25, [2006] 2 WLR 1235, [50].

[84] Nothing turns on the distinction between a town and a village green. These terms merely reflect the physical setting. Hereafter 'green' shall refer to both types.

green has 'significant practical effects',[85] it being an offence, for example, for such land to be built upon or damaged.[86] According to the Commons Registration Act 1965, land is registrable as a green if it satisfies one of three alternative definitions,[87] known judicially as Classes A, B and C respectively.[88] The one of relevance here is Class B, defined as land on which 'the inhabitants of any locality have customary right to indulge in lawful sports and pastimes'.[89] However, this type of green was registrable only until 1970.[90] As such, no longer do new discoveries of customary rights have the potential to transform the status of private land into a green.

(c) Summary

It is clear that the second mechanism is commonly used to explain the creation of property rights by long use. However, resort to the language of presumptions obscures the true position that it is the long use itself, and not a grant, that generates the property right.

Mechanism 3: Open Acknowledgement that Time Creates Rights

(a) Adverse Possession over Registered Land

When land is registered, the rules of limitation are inapplicable.[91] The mechanism by which a squatter acquires indefeasible title is much more transparent. After adversely possessing land for ten years, a squatter may apply to become the registered proprietor and will succeed if the present owner fails to object and then evict him.[92] The successful squatter acquires the dispossessed owner's registered estate, subject to the benefits and burdens that affected it when the dispossessed proprietor held it,[93] but not through any theory of fictitious conveyance.

---

[85]   *R v Suffolk CC, ex p Steed* (1996) 71 P & CR 463, 494 (Carnwath J).
[86]   Commons Act (1876) s 29; Inclosure Act (1857) s 12.
[87]   1(1)(a), 3(b), 13(b) and 22. See especially s 22(1)(b) which sets out the three definitions
[88]   See *New Windsor Corp v Mellor* [1975] Ch 380 (CA) 387 (Lord Denning MR) and *Sunningwell*, note 1 above, 347.
[89]   Commons Registration Act (1965) s 22(1). Note that Class A greens concern land 'allotted' by statute; Class C greens arise through mere long use and as such are dealt with under the third mechanism.
[90]   See *dicta* to this effect in *Sunningwell*, note 1 above, 348 (Lord Hoffmann) and *Oxfordshire CC* (HL) note 83 above, [140] (Baroness Hale).
[91]   Land Registration Act 2002, s 96.
[92]   *Ibid*, s 97, sched 6; Land Registration Rules 2003, r 189.
[93]   Land Registration Act 2002, sched 6, para 9. By exception, the registered squatter is not bound by pre-existing charges.

(b) Easements

It has been shown above that prescription of easements normally adopts the mechanism of presumed grant. Although there is conflicting case law, 'long' statutory prescription appears not to depend on any presumed grant. An 'absolute and indefeasible' easement arises by prescription after 40 years' use, even as against an incapable servient owner.[94]

(c) Village Greens

The Commons Registration Act 1965 provides that a right to register land as a green arises under Class C where 'for not less than twenty years, a significant number of the inhabitants of any locality, or of any neighbourhood within a locality, have indulged in lawful sports and pastimes as of right . . .'.[95] Parliament probably originally intended Class C merely to be a supplement to Class B greens. As explained above, Class B greens were registrable on proof of the existence of customary rights of recreation, which could be presumed after 20 years' use. However, the presumption was very fragile, being rebutted by any evidence that the use did not start until after 1189. It is likely that Class C was introduced to prevent rebuttal in this manner, and as such, being a method of presumed creation, would have fallen within the second mechanism.[96] However, Class C has since acquired a life of its own and now does not depend on any presumed customary rights, or past grant or dedication: a wholly new and modern green can be created after merely 20 years' use.[97] As a result, provided that the definition is met, it is possible to register any land as a green, even though it might not have the features of a traditional or customary village amenity. Remarkably, for example, a group of rocks and a quarry have both qualified for Class C registration.[98]

Upon registration as a green, the owner's ability to exploit the land is curtailed, as was seen above in relation to Class B greens. Furthermore, after a period of doubt as to whether or not the locals have any right to use

---

[94] Prescription Act 1832, ss 2 and 7. *Wright v Williams* (1836) 150 ER 353. *Cf Staffordshire and Worcester Canal Navigation*, note 50 above.

[95] s 22(1A), as amended by the Countryside and Rights of Way Act 2000 s 98. It is by virtue of s 13 of the Commons Registration Act and Commons Registration (General) Regulations 1966, SI 1966/1471, as amended by Commons Registration (New Land) Regulations 1969, SI 1969/1843, that new greens can be registered.

[96] See *Sunningwell*, note 1 above, 353 (Lord Hoffmann); and *Oxfordshire CC* (CA), note 75 above, [28] and [43]-[51] (Carnwath LJ).

[97] See eg *Sunningwell*, note 1 above, 359 (Lord Hoffmann). Note, however, that Lord Hoffmann in *Oxfordshire CC* (HL), note 83 above, says that once registered under Class C, land is 'conclusively presumed' to be a green: [53]. The language of presumption is misleading. Class C greens arise without the aid of presumptions.

[98] *Oxfordshire CC* (HL), note 83 above, [80].

a registered Class C green,[99] it has now been decided that registered greens of any Class are available for locals to use generally for sports and pastimes.[100] Owing to the restrictions imposed on the owner of a registered green, local residents frequently use (or abuse) the right to register a Class C green in order to prevent development of local land.[101] It should be noted that some changes to Class C greens will be made by the Commons Act 2006. These are considered below.

Conclusion

It is clear from the above survey that time's creative effect is significant and that, in accordance with common law method, the relevant rules have developed in an ad hoc manner in unconnected and isolated patches. The next section considers the problems of disguise and fragmentation which have resulted from this manner of development.

III. PROBLEMS OF DISGUISE AND FRAGMENTATION

Disguise

As the above survey demonstrates, time usually creates rights in the guise of either limitation or a fictitious presumption, rather than by direct acknowledgement that long use itself might create rights. Time's masked effect gives rise to problems of which four are identified here. Focus is largely confined to presumed grants, as this is where many of these problems lie.

First, the notion of a presumed grant is so fictitious that it offends common sense and is furthermore inconsistent with the technical requirements for prescription. The idea that prescriptive rights rest in a grant conflicts with the condition that prescriptive use must be *nec precario*. Any indication that the owner had given permission for another person to enjoy the land, whether by grant of an easement or merely a licence, will prevent a prescriptive right from arising.[102] For the doctrine to be internally inconsistent in this manner is unsatisfactory.

Secondly, in conjunction with the first point, the technical mechanism of presumed grant has led to an acceptance by many that the policy rationale

---

[99] *Mellor*, note 88 above; *Oxfordshire CC* (CA), note 75 above, [80].

[100] *Oxfordshire CC* (HL), note 83 above.

[101] A recent survey has shown that between one half and three quarters of all applications for Class C registration are made in order to frustrate development: ADAS *Town and Village Greens Project – Market Research Report* (2006, commissioned by Defra), p iv.

[102] *Sunningwell*, note 1 above, [72].

for prescriptive rights is 'acquiescence' by the servient owner in the other party's long-established enjoyment.[103] So long as there is a theory of grant, it follows logically that acquiescence is relevant. However, it is far from obvious that acquiescence *is* the policy rationale for prescription, for the following reasons. First, as apparent in the previous point, the requirement that use must be *nec precario* introduces an element of adversity into the prescriptive claim that cannot easily be explained by acquiescence.[104] Furthermore, it is often equally fictitious to assume acquiescence on the part of the servient owner as it is to presume a grant.[105] Finally, the assumption that acquiescence is the rationale for prescriptive rights fails to take account of the fundamental distinction between rights that arise by consensual grant and rights that arise otherwise, by operation of law. The policy behind the recognition of expressly granted rights can be explained by the law's respect for the wishes of legal actors when they are executed in legally recognised forms,[106] for which acquiescence is relevant. However, once it is accepted that prescriptive easements arise not by grant but by operation of law, it no longer follows that the policy justification for their existence is acquiescence. For these four reasons, it is inappropriate to rely unquestioningly on acquiescence as the policy justification for time's creative effect. Whilst acquiescence explains the effect of a grant, different policy reasons justify why rights arise by operation of law.

The third problem with time's masked effect is linked to the first two. Because the law has inappropriately tied itself to the mechanism of grant and the rationale of acquiescence, the questions that occupy the courts in prescription cases tend to concern whether or not the technicalities of a hypothetical conveyance are satisfied, including the capacity of the parties to make a deed of grant.[107] This focus comes at the expense of a proper consideration of why and in what circumstances long use should, as a matter of policy, give rise to a prescriptive right. Adherence to a presumption of grant avoids direct consideration of these substantial policy issues. Correlatively, it requires focus to be given to issues that might not be relevant.

For example, it is generally accepted that long use might create private easements over private land. However, the consequences of prescription by presumed grant go beyond issues between two private individuals. First, they extend to the creation of private rights over land that is currently enjoyed as a public amenity, to the detriment of the public. Secondly, and

---

[103] *Ibid*, 351–4 (Lord Hoffmann). See note 12 above and accompanying text.
[104] See Buckland and McNair, note 2 above, 139–40.
[105] P Jackson, *The Law of Easements and Profits* (London, Butterworths, 1978) 112–13.
[106] Eg, for the creation of an express legal easement, a deed is required: Law of Property Act 1925, s 52.
[107] See eg, D Fox, 'Illegality and Prescription' [2004] *Conv* 173, text to n 13.

conversely, long use can transform the private land into a publicly-enjoyed resource. The question as to whether or not it is appropriate for the effluxion of time to have these far-reaching effects cannot directly be addressed under a system that relies on presumed grant

The problem is well illustrated by the recent House of Lords decision in *Bakewell Management Ltd v Brandwood*.[108] Owners whose homes bordered a common had accessed their homes by driving over the common for more than 20 years. Under normal circumstances, they would undoubtedly have acquired easements to this effect. However, by statute it is an offence to drive on such land without the owner's authority.[109] Despite the long use being technically illegal, the Lords unanimously allowed the prescriptive claim, under the doctrine of lost modern grant. Two reasons for the decision are present in the judgment: a wide reason and a narrow one.[110]

The narrow reason relied on the existence of the common land owner's dispensing power to authorise and decriminalise driving over the common.[111] Because the owner could expressly have granted the easement, it was possible to presume such a grant, despite the illegality. In other words, the narrow reason draws heavily on the presumed grant theory to justify the creation of an easement. The problem with such an analysis is that prescription can operate in the face of illegal conduct only when the relevant offence contains a dispensing power. While the reasoning will apply to the offence of driving off-road,[112] which also contains a dispensing power, it will not apply to other similarly minor offences that may be committed by driving over commons,[113] where there happens to be no decriminalising option.

A wider reason was hinted at. It recognised the need to consider, as a matter of policy, whether or not a prescriptive right should arise. It involved considering whether the statutory purpose of the prohibition on driving over common land would be defeated by allowing a prescriptive right to arise.[114] The wider reason is preferable as it does not necessitate drawing arbitrary distinctions between offences, depending on whether or not the owner could lawfully have granted the easement. The existence of the fiction of a grant distracted in this case from proper consideration of the policy justifications for time's creative effect in these circumstances. It is inappropriate to mediate the creation of prescriptive rights through the presumption of grant.

---

[108] [2004] UKHL 14, [2004] 2 AC 519.
[109] Law of Property Act 1925, s 193(4).
[110] See A Goymour, 'Rabbits Beware: Residents Gain Rights to Drive over Common Land' [2005] *CLJ* 39.
[111] See *Bakewell*, note 108 above, [47] (Lord Scott, with whom the others agreed).
[112] Road Traffic Act 1988, s 34.
[113] Eg, Inclosure Act 1857, s 12; and Commons Act 1876, s 29.
[114] See generally the speeches of Lords Scott and Walker.

In short, it is important for long use to distance itself from the technical mechanism of grant and the corresponding rationale of acquiescence, in order to enable other, more relevant rationales to be explored.

The fourth problem regarding time's masked effect that might be observed is that many of these long use doctrines, whilst obscuring relevant issues, require judges to address unnecessarily complex questions. This has resulted in a large amount of litigation. Indeed, in recent history barely a year has passed without a case reaching the House of Lords.[115] The costs incurred are high, and disproportionately so.

Fragmentation

As well as being disguised, long use's creative effect is also fragmented across property law. This is in contrast to the approach of civil law systems, which tend to conceive long use more as one body of law.[116] The survey of the common law doctrines given in the last section suggests that the body of rules through which property rights might arise is extensive. However, because the individual doctrines have generally developed in isolation from one another, the body of law as a whole lacks coherence.

One of the symptoms of fragmentation is that of messy overlaps, especially the 'anomalous and undesirable . . . coexistence of three separate methods' by which a prescriptive easement might arise.[117] It is quite normal for the claimant to plead all three methods, although at his or her own risk as to costs. Another symptom of fragmentation is the development of inconsistencies between the doctrines. For example, it takes ten or twelve years to acquire full title to land by adverse possession[118] but 20 years for a mere easement. This cannot be justified other than by the accident of history.[119]

---

[115] *Sunningwell*, note 1 above; *Bettison v Langton* [2001] UKHL 24, [2002] 1 AC 27; *R (Beresford) v Sunderland CC* [2003] UKHL 60, [2004] 1 AC 889; *Bakewell*, note 108 above; *Oxfordshire CC* (HL), note 83 above. See also the comments of Carnwath LJ in *Oxfordshire CC* (CA), note 75 above, [55], where he described the registration of new greens as 'an area of unusually vigorous legal activity'.

[116] See eg Code Civil (France) arts 690–1 and 2219–83; Codice Civile (Italy) arts 1158–67 and 1061; and BGB (Germany) para 937 ff. See further EJ Cohn, *Manual of German Law*, 2nd edn (1968) 184.

[117] *Tehidy Minerals*, note 31 above, 543 (Buckley LJ).

[118] Ten years for adverse possession of registered land unless the owner objects; 12 years for unregistered land.

[119] It might be argued that a longer period of use is required for easements because the type of use is less continuous than for adverse possession. However, that argument falls away with respect to those easements that tend to be used continuously, such as rights of light and drainage. Furthermore, intermittent use might suffice for adverse possession, depending on the type of land: *Red House Farms v Catchpole* [1977] 2 EGLR 125.

Furthermore, the fragmentary approach means that there might be gaps in the law. Outlined in the previous section were those rights that *do* arise through mere use over time. What have not yet been discussed are the many rights over property that *do not* so arise. Examples include restrictive covenants, charges over property, leases and private trusts.[120] If, as this chapter seeks to demonstrates, time is an extensive mode of creation in its own right, there is no reason why its effect should necessarily be limited to those rights historically within its ambit.

Finally, the fragmentary nature of long use's legal effects has obscured an important pattern within the law. This is outlined in the next section and might usefully be drawn upon to inform the law's future direction.

IV. ADOPTING A PRINCIPLED APPROACH

Fictions and fragmentation have obscured the fact that long use gives rise to rights by operation of law, for policy reasons. This section sets out a principled approach for identifying exactly when long use should create property rights.

Identified in an earlier section were six possible rationales for time's creative effect. Although these rationales are valuable in giving justificatory force to the effect of time, they have limited use in determining in exactly what practical circumstances time ought to have creative effect. By contrast, the current case law is a rich source of guidance. The survey of the law given earlier reveals that time is seen as a more appropriate source of rights in some contexts than in others. Close examination of the cases reveals a pattern that, it will be shown, forms a rational basis for the future development of the law.

Identifying a Pattern in the Case Law

As explained above, long use frequently raises presumptions, some of which are easily rebutted; others of which, less so. At one extreme, for example, private easements, which allow one landowner to exercise a right over his or her neighbour's land, arise by operation of a very strong, almost irrebuttable presumption. At the other extreme, the rules for public rights of way, which open up land to the general public, employ a very weak presumption. Indeed, in a recent case concerning public rights of way, it was acknowledged that the rebuttable nature of the statutory presumption

---

[120] Note that tenancies at will and tenancies at sufferance are arguably created through long use. However they have little effect on the freeholders because they may eject the 'tenants' at any time: Megarry & Wade, note 45 above, paras 14.075 and 14.079.

'creates a delicate balance between, on the one hand, the interest of the public in having access to . . . highways . . . and, on the other, the interest of landowners in retaining control over their own land'.[121] The statute was deemed to provide 'an equilibrium between the interest of landowners and that of the public in respect of claimed rights of way'.[122] There is little room for such delicate balancing when a private right is in issue.[123]

These two examples form part of what will be shown to be a more general pattern. According to the pattern, where a presumed right is at issue, the more that the right will impinge on the owner's rights, the more readily rebuttable is the presumption. This means that time has a greater capacity for generating private rights than it does for public rights over land.[124] Doctrines that conform to the pattern include the following.

First, a presumed declaration of trust in favour of a locality opens up a landowner's property to a potentially large group of users. According to the pattern, the presumption ought not to be as strong as for private easements. The presumption of trust fits the pattern because it is rebutted relatively easily by evidence that no trust was in fact declared. Judges are generally reluctant to allow time to create these quasi-public rights. This is apparent both from the paucity of cases in which such trusts have arisen,[125] and also from statements to this effect in the cases themselves. For example, in *AG v Antrobus*,[126] a parish council brought an action against the private owner of Stonehenge, who had erected fences around the historic site. The council claimed, amongst other things, that the site was the object of a presumed trust in favour of the public and that therefore the fences surrounding the site should be removed. Farwell J, rejecting the assertion, was disinclined to find a presumed trust because 'it would be unfortunate if the Courts were to presume novel and unheard of trusts . . . from acts of kindly courtesy, and thus drive landowners to close their gates in order to preserve their property.'[127] It should be noted that there is little parallel concern against presuming private easements.

Secondly, presumed grants to presumed incorporations are similarly rare—and are even more easily rebutted than are presumed trusts. Indeed, there are indications in the case law that a grant might be rebutted even if it is merely 'unreasonable' to draw the conclusion that the Crown has

---

[121] *Godmanchester*, note 59 above, [56] (Auld LJ).

[122] *Ibid.*

[123] Note, however, that the courts are vigilant not to extend the recognised categories of easements to include new rights if to do so could give rise to a large number of prescriptive claims over a piece of private land. See eg, *Hunter v Canary Wharf* [1997] AC 655.

[124] See D Feldman, 'Property and Public Protest' in Meisel & Cook (eds), *Property and Protection: Essays in Honour of Brian W Harvey* (Oxford, Hart, 2000) 40.

[125] See note 64 above and the accompanying text.

[126] Note 56 above.

[127] *Ibid*, 198.

conferred such a right.[128] It is arguable that this invites the court to consider on the merits whether or not it is appropriate to find such a grant. This is in stark contrast to the automatic and non-discretionary application of the presumption of grant for private easements. Again, a possible explanation lies in the quasi-public consequences attaching to the finding of a presumed grant of extensive rights over Crown land.

Thirdly, along the same vein, it is also very easy to rebut a presumption of a customary right, which, by its very nature, would benefit a sector of the public. And similarly, some judicial reluctance towards allowing public rights to arise through mere lapse of time is evident in the recent flurry of cases relating to Class C greens.[129] It was explained in an earlier section that use as of right for 20 years allows local residents to apply for registration of land as a green, without resort to a presumption. Quasi-public status can thereby arise through mere lapse of time, followed by registration. Class C greens can therefore arise almost as easily as can private easements. Befitting the pattern, it is clear that some of the judiciary are 'uneasy' with the rule.[130] This is apparent from Lord Scott's speech in *R (Beresford) v Sunderland CC*, where he stated:

> [There] are important differences between private easements over land and public rights over land and between the ways in which a public right of way can come into existence and the ways in which a [green] can come into existence. To apply principles applicable to one type of right to another type of right without taking account of their differences is dangerous.[131]

Recently, residents are increasingly resorting to Class C green applications solely to frustrate proposed developments on local land. As Lord Walker said in *Beresford*, the doctrine allows 'normal developmental controls' to be 'bypassed'.[132] Such judicial comments lend support to the intrinsic desirability of the results that the pattern identified in this section would produce.

---

[128]   *Lord Rivers v Adams*, note 71 above, 367 (Kelly CB).
[129]   *R v Suffolk CC, ex p Steed* (1998) 75 P & CR 102; *Sunningwell*, note 1 above; *R (on application of Alfred McAlpine) v Staffordshire* [2002] EWHC 76; *Beresford*, note 115 above; *R (Laing Homes) v Bucks CC* [2003] EWHC 1578, [2004] 1 P & CR 36; *R (on application of Cheltenham Builders) v South Gloucestershire DC* [2003] EWHC 2803 (Admin), [2003] 4 PLR 95 [2004]; *R (Whitmey) v Commons Commissioners* [2004] EWCA Civ 951, [2005] QB 282; and *Oxfordshire CC* (HL), note 83 above
[130]   *Beresford*, note 115 above, [52] (Lord Scott).
[131]   *Ibid*, [34].
[132]   *Ibid*, [92].

Rationale for the Pattern

The pattern only emerges by piecing together the various fragmented rules on long use doctrines. Hence, it has not received direct judicial or academic attention. It might nevertheless be possible to rationalise why the pattern provides a suitable framework for rules relating to long use.

The creation of public rights over an owner's property is normally more burdensome to the owner than the creation of private rights. Furthermore, once created, public rights are more difficult to extinguish than private rights. Whilst it might be appropriate for long use alone to generate a private right, arguably something more should be required for the creation of public rights, in order to justify the extra impingement on the owner's rights that this entails. Two examples illustrate the point. First, private rights of way arise through effluxion of time by the operation of almost irrebuttable presumptions. However, it was seen in the previous section that the presumed dedication of a public right of way involves a 'delicate balance' between the interests of the public and the interests of the owner.[133] Factors over and above the mere effluxion of time are relevant.

Secondly, the creation of certain public rights might conflict with public planning law. This is particularly apparent when residents seek to register a green in order to obstruct a development for which planning permission has already been granted. It is not obviously appropriate for the *past* actions of residents over the last 20 years to be automatically determinative of the best *future* use of the land, particularly when this comes into conflict with planning decisions. It was seen above that this view has some judicial support.[134] According to the pattern, long use alone would not suffice for public rights to arise; other factors, such as planning decisions, would also be relevant.

Identifying Outlying Doctrines

The pattern identified accords with principle and is largely supported by authority. If long use is to be developed into a coherent mode of acquisition, the pattern, it is argued below, provides an appropriate basis upon which this can be done. However, owing to the ad hoc development of the law, it is inevitable that some doctrines fall outside the pattern. In the interests of consistency, the outlying doctrines should, if possible, be brought into line with the pattern, unless there are strong policy reasons for their current form. Three outlying doctrines are identified here.

---

[133] See note 121 above and accompanying text.
[134] See notes 131and 132 above and accompanying text. See also *Hunter v Canary Wharf*, note 123 above, 710 (Lord Hoffmann).

First, the presumption that rights in common have been created, thereby creating common land, is currently almost irrebuttable. This lies outside the general trend. It is inconsistent that a common might arise by operation of an almost irrebuttable presumption, whereas a presumed dedication of a public right of way is easily rebutted. According to the pattern, the right that is more burdensome on the owner—common land status—should be the one less easily acquired through the effluxion of time. The Commons Act 2006 represents an important step forward in this respect. Once the Act comes into force, rights of common will no longer be capable of arising through the effluxion of time at all.[135] This development is to be welcomed. It will have the effect of bringing the creation of commons more in line with the pattern.

The second outlying doctrine is the process by which Class C greens currently arise. It was seen above that through the mere effluxion of time private land might be converted into a green,[136] with potentially devastating effects for the owner. The doctrine is at odds with the pattern. Attempts have been made both by litigants and by politicians to curtail the doctrine, with varying degrees of success. Three different arguments, each aiming to narrow the doctrine, have been put before the courts, but each has ultimately been rejected by the House of Lords. First, it was argued that it was necessary for the locals who claimed the right to register a Class C green to believe that they were exercising a right claimed by the locality. The argument was accepted by the Court of Appeal in *Steed*[137] but rejected by the Lords in *Sunningwell*.[138] Secondly, it was argued in *Oxfordshire* CC and accepted by the Court of Appeal in that case that, following an amendment to the statute,[139] the relevant long use must continue right up until the green is actually registered.[140] According to this argument, as soon as an application for registration was made, the owner could prevent the use from continuing and thereby defeat the claim. It would therefore be extremely rare for a Class C green to arise. However, the argument's success lasted only for a brief period and failed when the case reached the House of Lords.[141] Finally, it was argued before the Lords in *Oxfordshire* CC that the Class C doctrine should be confined to such plots that would ordinarily be regarded as 'traditional' village greens.[142] Although their

---

[135] S 6(1). But note the ambiguity discussed in note 55 above.

[136] Provided that the green is registered. Registration, provided application is made within the relevant timeframe, occurs as a matter of course on proof of 20 years' use.

[137] Note 129 above.

[138] Note 1 above.

[139] Commons Registration Act 1965 s 22(1A), as amended by Countryside and Rights of Way Act 2000, s 98.

[140] *Oxfordshire* CC (CA), note 75 above.

[141] *Oxfordshire* CC (HL), note 83 above.

[142] See eg, *ibid*, [38] (Lord Hoffmann).

Lordships saw merit in the restriction as a matter of principle, a majority regarded it as incorrect as a matter of law.[143]

The Lords were probably correct to reject each of the three arguments as a matter of law. However, it is disappointing that in principle Class C greens are still capable of arising by mere lapse of time. The passage of the Commons Act 2006 presented Parliament with an opportunity to take on board the judicial criticisms of Class C greens and thereby bring the law more in line with the pattern. Unfortunately, however, the Act will have the opposite effect, by repealing the old legislative provisions relating to Classes A, B and C[144] and replacing them with an expanded version of Class C. Under the new provisions, as under Class C, a right to register land as a green arises automatically after inhabitants have indulged in lawful sports and pastimes on the site for at least 20 years. However, the timeframe in which the right to apply must be exercised is regulated by three different and alternative rules.

The locals will succeed under the first rule if they continue to use the land right up until the time of application.[145] This rule is almost an exact replica of Class C and puts onto a clear statutory footing the House of Lords' decision in *Oxfordshire CC*, which decided that for Class C, the long use must continue up until the time of application. Under the second rule, the locals are given a two-year grace period.[146] If their use of the land ceases after the Commons Act 2006 comes into force, they have two years in which they are entitled to register the land as a green. This provision is more generous to the inhabitants than the first. The third rule is potentially more generous still to the inhabitants: if they have ceased to use the land before the commencement of the Act, they are given five years after this cessation in which to apply for registration.[147] However, the third rule does not apply to certain land where its registration as a green would frustrate an ongoing development.[148] For land to be exempt from registration under the third method, planning permission must have been granted before 23 June 2006; construction work must have also started pursuant to the planning permission before that date; and the land must have become, or would become, permanently unusable for recreational activities by the public as a result. Because the exemption from registration is very narrow, the number of plots of land that will qualify are likely to be few in number.

---

[143] *Ibid* (Lords Hoffmann, Rodger and Walker). Lord Scott dissented; Baroness Hale refused to decide the point but expressed 'considerable sympathy' with Lord Scott's view: [145].
[144] Sched 6, Part I.
[145] S 15(2).
[146] S 15(3).
[147] S 15(4).
[148] S 15(5).

The combined effect of the three new rules will be to render it even easier to register a green after 20 years' use than it is under the current regime.

This effect will, however, be softened in one small respect. Under the current regime, it is possible for the owner of a registered green to apply to the Secretary of State for it to be deregistered but only on condition that exchange land is provided in return.[149] The minister takes into account the interests of all relevant parties when determining the application. The same is true under the new legislation, save for the fact that where the land sought to be deregistered is under 200 square metres in area, the owner will be able to apply for deregistration without having to provide land in exchange.[150] In such cases, the consequences of having one's land registered as a green might appear to be less severe than under the current regime. However, this appearance is misleading, for the fact that the owner of a small green provides no exchange land might count against his application for deregistration.[151]

On balance, the Commons Act provisions lie even further outside the pattern than Class C currently does. It is regrettable that Parliament missed the opportunity to contract the Class C doctrine and thereby bring it in line with the pattern.[152] Furthermore, the changes relating to greens are inconsistent with the provision in the Act that prevents commons from arising by the effluxion of time.

It would have been preferable for Parliament to acknowledge that factors other than long use, such as planning rules, ought to be relevant in determining whether public rights are created. There are hints at the relevance of planning law in the narrow exception in the third rule. However, it would have been more appropriate for the Act to have taken account of planning law more generally.

The third doctrine that falls outside the pattern is the law of limitation. Through limitation, an owner is not just deprived of some rights to enjoy the land or chattel, but deprived of everything. According to the pattern, one would expect the mere effluxion of time not to have such an effect. The rules are clear, however, that long possession suffices. But even though the doctrine lies outside the pattern, it can probably be justified. There is a strong public interest in land and chattels being marketable and their title certain. Limitation furthers this public interest by making certain, after the

---

[149]   Inclosure Act 1845, s 147.
[150]   Commons Act 2006, s 16.
[151]   *Ibid*, s 16(7).
[152]   During debate in the House of Commons Standing Committee, one member pointed out the inconsistency between the ways in which greens might arise and the fragile nature of the presumption of a public right of way. Ultimately, however, it was assumed that long use should of itself be sufficient to create a green. See HC Standing Committee D, cols 29 and 35–6 (25 April 2006).

limitation period has elapsed, that the current possessor has the best title.[153] The pattern can be seen to justifiably cede to this overriding public interest.

When title is registered, however, the public interest in certainty of title is satisfied by the register. Depriving the owner of title is no longer justified by this particular public interest. Therefore, one would expect that rules that deprive the registered owner of any rights should adhere to the pattern. And indeed this is the case today under the Land Registration Act 2002, which renders it difficult for a squatter to acquire title to register through mere long use. This should be contrasted with the position under the old regime for registered land, which employed the limitation mechanism. Under that system, long use, without more, operated to transfer the rights of beneficial enjoyment from the registered proprietor to the squatter.[154] The old regime did not adhere to the pattern.

Reasons for Adopting the Pattern

For two broad reasons, it would be advantageous to adopt the pattern and to bring the remaining outlying doctrines, unless justifiable in their own right, into line with it. First, adoption of the pattern would lead to a clearer, more rational and consistent body of rules. At the moment, like cases are not always treated alike. Identifying and following the pattern would help to draw the fragments of the law together and allow inconsistencies to be removed. This would be a significant improvement to the current position.

There is, however, a more pressing reason for bringing the law in line with the pattern. In its current state, part of the law might be incompatible with the European Convention on Human Rights (ECHR). The owner of land or a chattel is necessarily affected when someone acquires a property right through long use. The Human Rights Act 1998, which incorporates the ECHR, offers potential protection to the owner's rights in two respects. The Convention provides for the right to respect for one's home (Article 8) and protection against the deprivation and control of use of one's property (Article 1 of the First Protocol). Article 8 applies only to those cases in which long use deprives someone of their home; Article 1 of the First

---

[153] See Law Com 254, note 23 above, paras 10.5–10.10; and M Dockray, 'Why Do We Need Adverse Possession?' [1985] *Conv* 272. The difference in limitation periods between land (12 years) and chattels (6 years) can probably also be justified on the basis either that title to land, being generally more valuable than chattels, should command a greater level of protection; or that title to land is more easily discoverable, therefore the certainty of title conferred by limitation provisions is less pressing.

[154] Limitation Act 1980, ss 15 and 17; Land Registration Act 1925, s 75. After 12 years' adverse possession, the registered proprietor was deemed to hold the title on trust for the squatter.

Protocol applies to all property owners and is the more important article for the purposes of this chapter. Prima facie, it will apply whenever long use deprives a owner of some of his or her rights, for example by adverse possession, or when long use serves to control the type of use to which the property is put, for example when the land is registered as a green. The protection of both of these ECHR rights is not absolute but qualified. An infringement will generally only be permitted if it is sanctioned by national law, is in the public interest and crucially, is proportionate to the legitimate end pursued.

If any of the rules on long use are found to infringe the ECHR, the impact could be significant. For example, whenever legislation is found to be incompatible with the Convention, a judge, armed with the Human Rights Act 1998, must interpret the statute in a manner that is compatible with the Convention if that is possible;[155] if not possible, a declaration of incompatibility must be made.[156] Failing either of those two options, the person whose rights are infringed could take his case to the European Court of Human Rights (ECtHR).

Parts of the law on long use are potentially vulnerable to a human rights challenge. Indeed, one doctrine of long use has already been found to violate Article 1 of the First Protocol. The ECtHR decided in *Pye v United Kingdom* that rules of limitation, when applied to registered land, violated the Convention.[157] The facts of the case arose before the Land Registration Act 2002 came into force, when limitation provisions applied to both registered and unregistered land. The Court accepted that the deprivation of the owner's property rights was prima facie in the public interest. However, the deprivation was disproportionate to the legitimate aim of the doctrine and therefore infringed the ECHR. A 'fair balance' had not been struck between the owner's interests and the public interest in the existence of the rule. Significantly, in coming to this conclusion the court attached 'particular weight' to the fact that Parliament had considered it necessary to modify the law for registered land under the Land Registration Act 2002 in order to render it more difficult for squatters to acquire title.[158]

The pattern identified in this chapter is relevant here. First, the pattern itself seems to strike a sensible balance between the level of deprivation to the owner and the interest in long use creating rights. Indeed, under the pattern, the greater the owner's deprivation, the more difficult it is for long use to create rights. There might therefore be a strong correlation between the pattern and the level of permissible interference with another's property

---

[155]   Human Rights Act 1998, ss 2, 3 and 6.
[156]   *Ibid*, s 4.
[157]   Note 3 above. Note that the incompatibility was pre-empted by the High Court decision in *Beaulane*, note 3 above.
[158]   *Pye v UK*, note 3 above, [74].

rights under Article 1 of the First Protocol of the ECHR. It was suggested above that the application of limitation rules to registered land falls unjustifiably outside the pattern. It might be no coincidence therefore that that legal regime was found to be incompatible with the Convention in *Pye*.

Secondly, it is clear from *Pye* that the Strasbourg court was prepared to look at comparable domestic law doctrines when performing the proportionality test. If, as is suggested in this chapter, the pattern does form the backbone of domestic doctrines of long use, it might be appropriate, following *Pye*, to use the pattern as a yardstick whenever a particular long use doctrine is challenged under the Convention. This might mean that some of the doctrines that fall outside the pattern are incompatible with the Convention precisely because they fail to adhere to domestic law trends.

The creation of Class C greens was identified above as also being at odds with the pattern. It too has shown some signs of vulnerability in the face human rights challenges. In *Oxfordshire CC*, the Court of Appeal gave a very restrictive approach to the relevant legislation, partly out of concern that it might, on a wider interpretation, infringe the owner's rights under Article 1 of the First Protocol.[159] In the House of Lords, however, the doctrine was deemed inherently compatible with the Convention by Lord Hoffmann, with whom Lords Walker and Rodger concurred.[160] However, the point cannot be regarded as conclusively settled: first, the issue does not seem to have been fully argued before the Lords; secondly, Lord Hoffmann's reasoning was sparse and focused wholly on distinguishing *Pye* from the present facts rather than on the compatibility of Class C itself; and thirdly, Lord Scott, who was slightly more detailed in his analysis, considered that Article 1 of the First Protocol presented a 'potentially serious problem' *generally*, but on the very specific facts of the case, he agreed with Lord Hoffmann that there was no violation.[161] In the light of these three factors, and because it lies outside the pattern identified above, Class C might still be vulnerable to a Convention challenge.

---

[159] Note 75 above.
[160] Note 83 above, [58]-[59]. Note that Baroness Hale declined to comment on the issue.
[161] *Ibid*, [86]-[90]. He said that the local authority landowner would suffer no detriment, and therefore no infringement of Convention rights, upon the land being registered as a green. That was because the local authority retained a statutory power to re-appropriate the land for certain purposes.

V. CONCLUSION

At the start of this chapter, Lord Hoffmann is quoted as stating that any legal system should have rules to prevent the disturbance of long-established de facto enjoyment. It has been demonstrated that English law does indeed have such rules, and that these rules are very far-reaching. Their presence is, however, fragmented and often concealed beneath fictions. Although the current complex position can be explained by its history, it is desirable today to conceive time as a cohesive mode of acquisition in its own right. By drawing together and juxtaposing the fragments, time's role can be better understood, problems can more easily be seen and, most importantly, patterns emerge. These patterns can be drawn upon to guide the law towards a more principled and consistent approach.

In some respects, English law is slowly starting to recognise and scrutinise more openly time's creative effect. The approach taken to the reform of adverse possession in registered land is one example. However, further general recognition and analysis of long use is required. It is regrettable, for example, that the Commons Act 2006 failed to address the concerns surrounding Class C village greens. It is to be hoped that, in future reform proposals, the effect of the effluxion of time is acknowledged and properly understood.

9

An Adjudication Rule for Encroachment Disputes: Adverse Possession or a Building Encroachment Statute?

PAMELA O'CONNOR*

D
ISPUTES BETWEEN NEIGHBOURS over the position of boundaries are on the increase, due to closer settlement patterns and more intensive use of land. Discrepancies between the boundaries of land as occupied and the boundaries in the registered land descriptions are common and particularly likely to arise in new high-density residential developments.[1]

Boundary errors can be costly to rectify, generate damaging conflict between neighbours and impair the marketability of land. In an era of high land values and with the erosion of neighbourhood communities, landowners are increasingly unwilling to tolerate encroachments by adjoining landowners that diminish their landholdings. As land use becomes more closely regulated by planning controls, the existence of boundary disputes or an encroaching building creates uncertainty for purchasers, which tends to impair the marketability of both properties. Although disputes often involve very small areas of land, they occupy a disproportionate amount of the time for courts, local governments and complaints agencies.[2]

For all these reasons, the law needs to provide an appropriate rule or rules for adjudicating disputes over boundaries. English law has since 1833 used the rule of adverse possession to deal with possessory claims both by

---

* The author is indebted to Dr Elise Histed for her comments.
[1] Hansard HL vol 626 cols 1622–3 (19 Jul 2001), Baroness Scotland of Asthall, Parliamentary Secretary, Lord Chancellor's Department.
[2] 'Boundary disputes come before us with a regularity about which not all of us are happy considering what is at stake so often.' *Rimmer v Pearson* [1998] EWCA Civ 1847, 26 November 1998 (Gibson LJ).

squatters and by encroaching neighbours.[3] The Land Registration Act (LRA) (2002) introduced a variant of an adverse possession rule that differentiates between claims by neighbours adjacent to the property boundary and other claims against registered owners. An alternative rule, which appears not to have been considered by the Law Commission and HM Land Registry in their recent review of land registration law,[4] is the use of a building encroachment statute. This is a legislative scheme for discretionary adjustment of rights between neighbours in cases in which a building encroaches across a property boundary. Statutes of this type have a long history of successful operation in Canada, Australia and New Zealand.

This chapter compares and evaluates two approaches to the adjudication of boundary disputes: (1) the modified adverse possession rule introduced by the LRA (2002); and (2) a building encroachment statute coupled with a rule prohibiting the acquisition of title to the disputed land by adverse possession. It is argued that these two models are the best currently operating in land title registration systems in common law countries. This comparative study may provide some guidance for jurisdictions that are introducing systems of land registration (such as Hong Kong) or reviewing their rules for adverse possession and encroachment disputes.

I. THE PARAMETERS OF BOUNDARY DISPUTES

Boundary disputes between neighbouring landowners may raise two discrete legal questions that require different adjudicative processes. In a 'determination of boundaries' case, the question is the exact location of an original property boundary to which the land descriptions in the title register refers. In an 'encroachment' case, the question is whether a landowner (the 'encroaching owner') who has possessed or built upon a piece of land adjoining the boundary that lies within the registered landholding of a neighbour (the 'adjacent owner') thereby acquires or is permitted to acquire property rights to the piece of land (the 'boundary strip').

In practice, these questions are often conflated because 'possession is itself both title and evidence of title'. Long and unchallenged occupation is

---

[3] The Real Property Limitation Act (1833) abolished certain common law rules that prevented possession of part of a parcel being deemed to be adverse where the owner was in possession of the remainder. See S Jourdan, *Adverse Possession* (London, Butterworths LexisNexis, 2003) 23–33.

[4] Law Commission and HM Land Registry, 'Land Registration for the Twenty-first Century: A Conveyancing Revolution' (Law Com 271, 2001). See also Law Commision and HM Land Registry, 'Land Registration for the Twenty-first Century: A Consultative Document' (Law Com 254, 1998).

evidence that the land so occupied is that which the title confers, in the absence of original pegs or natural features determining the exact positioning of the boundaries to which the registered land description refers. And where a rule of adverse possession operates, the acquisition of rights by longstanding adverse possession of the boundary strip extinguishes the adjacent owner's title to it, making it unnecessary to determine the exact location of the original boundary.

Determination of Boundaries

Problems with boundary discrepancies occur under both the general boundaries and fixed boundaries methods of land description. England and Wales uses the general boundaries method, under which the location and boundaries of land are defined for purposes of the title register by reference to maps derived from the Ordnance Survey Map (a topographical map), which depicts permanent physical features such as hedges, party walls, fences, ditches and roads.[5] There are established presumptions as to where boundaries lie in relation to such features,[6] but otherwise the exact line of the boundary is left undefined.[7] The Registrar is empowered to determine the exact line of a boundary on application by the proprietor of a registered estate.[8]

Registered title systems derived from the Torrens model generally use the fixed boundaries method. On first registration, each parcel is surveyed by a licensed surveyor, and the boundaries are measured in metes and bounds from survey pegs and beacons emplaced in the ground. The parcel is registered with a full land description with reference to a plan of survey, which is deposited with the registry. Although Torrens boundaries are 'fixed' in this way, they are not guaranteed.[9] When there is disagreement as to the position of the parcel boundary, the measurements in the registered plan are not conclusive. Statutes commonly empower courts or a Registrar to determine the exact line of the boundary on application of a registered owner. The position of the boundary is treated as a question of fact, and the determination is made by reference to the survey measurements on the

---

[5] SR Simpson, *Land Law and Registration* (Cambridge, Cambridge University Press, 1976) 127; Scottish Law Commission, *Discussion Paper on Land Registration: Miscellaneous Issues*, DP 130 (2005) paras 2.1–2.10. (Scotland also uses general boundaries.)

[6] Jourdan, note 3 above, 563–4.

[7] Land Registration Act (2002) s 60(2) provides: 'A general boundary does not define the exact line of the boundary'. Simpson, note 7 above, 127

[8] Land Registration Act (2002) s 60 and Land Registration Rules (2003) No 1417, Part 10.

[9] Simpson observes that there is a common misconception that Torrens boundaries are guaranteed, due to confusion over the concept of 'fixed' boundaries: Simpson, note 7 above, 137.

ground.[10] When survey pegs or marks have been lost or displaced so that the boundary line of the original survey can no longer be ascertained, long and unchallenged occupation is taken as evidencing the location of the true boundary.[11]

Adjustment of Boundaries

Under both fixed and general boundary systems, landowners can be mistaken as to the exact position of a boundary. Errors occur when landowners construct fences and other structures on what they believe to be a boundary, without undertaking a survey to check the location of the boundaries. Sometimes the adjacent owner shares the mistake or is unaware that a neighbour is encroaching upon his or her land. The existence of an encroachment may be discovered some time later when further improvements are made or when a purchaser of one of the properties discovers a boundary discrepancy on survey and makes requisitions on title.

Legal Consequences of an Encroachment

A landowner whose building encroaches upon neighbouring land, whether by projecting onto or under the land or by overhanging it, is in an unenviable legal position. The adjacent landowner may either accept the encroachment as an accretion to his or her land or exercise the remedies provided by law.[12] The encroachment is actionable as a trespass and, if damage can be shown, as a nuisance.[13] The adjacent owner may sue for mesne profits for the use of his or her land, damages and an injunction for removal of the encroaching portion of the building.[14] In clear and simple cases that do not justify resort to legal proceedings, or in emergencies when it is necessary to protect the property rights of an adjacent owner, he or she

---

[10] *National Trustees, Executors and Agency Co of A'Asia Ltd v Hassett* [1907] VLR 404; *Leader v Beames* (2000) 1 Qd R 347; *Moore v Prentice* [1901] 20 NZLR 128; M Weir, 'The Uncertainty of Certain Boundaries' (2001) 9 *Australian Property Law Journal* 27, 35–6; Law Reform Commission of British Columbia, 'Report on Limitations (Project No 6): Part II—General' (1974) 50–1.

[11] *National Trustees, Executors and Agency Co of A'Asia Ltd v Hassett* [1907] VLR 404, 412 (Cussen J); Weir, *ibid*, 36.

[12] *Harrow London Borough Council v Donoghue* [1993] NPC 49 (EWCA).

[13] *Burton v Winters* [1993] 1 WLR 1077 (EWCA).

[14] For discussion of the remedies, see K and SF Gray, *Elements of Land Law*, 3rd edn (London, Butterworths, 2001) 147.

may be entitled to resort to self-help to remove the encroachment, provided that the act of demolition is not disproportionate to the loss suffered by the adjacent owner.[15]

In many common law jurisdictions, courts have discretionary power to refuse a mandatory injunction for the removal of the encroachment and award damages instead.[16] By exercising this discretion, a court allows an encroachment to continue subject to payment.[17] Since this can have the practical effect of a forced exchange,[18] the courts have laid down principles for the exercise of the discretion. In *Shelfer v City of London Electric Lighting Co*,[19] Smith LJ said that damages may be awarded in lieu of an injunction when the injury to the plaintiff's right is small, capable of being quantified and adequately compensated by a small monetary payment, and it would be oppressive to the defendant to grant an injunction in the circumstances of the case.[20]

All the circumstances of a case have to be considered in assessing whether it would be oppressive to the defendant to grant an injunction.[21] The extent to which the defendant has acted reprehensibly in trespassing upon the plaintiff's land is a major consideration, but is not determinative. In *Jaggard v Sawyer*, Sir Thomas Bingham MR said that 'it would weigh against a finding of oppression if the defendants had acted in blatant and calculated disregard of the plaintiff's rights.'[22] In *Ketley v Gooden*, Pill LJ (Hirst LJ agreeing) rejected the proposition of law that, irrespective of other considerations, a mandatory injunction must be granted when the encroachment resulted from a reckless disregard of the plaintiff's rights.[23]

Other relevant circumstances include whether removal of the encroachment would subject the defendant to a loss out of all proportion to the damage to the plaintiff.[24] Delay by the plaintiff in applying for relief may be a factor disentitling him or her to an injunction.[25] Through the application of these principles, the courts have in a number of cases allowed encroachments to continue by awarding damages in lieu of mandatory injunctions.[26]

---

[15] *Burton v Winters* [1993] 1 WLR 1077, 1080–2.
[16] The power derives from statutes adopting the reforms made by Lord Cairn's Act (Chancery Amendment Act (1868) (21 & 22 Vict c 27)) s 2.
[17] *Jaggard v Sawyer* [1995] 1 WLR 269, 286 (Millett LJ).
[18] *Shelfer v City of London Electric Lighting Co* [1895] 1 Ch 287, 315–16 (Lindley LJ); *Cowper v Laidler* [1903] 2 Ch 337, 341 (Buckley J).
[19] [1895] 1 Ch 287.
[20] *Ibid*, 322–3.
[21] *Jaggard v Sawyer* [1995] 1 WLR 268, 288–9 (Millett LJ).
[22] *Ibid*, 283.
[23] *Ketley v Gooden* (1997) 73 P & CR 303 (EWCA).
[24] *Jaggard v Sawyer* [1995] 1 WLR 268, 288.
[25] *Ibid*, 287. The plaintiff may be disentitled to relief by laches, acquiescence or estoppel.
[26] See eg, *Jaggard v Sawyer* [1995] 1 WLR 269; *Burton v Winters* [1993] 1 WLR 1077; *Ketley v Gooden* (1997) 73 P & CR 303 (EWCA); *Griffiths v Kingsley-Stubbs* [1987] CLY

II. APPROACHES TO ENCROACHMENT DISPUTES

Common law jurisdictions generally use one of three generic approaches to encroachment disputes, or a combination of them.[27] The first is a 'prohibition rule': no adjustment of the location of the boundary is permitted by reason of occupation, possession or encroachment subsequent to first registration of the parcel. The adjacent owner is *prima facie* entitled at any time to exercise his or her remedies against the encroaching neighbour. The second approach is an 'adverse possession rule', by which the encroacher, after the expiration of a statutory limitation period, is allowed to acquire title by adverse possession or to apply for registration as the new owner of the boundary strip. The third approach is a 'building encroachment' statute, which allows for discretionary adjustment of property rights in cases in which buildings encroach across boundary lines onto the lands of adjacent owners. Building encroachment laws are usually combined with a rule prohibiting adverse possession, so that the statutory scheme provides the only avenue for obtaining an adjustment of boundaries (other than by agreement).[28]

Miceli and Sirmans argue that the law should seek to advance two policy objectives in dealing with disputes arising from boundary errors.[29] The first is to encourage landowners to avoid making boundary errors before they undertake a sunk investment by making improvements (the 'deterrence objective'). The second is to limit the costs of boundary errors once they have occurred (the 'cost minimisation objective').[30] Each of the three generic rules can be compared and evaluated by reference to their tendency to promote the two policy objectives. In the following pages I evaluate, first, the prohibition of adverse possession and, second, systems that allow

---

1227 (EWCA). In *Harrow London Borough Council v Donohue [1993] NPC 49* (EWCA) it was held that that a landowner who had been totally dispossessed of his land by an encroachment was entitled to a mandatory injunction as of right, but this proposition was doubted in *Feakins v Department for Environment Food and Rural Affairs* [2005] EWCA 1513, [203]–[204] (Parker LJ).

[27] MM Park, *The Effect of Adverse Possession on Part of a Registered Title Land Parcel* (University of Melbourne, PhD thesis, 2003) <http://eprints.unimelb.edu.au/////.pdf> accessed 17 November 2006, ch 3.5. As an example of the use of rules in combination, Nova Scotia allows adverse possession as to part parcel claims not exceeding 20% of the area of the parcel, and a prohibition rule for all other claims: Land Registration Act, SNS (2001) c 6, s 75.

[28] This is the case with all the statutes except that of Western Australia, which does allow an encroaching owner to acquire title to the boundary strip by adverse possession (an example of using rules in combination).

[29] TJ Miceli and C F Sirmans, 'An Economic Theory of Adverse Possession' (1995) 5 *International Review of Law and Economics* 161, 161–5 and 170.

[30] *Ibid*. The names assigned to the objectives are my own.

boundary adjustment through adverse possession. I then evaluate provisions of Schedule 6 of the English LRA (2002), which combines these two approaches and compare them with the third approach, namely the building encroachment statutes.

Prohibition of Adverse Possession

Some jurisdictions prohibit or substantially restrict adverse possession claims to part parcels on the boundary while allowing claims to whole parcels.[31] Common justifications are to discourage trifling disputes over small pieces of land;[32] to prevent subdivision of land by adverse possession, which might undermine planning controls;[33] and to p&romote security of transaction by making the register and its land descriptions more authoritative.[34]

   The prohibition rule serves the deterrence objective, providing a strong incentive for landowners to avoid boundary errors prior to investing in improvements. As a deterrence measure, the rule produces 'overkill', since it visits the same disadvantages on the owner who created the encroachment and his or her successors in title, who may be blameless. At the same time, the rule does little to serve the cost minimisation objective. The adjoining landowner is entitled at any time to demand that improvements be removed, which may impose substantial costs and losses upon the encroaching landowner. Demolition of encroaching parts of buildings or footings could impair the stability of buildings on adjacent land, or contravene planning or building laws.[35] Restoring title boundaries may be prohibitively costly in some cases, as Baroness Scotland of Asthall explained in parliamentary debates on the Land Registration Bill (2001):

> One envisages, for example, an estate with 20 houses, where all 20 houses are one foot in the wrong position. Although all 20 houses have got the direct proportions the owners thought that they were buying, the man or woman on

---

[31] Land Transfer Amendment Act (1963) (NZ) s 21(e); Land Title Act (1994) (Qld) s 98; Real Property Act (1900) (NSW) s 45D; Land Titles Act (1980) (Tas) s 138Y (restricts adverse possession claims that result in 'sub-minimum lots').

[32] See Lord Goodhart's speech in support of his motion to amend the Land Registration Bill (2001) by deleting Sched 6, para 5(4): Hansard HL cols 1621–4 (19 July 2001). The Ontario Law Reform Commission was concerned that adverse possession 'would tend to stir up conflict': Ontario Law Reform Commission, 'Report on Land Registration' (Dept of Justice, 1971) 45.

[33] See, eg, the Tasmanian statute that restricts claims by adverse possession resulting in 'sub-minimum lots': Land Titles Act (1980) s 138Y; Park, note 29 above, 160.

[34] Registrar-General's Office of New South Wales, 'Working Paper on Application to Torrens Title Land of Laws Relating to Limitation of Actions' (1976) 4.

[35] See eg, *Droga v Proprietor of Strata Plan 51722* (1996) 93 LGERA 120 (NSWLEC), where beams supporting a six-storey building were embedded in the wall of a building adjacent to the boundary.

the end could say 'You have got a bit of my land'. To get his or her bit of land back, everyone would have to perform a very interesting dance.[36]

To avoid the loss that the adjacent owner ('A') can impose upon him or her, the encroaching owner ('E') will have to negotiate with A to buy or lease the boundary strip or to acquire an easement over it. The boundary strip is worth more to E than to A, because E's valuation is inflated by the investment that he or she has made in the building. The sunk cost represents a 'quasi-rent' that A may try to extract by holding out for a price in excess of his or her own valuation.[37] A rule that prohibits adjustment of boundaries other than by agreement facilitates rent-seeking behaviour by A, which tends to increase the costs of boundary errors once they have occurred.

The courts can in some circumstances provide limited relief to E by refusing to grant A a mandatory injunction for demolition of the encroachment. If A has taken advantage of E's inadvertence or carelessness and has attempted to extort money from him or her, the courts may find that it would be oppressive to grant A an injunction.[38] Provided, additionally, that the injury to A's rights is small, quantifiable and capable of being adequately compensated by a small monetary amount, the court may award damages instead.[39]

The court's discretionary power to withhold a mandatory injunction is a constraint upon A's rent-seeking, but its powers are limited. The court can, in effect, permit E to continue encroaching on A's land, subject to payment of damages, but cannot order A to transfer the boundary strip to E or grant E a property right. The marketability of E's land may be impaired if he or she is unable to provide a purchaser with title to the whole of the area of land occupied by the buildings. E can acquire property rights over the boundary strip only through a negotiated transfer, in which A can hold out for a price that is inflated by the quasi-rent.

Allowing Boundary Adjustment through Adverse Possession

Under an adverse possession rule, the expiry of the limitation period abruptly reverses the legal position of the parties. Until the statutory limitation period expires, the legal position of A and E are the same as under the prohibition rule (outlined in the previous paragraphs). All is

[36] Hansard HL col 1623 (19 July 2001), in support of an argument for the necessity of retaining an adverse possession rule in the LRA (2002).
[37] Miceli & Sirmans, note 31 above, 163; TW Merrill, 'Property Rules, Liability Rules and Adverse Possession' (1984–85) 79 *Northwestern University Law Review* 1131; A Bell and Gideon Parchomovsky, 'Pliability Rules' (2002) 101 *Michigan Law Review* 1, 58 and fn 199.
[38] *Jaggard v Sawyer* [1995] 1 WLR 269, 288 (Millett LJ).
[39] *Shelfer v City of London Electric Lighting Co* [1895] 1 Ch 297, 322–3 (Smith LJ).

changed when the statutory period expires or (depending on the terms of the rule) when the title register is amended upon an application by E. A's rights over the boundary strip are extinguished, and E gains the best title (or indeed a registered title).

Miceli and Sirmans theorise that the 'sudden death' aspect of adverse possession represents an attempt to balance two competing objectives—to discourage E from making boundary errors, and to encourage A to correct boundary errors promptly and thereby mitigate E's loss.[40] The mitigation principle assumes that E's sunk investment in the boundary strip (and so, the quasi-rent) is likely to increase the longer the error stands uncorrected.[41] The balance of objectives is achieved by allowing A a limited period of time in which to discover the encroachment and recover the boundary strip. As a result, both objectives are imperfectly achieved. Rent-seeking by A is still possible during the limitation period, and E may ultimately get to keep the boundary strip on expiry of the limitation period even though he or she may have encroached deliberately or carelessly.[42] Since small encroachments are difficult for A to detect, E might take a chance that A will fail to notice and object before the limitation period expires.

The adverse possession rule is notable for the considerations that it ignores. Under the English doctrine of adverse possession, a claim can succeed whether the original trespass was honest or dishonest.[43] Deliberate encroachers may eventually succeed in annexing boundary strips, while a landowner who trespasses through error can be required to remove an encroachment if the limitation period has not yet expired. Economic commentators have questioned the absence of a requirement of good faith in the law of adverse possession.[44] The law has no policy interest in upholding the claims of those who bypass the market and intentionally or carelessly take possession of the land of another.

The rule of adverse possession also fails to distinguish between adverse possessors who have made a sunk investment in improvements and those who have not. Although in the case of a boundary strip especially strong evidence of adverse possession may be required,[45] there is no requirement

---

[40]   Miceli and Sirmans, note 31 above, 161–5 and 170.
[41]   *Ibid*, 163.
[42]   *Ibid*, 163–4.
[43]   Jourdan, note 3 above, paras 3.24–3.26. Note that the LRA (2002) Sched 6, paras 3–6, discussed below, adapts the adverse possession rule to exclude deliberate or careless encroachers.
[44]   See, eg, Merrill, note 39 above, 1134; TJ Miceli, *Economics of the Law* (New York, Oxford, Oxford University Press, 1997) 132; and Miceli and Sirmans, note 31 above, 161–2.
[45]   *Rimmer v Pearson* (2000) 79 P & CR D21, D22 (Robert Walker LJ); Gray and Gray, note 16 above, 270, n 11. The courts will require evidence, in particular, that the acts of possession occurred on the boundary strip and not on the surrounding land: *West Bank Estates Ltd v Arthur* [1967] 1 AC 665, 679; *Williams v Underwood* (1981) 45 P and CR 235.

that the acts of possession include the construction of permanent improvements. The omission is puzzling, for without lasting improvements by E, there are no quasi-rents to obstruct bargaining and no opportunities for A to magnify the cost of E's error by engaging in rent-seeking behaviour.

Notwithstanding these doctrinal 'blind spots', a possible justification for using an adverse possession rule is the fact that its very simplicity reduces the cost of adjudicating disputes and simplifies the task of purchasers in identifying who owns the land. Adverse possession claims are determined by reference to observable conduct and the reckoning of time periods, rather than discretionary considerations or disputable facts such as mistake or good faith. In practice, many adverse possession claims raise significant dispute about questions of fact, and adjudication is often complicated by counter-claims alleging agreements or estoppel by acquiescence. Nevertheless, it seems that the use of an adverse possession rule for boundaries does provides some confidence to the market that the legal boundaries of the land correspond to the boundaries of the land as actually occupied, so that 'what you see is what you get'.[46] This is perhaps the most tenable justification for using the rule.

III. THE LRA (2002): A CONDITIONAL VETO RULE OF ADVERSE POSSESSION

The Land Registration Act (2002) introduced a new rule of adverse possession that makes separate provision for disputes over boundary strips. The rule is of a kind that Park calls generically a 'veto' rule, which allows registered title to be extinguished only by alteration of the register following an application by the adverse possessor, and gives the registered owner a right to object to and effectively to veto the application.[47] In the form in which the rule was originally used in Australia, the registered owner's right of veto was absolute and unqualified.[48] In their proposals for the LRA (2002), the Law Commission and HM Land Registry recognised that the veto rule could be modified so that the registered proprietor would have an effective veto against some adverse possession claims but not others.[49] In this way it would be possible to filter the applications to register an adverse possessor, without altering the content of the common law rules of adverse possession.

---

[46] MM Park and I P Williamson, 'The Need to Provide for Boundary Adjustments in a Registered Title Land System' (2003) 48(1) *The Australian Surveyor* 50, 51; Park, note 29 above, 266.

[47] Park, note 29 above, ch 6.3.2.

[48] The original veto rule was introduced in South Australia and later adopted by New Zealand and Queensland, although Queensland repealed its provision.

[49] Law Comn No 271, note 4 above, para 2.73, fn 146 indicates that the starting point was the Queensland provision, which was then modified.

Schedule 6 of the LRA (2002) uses a conditional form of the veto rule as the basis for a set of provisions that: (1) confines the circumstances in which a registered proprietor can veto a first application by an adverse possessor to be registered; and (2) allows subsequent applications in all cases to succeed when the registered owner has failed within a further two years to take action to recover the land from the adverse possessor.

The scheme of Schedule 6, so far as it relates to boundary disputes and omitting transitional provisions, may be summarised as follows. Under s 15 of the Limitation Act (1980), the limitation period for recovery of land is disapplied to registered land, so that registered title can no longer be extinguished by expiry of time but only by the registration of the adverse possessor as the proprietor.[50] A person may apply to be registered as proprietor of an estate in land if he or she has been in adverse possession for the previous ten years either personally or through a predecessor in title.[51] A person is deemed to be in adverse possession if, but for section 96 (which disapplies the Limitation Act), a period of limitation under section 15 of that Act would have run in his or her favour.[52] So far, there is no alteration of the common law requirements of adverse possession, which the applicant must satisfy.

The next set of provisions applies the filter. The registrar must give notice of the application to the registered proprietor and certain other interested parties. A person given notice by the registrar may require that the application be dealt with under paragraph 5 (the 'conditional veto' provisions). Under those provisions, the applicant is only entitled to be registered as the new proprietor if one of three conditions apply.[53] The first is that 'it would be unconscionable because of an equity by estoppel for the registered proprietor to seek to dispossess the applicant', and the circumstances are such that the applicant ought to be registered.[54] The second is that the applicant is for some other reason entitled to be registered.[55] The two conditions, which apply to any application by an adverse possessor, effectively nullify the registered owner's veto when the applicant is entitled to be registered as owner of the estate or interest on grounds other than adverse possession.

The third condition narrows the registered owner's power to veto an application relating to land adjacent to the adverse possessor's land.[56] Most such claims relate to part parcels adjoining the boundary ('boundary strips'). If the exact boundary has not been determined by the registrar, and

[50] LRA (2002) s 96, Sched 6, para 9(1).
[51] *Ibid*, paras 1 and 11(1)(2).
[52] *Ibid*, para 11(1) and (3).
[53] *Ibid*, para 5(1).
[54] *Ibid*, para 5(2).
[55] *Ibid*, para 5(3).
[56] *Ibid*, paras 1 and 3–5.

the applicant (or any predecessor in title) has been in adverse possession for at least ten years in the reasonable belief that the land belonged to him or her,[57] the registered owner will be unable to veto a first application for registration by the adverse possessor.[58] The registered owner must subsequently recover the land from the adverse possessor, or a further application for registration after two years will succeed.[59]

A questionable aspect of the third condition is that it is confined to cases in which the exact line of the boundary has not been determined by the registrar.[60] The power to determine a boundary arises under Part 10 of the Land Registration Rules (2003).[61] Once the boundary has been determined in this way, it is noted on the register to each affected parcel.[62] The Law Commission and HM Land Registry explain that when boundaries have been fixed in this way, 'then the register is conclusive as to the boundary and the justification for the third condition is, therefore, absent'.[63] They suggested that the determination procedure might be invoked 'where the legal boundaries and its apparent physical boundaries do not coincide'.[64]

This approach seems to conflate determination of boundaries with adjustment of boundaries under an adverse possession rule. The purpose of the determination procedure is to clarify the often imprecise location of general boundaries. While longstanding and unchallenged occupation may be evidence of the location of the boundary, the Rules do not empower the registrar, when making a determination, to adjust the legal boundaries to take account of physical possession.

A further difficulty is that the Act precludes adjustment of boundaries at any time after boundaries have been determined. In effect, the titles affected by a determination are placed thereafter under an absolute veto rule. Park and Williamson have persuasively argued that systems of registered land need to provide a mechanism for adjustment of boundaries to take account of changes in occupation over time, and that the LRA (2002) is inadequate in this respect.[65]

---

[57]   *Ibid*, para 5(4)(c) appears to allow that, provided the period of adverse possession has continued to the date of the application, the ten years of reasonable belief can end on an earlier date.

[58]   *Ibid*, para 5(4).

[59]   *Ibid*, para 6.

[60]   *Ibid*, para 5(4)(b).

[61]   The enabling provision is s 60(3) of the LRA (2002). The Law Commission and HM Land Registry report that the procedure under the Land Registration Rules (1925) r 276 was used extremely rarely, but they expect that under the new Rules, it will become much more common: Law Comn 271, note 4 above, paras 9.10–9.11 and 14.49.

[62]   Land Registration Rules (2003) r 120.

[63]   Law Comn 271, note 4 above, para 14.49.

[64]   *Ibid*.

[65]   Park & Williamson, note 48 above, 56–7. Park predicts that, because the scheme is too restrictive, building encroachment laws may be necessary to provide for adjustment of boundaries: Park, note 29 above, 150.

Compared to a 'pure' rule of adverse possession, the conditional veto regime in Schedule 6 strengthens the incentive to avoid making boundary errors. No period of adverse possession will relieve the liability of a dishonest or careless trespasser, so long as the registered proprietor objects. But the rule does nothing to limit the costs of boundary errors once they have occurred. It provides no relief to a landowner who has within the previous ten years invested in a building that in fact encroaches across a boundary line, even if the encroachment resulted from an honest and reasonable mistake about the location of the boundary. Rent-seeking by the adjacent owner is still possible for at least ten years after the encroachment commences—and in some cases indefinitely.

Purchasers of land from which an encroachment emanates may never be in a position to invoke the third condition, even if they bought in ignorance of the existence of the encroachment. If the purchaser first learned of it or ought reasonably to have known of it within ten years of purchase,[66] he or she will not be able to rely solely on his or her own period of adverse possession with 'reasonable belief' that the boundary strip was his or hers. The purchaser will additionally need to prove that his or her predecessor in title was in adverse possession of the boundary strip in the reasonable belief that it belonged to him or her.[67] Otherwise, the registered owner will be able to veto the application to register.[68] The purchaser's liability for the encroachment, and that of his or her successors, can continue indefinitely.

IV. BUILDING ENCROACHMENT LAWS

Boundary encroachment laws in Australia originated with the Encroach-ment of Buildings Act (1922) (NSW), a model that has been adopted in three other Australian jurisdictions. A differently worded provision is used

---

[66] In cases decided under building encroachment laws, Australian and New Zealand authority indicates that it is not necessarily unreasonable to build without survey, when other steps are taken to locate the true boundary: *Collins v Kennedy* [1972] NZLR 939, 941 (NZSC); *Attard v Canal* (unreported, [2005] NSWLEC 222), [54]–[56]. Local conveyancing and building practices will affect the assessment of what is reasonable.

[67] Sched 6, para 5(4)(c) cannot have been intended to mean what is says. Literally, it requires that *either* the applicant *or* any predecessor in title have been in adverse possession for ten years with the required belief. This follows literally from the words '(or any predecessor in title)'. It seems unlikely that Parliament intended that an applicant who has at no time held the required belief could satisfy para 5(4)(c) on the basis that his or her predecessor did. It may be that the 'or' is a shorthand way of saying 'or, if there has been another owner, or other owners, during the ten-year period, the applicant and that other owner or those other owners'.If this interpretation is correct, an applicant who has been in adverse possession for less than ten years with the requisite belief can add his or her period to that of a predecessor, to make up the required ten years.

[68] Assuming that the other two conditions in para 5 of Schedule 6 are inapplicable.

in Western Australia and New Zealand.[69] Three Canadian provinces have an encroachment statute of a type known generically as a 'statute of unskillful survey', based on an Ontario provision enacted in 1818.[70] Three other Canadian provinces use 'mistaken improver' statutes to provide relief to persons who make improvements on another's land under a mistake as to boundaries.[71] For purposes of clarity, the discussion below focuses on the New South Wales provision and its analogues in Queensland, South Australia and the Northern Territory.[72]

The New South Wales statute was enacted to relieve against difficulties created by a rule prohibiting the acquisition of title to registered land by adverse possession.[73] There was a perceived need to control rent-seeking by adjacent landowners in cases in which buildings encroached across boundaries through inadvertence of the encroaching owner or through the fault of his or her predecessor in title. At the time, boundary errors were common, and it was widely recognised that in many cases the fault lay with deficiencies in early surveys to which registered land descriptions referred. In his Second Reading Speech, the Minister identified the mischief to which the measure was directed:

> [A]lthough encroachments may arise without wrong intent through human error, yet when they are discovered human avarice takes advantage of the opportunity, with the result that innocent men are blackmailed, in respect of an inch or two of land to an unconscionable extent.[74]

Accordingly, the Act is regarded as remedial legislation and is given a 'fair, large and liberal interpretation'.[75] There is no presumption against granting relief to an encroaching owner or allowing an encroachment to continue.

---

[69]   Property Law Act (1952) (NZ) s 129; Property Law Act (1969) (WA) s 122.

[70]   British Columbia: Property Law Act (1996) (RSBC) c 377, s 36; Manitoba: Law of Property Act, CCSM, c L90, s 28; Nova Scotia: Land Registration Act (2001) (SNS) c 6, s 76(3). The provisions are modelled on an Ontario provision dating from 1818 that was repealed in 1911. The provisions are very brief. The courts have developed principles for the exercise of their discretion, the 'Vineberg' principles, drawn from cases interpreting 'mistaken improver' statutes: see *Taylor v Hoskin* 2003 BCSC 1843, 17 RPR (4th) 123, para 91 (BCSC).

[71]   The provinces are Saskatchewan, Alberta and Ontario. Mistaken improver statutes are primarily remedial in purpose. There are difficulties in applying them to encroachment cases, since encroaching buildings are usually a detriment rather than a benefit to the adjacent landowner.

[72]   The relevant provisions are: Encroachment of Buildings Act (1922) (NSW); Property Law Act (1974) (Qld) Pt 11, Divn 1; Encroachment of Buildings Act (NT); Encroachments Act (1944) (SA).

[73]   New South Wales subsequently legislated to allow adverse possession as to whole parcels only: Real Property Act (1900) (NSW) s 45D.

[74]   NSW *Hansard*, 13 September 1922 (Mr Ley), as cited in *Googoorewon Pty Ltd v Amatek Ltd* (1991) 25 NSWLR 330, 333–4 (NSWCA, Mahoney JA).

[75]   *Clarke v Wilkie* (1977) 17 SASR 134, 139 (Wells J); *Hardie v Cuthbert* (1988) 65 LGRA 5, 6 (Young J); *Boed Pty Ltd v Seymour* (1989) 15 NSWLR 715, 719 (Bryson J):

The Act makes separate provision for the determination, marking and recording of existing boundaries (section 9) and for relief in respect of encroachments (section 3). These are discrete procedures, and the making of an application or order under section 9 does not preclude an application or order under section 3 in respect of the same boundary.[76] In some cases it may be necessary or desirable to have the existing legal boundary determined in order to establish whether an encroachment exists and what the extent of it is.

Relief in Cases of Encroachment

An 'encroachment' for the purposes of the Act is defined to mean an encroachment by a building, including an overhang of any part or an intrusion of any part in or upon the soil.[77] 'Encroachment' means an encroachment over a boundary line between contiguous parcels of land and does not include an improvement that stands entirely within one parcel of land.[78] 'Building' is undefined in the legislation and has been given an expansive and purposive construction. It is an encroachment that is man-made, of a substantial and permanent character.[79] It need not be an enclosed structure such as an encroaching garage or shed but rather can include a concrete driveway,[80] a swimming pool,[81] a tennis court fence[82] or a carport.[83]

Bunney v State of South Australia (2000) 77 SASR 319, para 9 (Debelle J); *Googoorewon Pty Ltd v Amatek Ltd* (1991) 176 CLR 471, 477 (HCA); *Re Melden Homes (No 2) Pty Ltd's Land* [1976] Qd R 79, 81; *Executive Seminars Pty Ltd v Peck* (unreported, [2001] WASC 229, 29 August 2001), paras 154–6.

[76] *Cf* the contrary position assumed by the LRA (2002) Sched 6, para 5(4)(b).

[77] Encroachment of Buildings Act (1922) (NSW) s 2.

[78] *Googoorewon Pty Ltd v Amatek Ltd* (1991) 176 CLR 471, 477 (HCA). A similar view is taken of the New Zealand provision: *Blackburn v Gemmell* [1981] 1 NZCPR 389 (NZHC).

[79] *Ex p Van Achtenberg* [1984] 1 Qd R 160, 162 (SCQ); *Ward v Griffiths* (1987) 9 NSWLR 458, 460.

[80] *Ward v Griffiths* (1987) 9 NSWLR 458 (NSWSC); *Clarke v Wilkie* (1977) 17 SASR 134 (SASC); *Shadbolt v Wise* (2003) 126 LGERA 59 (QCA); *Gladwell v Steen* (2000) 77 SASR 310 (SASC).

[81] *Cuthbert v Hardie* (1989) 17 NSWLR 321 (NSWCA); *Shadbolt v Wise* (2003) 126 LGERA 59 (QCA).

[82] *Uechtritz v Watson* (1993) 6 BPR 13,582 (NSWSC).

[83] *Gladwell v Steen* (2000) 77 SASR 310 (SCSA).

Either the 'encroaching owner'[84] or the 'adjacent owner' may apply to the court[85] for relief in respect of an encroachment.[86] Since 'owner', by extended definition, means anyone entitled to an estate in freehold in possession, whether legal or equitable and including a registered mortgagee in possession,[87] any such person can apply for relief. The court is empowered to order: (1) the payment of compensation to the adjacent owner; (2) the conveyance, transfer or lease of the subject land to the encroaching owner;[88] (3) the grant to the encroaching owner of any estate or interest, easement, right or privilege in relation to the boundary strip ('the subject land');[89] and (4) the removal of the encroachment.

The court is empowered to grant or refuse relief as it deems proper in the circumstances of the case.[90] The Act sets out a non-exhaustive list of discretionary considerations that the court may take into account, including: whether the application is made by the encroaching owner or the adjacent owner;[91] the situation and value of the subject land; the nature and extent of the encroachment; the character of the encroaching building and the purposes for which it may be used; the loss and damage that has been or will be incurred by the adjacent owner; the loss and damage that would be incurred by the encroaching owner if he or she were required to remove the encroachment; and the circumstances in which the encroachment was made.[92] Other relevant considerations identified in the cases

---

[84] '"Encroaching owner" means the owner of land contiguous to the boundary beyond which an encroachment extends': s 2. Note that the term includes the owner for the time being, who might not be the person who erected the encroachment.

[85] The Land and Environment Court of New South Wales, or the Supreme Court of the relevant State or Territory.

[86] Encroachment of Buildings Act (1922) (NSW) s 3(1).

[87] *Ibid*, s 2.

[88] Only the land over which the encroachment extends can be the subject of such an order. The court has no power to order the transfer of any additional land as curtilage, or to regularise the boundary line: *Tallon v Proprietors of Metropolitan Towers Building Units Plan No5157* [1997] 1 Qd R 102, 107 (SCQ); *Carlin v Mladenovic* (2002) 84 SASR 155, 160–2 (SCSA).

[89] See, for example, *Ward v Griffiths* (1987) 9 NSWLR 458, where the court granted encroaching owners an easement of right of way permitting them to continue to use an encroaching concrete driveway to gain access to their premises. In some cases where an encroachment was built when the adjacent properties were in common ownership, the grant or reservation of an easement may be implied: *Wherry v Trustees of the Sisters of Charity of Australia* (2000) 111 LGERA 216; (2001) 75(10) ALJ 591(NSWLEC).

[90] Commentaries on how courts interpret and apply the statutes are scant. On the Queensland and New South Wales statutes, see C MacDonald, L McCrimmon and A Wallace, *Real Property Law in Queensland* (Sydney, LBC, 1998) 98–104; P Butt, *Land Law*, 5th edn (Sydney, Lawbook Co, 2006) [319]–[324]. Decisions made under one statute are persuasive authority in the interpretation of a similarly worded statute in another State.

[91] Little weight is usually attached to this consideration. Parties sometimes use it to support a claim that they are demonstrating their bona fides by coming to court: *Austin v Scotts Head Lifestyle Homes Ltd* (unreported, [2002] NSWLEC 241, 20 December 2002), [43] (Pain J).

[92] Encroachment of Buildings Act (1922) s 3(3).

include: whether the adjoining owner was aware of or consented to the encroachment;[93] the length of time for which the encroachment has existed;[94] and the conduct of the parties in resolving the issues resulting from the encroachment.[95]

Criteria for Exercising the Discretion

In exercising the discretion to grant or refuse relief under the statutes, courts consider many of the same factors that would be relevant to the exercise of the equitable jurisdiction to withhold a mandatory injunction for trespass.[96] There are three main sets of considerations. The first set relates to the conduct of the encroaching owner and serves the deterrence objective.[97] The second set relates to the conduct of the parties in response to the encroachment and include matters such as delay in seeking relief and the making of rent-seeking or punitive demands by the adjacent owner.[98] These factors curb the oppressive use of legal rights by the encroaching owner, and limit the cost of the encroachment. The third set of factors is directed at finding a *balance between the loss and damage to either party if the other party is to succeed.*[99] *These considerations serve the policy objective of minimising the cost of boundary errors once they have occurred.*

No single factor is given determinative weight under the statute. The conduct of the encroaching owner is a consideration of the first importance. Even a deliberate encroacher is not absolutely barred from relief, although it has often been said that 'it would be a rare and exceptional

---

[93] The fact that the adjacent owner or a predecessor in title has at one time consented to the existence of the encroachment does not make it any the less an encroachment, but it is relevant to the exercise of the court's discretion: *Boed Pty Ltd v Seymour* (1989) 15 NSWLR 715 (SCNSW).

[94] Eg, in *Morris v Thomas* (1991) 73 LGRA 164, the adjacent owner had known of the encroachment for 20 years and only sought its removal when the relationship soured.

[95] *Farrow Mortgage Services (in liq) v Boscaini Investments Pty Ltd* [1997] ANZ ConvR 349 (SASC). The relevant conduct can include whether the adjacent owner has failed to mitigate his or her loss *Re Melden Homes (No 2) Pty Ltd's Land* [1976] Qd R 79.

[96] See text accompanying note 21ff above.

[97] See text accompanying note 31ff above. The deterrence and cost minimisation objectives referred to are non-statutory policy objectives, proposed by Miceli and Sirmans and used here to evaluate the rule.

[98] For an example of rent-seeking, see *Re Melden Homes (No 2) Pty Ltd's Land* [1976] Qd R 79 (where encroachment resulted from error, and adjacent owners demanded a price vastly in excess of the value of the land).

[99] *Mark Dawkins v ARM Holdings Pty Ltd* (unreported, [1994] NSWLEC 54, 14 April 1994), [58], cited with approval in *Attard v Canal (No 1)* (unreported, [2005] NSWLEC 222), 12 May 2005), [50].

case in which the court would make an order under this Act in favour of a person who, with full knowledge, encroached on his neighbour's land.'[100]

If an encroaching owner fails to satisfy the court that the encroachment was not intentional and did not arise from negligence,[101] he or she must pay three times the unimproved capital value of the boundary strip if the court makes an order for compensation for the transfer, lease or grant of the subject land to him or her.[102] This civil penalty provision has caused difficulties in several jurisdictions. The mandatory trebling of compensation is excessive and arbitrary, and the provision is cast in such broad terms that it makes the encroaching owner liable to the penalty, whether the encroachment was caused by his or her own intentional or negligent act or that of a predecessor in title or independent contractor.[103] The existence of the penalty provision may discourage courts from awarding compensation, since the penalty provision does not apply unless an award of compensation is made.[104]

A preferable provision is found in the Western Australian and New Zealand statutes. An encroaching owner can get no relief under those statutes unless he or she proves that the encroachment was not intentional and did not arise from gross negligence, *or* that the building was not erected by him or her.[105] When relief is granted, the encroaching owner may be ordered to pay compensation on such terms as the Court thinks fit.[106] There is no mandatory penalty provision.

---

[100]   *Haddans Pty Ltd v Nesbitt* (1963) 57 QJPR 21, 22 (SCQ, Gibbs J). See also *Morris v Thomas* (1991) 73 LGRA 164, 168 (Bignold J); *Austin v Scotts Head Lifestyle Homes Ltd* (unreported, [2002] NSWLEC 241, 20 December 2002), para 52; *Shadbolt v Wise* (2003) 126 LGERA 59, [16] (QCA). Cf *Jaggard v Sawyer* [1995] 1 WLR 269, 283 (Sir Thomas Bingham MR) and 288 (Millett LJ) (see note 23ff above and accompanying text).

[101]   *Shadbolt v Wise* (2003) 126 LGERA 59 (QCA); *Droga v Proprietor of Strata Plan 51722* (1996) 93 LGERA 120 (NSWLEC).

[102]   Encroachment of Buildings Act (1922) (NSW) s 4(1); Property Law Act (1974) (Qld) s 186(1); Encroachment of Buildings Act (NT) s 7(1); Encroachments Act 1944 (SA) s 5(1).

[103]   *Healam v Hunter* [1992] ANZ ConvR 592; (1991) NSW ConvR 55–569, paras 11–12 (Waddam CJ); *Gladwell v Steen* (2000) 77 SASR 310, para 21 (Debelle J).

[104]   In *Gladwell v Steen* (*ibid*), Debelle J discussed the various options that courts have to avoid the necessity of imposing the penalty upon an innocent encroaching owner who has purchased without knowledge of the encroachment. One option is to award no compensation, since compensation is not mandatory on the creation or transfer of an interest: *Carlin v Mladenovic* (2002) 84 SASR 155 (SCSA, Full Ct), paras 32–9; *Melden Homes (No 2) Pty Ltd's Land* [1976] Qd R 79, 81; *Morris v Thomas* (1991) 73 LGRA 164, 169; *Butland v Cole* (1995) 87 LGERA 122; *Bunney v State of South Australia* (2000) 77 SASR 319, paras 9 and 30–4 (Debelle J).

[105]   Property Law Act (1952) (NZ) s 129(2); Property Law Act (1969) (WA) s 122(1). This provision still leaves the encroaching owner without relief when the error was caused through the negligence of a contractor such as a surveyor. The encroaching owner's remedies against the negligent contractor may already be barred by statute when the encroachment arises.

[106]   Property Law Act (1952) (NZ) s 129(4); Property Law Act (1969) (WA) s 122(4).

A Case Study Comparison

The following case adjudicated under a South Australian building encroachment statute highlights some key differences between the operation of such a law and the LRA (2002) Schedule 6. In *Gladwell v Steen*,[107] the applicant and respondents each purchased their respective land in the belief that the Steens' carport and driveway stood wholly on the Steens' land, but they subsequently discovered that the buildings encroached onto Gladwell's land by a one-metre strip. The predecessors in title of both parties had known of the encroachment and allowed it to continue. The Steens learned of the encroachment shortly after they purchased the land, but it did not become an issue until three years later, when the neighbours had a falling out and Gladwell sought an order for removal of the encroachments.

The Supreme Court of South Australia (Debelle J) found that encroachments caused no inconvenience to the applicant and did not prejudice the use of his land. The removal of the encroachments would deprive the Steens of vehicular access to their land and diminish its value by an amount greater than the value of the boundary strip. The court ordered that the applicant transfer the boundary strip to the Steens but did not require them to pay compensation for the transfer. Debelle J reasoned that, since Gladwell had never expected to acquire the boundary strip when he bought his own land, compensation would represent a windfall to him.[108] The effect of the order was to make good the expectations actually held by both the applicant and the respondents when they bought their respective properties

If the dispute in *Gladwell v Steen* were adjudicated under the LRA (2002), the Steens, who learned of the encroachment shortly after purchase, would never acquire title to the boundary strip. Although they believed at the time they purchased their land that it included the land on which the buildings stood, neither they nor their predecessors in title had been in adverse possession for ten years in the reasonable belief that it belonged to them.[109] The Steens would have to rely on the discretion of the court to withhold the injunction sought by Gladwell and award damages.

---

[107] (2000) 77 SASR 310 (SCSA).
[108] The decision not to award compensation may have been affected by the fact that if the court had made an order for compensation, the mandatory penalty provision would apply, and the Steens would have to pay three times the market value because of their inability to prove that the encroachment by their predecessors in title was neither intentional nor caused by negligence: *ibid*, paras 16–25, and note 106 above.
[109] LRA 2002, Sched 6, para 5(4)(c). Note the ambiguity in this provision as to whether the applicant can reckon the requisite ten year period by adding his or her own period of adverse possession with reasonable belief to that of his or her predecessor, where neither period had lasted ten years: note 69 above.

While it is likely that the court would exercise its discretion in their favour, it could not order the transfer of the boundary strip; and without title to it, the value of their land would be diminished. And if the Steens were permitted to continue using the encroaching buildings, they would be liable to pay damages.

V. CONCLUSION

A building encroachment statute, in conjunction with a prohibition rule excluding the acquisition of title to a boundary strip by adverse possession, offers the following advantages in comparison with the conditional veto rule of adverse possession rule in the LRA (2002):

1. It excludes the acquisition of title to a boundary strip by an adverse possessor who has made no lasting and substantial improvement. This is consistent with a view that the law has no policy interest in facilitating a non-market transfer when there is no sunk investment or quasi-rent to impede private bargaining.
2. It allows courts to balance the deterrence objective with the cost minimisation objective, by weighing the encroacher's conduct with all other relevant circumstances. This flexibility enables the courts to provide a disincentive to encroachment while providing relief to those who have inadvertently or carelessly placed themselves in a position where they are subject to rent-seeking or punitive demands by the adjacent owner, or otherwise facing a substantial loss.
3. The court can act on the application of either party, and its powers are not confined to vindicating existing rights or restraining their exercise. It can adjust the property rights of the parties and award compensation. This promotes a final resolution of the dispute and removes a title cloud that may impair the marketability of both properties.
4. By empowering the court to award compensation, the statutes allow the court to distribute the cost of the boundary error more equitably than is possible under adverse possession or a prohibition rule.

The adverse possession rule provided by Schedule 6 of the LRA (2002) has the advantage of providing a degree of assurance to purchasers that the registered owner is able to pass title to the land as physically occupied by him or her. It effectively operates as an absolute veto rule in some cases, such as when landowners encroach inadvertently at any time after the registrar has made a boundary determination, or when registered owners learn of a pre-existing encroachment within ten years of purchase. In these cases, and in other cases in which the statutory 'limitation' period has not run, encroaching owners may be exposed to rent-seeking or punitive demands by the adjacent owner.

Encroaching owners may be able to obtain negative relief through the exercise of the court's discretion to withhold a mandatory injunction, but they cannot initiate the proceedings nor ask the court to order a transfer or the grant of a property right. Although the Schedule 6, LRA (2002) provisions and the equitable discretion to withhold an injunction have a complementary operation, there is no procedural or policy articulation between them. A building encroachment law similar to the New South Wales model would bring together all the relevant provisions into a unified and coherent discretionary scheme that is procedurally accessible to both parties and provides positive relief.

10

de Soto Discovers the Prairies:
Of Squatters and the Canadian West

BRUCE ZIFF AND SEAN WARD*

[P]olicy-makers ordinarily use history badly. When resorting to an analogy, they tend to seize upon the first that comes to mind. They do not search more widely. Nor do they pause to analyze the case, test its fitness, or even ask in what ways it might be misleading. Seeing a trend running through the present, they tend to assume that it will continue into the future, not stopping to consider what produced it or why a linear projection might prove to be mistaken.

ER May, *'Lessons' of the Past: The Use and Misuse of History in American Foreign Policy*[1]

INTRODUCTION

L AND ACQUISITION BY illegal occupation—or in common parlance, squatting—has a long if not venerable history in the settler colonies within the British Empire as well as in post-Revolutionary America and elsewhere. It became commonplace for pioneers, hungry for lush, arable or otherwise valuable realty, to set out ahead of the governmental systems designed to facilitate the orderly settlement of the frontier. Vast expanses of what was seen as available unclaimed wilderness beckoned the hearty and resolute. Each land rush episode was, of course, somewhat unique. But there were some common features. Settlers ventured out, staking claims that had no initial legal standing. Conventions emerged to determine entitlements among the squatting population, including informal devices to enforce rights, such as vigilante organisations. Attempts were made by governments to dislodge wilful freebooters[2] and to prevent others from following in their tracks. A predictable by-product

---

* The authors wish to thank Russ Brown, Larissa Katz and an anonymous reviewer for their helpful comments.

[1] (New York, OUP, 1973) xi.

[2] JC Weaver, *The Great Land Rush and the Making of the Modern World, 1650–1900* (Montreal & Kingston, McGill-Queen's University Press, 2003) 21.

was animosity between squatters and the state. Almost always the authorities eventually capitulated, according recognition to unlawfully acquired rights in some way. Over and over again in the development of the (now) developed world, rights sprouted up in this fashion.

The Australian story is well known. In New South Wales, squatters acquired the lands, mainly for grazing, west of Sydney during the 1830s and 1840s, though there was also squatting in the preceding decade. Where sparsely vegetated lands were involved, large tracts were occupied to sustain the sheep and cattle runs. In due course, officialdom abandoned hopes for its planned development of a society of farmers and sanctioned the brazen acts of confiscation by the pastoralists. Certain half-measures were initially offered, including licenses of various sorts, but the squatters held out for and won far more. As of 1847, they were entitled to obtain pastoral leases for up to fourteen years and were permitted to purchase the freehold of these lands—at its unimproved value—during or at the end of the lease term.[3] Meanwhile, squatting continued apace elsewhere, particularly in Queensland.[4] The upshot was the creation of a wealthy squattocracy, as it came to be called.

In the United States, the process began far earlier and was at least as extensive.[5] Squatters were taking up lands in Massachusetts in the first half of the seventeenth century. From there the practice spread to Maryland, Vermont, Maine and other colonies along the eastern seaboard. Elaborate conventions arose to define and perfect claims, some of which migrated as the western frontier was opened up. In the west, claims clubs and other settler associations were created to protect the interests of those on the land from the challenges of claim jumpers and speculators. Vigilantism was common, with violence and other acts of reprisal being carried out or threatened, as a means of enforcing established ownership norms. The sundry efforts of Congress to curb the tide fell far short. In fact, the system of land sales adopted in the late eighteenth century almost certainly served to fuel illegal occupations, for the prices sought were simply too high for the market. Land theft was far preferable.

As in Australia, the ultimate capitulation of the state occurred in stages. A host of pre-emption statutes were passed in the early part of the nineteenth century, leading to legislation in 1841 under which Congress conferred pre-emptive rights of purchase for those in occupation of surveyed federal property. Later on, the scope of that pre-emption law was

---

[3]   B Kercher, *An Unruly Child: A History of Law in Australia* (St Leonards, NSW, Allen & Unwin, 1995) 122.

[4]   See SH Roberts, *The Squatting Age in Australia, 1835–1847* (London, CUP, 1964 (1935)).

[5]   See further PW Gates, *Landlords and Tenants on the Prairie Frontier* (Ithaca, Cornell University Press, 1973).

expanded to include unsurveyed land. Twenty years later, the Homestead Act (1862) provided for acquisition of land on payment of a fee of $10. As a condition of the grant, the land had to be occupied for a minimum of five years and improved during that time.

Recently, the Canadian historian John Weaver completed extensive work on the undulating courses of frontier settlement. In *The Great Land Rush and the Making of the Modern World, 1650–1900*,[6] he describes and assesses at length both government policies and the squatter phenomena in relation to European settlement in Australia, South Africa, the United States, New Zealand, Argentina and Canada. However, his treatment of illegal land-grabbing in Canada in general, and in Western Canada in particular, is quite limited. All in all, the Canadian experience was a fairly tame affair. Although both squatting and illegal timber stripping were prevalent in Upper and Lower Canada (roughly present-day Ontario and Quebec),[7] the process of land acquisition was less turbulent than that occurring at about the same time on the American frontier. The rugged individualism found in Canada was not quite as rugged as that in the United States, for there was more deference to authority among the Canadian settlers. The acquisition of land for grazing played a major role in the American West but was far less significant in Canada, especially in the East. Land was used principally for farming, and the holdings, whether lawfully acquired or not, tended to be small. Overall, however, some common features are evident in the Canadian experience: settlement was messy, government procedures proved inadequate to the task and informal rule systems arose that eventually crystallised into *de jure* rights.

The Canadian prairie—cold, distant, immense—was the last place in the British Empire to experience a major land rush. As a result, when that process began in earnest in the 1870s, many of the mistakes and oversights affecting formal settlement procedures, relating to such matters as surveying and land dispersal, had been addressed. As a consequence, it was in the Canadian West, uniquely, that the there was both time and money to plat the land properly before settlers arrived. Owing to the hard-learned lessons of the past decades, plus a cadre of competent bureaucrats, not to mention a measure of good fortune, Canada's westward expansion gave rise to 'few murderous conflicts, no extended warfare, minimal pastoral landhunting, modest squatting, and sound land titles'.[8] The squatting that did occur has been said to involve small acreages near river valleys, where acquired land was mainly used for hunting and fishing.[9]

---

[6] Note 2 above.
[7] *Ibid*, 265.
[8] *Ibid*, 251.
[9] *Ibid*, 252.

However, in this chapter we will suggest that there was a more extensive and interesting pattern of squatting in Canada's northwest territories than has been appreciated to date. In fact, it may be that the scale of extra-legal occupation was significant. For example, much of the central area of the modern city of Edmonton, now the capital of the province of Alberta, was unilaterally appropriated by settlers within a year of the region having been acquired by Canada. And dozens of homesteads in the outlying lands near Edmonton were obtained in the same fashion. Claims were staked and recognised all within a short span of time (ie, the period from 1871 to 1886). This chapter deals with that less-known and under-theorised moment of frontier squatting.[10] It is absent from Weaver's otherwise masterly account, and it seems never to have been placed within the meta-narratives of frontier development.

In recent years the settlement practices of the nineteenth century have been invoked by the Peruvian economist Hernando de Soto as applicable in a contemporary setting. His runaway bestseller *The Mystery of Capital*[11] advances some provocative ideas about development strategies for third-world and former communist states. It is a central precept of de Soto's work that developing nations are not poor but rather have considerable wealth. Yet these countries have low standards of living because that wealth takes the form of *de facto*, and hence insecure, claims to land; in short, much of the land is illegally held. Because title is precarious, the exchange values of these hardscrabble patches are depressed. Even more important, the land's full value cannot be unlocked because it cannot be used as loan security. It is, in his words, dead capital. By comparison, Western nations have well-oiled *de jure* legal structures to protect and record titles. This, he argues, makes all the difference.

In brief, the de Soto thesis starts on the safe ground that property rules require juridical protection to be effective and efficient. If developing nations take that step, a host of significant benefits will be fostered, including cheaper and better built homes for the poor and reduced crime.[12] Accordingly, it is proposed that unlocking the capital potential of real property can be accomplished by giving legal status to the immense extra-legal holdings now in existence. That response, in turn, holds significant implications for the extent and purpose of foreign aid. In essence, de Soto suggests that there is no need for an infusion of capital to

---

[10] For earlier accounts, see EA Mitchner, 'The North Saskatchewan River Settlement Claims, 1883–84' in LH Thomas (ed), *Essays on Western History* (Edmonton, University of Alberta Pr, 1976) 129; and JF Gilpin, 'The Edmonton and District Settlers' Rights Movement, 1880 to 1885' in RC Macleod (ed), *Swords and Ploughshares: War and Agriculture in Western Canada* (University of Alberta Pr, Edmonton, 1993) 149.

[11] H de Soto, *The Mystery of Capital: Why Capitalism Triumphs in the West and Fails Everywhere Else* (New York, Basic Books, 2000).

[12] *Ibid*, 176–8.

bolster the local economy. Instead, aid should be directed at allowing extant landholdings to be protected in a way that optimises their marketability.

The core idea—the importance of stable property rights—is of course not de Soto's brainchild. Moreover, proposals to affirm squatter titles within peri-urban communities have been floated from time to time over the last thirty years.[13] Nevertheless, *The Mystery of Capital* has garnered attention in development literature and beyond. His reform proposals may seem extreme, but a key component of de Soto's thesis is that the transformation of illegal land-grabs into valid holdings can be found in the economic histories of the developed world. His plan may well be radical, but it is not unprecedented.[14]

This use of history forms a central link in de Soto's line of argument. In chapter 5 of *The Mystery of Capital*, 'The Missing Lessons of US History', he reviews the American experience alluded to above. History has shown, he argues, that the tide cannot be readily turned against informal appropriation of property. Moreover, he regards the American response to squatting—namely surrender—as a significant factor leading to the economic strength of the United States during the settlement period and beyond. Importantly, the American situation as it stood over 150 years ago is seen as comparable to the current state of affairs in the developing world and the former Soviet Union. Governments are lagging behind popular initiatives and hence losing control. The primary—and hitherto missing—lesson is that 'pretending extralegal arrangements do not exist or trying to stamp them out, without a strategy to channel them into the legal sector, is a fool's errand—especially in the developing world . . .'[15]

The Mystery of Capital has been subjected to critique on a number of fronts. The empirical claims as to the extent of untapped wealth in the developing world have been doubted, and the treatment of property law reform as *the* key to development has come under question. Many other elements must be in place. Capital markets cannot flourish without stable financial institutions.[16] A (costly) government infrastructure to maintain a

---

[13] See A Varley, 'Private or Public: Debating the Meaning of Tenure Legalization' (2002) 26 *Int'l J of Urban & Regional Research* 449, which reviews some of the earlier writing.

[14] He also argues that the red tape required to acquire title, incorporate businesses and so forth, should be drastically cut.

[15] de Soto, note 11 above, 150.

[16] See further RG Rajan and L Zingales, *Saving Capitalism from the Capitalists: Unleashing the Power of Financial Markets to Create Wealth and Spread Opportunity* (New York, Crown Business, 2003).

proper record of titles is required.[17] Adequate creditors' remedies, bankruptcy laws and a sound judicial system are also essential ingredients. The sequencing of these interconnected reforms has also been raised as a concern.[18] Even the tendency of validated titles to support an increase in secured lending has been questioned.[19] More generally, concerns have been voiced that the abrupt introduction of market and rule of law reforms can have unexpected and catastrophic social and cultural consequences, including the inflammation of existing ethnic tensions.[20]

In this chapter we do not directly engage these matters. Instead, the focus will be on de Soto's use of history to buttress his main argument; less seems to have been said about that aspect of his thesis.[21] In some important ways, the events at Edmonton Settlement provide, in a microcosm, the so-called missing lessons of history upon which de Soto relies. At the same time, however, this epitome raises questions about the degree to which these lessons are truly germane to the modern setting. In other words, we will use the story of the Edmonton Settlement to interrogate de Soto's historical narrative.

THE EMERGENCE OF EDMONTON SETTLEMENT

On 2 May 1670, King Charles II granted land in North America to the Governor and His Company of Adventurers Trading into Hudson's Bay (HBC). The grant conveyed all lands covered by the Hudson's Bay drainage basin, some 1.5 million square miles of land spanning the western portions of modern-day Quebec through to most of the Province of Alberta and into what is now the northern United States. The first Governor was Prince Rupert, and the lands became known as Rupert's Land. The HBC governed these territories for 200 years. Rupert's Land was a commercial fiefdom, a 'company town writ large'.[22] In 1870, three years after Confederation, the HBC lands were sold to Canada. The company retained significant

---

[17]   See further R Home, 'Outside de Soto's Bell Jar: Colonial/Postcolonial Land Law and the Exclusion of the Peri-urban Poor' in R Home and H Lim (eds), *Demystifying the Mystery of Capital: Land Tenure and Poverty in Africa and the Caribbean* (Portland, Cavendish, 2004) 11.

[18]   See J Manders, 'Sequencing Property Rights in the Context of Development: A Critique of the Writings of Hernando de Soto' (2004) *Cornell Int L J* 177.

[19]   See 'The Mystery of Capital Deepens', *Economist*, 26 August 2006, 62 and the references cited there.

[20]   See especially A Chua, *World on Fire: How Exporting Free Market Democracy Breeds Ethnic Hatred and Global Instability* (New York, Anchor Books, 2003).

[21]   That facet is briefly considered in R Skidelsky, 'The Wealth of (Some) Nations', *New York Times Book Review*, 24 December 2000) 8. See also W Bole, 'The Clash of Me and We', book review, *America*, 19 February 2001, 24, who notes the importance of labour law reform in the United States; and also Manders, note 18 above, 190–1.

[22]   PC Newman, *Company of Adventurers* (Markham, ON, Viking, 1985) vol 1, 1.

landholdings (approximately 7 million acres of fertile terrain) and was entitled under the terms of the surrender to reserve up to 3,000 acres around established trading forts. There had been a fort in Edmonton since 1795, and the full 3,000 acres was reserved there. The reserve area was surveyed in 1873, but the surrounding lands were not.

One can be forgiven for assuming that a well-ordered community of pioneers would emerge from the vacuum created following the sale of Rupert's Land and the withdrawal of the HBC. That was not to be. Within a year of the sale, people began staking claims, mainly east of the reserve lands. The first two claims were taken by the Reverand George McDougall for a Methodist mission and a parsonage respectively. A string of easterly claims followed along the crest of the North Saskatchewan River valley. There was one large claim to the west of the reserve, as well as a cluster of sizable parcels south of the river. A number of these original squatters were former HBC employees. A consensus appeared to develop among them at an early stage that squatters were generally entitled to claim up to a 200-yard frontage (20 chains) for the highly prized river lots.[23]

By 1880 there had still been no official survey, and no patents had been issued for lands along the river. However, there was a bustling community of about 300 souls, with shops, wood-frame houses and a coal mine. By 1874, the great westward trek of the North-West Mounted Police (later to become the Royal Canadian Mounted Police) had been completed, so there was a police presence nearby. By 1881, the Edmonton Settlement had been connected by telegraph to Winnipeg, 1,200 kilometres away,[24] and a weekly newspaper, the *Edmonton Bulletin*, conveyed the news from the East as well as chronicling local events. The *Bulletin* was owned and edited by Frank Oliver, who arrived in the settlement in 1876. It operated on lands that Oliver purchased from an original squatter. The paper became, in essence, the voice of the squatters. By the early 1880s, the push had begun for the transformation of the *de facto* land rights into *de jure* titles, and all of the important moments in that struggle were narrated weekly in the newspaper.

The most notorious moment of the squatter period occurred in early 1882. Quite predictably, there were several attempts to claim jump. By 1882, the *Bulletin* reported that trouble had been 'brewing, as the settlers became thicker and the land became more valuable'.[25] The first confrontation involved one of the earliest lots to be staked, which in the ensuing ten-year period had been transferred three times. Several people in the

---

[23] 'The Land', *Edmonton Bulletin*, 11 February 1882.
[24] OD Jones, 'The Historical Geography of Edmonton, Alberta' (MA Thesis, University of Toronto 1962) 31.
[25] 'On the Jump', *Edmonton Bulletin*, 11 February 1882.

settlement had been 'casting a longing eye'[26] at this large plot, thought to be valued at between $5,000 and $10,000. There was a small commercial building on the property, under lease as a store, but little more. No one was residing on the land, and to some it seemed ripe for the picking.

On Saturday, 4 February 1882, an American, referred to only as L George in the *Bulletin* account, arrived on the lot, drove in boundary stakes and, with the help of several hired hands, began building a small (10' x 20') frame house. News of these events circulated at once, and two days later a vigilante group, estimated to be 150 strong, descended on George and his crew. There was a mounting apprehension that a chain reaction of claim jumping might ensue and that this was a test case of the durability of the squatter claims. There was an initial war of words between the proprietors and George; this produced a standoff. George then retreated into the unenclosed frame of the building and drew a revolver. He was summarily disarmed. The gang then efficiently relocated the house frame to the bottom of the river valley, about 200 feet below, at which point the firearm was returned to George.

The creation of this vigilante group was ad hoc, but that night a meeting was called, the purpose of which was to create a more permanent organisation, a 'mutual protection society'. The upshot of that meeting was the formation of a vigilance committee. It was to operate as a secret society (whatever that might mean), so as to allow its members 'greater freedom of action' in carrying out its stated functions.[27] It was not long before the committee was pressed into service. On 21 February, a second claim jump was attempted, this time by one JM Bannerman, who happened to be the brother of a Member of Parliament for an Ontario constituency.[28] Bannerman, by letter to the newly formed vigilance committee, announced his intention to occupy and build on the mission property, at that point occupied by one Matthew McCauley. Bannerman claimed that he had the approval of the Minister of the Interior to proceed and was therefore not affected by any local rule that might have been established by the committee.

The vigilantes resolved to protect the mission claim, now of some eleven years' standing, and to 'apply the necessary persuasion'[29] to ensure that the claim jump did not pre-empt a decision by the authorities as to the mission's right to receive a patent for that property. At the appointed hour they arrived, making no attempt to conceal their identities or purpose. They were well-prepared for the task at hand. The dwelling was hoisted by rope onto two bob-sleighs, then drawn by a team of horses for a quarter of

[26]   *Ibid.*
[27]   'The Vigilance Committee', *Edmonton Bulletin*, 18 February 1882.
[28]   William Bannerman, Sr (1841–1914), MP for Renfrew South, Ontario, 1880–82.
[29]   'Next!', *Edmonton Bulletin*, 25 February 1882.

a mile. There, Bannerman's partially built shanty suffered the same fate as George's wood frame.[30] Whether the chosen route was necessitated by the location of the precipice or was designed to visit a little rough music on Bannerman through a very public display, is not known.

Following the first claim jump, George had threatened legal action, but nothing came of it.[31] However, following this second encounter there were legal repercussions. Several men, including Frank Oliver, were charged with the offence of malicious injury to property. A civil suit was also filed. The jury returned a verdict of not guilty on the criminal charges. The defence was premised in part on the protection of Matt McCauley's prior property rights.[32] Likewise, in the civil action it was held that McCauley's pre-existing claim, even if adverse to that of the Crown, was superior to those of the claim jumper. That outcome accords with long-established common law doctrine.[33] The plaintiff did recover against one of the vigilantes for the destruction of the building.

Another major event of 1882 was the decision by the Hudson's Bay Company to subdivide and sell off portions of the reserve lands. The company made available some, but only some, of the lots in the initial offering. A similar approach was adopted for the equally large reserve lands at Winnipeg, where real estate sales had been a robust success. In Edmonton, the location was 'high and dry', and the prices and terms were attractive. As expected, there was an extremely strong demand for the properties, and over the span of just a few days, about 400 lots were sold. Sales grossed $12,000 (about $25 to $30 per lot). Once the company suspended the sales, a number of the lots that had been sold in this initial flurry fetched much higher prices in the secondary market that quickly emerged.

While squatters were selling river lots, and the HBC was developing its own land market, there was another regime, indeed the main system of land allocation, in operation. The government of Sir John A Macdonald was bent on rapid and aggressive westward expansion, as part of the government's National Policy. As a result, following closely on the heels of the purchase of Rupert's Land, a homesteading system drawn extensively from the 1862 American homestead legislation was implemented. Most of Rupert's Land was surveyed under a township system, which created mile-square sections (640 acres) bordered on all sides by road allowances.

---

[30] 'Court', *Edmonton Bulletin*, 17 June 1882.

[31] George filed a complaint with the federal government, seeking $10,000 in damages. The *Bulletin* offered that this was '[n]ot a bad price for a hundred dollar shanty': *Edmonton Bulletin*, 18 February 1882.

[32] 'Court', note 30 above.

[33] See eg, *Asher v Whitlock* (1865) LR 1 QB 1.

By virtue of the Dominion Lands Act, settlers could acquire quarter-sections (160 acres) for a nominal fee, with a pre-emptive right to acquire an additional quarter-section and a right to purchase a third at a still higher rate. In 1882, the pre-emption prices for quarter-sections were set at between $320 and $400 ($2.00 to $2.50 per acre).[34]

Throughout these turbulent times, the accounts portrayed in the *Bulletin* represented the squatters as those on the moral (and mainly the literal) high ground. They were not land thieves but valuable—yet undervalued—trailblazers. In an 1882 editorial, Frank Oliver described the squatters in the northwest as 'the scouts, the pickets, the advance guard of Canadian settlement'.[35] Their importance to the Canadian national policy meant that they should not be bullied by 'any company' (read the HBC), any 'syndicate' (probably meaning the Canadian Pacific Railway or the colonisation societies) or the federal government.[36] Every Canadian was entitled to share the country's bounty, whether or not government regulations were followed:

> The squatter who strikes out ahead of his fellows and seeks new fields is the man who deserves well of his country. He answers for geological and meteorological observatory. He injures no one inasmuch as he takes up land where no one else would have it before, and it is only right that he should receive every advantage that his enterprise brings him, and when the government tries to displace him for any cause, they are working themselves as much injury as they are to him.[37]

It must be stressed that these squatters' rights were taken as belonging to 'Canadians', a term that had already taken on a distinct, coded meaning. Protection was being sought for native-born Canadians, or for men from countries who had 'thrown in their lot completely with Canada' and who therefore had the same entitlements as those born on Canadian soil. Left out were 'Mennonites, . . . Jews, or chinamen, or any foreign nation or strange class'.[38]

Land speculators, long the whipping boys of American settlement politics, also attracted Oliver's acid criticism. However, the greatest contempt was reserved for the railways and colonisation societies, both of which had received massive landholdings in the northwest. There were also speculative purchasers and speculative (ie, non-resident) squatters. These were all distanced from the *bona fide* squatters. Of course, they too were speculators of a sort, since it was expected that their holdings would appreciate as new waves of homesteaders arrived in search of the best

---

[34] 'The Very Latest', *Edmonton Bulletin*, 4 March 1882.
[35] 'The Last Land Act', *Edmonton Bulletin*, 10 June 1882.
[36] 'Squatters and Squatting', *Edmonton Bulletin*, 5 May 1883. See also 'The Answer', *Edmonton Bulletin*, 28 July 1883.
[37] 'Speculative Squatting', *Edmonton Bulletin*, 12 January 1884.
[38] 'The Last Land Act', note 35 above.

parcels. But their rights to the land had been earned, as John Locke might have argued, by virtue of the improvements to and settlement on the very lands they claimed.[39]

Over this period there was a festering resentment of the government in Ottawa, a recurring theme in Alberta politics that can fairly be said to have been born at this point. Requests had been made for pre-emptive rights for squatters *à la* American homestead law, and prior to that some sought the implementation of formal rules for establishing boundaries applicable to squatters *inter se*. The prevalence of squatting in the region was blamed on the Department of the Interior, which was criticised for its inability to keep abreast of the demand for land by those willing to pioneer the West. Moreover, Oliver's editorials complained that the bureaucratic delays in resolving squatters' rights were inducing Canadians to leave in search of greener pastures south of the border:

> The numbers of Canadians who leave their country and settle in the States has long been and is yet a subject of remark and wonder. Had this human tide been flowing into the North-West, Canada would no doubt occupy now a prominent position among the nations, but when it is considered that especial inducements are given to Canadians to emigrate to the United States, and every hindrance possible is thrown in the way of their coming to the North-West, while special encouragement is given to Jews and heathens, paupers and criminals, hypocrites and swindlers from other countries to come in and possess the land, the wonder is, not that so few, but that any come.[40]

While the intransigence of government on the land rights question may have seemed to last an eternity to Oliver and others, in fact there was considerable work afoot. In 1882, a land surveyor named Michael Deane was dispatched by the Department of the Interior to collect data on Edmonton Settlement. Deane's instructions were to create an inventory of improvements and their estimated value, as well as the extent of cultivation in the area. He was not supposed to set out lot lines, for there were concerns that by doing so he would be placing an imprimatur of legitimacy on the claims and their delineation. Perhaps predictably, he succumbed to local pressure to do just that, and, as feared by Ottawa, the resulting cadastre was viewed by the settlers as possessing some ill-defined air of legitimacy. Figure 10.1 shows the Deane survey. It is, in effect, Edmonton's first published work of fiction.

As we have seen, Frank Oliver was a relentless advocate for squatter's rights, using the *Bulletin* to rally and cement support and pressure. He was

---

[39] See further 'Squatters and Squatting', *Edmonton Bulletin*, 5 May 1883; 'Speculative Squatting', note 37 above; 'Speculative Squatting', *Edmonton Bulletin*, 26 April 1884. See also Robert Watson, MP for Marquette, *House of Commons Debates (Canada)*, 28 February 1883, 86.

[40] 'The Last Land Act', note 35 above.

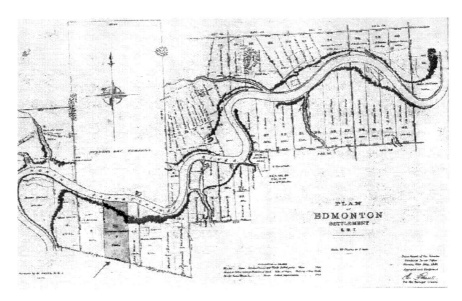

not alone, for the issues that emerged in Edmonton had counterparts elsewhere in the territories. In Ottawa there was both a desire to resolve the squatting question as well as support for the squatters' claims.[41] As a consequence, in 1883 the federal government made major concessions: amendments to the homesteading legislation recognised squatters' claims to specified lands. A settler who was in *bona fide* occupation and had made improvements prior to survey on lands earmarked for homesteading would be granted a pre-emptive right to obtain free homestead entry.[42] This provision did not cover all squatting and certainly not the lands in the Edmonton Settlement, but it nonetheless held great practical and symbolic significance for the river lots. In the same year, the Department of the Interior acceded to requests from delegates from several settlements to recognise their land rights. '[J]ustice has been guaranteed the original river settlers', announced the *Bulletin* triumphantly.[43]

With legislative reforms in place, the final step was to confirm entitlements on the ground, a task that fell to William Pearce, a senior civil

---

[41]   See, eg, Malcolm Cameron, MP for Huron West, *House of Common Debates (Canada)* 30 January 1884, 75–6.

[42]   SC 1883, c 17, s 28. Once the Province of Alberta acquired authority over public lands in the province, it put an end to this legal indulgence. Section 16 of the Provincial Lands Act (SA) (1931) c 43 provided that 'The occupation of land[,] without entry as provided by this Act[,] gives to the occupant no right thereto and the occupant may be ejected as a trespasser and any improvements made by him shall thereupon be forfeited to the Crown.' That provision forms the basis of the current law: Public Lands Act (RSA) (2000) c P-40, s 4.

[43]   'The Answer', *Edmonton Bulletin*, 28 July 1883.

servant.[44] Arriving in 1884, he was required to deal with some 240 disputes, the lion's share pertaining to pre-survey homesteaders in the Edmonton vicinity. These were routine claims, and as a general rule, homestead rights were conferred with pre-emptive rights to a second quarter-section being offered to the settlers for $160.00. About two dozen files concerned boundary disputes, mainly within Edmonton Settlement. Faced with the Deane survey and the sense of entitlement that had congealed around it, Pearce elected to preserve the *status quo* whenever possible; only three deviations were made to the Deane plan. Shortly afterwards, a protocol was established for the issuance of letters patent for the Edmonton Settlement claims. Among other things, title would be granted on the payment of a $10 fee, the same as levied for homestead entry.

APPLYING THE DE SOTO TEMPLATE

As noted earlier in this chapter, de Soto places stock in the history of frontier settlement in the West as a guide to contemporary development economics. He recognises that American responses to informal land rights should not be slavishly followed; there is also an appreciation of cultural and historical contingencies. Nevertheless, de Soto insists that 'the American experience is extremely significant'[45] and that it is 'very much like what is going on today in Third Word and former communist countries'.[46] At a level of great generality, it is indeed difficult to dismiss three key lessons identified by de Soto. First, informal rights that take root are highly resistant to destruction. Attempting to destroy them is, as he suggests, a fool's errand. Second, *de jure* rights are likely to fare better than *de facto* ones. Third, the validation of illegal occupation has been tried before, and the sky has not fallen.

The events at Edmonton Settlement provide yet another case in point. In Edmonton and environs, pioneers pressed forward in advance of the official system, taking either land not yet surveyed or parcels before they were officially released for homestead entry. Local informal laws quickly emerged to provide a measure of stability. At the earliest moments, a convention appeared to develop regarding the acceptable measure of entitlement: a frontage of 200 yards. Moreover, apart from some exceptional cases, the Deane survey and the Pearce commission were undertaken

---

[44] Largely unsung, William Pearce (b 1848, d 1930) had a storied career aiding development in the West, especially in Alberta. See further EA Mitchner, *William Pearce and Federal Government Activity in Western Canada 1882–1904* (PhD Thesis, University of Alberta 1971).

[45] de Soto, note 11 above, 148.

[46] *Ibid*, 149.

with little local turmoil.[47] In addition, one sees here, as in other frontier episodes, a tension between the governmental bureaucracy and the demands of the settlers. The attitude among those in the pioneer community was a mix of entitlement, impatience and, in some measure, apprehension. But in the end, the state conceded. The counter-hegemonic action of the squatters was co-opted by the state; they were brought in from the cold, and the informal practices that developed were incorporated into federal law and policy.

The events in Edmonton Settlement also provide a setting in which the market-worthiness of informal titles can be assessed. Reflect back on the events of 1882, and in particular the decision by the Hudson's Bay Company to sell off lots within its reserve. A plan of subdivision was drawn up, and titles to the lots sold there were rock-solid as far as Canadian law was concerned. Following the initial sales, a brisk secondary market soon emerged. Directly to the east of the HBC reserve were the squatter-owned river lots, which existed on a legal no-man's land. These properties were also subdivided, and secondary sales were not uncommon. These two markets, literally side-by-side, created laboratory conditions—a kind of real estate petri dish—under which one can assess the degree to which security of title affected the value of land.

HBC lots that originally sold for $25 at the beginning of 1882 were going for $300 just a few months later.[48] The Edmonton Settlement lands also sold well, often at prices far in excess of the reserve-land sales (owing to the size and location of the river lots). Even so, Frank Oliver understood that the river-lot transactions were being conducted under a cloud, since 'not a line was surveyed or the remotest prospect of a deed ever being given or received was in view.'[49] Likewise, 'as the original settlers held no titles they were afraid to sell lest their rights to the balance of their claims should be prejudiced and *buyers were, of course, afraid to invest in more than they actually needed for present use.*'[50] De Soto would not be surprised in the slightest.

However, as much as these events seem to support certain ineluctable conclusions, drawing parallels between past and present circumstances is somewhat counter-intuitive. Do the property holdings in the *pueblos jovenes* that surround Lima, Peru, or the *favelas* located on the outskirts of the major cities of Brazil, or the townships of South Africa, or the

---

[47] Although Oliver was deeply displeased with some of Pearce's decisions: 'Land Decisions', *Edmonton Bulletin*, 28 March 1885.

[48] 'Dry Facts', *Edmonton Bulletin*, 29 April 1882.

[49] 'The Boom', *Edmonton Bulletin*, 4 February 1882.

[50] *Ibid* (emphasis added).

communally worked rural landscapes throughout the third world, truly compare to the plots found in places such as nineteenth-century America, Australia and Western Canada?

There are some obvious differences. The land available on the frontiers was plentiful and valuable. Naturally, the first-comers sought out the best sites and, having regard to the various logistical factors that limited acquisition, asserted rights over as much terrain as possible. By contrast, the lands that are squatted in many third-word locales are leftovers. Moreover, they are densely populated. Frontier squatting occurred on state-owned land, but that is not invariably so for current peri-urban communities.

Importantly, there was a very close synergy between the aspirations of the squatters in places such as Edmonton Settlement and the policies being pursued by the authorities. These two groups needed each other. The motivations for inducing settlement in Western Canada, the United States and elsewhere depended on historically particular imperatives and goals, but in each case large-scale settlement was the chosen policy. The process of formalising property rights in the United States, as chronicled by de Soto, occurred in part because of the desire of the government to encourage prompt development.

That was equally so on the Canadian Prairies, where settlement was a cornerstone of the National Policy. Rupert's Land was not designed to be a colonial plantation when it was granted to HBC in 1670. It had been under British control for 200 years, but virtually no settlement infrastructure had been developed over that time except within the confines of the trading fort pallisades and the odd failed settlement experiment. To European eyes it remained a pristine wilderness that had to be developed quickly and from scratch. Canadians were lured westward with grandiose promises of the good life.[51] Hence, what the squatters did in Edmonton and the surroundings, as Frank Oliver claimed, was wholly consistent with the needs of the newly formed federal government. Oliver was right: the squatters were scouts.

Despite the expressed concerns that the government would let them down, the squatters had in fact little reason to fear that they would not prevail in the end. After all, the earlier American episodes were a matter of record. Likewise, in Upper Canada during the mid-nineteenth century it had become the 'usage' that in disposing of Crown lands, preference was afforded to squatters who had already defined, cleared and cultivated a plot.[52] Land was plentiful, and it had to be filled in some way. In other words, the futility of trying to displace the squatters does not on its own

---

[51] See generally D Owram, *Promise of Eden: The Canadian Expansionist Movement and the Idea of the West, 1856–1900* (Toronto, UTP, 1992 (1980)).
[52] In *Cosgrove v Corbett* (1868) 14 Gr 617 (Ont Ch) 620, this practice is acknowledged.

account for their successes. It was simply *pointless* to try to stop them. Granted, the squatters refused to play by the rules, but they were really more like queue-jumpers than outright thieves.

The founders of Edmonton Settlement, like countless others beforehand, started out as economic outsiders. They were in search of prosperity, which they found on those river lots near the HBC fort. Their hopes, mostly realised, were to participate in the mainstream economy. However, the squatters were almost all insiders in another sense: they were not 'jews, chinamen, mennonites' and so forth.

There were no significant class or ethnic divisions within Edmonton Settlement. Moreover, once established in the West, the squatters were not just equal participants in the newly forged society; they *were* the new society. Many ascended to positions of power, including Frank Oliver, who was elected the member of parliament for the region and who, during his political career, served as the Minister for the Interior, the federal department responsible for western settlement.[53] Those living in peri-urban communities of the third world are on the periphery of society in all imaginable ways. The first denizens of Edmonton were certainly not.

In addition, the transition from informal rights to *de jure* titles was seamless. Quit claim deeds were often used in sales of the lots. Real estate deals resembled in every way the conventional modes of conveyancing. Indeed, as a general rule, second- or third-generation squatters were required to provide proof of what was, in essence, a good root of title as part of the patent application process.

It may be that these factual differences are of no consequence to de Soto's main claim. One could never expect circumstances to be precisely on all fours, and indeed John Weaver's treatment of the great land rushes exposes many nuanced differences and variations on the principal themes. Still, there is at least one difference between then and now that arguably does matter. Extra-legality served no purpose to the nineteenth-century squatters that could not be better served by the validation of rights. The squatters knew this well. There was more money to be made and fewer monitoring and enforcement costs to be borne, if they could secure state-backed claims. But in at least some peri-urban settings, the enigma of informal ownership might well be useful because it inhibits marketability outside of the informal community itself. Of course, the conditions of living are appalling, and informal titles are inherently problematic.[54] But frail titles held under inscrutable rules form a buffer against outsiders entering this grey market. De Soto's entire theory is premised on this same

---

[53] Likewise, in New South Wales the squatters exerted considerable political influence and power: Kercher, note 3 above, 120–1.

[54] See further W King, 'Illegal Settlements and the Impact of Titling Programs' [2003] *Harv Int'l L J* 433.

idea: investors prefer the certain, familiar and intelligible, and they shy away from unnecessary risks. In this way, informality engenders its own means of ensuring stability and continuity by deterring other private interests from entering this unusual land market.[55]

In addition, perhaps de Soto overplays his hand, leading him to misconstrue some of the missing lessons of history.[56] He argues that '[t]he recognition and integration of extralegal property rights was a key element in the United States becoming the most important market economy and producer of capital in the world.'[57] That is a very bold claim. Let us put to one side the myriad other geographical, political and social factors that might logically be more central to the creation of a vibrant American economy, and focus solely on frontier development. Squatting, while prevalent, was the secondary mode of settlement; it was derivative of the official plan. It seems doubtful that it could have flourished as it did without state involvement.

Furthermore, it is by no means generally accepted that the strategy for settling the American and Canadian western frontiers was economically optimal. This critique emerges partially from the extravagant giveaways to railway companies and other ventures. But more significantly, the rush to secure land came at a cost. Because settlements were offered on a first-come, first-served basis, homesteaders may have been induced to develop and clear some regions prematurely. While squatters sought and often acquired prime real estate, the deprivations resulting from the absence of an adequate infrastructure produced hardship. And squatting and legal homesteading in more remote areas was sub-optimal whenever access to markets was limited or costly.[58]

---

[55] We are indebted to Larissa Katz for the kernel of this idea.

[56] De Soto seems to misunderstand pertinent aspects of the common law. He maintains, for example, that the English common law had no means to resolve disputes when land with 'dubious title' was acquired: *Mystery of Capital*, note 11 above, 111. Likewise, it is stated that in England long-term occupation was simply illegal: note 11 above, 113. Hence, there is no appreciation of the priority accorded to first possessors as against latecomers. Nor, of course, is account taken of the law of adverse possession. It is scarcely surprising, therefore, that the notion of occupancy ripening into full-bodied ownership is treated as a monumental step. But it is not. And he describes the Northwest Ordinance (US), which was promulgated in 1787, as '[n]otably . . . establish[ing] the concept of "fee simple ownership"'! See de Soto, note 11 above, 122.

[57] *Ibid*, 148.

[58] See further C Southey, 'The Staples Thesis, Common Property and Homesteading' (1978) 11 *Can J of Econ* 547. In K Norrie & D Owram, *A History of the Canadian Economy*, 2nd edn (Toronto, Harcourt Brace, 1996) 231, the authors regard this reasoning as elegant but as yet unsubstantiated. See also TJ Anderson & PJ Hill, 'The Race for Property Rights' (1990) 33 *J Law & Econ* 177; RL Stroup, 'Buying Misery with Federal Land' (1988) 57 *Public Choice* 69. For a defence of American settlement policies, see DW Allen, 'Homesteading and Property Rights; Or, How the West was Really Won' (1991) 34 *J Law & Econ* 1.

CONCLUSION

This essay begins with a quotation from Ernest May on the uses and misuses of history in the formation of foreign policy. May warns against the unreflective adoption of historical precedent. In brief, in this chapter we have sought to demonstrate that May's warning is apt when assessing Hernando de Soto's contributions to development theory. While the history of Edmonton Settlement reflects some of the central claims advanced by de Soto, it is just as important to appreciate that that history, as with those like it, is far removed in so many ways from the circumstances that prompted de Soto's efforts to solve the mystery of capital. These historical differences are quite possibly significant enough to undermine the capacity of what he terms the missing lessons of history to advance his main thesis.

IV

Property, Empire and Indigenous Title

11

Land Law and The Making Of The British Empire

PATRICK McAUSLAN*

INTRODUCTION

T HIS IS A story about land, law and empire. I aim to show how a particular part of the common law—the land law—was used as the principal legal tool for the advancement of the British empire from the sixteenth century onwards; how this necessary blending of public and private in the law, which such an evolution of law required, was brought about; how it was continued in countries that were once part of the empire but then became independent; and how this approach was adapted for the acquisition of land in African dependencies in the late nineteenth and early twentieth centuries.

The story starts off in England with an overview of the origins and development of English land law. English land lawyers recount the origins of our land law without any real sense of its uniqueness, its blend of public and private law and its fundamental impact on the development not just of the details of the law but of our whole outlook on land and law. My argument is that the use of land law as the legal spearhead of English colonialism can only be properly understood if we go back to the beginning of our law and trace its development and use in England, where the tools and ideologies were forged and eventually proved so potent a force for colonial expansion.

Karsten's work refers only briefly and in passing to Ireland,[1] but Wood has drawn my attention to England's 'brutal colonial enterprise'[2] in Ireland in the sixteenth century and beyond and the enormously important role it played in the early development of land law as a vital tool of colonialism.

---

* This chapter is part of a forthcoming book by the author.
[1] P Karsten, *Between Law and Custom: 'High' and 'Low' Legal Cultures in the Lands of the British Diaspora—The United States, Canada, Australia and New Zealand, 1600–1900* (Cambridge, Cambridge University Pres, 2002).
[2] E Meiksins Wood, *Empire of Capital* (London, Verso, 2003) 75.

Ireland is perhaps underrated as the legal seed bed for the expansion of the British empire, and this accounts for the attention given to it here.

My present concern is to show how the basic fundaments of the law were used in the colonial enterprise to justify setting aside indigenous land laws and customs and impose in their stead rules of English land law, which provided the formal legal backing for the land grabbing that was and is at the heart of any colonial enterprise. Attitudes to indigenous land laws and agreements with indigenous peoples with respect to their land are of greater importance here than the finer points of land law in, for example, New Zealand, Kenya or the USA.

Empire's land law was an early example of globalisation—common rules applicable across and throughout many different lands. This form of colonial globalisation was in a way internationalised after the First World War, when, as Anghie has shown,[3] the international community's involvement in colonial governance was continued to provide an intellectual justification for displacing local laws and practices with imposed laws to facilitate the colonial exploitation of the territories subjected to mandate and trusteeship status.

That form of globalisation did not disappear when empire, mandates and trusteeships wound down by the late 1950s. The new globalisation has attempted to build on the old, and the legal face of this new globalisation is a familiar one: Anglo-American common law. The new globalisation has followed the old one too in its involvement with land law and its attempts to develop land laws that displace local laws and to put in place laws based on 'best practice' or international norms that can be used to justify such displacement and continue the practice and ideology of strong central government involvement in land management. This part of the story of the evolution of land law in the developing world, however, cannot be dealt with in detail here.

ENGLAND: THE FEUDAL ORIGINS OF COLONIAL LAND LAW

We must return to the beginning of the modern history of England, the Norman conquest of William I in 1066. Conquering England meant asserting *imperium*, that is, sovereignty over England. Initially, William attempted to govern England through the existing persons who had held office under Edward the Confessor, whose heir William claimed to be, but after the great rebellions of 1069, more and more land passed from English

---

[3] A Anghie, 'Time Present and Time Past: Globalization, International Financial Institutions and the Third World' (2000) 32 NYU *Journal of International Law and Politics* 243.

hands into Norman ones.[4] The invasion of 1066 coupled with the rebellions of 1069 enabled William to act on the basis that all the land in the country was forfeited to him; he obtained *dominium* or absolute ownership of the land of England, which then allowed him to determine who subsequently obtained what land and on what terms. In practice and in law, no distinction was made between conquering the country and acquiring absolute ownership of that country's land.

If this was and remains one fundament of English land law—that the monarch owns all the land in England and derives his or her ownership from being the supreme lord in the country—the other fundament was feudalism. Maitland has elaborated and explained the connection between the land law aspect of feudalism and public law:

> It may seem strange that we begin our survey of public law by examining the system of landed property . . . but . . . if we examine our notion of feudalism does it not seem this, that land law is not private law, that public law is land law, that public and political rights and duties of all sorts are intimately and quite inextricably blended with rights in land? Such rights carry with them the right to attend the common council or court of the realm, the common council or court of the county; jurisdictions, military duties, fiscal burdens, are consequences of tenure; the constitution of parliament, of the law courts, of the army, all seems as it were a sort of appendix to the law of real property . . .[5]

The origins of English land law then lie in conquest, confiscations, plantations of foreigners and the 'depression' of the native English by such plantations, and overall, the duties owed by all those holding land, by whatever tenure, to the king, from whom all land was held mediately or immediately. Not only does this ensure the close connection between land law and government, but it also and necessarily carries with it the implication that the monarch (and later, governments acting in the name of the monarch) has supreme power over the land and all who occupy and use the land. Feudalism in a sense then involves the continued intermingling of *imperium* and *dominium* with respect to land.

THE COLONISATION OF IRELAND: THE EARLY DEVELOPMENT OF COLONIAL
LAND LAW

The story of the engagement of the English with Ireland demonstrates the truth of this intermingling of *imperium* and *dominium* and provides too an early example of English legal attitudes and actions towards customary

---

[4] FM Stenton, *Anglo-Saxon England*, 2nd edn (Oxford, Oxford University Press, 1947) 617–18.

[5] FW Maitland, *The Constitutional History of England* (Cambridge, Cambridge University Press, 1926) 23, 157.

laws that conflicted with and impeded colonial expansion and settlement, or plantation, as it was then called.[6] In the eleventh and twelfth centuries, at the time of the first English invasions and plantations in Ireland, that country consisted of several small kingdoms. There was, however, a more or less national system of customary law—the Brehon Laws, the product of a hereditary caste of lawyers. Within the Brehon Laws there was a complex Irish land system, which reflected an equally complex social system.

Kolbert and O'Brien have drawn attention to a specific strength of the Brehon system:

> The old Irish politico-legal system, particularly in its application to agrarian conditions . . . had its imperfections, but, whatever its weaknesses it has this great strength: under its rule it was exceedingly difficult to disturb any tenant in the occupation of his share of the clan lands . . . and this feature, this freedom from eviction and *a fortiori*, from wholesale clearances, was doubtless one of the reasons for the remarkable tenacity of the Brehon laws and for their survival, in the face of great official [English] hostility, until the seventeenth century.[7]

The 'great official hostility' is worth noting. In the fourteenth century, during the reign of Edward III, four steps were taken to break the power and wealth of the descendants of the first Anglo-Norman conquerors of Ireland.

> The first step taken was 'a general resumption of all the lands, liberties, seigniories, and jurisdictions that had been granted in Ireland not only by Edward the Third himself but also by his father'. Next followed in 1342 the removal of the Anglo-Irish from offices under the crown; and in 1355 came a series of ordinances forbidding intermarriages betwixt English and Irish, and rendering illegal the practice of fostering which was largely carried on . . . At length in 1367 was passed the memorable Act known as the Statute of Kilkenny . . . by [which] it was made treason for one of English birth or blood to accept or rule by the Brehon Law . . . while the penalty of forfeiture was attached to those who adopted the names, tongue, or manners of the mere Irish.[8]

As Montgomery has noted, these and later efforts were on the whole futile, and despite various attempts to enforce them by military expeditions from England, the 'circle of the English colony grew steadily less' during the fourteenth and fifteenth centuries.

---

[6] What follows is derived from WE Montgomery, *The History of Land Tenure in Ireland* (Cambridge, Cambridge University Press, 1889) and CF Kolbert and T O'Brien, 'Land Reform in Ireland' (Cambridge University Department of Land Economy Occasional Paper No 3, 1975).

[7] Kolbert and O'Brien, *ibid.*, p.7.

[8] Montgomery, note 6 above, 52.

The Tudor monarchs made considerable efforts to reassert English rule over Ireland, and did so by means that foreshadowed later colonial adventures. Reorganisation of land rights were key. There were three elements of this approach:

(a) **Surrender and Regrant:** In the 1540s, officials of Henry VIII negotiated with previously independent lords, of both Irish and Anglo-Irish descent, to surrender their lands in return for regrants in knight service at a rent.

(b) **Plantations:** The plantation process replaced the primary producers on the land with immigrants. It involved a two-stage legal process. First, the previous lords or occupants of the land lost their rights by forfeiture for what the English Crown and the courts considered treason in resisting English rule. This act of forfeiture left the title to the Crown. Next, new grants were made to settlers as quasi-feudal tenants of the Crown.

(c) **Composition:** This was the method used in Connaught. A commission established in 1585 inquired into the ownership of land in the area. The commission entered into agreements with persons successfully claiming land, whereby the persons could have their titles confirmed. Landowners usually agreed to hold their land in knight service from the Crown.[9]

Thus by the beginning of the seventeenth century, most of the land of Ireland had passed into or through the hands of the English Crown by various legal subterfuges and was held on some form of English tenure. The stage was set for the final step in the process of the legal colonisation of Irish land: the substitution of Irish Brehon Laws by English land law.[10]

> The history of the final abolition of the Irish Code is simple. Two decisions of the Courts in the reign of James the First whereby the whole land system of the Brehon law was crumbled into dust, became of great importance, since they followed the conquests of war, and hence affected practically the whole of Ireland. One by one the decisions of all the judges . . . declared void in law the Irish custom of Gavelkind succession, while the other abolished Tanistry.
>
> [In relation to Gavelkind,] the judgement . . . says that . . . 'because all the said Irish countries and the inhabitants of them from henceforward were to be governed by the rules of the Common Law of England, it was resolved and declared by all the judges that the said Irish custom of Gavelkind was void in law, not only for the inconvenience and unreasonableness of it but because it was a mere personal custom and could not alter the descent of inheritance . . ..

---

[9] A Lyall, *Land Law in Ireland* (Dublin, Oak Tree Press, 1994) 62–3.

[10] Omitted is any discussion of the evolution of the colonial judicial and legal system in Ireland, which created the conditions for the judicial decisions discussed in the text. For a survey, see DT Konig, 'Colonization and the Common Law in Ireland and Virginia, 1569–1634' in JA Henretta and SN Katz (eds), *The Transformation of Early American History, Society, Authority and Ideology* (New York, Knopf, 1991) 70–92.

> [In relation to Tanistry,] it was . . . finally settled by the Court that 'the said custom of Tanistry was void in itself and abolished when the Common Law of England was established.' By these two decisions the law of a nation, which, whatever its faults, was ingrained in their national life, and regarded by them with unreasoning devotion . . . was swept away . . ..
>
> The injury inflicted upon the Irish peasantry lay . . . not so much in the introduction of the English tenures as in the refusal to recognize the rights of the tenantry established under the compulsory reorganisations of the land system . . .[11]

Kolbert and O'Brien have noted that had the substitution of the English common law for Brehon Law in 1613 been the chief bequest of the Stuarts, 'much would have been forgiven them, particularly had it been carried out in spirit and letter.' Montgomery too has noted that the rules developed especially for the settlement of Ulster appeared to have been framed in a liberal and thoughtful spirit. Practice, however, was very different. Severe though Montgomery has been on the practice,[12] Kolbert and O'Brien have been even more damning. Writing of the confiscations of the Stuarts and the settlement of William III, they state:

> One of the fatal lessons it taught the Irishman was to put no faith in English law as it was administered in Ireland, and in particular, to put no reliance on a title based on that law as a guarantee of security of tenure for his land. As Lecky remarks of this new machinery for expropriation: 'Every man's enjoyment of his property became precarious, and the natives learnt with terror that law could be made in a time of perfect peace, and without any provocation being given, a not less terrible instrument than the sword for rooting them out of the soil.'[13]
>
> . . . The conditions that followed the 'Revolutionary Settlement' [of William III] . . . put the whole power, prestige and authority of the country exclusively into the hands of a small minority, little more than a tenth of the people . . . It had immense, and in many things virtually absolute, powers, particularly in reference to land, as the main aim of the Settlement was to secure that there would be no Catholic interest therein of the slightest consequence . . . The provisions were . . . intended to make it impossible for any Catholic ever again to own any land in his own country.[14]

The introduction of English land law into Ireland has been dealt with here for two principal reasons. First, it is not a subject about which much has been written in the context of colonialism. Second, when placed in the

---

[11] Montgomery, note 6 above, 67–9, 72 and 73. For Gavelkind and Tanistry, see Montgomery, 6–10.

[12] *Ibid*, 75, 86–8 and 91–3.

[13] WEA Lecky, *A History of Ireland in the Eighteenth Century* (London, Longmans, 1892) 28.

[14] Kolbert and O'Brien, note 6 above, 18, 22 and 23.

context of empire, as Wood has recently done, it can be clearly seen as the precursor of the use of land law to advance the colonial acquisition and occupation of foreign lands.

What were the key elements of the imposition of English land law on Ireland? First, a combination of military adventurism and colonial settlement—the former a necessary prelude to the latter. Second, an assertion of sovereignty—*imperium*—by the monarch, followed by, third, the assertion of dominium over the land through the granting of land to Englishmen and the 'granting' of land to natives who were already in possession of land under their own laws using feudal arrangements aimed at creating a land-related governance bond between the monarch and the holders of land in Ireland. This in turn led to, fourth, the provision of a legal veneer for the forfeiture of land to the English Crown when the natives 'rebelled' against colonial occupation. Fifth, land thus acquired by the English Crown was then made available for planned settlements—plantations—and more generally, for 'adventurers' to take up and exploit. Sixth and finally, a combination of judicial decisions, legislation and executive action set aside the existing native land law and substituted English land law *tout court* as a final step in a legal process that had over the preceding years made it more and more difficult for the native land law to operate within Ireland. The way was then open to use English land law consciously and deliberately to deprive the Irish of rights to land in their own country and to ensure legal backing for the colonial occupiers and settlers.

What is missing from this account is any attempt at a justification of this course of action. Wood highlights the justification provided by Sir John Davies, lawyer and English Attorney-General for Ireland who was the principal architect of the legal arrangements for the settlement of Ulster in the early years of the seventeenth century and the formal replacement of Irish land law by the English common law. His justification has echoed down through the ages and has been repeated again and again as the justification for colonialism and the displacement of indigenous law by colonial law:

> In a letter to the Earl of Salisbury in 1610, having argued that the king has supreme rights over the land not only by English common law but by Irish customary law (which was, in any case, no law at all but just 'lewd' and 'unreasonable' custom) Davies went on . . .:

> 'His Majesty is bound in conscience to use all lawful and just courses to reduce his people from barbarism to civility . . . Now civility cannot possibly be planted among them by this mixed plantation of some of the natives and settling of their possessions in a course of Common Law; for if themselves were suffered to possess the whole country, as their septs have done for many hundred of years past, they would never, to the end of the world, build houses, make townships,

or villages or manure or improve the land as it ought to be . . . when his Majesty may lawfully dispose it to such persons as will make a civil plantation thereupon.

Again, his Majesty may take this course in conscience because it tendeth to the good of the inhabitants in many ways.'[15]

The language may be old, but the sentiments have lived on: natives have no law and no capacity to develop a modern state and society; it is for their own good that their land is taken from them and given over to those who will make more effective use of it, and that their 'lewd' customs are replaced by a proper system of law.

THE COLONISATION OF AMERICA: THE BEGINNINGS OF THE
GLOBALISATION OF LAND LAW

The seventeenth century was an era of English imperial expansion; besides the aggressive colonisation of Ireland, the period saw the beginnings of colonial expansion into North America and the Caribbean. This section will discuss the expansion and development of English land law in North America, which culminated in the seminal decision of the US Supreme Court in *Johnson v M'Intosh*[16] in 1823. Robertson's recent study of this case[17] shows its fundamental importance in providing the legal justification for the expansion of the new United States of America into indigenous America and the seizure of the lands of the indigenous peoples by the European-American colonialists. It would be a mistake to assume that that decision came out of the blue: it built on a long line of thinking and action by European-Americans with respect to the taking of indigenous lands from the seventeenth century onwards.

There were basically two contrasting approaches to relations with indigenous Americans with respect to land. One approach was to deal with them more or less as equals either in the market place—with the colonial government and then the US government buying land from them—or as part of an international community by concluding treaties with them about sharing with or acquiring land from them. These actions involved a recognition of customary land tenure as a valid operative form of tenure. This was the predominant approach in the early years of the colonisation of America.

The alternative approach was in effect to deny that indigenous Americans had property rights recognisable by the common law and that indigenous American nations were entities entitled to be seen and treated

---

[15] Wood, note 2 above, 81–2.
[16] 21 US (8 Wheat) 543 (1823).
[17] LG Robertson, *Conquest by Law: How the Discovery of America Dispossessed Indigenous Peoples of Their Lands* (New York, Oxford University Press, 2005).

as a separate sovereign peoples. As a consequence—or if not as a consequence, then as part and parcel of the denial of property rights to such people—their land could be taken and used by incoming colonial settlers. This was the position adopted on the ground in many cases, with either squatters ignoring the formal law and simply moving onto Indian lands or individual speculators buying land from the Indians.[18]

This 'political' position had legal backing. Two important English legal rulings in the eighteenth century provided broad juridical justification for such an approach. First, a ruling by the Privy Council in 1722 provided that 'if there be a new and uninhabited land found by British subjects, as the law is the birthright of every subject, so wherever they go they carry their law with them.'[19] 'Uninhabited' must be understood as a term of art: it did not mean empty of people but empty of 'civilised' people who recognised private property rights in land. Second, the famous decision in *Campbell v Hall*[20] in 1774 reiterated the earlier Privy Council ruling that when Englishmen found a colony in a previously uninhabited or savage country, they carry English law with them insofar as it is applicable there.

Such rulings found legal support within America. It was Chief Justice Marshall's judgement in the Supreme Court decision of *Johnson v M'Intosh*[21] that in effect brought together the practice on the ground, the philosophical justifications for such practice and the law—thereby providing a legal framework not just for what Robertson has pithily summed up as the judicial conquest of Native America[22] but also for later US and British colonial adventures throughout the world. Robertson has shown the background to the decision and the reasons that impelled Marshall to develop the arguments that he did. They involved him trying to curry favour with the state of Virginia, which was at the time very resentful of certain Supreme Court decisions, by setting out principles that would favour Virginia over Kentucky in a different dispute over the grant by Virginia of lands to their military veterans (of which Marshall was one). These principles not strictly necessary for the instant case.

---

[18]   *Ibid*, 103–7.
[19]   A ruling of the Privy Council (the body that from the late seventeenth century administered colonies) in 1722. Quoted by V Strang, 'Not so Black and White: The Effects of Aboriginal Law on Australian Legislation' in A Abramson and D Theodossopoulos (eds), *Land, Law and Environment, Mythical Land, Legal Boundaries* (London, Pluto Press, 2000) 113, fn 1. Konig refers too to the opinion of the King's Bench in 1693 in *Blankard v Galdy* 90 ER 1089 that 'in case of an uninhabited country newly found out by English subjects, all laws in force in England are in force there . . .'
[20]   (1774) 20 St Tr 239. This case also affirmed that existing law remains in force, but as later events showed, 'law' meant 'systems of law not totally dissimilar to the common law system', which opened the way for the disregard of customary law when it was convenient so to do.
[21]   21 US (8 Wheat) 543 (1823).
[22]   Robertson, note 18 above, 44.

The basic facts of the case are relevant to the broad argument being advanced here, as they show how the decision provided retrospective legal justification for private speculative actions in the land market, which at the time they were undertaken were of highly dubious legal provenance—a characteristic of judicial decisions regarding land disputes involving indigenous land rights. The case involved 43,000 square miles of 'lush, rolling farmland commanding the junctures of four major river systems in Indiana and Illinois'[23] and goes back to the Proclamation of George III (1763), which

> declared the lands west of the Allegheny Mountains to be reserved for the use of Indians; barred colonial governors from authorizing surveys or issuing patents establishing title to these lands; forbade individual colonists to purchase, settle or take possession of any of them without a license from the Crown; and ordered squatters to leave immediately. The Crown claimed a 'pre-emption' or 'preemptive' right to these lands (i.e., an exclusive right to purchase, whenever the Indian owners should be willing to sell).[24]

The Proclamation was very unpopular with most colonists and led to 'crafty speculators' trying to find a way round it.

> One such speculator was William Murray ... who was convinced that the proclamation's prohibition of individual land purchases from Indians was bound to be repealed ... Although the circumstances remain ... murky, sometime prior to the spring of 1773 Murray obtained an altered copy of an opinion issued in 1757 by ... England's attorney general ... and solicitor general. It related to the right of the British East India Company to purchase land directly of 'the Mogul or any of the Indian princes or governments.' ... The opinion helpfully provided that the king's 'Letters Patent' were *not* necessary for lands 'acquired by treaty or grant from the Mogul or any of the Princes or Governments ... the property of the soil [ie, title to the property] vesting in the Company'. The altered transcription that came into Murray's hands omitted the reference to 'the Mogul' and substituted for 'the Company' 'the grantee' ... If one believed that the Camden-Yorke opinion had been issued after the proclamation, as Murray was prepared to intimate, it might be read to supersede the Crown's prohibition of individual purchases west of the Allegheny Mountains.

> Thus, from a scheme hatched on the eve of the Revolution and predicated on fraudulent legal authority, was born the land speculation that would give rise to the *Johnson v M'Intosh* litigation.[25]

For the next 40-odd years, this 'large land purchase' was the subject of numerous attempts to get official approval from either or both Congress and the US government. All failed. For reasons that need not be rehearsed

---

[23]   *Ibid*, 6.
[24]   *Ibid*.
[25]   Robertson, note 18 above, 7 and 8.

here, it was not possible until 1817 to mount a case concerning the validity and legality of the land purchase in a federal court, which could be appealed to the Supreme Court.

A federal court could hear a case between citizens of different states (the diversity of citizenship principle allowing an out-of-state party access to a federal court) only if the amount in controversy equalled or exceeded the then limit of $2000, so it was necessary to find a shareholder plaintiff and defendant from different states claiming title to land in the claim area valued at $2000 or more. Johnson and M'Intosh were two persons who agreed to be the parties in the action. The action was a collusive one, a pretended trespass and ejectment with an agreed statement of facts—both parties agreeing to go through with this charade with which the judge joined in, finding for the defendant M'Intosh. The plaintiff Johnson then appealed to the Supreme Court on a statement of facts that could not be challenged in the court and that counsel for Johnson considered he could win the case on. The fundamental case presented to the Supreme Court was the effect of the Royal Proclamation of 1763 on a pre-Revolutionary War land purchase.

On this narrow ground, the Court found against the plaintiff: the Proclamation of 1763 was considered to constitute an objection to the title of the plaintiff, and the claim was therefore barred. However, Marshall was concerned to use the case to 'lay the groundwork for the successful resolution of the claims of Virginia militia grantees and their transferees'[26]. What was required to achieve this was a finding that Virginia owned the land that was taken from the Chickasaw and granted to the militia, in fee simple.

As recounted by Robertson, Marshall set out to demonstrate that Virginia did indeed own the land by reference to history 'of dubious reliability and relevance'.[27] He also re-phrased the issues before the Court to bring them within the framework and principles that he wanted to use to achieve the ends that he had set himself:

> On the discovery of this immense continent, the great nations of Europe were eager to appropriate to themselves so much of it as they could respectively acquire. Its vast extent offered an ample field to the ambition and enterprise of all; and the character and religion of its inhabitants afforded an apology for considering them as a people over whom the superior genius of Europe might claim an ascendancy . . .

> But as they were all in pursuit of nearly the same object, it was necessary, in order to avoid conflicting settlements, and consequent war with each other, to establish a principle, which all should acknowledge as the law by which the right

---

[26] *Ibid*, 95.
[27] *Ibid*, 96.

of acquisition, which they all asserted, should be regulated as between themselves. This principle was, that discovery gave title to the government by whose subjects, or by whose authority, it was made, against all other European governments, which title might be consummated by possession . . .

[The Indians] were admitted to be the rightful *occupants* of the soil, with a legal as well as a just claim to retain *possession* of it and to *use* it according to their own discretion; but their rights to complete sovereignty as independent nations, were necessarily diminished, and their power to dispose of the soil at their own will, to whomsoever they pleased, was denied by the original fundamental principle, that discovery gave exclusive *title* to those who made it.[28]

Thus at a stroke, Marshall asserted that the European 'discoverers' of America had unilaterally and as a *consequence of discovery* converted the absolute title of the Indians—the title to the soil—to a mere right of occupancy. Following that logic, Marshall went on:

While the different nations of Europe respected the right of the natives as occupiers, they asserted the *ultimate dominion* to be in themselves and claimed and exercised, as a consequence of this ultimate dominion, a power to grant the soil while yet in possession of the natives. These grants have been understood by all, to convey a title to the grantees, subject only to the Indian right of occupancy.[29]

What is this but a reprise of the old feudal notion used by William I that acquisition of a country as a conqueror involves acquisition of the land and the consequent right to dispose of that land to whomsoever the conqueror/discoverer determines? Marshall went on to assert that 'no one of the powers of Europe gave its full assent to this principle [of discovery] more unequivocally than England'.[30] He concluded 'somewhat disingenuously'[31]:

The United States . . . have unequivocally acceded to that great and broad rule by which its civilised inhabitants now hold this country . . . They maintain . . . that discovery gave an exclusive right to extinguish the Indian title of occupancy, either by purchase or by conquest . . . An absolute title to lands cannot exist, at the same time, in different persons, or in different governments.[32]

Thus, on the basis of a fraudulent land purchase, a collusive action, questionable and deficient history, disingenuous reasoning and a personal interest, the great Chief Justice Marshall rewrote the land law of early America and so facilitated the dispossession, dispersal and degradation of

---

[28] *Johnson v M'Intosh* 21 US (8 Wheat) 543, 572–4 (1823), quoted in *ibid*, 99–100. Emphasis added by Robertson.
[29]   *Ibid*, 574, quoted in *ibid*, 100, emphasis added.
[30]   *Ibid*, 576, quoted in *ibid*, 102.
[31]   Robertson, note 18 above, 111.
[32]   *Johnson v M'Intosh*, note 28 above, 587–8, quoted in *ibid*, 111–12.

the Native Americans, which took place at an ever increasing pace in the nineteenth century. He set aside all the evidence of almost two hundred years of attempted honest and straightforward dealing on the basis of law between the Native Americans and the colonists, preferring to support and give legal authority to those who had ignored the law as it had been clearly laid down and who had refused to accord full recognition to the Native Americans or their rights to their own land. His judgement opened the way for the use of land law as the primary tool for the forcible displacement of native inhabitants, the removal of their rights to their land and their replacement by colonial settlers, the whole given justification by references to the superior civilisation of the colonists when compared to that of the natives.

But it is important not to attach too great a uniqueness to the decision. Given the theoretical justifications put forward for colonisation by Grotius, Locke and Vattel,[33] with particular reference to the taking of land from native inhabitants of colonised countries and its conversion to more 'productive' use, *Johnson*, or, perhaps more accurately, Marshall may more correctly be seen as responding to these justifications and giving them a legal veneer rather than developing an original approach to colonial land grabbing. I would argue too that the discovery doctrine, with its elision of *imperium* and *dominium*, emerged in a direct line from the Norman Conquest and the feudal approach to governance: ownership of land is the key to control and governance of the state.

THE COLONISATION OF AUSTRALIA AND NEW ZEALAND: REFINING THE WEAPON OF LAND LAW

During the almost fifty-year period of the land purchase saga that culminated in *Johnson v M'Intosh*, the English also began to acquire Australia and New Zealand, where the pattern of using land law as the spearhead of colonial penetration was further developed in order to ensure a more complete colonial and settler control of land. In some respects, one might say that the legal tools were refined. The 'mistake' of American colonisers—early official and judicial acceptance that the indigenous inhabitants owned the soil (the term used to describe the ultimate ownership of the land)—was not repeated in Australia and New Zealand. Early colonial administrators in Australia were prepared to recognise aboriginal ownership of the soil but acted on the basis that *imperium* over the country gave the Crown rights over the land that were superior to the rights of the aboriginal inhabitants.

---

[33] Wood, note 2 above, especially 68–72 and 94–101.

In many respects, the imposition of the whole panoply of English land law on the Maoris in New Zealand is the most egregious example of land law as a weapon of colonisation outside of Africa, and it merits a fuller discussion.[34] The Treaty of Waitangi in 1840 between the British government and the Maoris appeared to provide protection for Maori land rights of a more extensive scope than anything that existed in Australia and, by that time, than any treaty was likely to in America. Parsonson, however, has noted:

> From the beginning there were ominous signs foreshadowing the Government's sustained assault on Maori rights . . . The limitation of Maori land rights began with the Crown's introduction of feudalism to New Zealand based on the early decision that land titles in the colony must derive from Crown grant; it was evident in the first piece of legislation passed in New Zealand that directly affected Maori land rights, the Land Claims Ordinance 1841 . . . [I]t enacted the Crown's sole right of pre-emption and . . . also spelt out the extent to which Maori rights were to be recognised; 'all unappropriated land within the . . . Colony . . . subject however to the rightful and necessary *occupation and use* thereof by the aboriginal inhabitants of the said Colony are and remain Crown and Domain Lands of Her Majesty.[35]

Parsonson is correct in seeing the basic limitation on Maori land rights as stemming from the introduction of feudal law into New Zealand, although she perhaps was not fully aware of the rationale of the feudal rule that title to land must derive from a Crown grant: the elision of *imperium* with *dominium*.

As each colonial acquisition built on the legal structures developed in the last acquisition—America on Ireland, the Antipodes and South Africa on America—so too here: the exercise of power by the British government over Maori land in the 1840s and beyond lay the legal foundations for the exercise of British colonial power over land in Africa in the late nineteenth and early twentieth centuries.

A particular problem for the colonial authorities was that the Maori were entering into various kinds of leasing arrangements with settlers both prior to and after the Treaty of Waitangi. This assumed that the Maori had rights to dispose of the land, which was inconsistent with the British understanding of the effect of the treaty. It also interfered with the Crown's

---

[34] What follows draws on Karsten, note 1 above; and A Parsonson, 'The Fate of Maori Land Rrights in Early Colonial New Zealand: The Limits of the Treaty of Waitangi and the Doctrine of Aboriginal Title' in D Kirkby and C Coleborne (eds), *Law, History and Colonialism: The Reach of Empire* (Manchester, Manchester University Press, 2002) 173–89; and J Weaver, 'The Construction of Property Rights on Imperial Frontiers: The Case of the New Zealand Native Land Purchase Ordinance of 1846' in D Kirkby and C Coleborne (eds), *Law, History and Colonialism: The Reach of Empire* (Manchester, Manchester University Press, 2002) 221–39.

[35] Parsonson, *ibid*, 173 and 174 (emphasis added).

monopoly right of pre-emption, which would enable it to acquire land from Maoris cheaply. In 1841, Governor Hobson was directed to promulgate an ordinance to declare the absolute invalidity of any conveyance, contract or will for the disposal of land by any native chief or chiefs to a European and to forbid all Europeans from acquiring land or any interest in land in that way. This ordinance was not enforced, and leases were tolerated. However, the Native Land Purchase Ordinance (1846) attempted to put more legal teeth into the policy, and the Constitution Act (1852) elevated the ban on transactions between Maoris and Pakeha into constitutional status.

The basic British aim behind the treaty and the ordinances was to reinforce the imposition of English feudalism on the Maoris with respect to rights to land and to ensure that the colonial authorities had the necessary authority to determine not merely what rights Maoris had in the land but also where Maoris would be allowed to live. It was a logical consequence of the Crown's right of pre-emption, which in practice amounted to something very close to compulsory acquisition of land with no opportunity to challenge the amount of compensation: the Crown would also determine what land would be left for the Maoris, or to put it another way, where Maoris might live. In other words, it was a policy of Native Reserves. As described by Parsonson, these reserves and their management sound very familiar to those who are knowledgeable about colonial land management practices in Africa:

> [Governor] Grey's policy was based on the systematic extinguishment of customary title, control by Crown officials of the size and location of Native Reserves created at the time of purchase [of land by the colonial government], denial of Maori control and management of the reserves, and recognition only of a Maori right to 'use and occupy'.[36]

Eventually, colonial policies and laws pushed the Maori into war in the 1860s, which in turn—just as in Ireland in the sixteenth and seventeenth centuries—led to confiscations of land, the further downgrading of Maori property rights and the denial that they could enforce any right to own or occupy land in the courts. Parsonson has concluded that the war and its aftermath 'conveyed in unmistakeable terms a message until then quietly tucked away in legislation and in policy documents . . . that Maori law was to be ignored'.[37] This conclusion, difficult to disagree with, neatly juxtaposes war and law: the colonial common law of land is used to take away the land of indigenous populations, to set aside the land laws of indigenous populations and the rights in land that those laws enshrine and protect; but

---

[36] *Ibid*, 182.
[37] *Ibid*, 183.

if colonial law is resisted, then colonial military force is used to enforce it. The weapon of law and weapons of war are two sides of the same coin.

THE COLONISATION OF AFRICA: THE EXPANSION OF THE JURISDICTION OF LAND LAW

The countries hitherto considered have one thing in common, besides being colonised by Britain (or by England in the case of Ireland): they were all colonies acquired and used for purposes of settlement. From their very origins as dependencies, they were colonies and became part of the dominions of the Crown so that there was a kind of logic—perverted in practice though it was—in applying a feudal land law to these colonies and using it to dispossess the native inhabitants of their lands and their rights, the more easily to replace them with colonists.

In the case of the colonisation of countries in Africa, however, the position was very different. Although many countries in Africa ultimately became colonies, there were, both in British colonial constitutional law and in international law, very important differences between a colony that was a part of the Crown's possessions and those dependencies that were not. Yet powers over land within these dependencies slowly developed in the last two decades of the nineteenth century through various legal subterfuges, until they equalled the plenitude of powers taken by the Crown in the colonies, and English land law was specifically applied to these dependencies.

The legal basis for the exercise of British power in Africa in the nineteenth century was provided by the Foreign Jurisdiction Act (1843), the major purpose of which was to regulate Crown jurisdiction over British subjects who lived outside British dominions and yet were not, in whole or in part, subject to the jurisdiction of the country in which they were living.[38] The Act was drawn in very wide terms. It permitted the Crown to exercise jurisdiction wherever 'by treaty, capitulation, grant, usage, sufferance or other lawful means', it had come to enjoy such power. The extent of the power permitted by the Act was:

> to hold, exercise, and enjoy any power or jurisdiction which Her Majesty now hath or may at any time hereafter have within any country or place out of Her Majesty's dominions, in the same and as ample a manner as if Her Majesty had acquired such power or jurisdiction by cession or conquest of territory.[39]

The Foreign Jurisdiction Act (1843) was amended several times over the years and was replaced by the Foreign Jurisdiction Act (1890), which

---

[38] The two principal countries in which the Crown exercised jurisdiction over British subjects were the Ottoman Empire (from 1579) and China.
[39] S 1.

repeated the substance of section 1 of the 1843 Act. During the currency of the 1843 Act, the concept of jurisdiction was constantly expanded by the British government, particularly in relation to protectorates in Africa.

International law acknowledged the type of relationship in which a powerful state takes over the duty of protecting a weaker state and conducts its external affairs. The protected state remains an entity in international law. However,

> During the course of the nineteenth century ... European states began to exercise powers of protection over countries in Asia and Africa regarded by international law as imperfectly civilised and barbarous, such powers arising either as a consequence of treaties or as a result of the gradual assumption of control ... [T]hese protectorates were considered as debarring other civilised states from maintaining relations with the protected state ...

> In international law, the majority of these new protectorates ... were not recognized as persons, and treaties conferring jurisdiction were not considered binding on the protecting power. Indeed such treaties were merely regarded as statements of limitations which the protecting power would place on its own action ...

> In English municipal law protectorates were nowhere defined, but it has been recognized that for purposes of the Foreign Jurisdiction Acts, a protectorate 'means territory outside the dominions of the Crown, but over which the Crown exercises some jurisdiction' ...

> The colonial protectorates eventually differed from Crown colonies in little more than name, apart from the fact that they were not formally annexed, were administered by Orders [in Council] under the Foreign Jurisdiction Act and did not form a portion of British territory.[40]

As far back as 1833, the British Government had been advised by law officers that the exercise of protection over a state did not carry with it power to alienate the land contained therein.[41] The government was advised that unless a right to deal with waste and unoccupied land was specifically reserved in an agreement or treaty of protection, no such right could be allowed in a protectorate, and even in respect of waste and unoccupied land, it was not clear whether it could be alienated. This position represented a major obstacle to the British government, for if it could not grant land, it would be unable to attract settlers. Our focus will

---

[40] C Palley, *The Constitutional History and Law of Southern Rhodesia, 1880–1965* (Oxford, Oxford University Press, 1966) 44–6. The quotation in this passage is from the judgement of Farwell LJ in *R v Crewe (Earl) ex parte Sekgome* [1910] 2 KB 576, 611.

[41] AD McNair, *International Law Opinions*, vol I (Cambridge, Cambridge University Press, 1956) 39.

be the position in what is now Kenya (but was first part of the Sultan of Zanzibar's dominions and then the East African Protectorate).[42]

Within the East African Protectorate, declared in 1895, the colonial administration promulgated the Land Regulations in 1897.[43] These drew a distinction between land within the Sultan of Zanzibar's mainland dominions and land elsewhere in the protectorate. In the Sultan's dominions, the colonial authorities were empowered to sell the freehold of Crown land, not being the private property of the Sultan. In the rest of the protectorate, the colonial authorities could only offer 99-year certificates of occupancy, which did not appeal to would-be settlers.

Such a situation could not long continue, nor did it. In 1899, the law officers vouchsafed a new set of 'principles' to the government:

> On being informed by the Foreign Office that the natives of certain regions were 'practically savages without any proper conception of ownership of land' the Law Officers replied that the right of dealing with waste and unoccupied land accrued to the Crown by virtue of its protectorate, since protectorates over territories occupied by savage tribes 'really involve the assumption of control over all lands unappropriated. Her Majesty might, if she pleased, declare them to be Crown lands or make grants of them to individuals in fee or for any term'.[44]

Thus, the old feudal intermingling of *imperium* and *dominium* was applied to land in the African protectorates, laying the foundation for large-scale land grabbing in Anglophone Africa.

The East Africa (Lands) Order in Council (1901) gave effect to the law officers' opinion in the East African Protectorate. This Order vested Crown land in the whole of the protectorate in the Commissioner and Consul-General (the forerunner of the colonial Governor) for the time being to be held in trust for Her Majesty. The Commissioner was empowered to make grants and leases of Crown land on such terms as he might think fit. The following year the Commissioner promulgated the Crown Lands Ordinance, which provided for outright sales of land and leases of 99 years' duration. The rights and requirements of Africans to which regard was to be had in dealing with Crown land were seen in terms of actual occupation only; when land was no longer occupied by Africans, it could be sold or leased as waste or unoccupied land.

---

[42] See chapter 1 of YP Ghai and JPWB McAuslan, *Public Law and Political Change in Kenya* (Nairobi, Oxford University Press, 1970) for the tale of the colonial legal origins of Kenya.

[43] The Regulations were issued under the authority of the East Africa Order in Council SRO 1897 No 575, which made provision for the governance of the East Africa Protectorate and provided for the reception and application of the common law and the doctrines of equity to the new protectorate. So land granted under the Land Regulations was governed by English land law.

[44] Palley, note 39 above, 82, quoting FO 834/19, Law Officers to Foreign Office, 13 December 1899.

The Crown Lands Ordinance (1915) completed the process of equating British governmental powers over land in a protectorate to that exercised over a land in a colony. It redefined Crown lands so as to include land occupied by native tribes and land reserved by the Governor for the use and support of members of the native tribes. But it was declared that 'such reservation shall not confer on any member of any tribe any right to alienate the land so reserved or any part thereof.'[45] The disinheritance of Africans from their land was thereby complete, and the conversion of most of the East African Protectorate into the Colony of Kenya in 1920[46] made no difference to indigenous rights to land—or the lack of them.

The notorious case of *Ol le Njogo v The Attorney General* (the '*Masai Case*')[47]—the Kenyan equivalent of *Johnson v M'Intosh*—demonstrates both the full extent of the powers over land and people in an African protectorate and the continuity of approaches to acquisition of land through legal stratagems in British colonial policy.[48] It was early discovered that the traditional grazing grounds of the Masai consisted of rich agricultural land and were therefore very suitable for settlers. In 1904, the Laibon of the Masai, together with some other senior members of the tribe were induced to agree, on behalf of the Masai, to vacate some of this land and be 're-grouped' in two other areas, on the condition, inter alia, that the Agreement 'shall be enduring so long as the Masai as a race shall exist, and that Europeans or other settlers shall not be allowed to take up land in the Settlements'[49].

This Agreement lasted seven years, but well before its formal demise and replacement in 1911, the settlers pressed for it to be abrogated and the Masai to be moved once again. After a period of indecision, the government of the protectorate gave way. It concluded another 'agreement' with the Masai, under which the Masai 'agreed' to move, in the face of considerable pressure and threats. With a great deal of mismanagement, which caused considerable hardship and loss of life to the Masai and their cattle, the government carried out the move.

The plaintiff, on behalf of some of the Masai who had been compelled to move, brought an action for breach of the 1904 Agreement on the ground that the Agreement was a civil contract that was still subsisting, the Agreement of 1911 not having been made with those Masai capable of

---

[45] Crown Lands Ordinance, No 12 of 1915, ss 5, 54 and 56.
[46] The coastal strip of Kenya under the nominal sovereignty of the Sultan of Zanzibar remained a protectorate until the whole of Kenya became independent on 12 December 1963.
[47] (1914) 5 EALR 70.
[48] The account that follows is based on Ghai and McAuslan, note 41 above, 20–2. See too L Hughes, 'Malice in Maasailand: The Historical Roots of Current Political Struggles' (2005) 104 *African Affairs* 207–25.
[49] As quoted in *Masai Case* at 92.

binding the whole tribe. Preliminary objections were raised by the protectorate authorities that the courts had no jurisdiction, since the Agreements of 1904 and 1911 were treaties, not contracts, and were Acts of State, not cognisable in a municipal court. These arguments were successful both at first instance before Hamilton CJ[50] and before the Court of Appeal for Eastern Africa (EACA). On the treaty point, the EACA decided that as the protectorate was a foreign country vis-à-vis Great Britain, it followed that the Masai were foreigners in relation to the protecting power. They were 'subjects of their chiefs or their local government whatever form that government may take'.[51] Furthermore the Court held that the Masai still retained some element of sovereignty, and treaties could therefore be made with them, even though they would not be governed by international law but 'by some rules analogous to international law and [would] have similar effect to that held by a treaty and must be regarded by Municipal Courts in a similar manner'.[52]

Just what elements of sovereignty the Masai retained was not clear. It was admitted that they were entirely subject to the administrative and judicial control of the protectorate authorities. However, holding that the Masai retained some element of sovereignty enabled the court to take refuge in another rule of British colonial constitutional law: the doctrine of act of state.

> In my opinion an action will not lie against these Defendants for doing these acts which are acts of state and not cognisable by the Court as being committed in a foreign country against foreigners who belong to the tribe with whom the treaty was made.[53]

There was only one possible ground on which a court could hold that the Masai as such retained a residual sovereignty: that the radical or allodial title to their land was still vested in them, but as we have seen, the effect of the East Africa (Lands) Order in Council (1901) and the Crown Lands Ordinance (1902) had been to take that title away from them: they were, in the eyes of the received English land law, merely occupiers of land—tenants at will of the Crown. Three hundred years earlier, the imposition of

---

[50] Registrar, Judge and Chief Justice of the East Africa Protectorate (1897–1920) and later a Conservative MP.

[51] Masai Case, 93.

[52] Ibid.

[53] Ibid, 96. Morris Carter CJ comforted himself with this conclusion by repeating (at 97) the words of Vaughan Williams LJ in R v Crewe (Earl of) ex parte Sekgome [1910] 2 KB 576 (a case dealing with the writ of habeas corpus in the Bechuanaland Protectorate, now Botswana): 'The idea that there may be an established system of law to which a man owes obedience and that at any moment he may be deprived of the protection of that law, is an idea not easily accepted by English lawyers . . . It is made less difficult if one remembers that the Protectorate is over a country in which a few dominant civilised men have to control a great multitude of the semi-barbarous.'

the common law of land in Ireland and key judicial decisions undermining customary Irish land law had had the same effect on the tenure rights of the 'natives' of Ireland: they lost their rights and had only a precarious occupancy of their own land thereafter, with the English settlers obtaining freehold title to the land.

With the important exceptions of South Africa and Zimbabwe (formerly Southern Rhodesia),[54] where incoming European settlers seized the bulk of the land from the indigenous African population for themselves and applied 'European' (Roman-Dutch) law to that land, the major difference between the countries discussed earlier—Ireland, the USA, Australia and New Zealand—and Britain's African dependencies was that European settlement in the African dependencies was small and did not take over a significant amount of the land—even in Kenya only 7 per cent of the land area was reserved for European settlement, although it was the best land in the country. Whereas in the aforementioned countries, the intermingling of *imperium* and *dominium* and the application of the common law of land was but a prelude to the seizure of indigenously-owned land and its allocation to settlers, in African dependencies, the same process left the Crown (the British Government) as owner and controller of most of the land in the countries it ruled over and left the indigenous population as tenants at will of the Crown (in practice, the colonial authorities), although the 'internal incidents' of that tenancy at will were regulated by customary law.

Customary law and customary tenure in Africa were once presented as systems indigenous to Africa and Africans. Recent scholarship, particularly that by Chanock,[55] has shown how 'models of the customary law of land tenure were, to a significant extent, instruments of colonial land policies.'[56] An explanation will show how the colonial authorities used customary tenure to bolster their land policies and how these policies reflected and furthered the age-old approach to colonial land management.

Fundamental to the British colonial approach to customary tenure in Africa was the view of property rights to which Wood has drawn attention as being at the root of all English (later British) colonial enterprise and going back to Thomas More's *Utopia*: the right, under natural law, of colonists and settlers to seize lands that were unused or uncultivated or simply were not being cultivated fruitfully enough.[57] This approach was

---

[54] DL Carey Miller with A Pope, *Land Title in South Africa* (Kenwyn, Juta, 2000).

[55] M Chanock, *Law, Custom and Social Order: The Colonial Experience in Malawi and Zambia* (Portsmouth, Heinemann, 1998); and M Chanock, 'Paradigms, Policies and Property: A Review of the Customary Law of Land Tenure' in Kristin Mann and Richard Roberts (eds), *Law in Colonial Africa* (Portsmouth, Heinemann, 1991) 61–84.

[56] Chanock, *ibid*, 62.

[57] Wood, note 2 above, 75.

given a more comprehensive ideological structure by John Locke towards the end of the seventeenth century. Wood writes:

> In effect John Locke provided a theoretical structure for the principle already enunciated by Sir John Davies in Ireland: that the essential criterion in the justification for colonial exploitation was *value*. . . For Locke, America was the model state of nature, in which all land was available for appropriation because, although it was certainly inhabited and even sometimes cultivated, there was no proper commerce, hence no 'improvement'; no productive and profitable use of the land and therefore no real property . . .
>
> Commentators have pointed out that Locke introduced an important innovation into the *res nullius* principle by justifying colonial appropriation of unused land without the consent of any local sovereign and that he provided settlers with an argument that justified their actions on the basis of natural law, without any reference to civil authority.[58]

The labour theory of property became the dominant theory of property in England thereafter. Bentham, JS Mill and Green all accepted and espoused this theory in the nineteenth century, and this intellectual climate influenced, albeit subconsciously, the Government's law officers when they advanced their view that the Government could take control of all unappropriated land in an African protectorate without seeking the consent of the local rulers who were being protected.

The labour theory of property might provide the justification for seizing land from Africans and granting individual titles to settlers, but more was needed to ensure that Africans could not themselves seek to emulate the example of the Europeans and acquire individually owned plots of land and enter the market economy in competition with Europeans. This is where the colonial construction of customary tenure became crucial.

To summarise the arguments of Chanock, the British developed a feudal model of customary tenure that 'fitted British ways of thinking about state and society'.[59] The colonial authorities adapted and used the institution of chieftaincy, endowing the institution with sets of powers quite different to those that it had before the advent of colonialism.

> In the broad approach to the institutions of primitive government the chiefs were seen as the holders of land with rights of administration and allocation. Rights to land were seen as flowing downward. Whatever they were, they were derived from political authority rather than residing in the peasantry. This essentially feudal model not only fitted British ways of thinking about state and society, but was necessary if there were to be any linkage between British land law and African . . . British policy aimed at limiting the legal recognition of chiefs as

---

[58]   *Ibid*, 96–7.
[59]   Chanock (1991), 64.

owners in the sense of English law. But it conceded that they had political rights, as trustees for the community as a whole, and as allocators . . .

Against this background of notions of African economic behaviour, and the powers of chiefs, the colonial legal system etched its version of customary land law, a version essentially necessitated by the need to validate early land alienations. The summoning into existence of the customary regime was hugely convenient, for to treat indigenous rights as if they were the equivalent of rights recognised in English law would have created a plethora of embarrassing problems. And to treat Africans as people who had not 'evolved' the institution of private property . . . gave vastly greater scope to the state . . . [C]olonial regimes would handle land in the best interests of the population. Attempts to assert individual rights could gain no recognition because they were by definition not legal.[60]

CONCLUSION

In the colonial appropriation of land in Africa, one can see the culmination of over three hundred years of development of a colonial land law designed to facilitate plantations, colonists and settlers and to deprive indigenous populations of their laws, their rights and their land. Throughout this period, there was an underlying continuity of approach and attitude stemming from the fundamentals of the feudal system of English land law. First, the elision of *imperium* and *dominium—dominium because of imperium*: so important for the colonial enterprise was absolute ownership of the land that even where *imperium* was not technically acquired (eg, the African protectorates), the law officers of the Crown ignored this inconvenience and gave the green light for *dominium*.

Second, and following on from the first point, the English government and later the British government and its colonial offshoots—the US, Australian and New Zealand governments and various African colonial governments—claimed the right to determine who obtained or retained what land on what terms. Third, by and large, indigenous peoples were relegated to permissions or licences to occupy and use land, while incoming settlers obtained freehold titles, which amounted, in the eyes of the common law, to rights in the land. Fourth, indigenous peoples were herded into reserves, and detailed governmental controls were exerted over their use and occupancy of land; in particular, strenuous legal and administrative efforts were made to prevent them entering or operating in the land market, and if necessary criminal penalties or worse were imposed on them if they did. Fifth, the English courts and later the Judicial Committee of the Privy Council—technically not an English court but in

---

[60] Chanock, (1991), 64 and 66.

terms of personnel always regarded as such—played a key role in providing the Empire-wide legal justification for these exercises in invasions and land seizures. In short, the common law, so often represented as one of the great benefits of British colonialism, is better regarded as one of its more pernicious progenitors.

12

Translating Native Title to Individual 'Title' in Australia: Are Real Property Forms and Indigenous Interests Reconcilable?

LEE GODDEN AND MAUREEN TEHAN*

INTRODUCTION: NATIVE TITLE AND ITS TRANSLATION TO PROPERTY

A SHIFT HAS occurred in the parameters of the debate about indigenous landholding within Australia in the last few years. This shift has operated in concert with a policy reorientation in the ongoing relationship between settler Australia and Australia's indigenous peoples. *Mabo v Queensland (No 2)*[1] is generally regarded as a pivotal point in the relationship between aboriginal people, the Australian settler society and its legal institutions. Its prominence is ascribed to its symbolic as well as legal acknowledgment of pre-existing aboriginal claims to land,[2] through the recognition of native title. Recognition of native title generally has proceeded upon the basis that what is 'recognised' as native title[3] may constitute a 'property-like' interest, although there remains confusion about the exact parameters of its proprietary characteristics.[4]

An equivocal conflation of native title and Western property concepts was a feature of *Mabo (No 2)* itself[5] and in commentary in the immediate

---

* The authors acknowledge the assistance of the Australian Research Council Discovery grant 'Managing Competing Claims to Land and Resources: Does Property Law Promote Sustainability?' and the constructive comments of an anonymous referee.
[1] (1992) 175 CLR 1 (hereinafter '*Mabo No 2*').
[2] Recognition of rights over waters was subsequently extended by both the Native Title Act (Cth) (1993) s 223 and *Commonwealth v Yarmirr* (2001) 208 CLR 1.
[3] *Mabo No 2* (per Brennan J) and Native Title Act (Cth) (1993) s 223.
[4] Kirby J finds native title to be a sui generis interest in *The Wik Peoples v State of Queensland* (1996) 187 CLR 1 (hereinafter '*Wik*').
[5] See J Gray, 'Is Native Title a Proprietary Right?' (2002) 9 *E-Law: Murdoch University Electronic Journal of Law* 2.

post-*Mabo* phase.[6] Various justifications have been provided for why native title is—or is not—property,[7] but these concerns have not been as prominent in more recent reflections on the nature of indigenous landholding. Rather, current policy debates in Australia about indigenous land tenure appear simply to assume a proprietary character for native title. Indeed, the debates have centred upon whether moves to create individual title from communal indigenous title would provide a basis for the long-term economic and social viability of aboriginal communities.[8]

A clear assumption in such policy positions is the view that individual property rights are the cornerstone of economic prosperity.[9] Of necessity, this approach views the translation of indigenous landholding forms to Western commercial property forms as relatively unproblematic. Accordingly, the thrust of much new policy adopts individual land title,[10] or some form of individual autonomy over aboriginal lands,[11] as one of the major foundations for economic, social and cultural sustainability. This economically-oriented policy stands in contrast to the earlier rationale for granting aboriginal land rights and native title, which was embedded more directly in a human rights and cultural integrity framework.[12]

Research in a range of overseas jurisdictions suggests that the move to individual title over indigenous lands, by itself, has not produced significant gains for indigenous communities in terms of economic improvement

[6]   See eg, P Lane, 'Native Title: The End of Property as We Know It?' (2000) 8 *Australian Property Law Journal* 1; R Bartlett, 'The Proprietary Nature of Native Title' (1998) 6 *Australian Property Law Journal* 77; A Howe, 'A Post-structuralist Consideration of Property as Thin Air: *Mabo*, a Case Study' (1995) 2 *E-Law* 21; G Nettheim, 'Judicial Revolution or Cautious Correction? *Mabo v Queensland*' (1993) 16 *UNSW Law Journal* 1.

[7]   See eg, M Tehan, 'To Be or Not To Be (Property): Anglo-Australian Law and the Search for Protection of Indigenous Cultural Heritage' (1996) 15(2) *University of Tasmania Law Review* 267.

[8]   W Mundine, 'Aboriginal Governance and Economic Development', National Native Title Conference, Coffs Harbour, 2005.

[9]   The classical thesis in this regard is H de Soto, *The Mystery of Capital: Why Capitalism Triumphs in the West and Fails Everywhere Else* (New York, Basic Books, 2000). For an application in the Australian context see N Pearson and L Kostakidis-Lianos, 'Building Indigenous Capital: Removing Obstacles to Participation in the Real Economy' (Cape York Institute for Policy and Leadership Viewpoint paper, July 2004) <http://www.cyi-staging.net/.aspx?article=EG088DQNZMZG1O33R3IN> accessed 27 February 2006. See also chapter 10 in this volume.

[10]   H Hughes, 'The Economics of Indigenous Deprivation and Proposals for Reform' (2005) 63 *Centre for Independent Studies Issues Analysis*.

[11]   See amendments to the Aboriginal Land Rights (Northern Territory) Act (C'th) (1976) in the Aboriginal Land Rights (Northern Territory) Amendment Bill (2006); see also Australian Parliament, 'Report of the Senate Community Affairs Committee on the Aboriginal Land Rights (Northern Territory) Amendment Bill 2006', Canberra, 1 August 2006; Human Rights and Equal Opportunity Commission, 'Social Justice Report 2005', Sydney, 2005.

[12]   For an overview of the operation of the aboriginal land rights legislation in the Northern Territory, see Justice J Toohey, 'Aboriginal Land' (1985) 15 *Federal Law Review* 159.

and social justice. Rather, in many instances, the process has lead to a significant loss of indigenous lands. However, an exploration of the wide-ranging social consequences of the move to individual title is not the central focus of the chapter.[13]

By contrast, we want to refocus the debate on the highly problematic process of conceptualising indigenous relationships with land at law, as a form of individual title. Therefore, this chapter seeks to re-open the question of the character of native title interests. Indeed, the very notion of individualising native title draws the legal nature of the concept into sharp relief and necessitates an exploration of both the possibilities of such individuation and its relationship with Western property forms.[14] In this regard, this chapter considers whether it is appropriate and effective to conceive of native title as an entity akin to Western real property. Such an examination requires a review of central tenets of property theory to probe whether the rights typically designated as native title can be accommodated within a proprietary framework—and what may be 'lost in translation'. The analysis therefore involves a brief and admittedly rather selective account of the transition in Western property law from physically-oriented constructs based around possession, to more abstract forms.

Ironically, though typically, the 'rights' designated by law as native title may not involve exclusive possession.[15] This is especially so as a result of legislative characterisation of native title.[16] Instead, they may include a mixture of corporeal and incorporeal elements. Nonetheless, such rights may be integrally linked with particular communities as an expression of wider social and spiritual networks.[17] To incorporate such intangible relationships within a proprietary-type framework obscures many of these relationships. In exploring this issue, this chapter engages with conceptual debates about the nature of Western real property and native title rather than a directly substantive analysis of how communal customary landholding forms have been equated to individual landholding forms in other jurisdictions and historical periods.

---

[13] These issues are explored by M Stephenson in this volume.

[14] While much of the argument about the justifications, implementation and cultural consequences of such a policy also relates to individualising statutory aboriginal title under the various State and Federal land rights legislation, the nature of statutory title, largely grants of estates in fee simple, does not raise the conceptual issue that arises in our consideration of native title.

[15] Although see the contrary view by N Pearson, to the effect that if what is recognised is 'true' to indigenous occupation then it necessarily involves possession. N Pearson, 'Land is Susceptible of Ownership' in M Langton et al (eds), *Honour Among Nations: Treaties and Agreements with Indigenous People* (Melbourne, Melbourne University Press, 2004) 98–100.

[16] Native Title Act (Cth) (1993) ss 223, 225 and generally.

[17] *De Rose v South Australia* (2003) 133 FCR 325; and *De Rose v South Australia* (2005) 145 FCR 290.

Property Law as 'Translation'

After considering the first phase of translation that occurs with the recognition by the common law and statute of indigenous relationships with land, ie, the process of deriving native title, this chapter will discuss the next translation that is being contemplated for indigenous landholding. Accordingly, the chapter examines whether it is desirable and feasible for interests, such as native title, to operate in a similar manner to Western property as a catalyst for economic development.[18]

In the course of the historical 'translation' of common law property to its current doctrinal and social form, there are many instances of the generic 'property' concept being able to accommodate new substantive and economic content.[19] Typically though, the paradigmatic form for such incorporation has involved an acknowledgement of a particular physical manifestation of more inchoate cultural and social rights.[20] This pattern is exemplified in areas such as literary works and the recognition of intellectual property as an expression of the rights of an author in the works.[21] In this translation paradox, the property form has become increasingly 'abstracted' and 'generic' in order to better accommodate a greater degree of alienability and practical, market 'outcomes', even though it may not have entirely lost an empirical grounding.

Given this trajectory for Western property, we argue that any contemplated 'translation' from native title to individual 'economic' title may not be as straightforward as many have claimed, particularly when this process operates as a reduction to market-value precepts. Such reductionism, by virtue of its focus on economic objectives and value, may operate to emphasise the physically-oriented access and use components of native title and to minimise the cultural connections and the broader relationship context for native title. We do not suggest that there is not or should not be an economic component of native title that might be exploited. However, we argue that it is imperative to acknowledge the effect on relationships of the particular legal forms generated to achieve economic objectives. Moreover, the difficulties of translating native title into a vehicle for economic and cultural sustainability do not pertain only to what may be altered in the discrete conceptual and doctrinal translation exercise. There are considerable difficulties in reconciling native title at an institutional and organisational level with individual title, or even with lesser forms of

---

[18] This aspect leaves aside the debates about whether individual property interests do stimulate and sustain broader economic development—an issue debated over many centuries.

[19] K Gray, 'Property in Thin Air' (1991) 50 *Cambridge Law Journal* 252.

[20] See eg, *Pacific Film Laboratories Pty Ltd v FCT* (1970) 2 CLR 154.

[21] B Sherman and L Bentley, *The Making of Modern Intellectual Property Law: The British Experience, 1760–1911* (Cambridge, Cambridge University Press, 1999).

individual control over the communal interest. Questions that arise include: who can hold such rights; how can the interests of third parties be dealt with; how can the interest be transmitted within the group; and more broadly, how would the interest interface with land title registration systems such as Torrens title systems and planning regulations? This chapter offers exploratory discussion of these institutional and implementation issues.[22]

WESTERN PROPERTY AND THE TRANSLATION PARADOX

Defining Native Title in the Shadow of Property Law

Since 1992, Australian law has recognised native title, and there have been a series of claims and settlements made under the Native Title Act (1993).[23] Considerable pressure remains for more comprehensive social and political recognition of indigenous claims to land and waters, much of which is taking place through a negotiated, agreements-based process, as much as through formal litigated claims.[24] Given the rapid proliferation of native title claims over the past decade or so, it is imperative to examine how native title interests are constructed in their relationship with Western settler property within Australia and thus whether native title can, and should be, equated to Western commercial real property interests as a form of individual tenure.

In order to examine this interaction, it is necessary to provide at least a working definition of 'property'. To state that the meaning of property has varied over time and context risks cliché.[25] Even within the more tightly circumscribed sphere of the common law, the precise attributes, characteristics and referents of 'property' remain open. Given the indeterminacy of language, perhaps it necessarily will remain so, until fixed by reference to a

---

[22] The authors are aware of the many historical and contemporary examples in which indigenous communal land titles have been 'translated' into individual title. Classic examples are the nineteenth-century situations in North America under the US Indian 'allotment policy' and the processes operative under the Maori Land Court in New Zealand. However this chapter does not deal with these comparative examples, given the excellent discussion by Margaret Stephenson in this volume.

[23] For details of the scope and range of these settlements, see the ATNS database <http://www.atns.net.au> accessed 1 December 2006.

[24] For a discussion, see M Langton and L Palmer, 'Modern Agreement Making and Indigenous People in Australia: Issues and Trends', paper presented to the 13th Commonwealth Law Conference, Melbourne, April 2003. See also G Hiley and K Levy, *Native Title Claims Resolution Review* (2006); 'Government Response to Native Title Claims Resolution Review' (2006).

[25] Gray, note 19 above.

given context.[26] Sackville J has written judicially on the idea that any definition of property will be dependent upon the context in which the question 'what is property?' is raised and the purpose for which the answer is to be supplied.[27]

Further, the progression of common law property itself has shown particular ambivalence about the definition of real property, which putatively has been characterised as a move from the physicality of possessory concepts[28] toward the abstraction of either a bundle of rights or a socially and legally mandated power of control.[29] Gray and Gray write:

> The common law world has never fully resolved whether property in land is to be understood in terms of empirical facts, artificially defined jural rights, or duty-laden allocations of social utility. Although these three perspectives sometimes intersect and overlap, it remains ultimately unclear whether the substance of property resides in the raw datum of human conduct or in essentially positive claims of abstract entitlement or in the socially directed control of land use. In short, the idea of property in land oscillates ambivalently between the behavioural, the conceptual and the obligational, between competing models of property as a fact, property as a right and property as responsibility.[30]

While conceding the ambivalence with which law approaches the definition of property, this chapter argues that within Australian law, the dominant trajectory in the conception of settler real property interests has been a growing ascendancy of the model of property as an artificially defined jural right.[31] However, there has been some blurring of the notion of property as right with a conception of property as a socially endorsed concentration of power or control.[32] Indeed, a recent attempt to circumscribe the requisite rights or elements associated with property in water

---

[26] For a discussion of the role of language 'forms' in providing a meaning for property see, J Penner, 'The Bundle of Rights Picture of Property' (1996) 43 *UCLA Law Review* 711, 712.

[27] *Wily v St George Partnership Banking Ltd* (1999) 84 FCR 423, 426.

[28] 'Anyone who frees himself from the crudest materialism readily recognises that as a legal term property denotes not material things but certain rights.' M Cohen, 'Property and Sovereignty' (1927–28) 13 *Cornell Law Quarterly* 8, 11. See also J Waldron, 'The Normative Resilience of Property' in J McLean (ed), *Property and the Constitution* (Oxford, Hart, 1999).

[29] *Yanner v Eaton* (1999) 210 CLR 351 (per majority).

[30] K Gray and S Gray, 'The Idea of Property in Law' in S Bright and J Dewar (eds), *Land Law: Themes and Perspectives* (Oxford, Oxford University Press, 1998) 18.

[31] This trend has been influenced by academic literature, in particular the seminal work of K Gray on the nature of property. See eg, the extensive use of Gray's work in *Yanner v Eaton*, note 29 above.

[32] See generally L Godden, 'Grounding Law as Cultural Memory: A Proper Account of Property and Native Title in Australian Law and Land' (2003) 19 *Australian Feminist Law Journal* 63.

concluded that it contained the following elements: definition, identification, assumption, permanence, stability, transferability, value and protection.[33] This collection of requirements was augmented by the overriding need for there to be exclusivity—which was deemed by definition 'fundamental to the concept itself'.[34]

Notwithstanding the dangers of pronouncing any element 'fundamental' to property, the emphasis on exclusivity can be seen to continue the ambiguous oscillation from behavioural to abstract conceptions of property. Thus despite the move to more abstract forms, there remains a residual reliance upon a form of indirect 'physicality', which is denoted by exclusive possession, and thus on the power to exclude others. Clearly, the current legal conception of exclusive possession in some respects echoes an earlier behavioural mode of property identified by Gray and Gray whereby an extended form of physical control is germane to the identification of basic proprietary characteristics.

The deference to an earlier regime of physical possession continues to be manifest in the availability of equitable remedies, such as specific performance, that are available to protect proprietary interests.[35] However, issues of the identification of a proprietary interest at common law are less compelling in a statutory-based land registration system in which 'title' (and thus in many ways the interest itself) is conclusively determined through an administrative process that culminates in 'indefeasible title'.[36] In the routine of everyday property transactions, it is this more abstract understanding of real property that prevails. Courts are rarely called upon to distinguish from first principles, proprietary interests that are related to

---

[33] D Fisher, 'Rights of Property in Water: Confusion or Clarity?' (2004) *Environmental Planning and Law Journal* 200, 211.

[34] *Ibid*. This view has not been accepted unequivocally. Moreover, the concentration on exclusivity as denoting property requires some clarification. There are two pertinent qualifications. First is that exclusivity is related to the power to exclude others from a given entitlement. This 'power' operates as much in relation to a fee simple as it does to a profit. For example, if one holds a profit in relation to rabbits for a given field then the rights are exclusive, even if this right does not confer on the holder the right to exclude others from using the relevant field—that right, of course, sits with the holder of the fee simple estate. Under this conception of exclusivity it is possible then to have various proprietary interests operating with respect to the one piece of land. Some of these rights will confer a power, amongst others, to exclude other people from the use of the land. Others, such as an easement, confer more limited rights. This analysis, which highlights the variable function of 'exclusivity', also points to the change from direct physical control to a bundle of rights concept.

[35] Eg, *National Provincial Bank Ltd v Ainsworth* [1965] AC 1175; *Brown v Heffer* (1967) 11.

[36] In Australia the classic exposition of this view appears in *Breskvar v Wall* (1971) 126 CLR 376 (per Barwick CJ).

exclusive possession or other physical parameters.[37] Nonetheless, it is very clear that the ambivalence about how property is to be conceived has not been dispelled.[38]

A double movement occurs. At one level there is an overriding impulse to fashion Western real property as generic and abstract. Thereby, what seems to distinguish real property in Australia is its purported distance from the raw datum of human experience; from cultural and social practices and from a direct 'legal' recording of physical existence. In short, real property under this approach is to be understood as not 'real' in the sense that it is not primarily constituted at law in the realm of the factual that takes into account its situated existence. If real property is represented as an abstract right, then strategically, this characterisation can be used to highlight how these interests are intrinsically different from the rights that the law regards as comprising native title. If real property and native title are intrinsically different, then the implicit corollary would seem to be that the two groups of rights can be treated in different ways through the legal process.[39]

However, at another level, a closer examination of the apparent distinction between Western real property concepts and native title reveals that the gulf is not as wide as the current emphasis upon real property as abstract rights would suggest. Indeed, the artificiality of any supposed disjunction between real property and the rights that the law is prepared to recognise as native title is discussed in detail below. Nonetheless, real property interests in Australia tend to be constructed as pertaining to relationships denoted by generic rights of exclusivity, control and access. On the other hand, native title is constructed by reference to factually contingent relationships that have a direct possessory anchoring in a particular place or that are linked to an identified group or community. The manner in which these two different constructions of rights are derived[40] requires an overview of the progressive development of Western property and its interaction with indigenous rights to land and water.

---

[37] However, the confounding of Torrens title systems by the 'exception' of adverse possession is well recognised. For a discussion, see the contribution by P O'Connor in this volume. It is recognised that indefeasible title typically does not extend to guaranteeing the actual physical measurements of the land. Extrinsic evidence can be brought to establish land boundaries. For a discussion, see A Bradbrook, S MacCallum and A Moore, *Australian Real Property Law* , 3rd edn (Sydney, LawBook Co, 2002) 608–10.

[38] There are instances in which a reference to physical possession and the physical context of land is significant. For example, the doctrine of accretion may modify 'abstract' property rights. For a discussion, see A Moore, 'Land by Water' (1968) 41 *ALJ* 32.

[39] As a counterpoint to this argument see the views of Sean Brennan, who suggests that native title should be treated as comparable to Western property interests in relation to issues of constitutional recognition and compensation: S Brennan, 'Native Title In the High Court of Australia a Decade after *Mabo*' (2003) 14 *Public Law Review* 209.

[40] See generally S Motha, '*Mabo*: Encountering the Epistemic Limit of the Recognition of Difference' (1998) 7 *Griffith Law Review* 79.

Property and Its Progress

Two trends appear to have dominated in the trajectory that brings us to the conception of property as artificially defined jural rights. First there is a progressive abstraction and de-physical conception consistent with broader movements within law itself, and secondly the increasing focus upon real property as property 'ownership'. An emphasis upon abstraction and alienability in modern real property forms operates to obscure the specificity of belonging that links people to land even when property is characterised as denoted by reference to a socially endorsed concentration of power.[41]

By contrast, we would suggest that despite law's pretension to abstract right, real property law seeks to conceal its own history in materiality and factual manifestation,[42] so that now it may be distanced from the socially embedded, factually dependent and culturally constructed conception that is 'recognised' by law as native title. Such an empirical and factual grounding for native title renders it acutely vulnerable to 'the tide of history',[43] to extinguishment by the sovereign power that brought common law property to Terra Australis.[44] Moreover, within Australian law, we can contrast this historical imperative of the vulnerability of native title with a corresponding oscillation away from a 'real property as fact' model to a property as a bundle of rights.

These double movements are part of current attempts to illuminate a distance between property and native title. Nonetheless, we suggest that Australian law is clearly self-referential in its demand of native title that it demonstrate physical 'connection'[45] and provide strict evidence of its factual, material grounds. This demand reiterates the earlier history of common law property itself with its origins in a localised agrarian and feudal regime.[46] For despite the emphasis given to more abstract formulations in recent theories, property law has its beginnings in an order of

---

[41] The reference here is to the Australian High Court and the majority judgment in *Yanner v Eaton*, note 29 above.

[42] 'For the inaugural inaugurates nothing at all; it consists in saying what must be said, in making that which must be made, in putting texts in their place and in putting into play our relation to the gods.' P Legendre, *Le Desir Politique de Dieu: etude sur les montages de l'Etat et du Droit* (Paris, Fayard, 1988) 234, quoted in Y Hachamovitch, 'The Ideal Object of Transmission' (1991) 11 *Law and Critique* 85, 88.

[43] The euphemism of a tide of history has been used in a number of native title cases to suggest that the extinguishment of indigenous interest in land was due to an overwhelming historical process.

[44] Australia was shown on many maps prior to colonisation as 'Terra Australis Incognito'.

[45] Strictly speaking the term 'possession' is not employed so much as a requirement for 'connection', ie, a capacity to provide the indicia of physical control and use that for law denotes connection. Moreover, extinguishment means both loss of connection and by operation of inconsistent crown action, ie, the implementation of property as jural right.

[46] On the self-referential aspect, see Motha, note 40 above.

factual control and empirical possession. These origins lie in the age-old rites and rights of land use in an agrarian society, which leave 'permanent marks upon the land'.[47] As 'the earth is the first space of precedent',[48] so the institution of the law of property has its ontological moment in earth that is now constructed by law as abstract right. Indeed a considerable body of scholarship demonstrates the close association between Western European (including common law) views of property and the privileging of agricultural systems.[49] The onset of civilisation, property and law was equated with the instigation of agricultural societies,[50] characterised by the very grounding and marking by physical possession that once again seems to be demanded of native title claimants.

However, during the period of colonial expansion, real property increasingly came to be associated with historical progress, and historical progress with material advancement.[51] To proclaim the progress of Western society required a base against which progress could be measured. The evolutionary model of history provided this measure, and its calibration of civilisation was the denominator of property. Any stage prior to agriculture was a state of nature[52] and therefore 'pre-law' and 'pre-property'.[53] Or as designated in the context of Australian colonisation, the land was *terra nullius*.[54] *Terra nullius* was part of the British attempt to classify an unknown land in familiar property terms.[55] According to the fiction, Australia was held to be a land that was unoccupied, not because there were no inhabitants, but because aboriginal people did not occupy it in a civilised fashion.[56]

---

[47] A classical example here is an easement acquired by prescription or long user where it is necessary for there to be permanent marks of the use of land as a right of way to ground the claim for an easement.

[48] Hachamovitch, note 42 above, 90.

[49] See eg, T Flannigan, 'The Agricultural Argument and Original Appropriation: Indian Lands and Political Philosophy' (1989) 22 *Canadian Journal of Political Science* 589.

[50] E Vattel, *Droit des gens ou pinciples dela loi naturelle applique aux affairs des nations et des souvrains*, Chitty (ed) (London, T& JW Johnson, 1863 (1758)) 35.

[51] See for example the discussion of Hegel's philosophy of history by P Singer, 'History with a Purpose' in R Scrutton, et al (eds), *German Philosophers* (Oxford, Oxford University Press, 1997) 124–37.

[52] T Griffiths, *Hunters and Collectors: The Antiquarian Imagination in Australia* (Cambridge, Cambridge University Press, 1996) 5–8.

[53] T Murphy and S Roberts, *Understanding Property Law* (London, Sweet and Maxwell, 2003).

[54] P Fitzpatrick, *Enacted in the Destiny of Sedentary Peoples: Racism, Discovery and the Grounds of Law*, paper, Queen Mary and Westfield College, University of London, 1999, 9.

[55] See generally *Miliripuum v Nabalco Pty Ltd and the Commonwealth (Gove Land Rights Case)* (1971) FLR 141.

[56] *Mabo (No 2)*, note 1 above, 27 (Brennan J).

Native Title as Ownership?

The imperative of occupying and possessing the land in a civilised manner was played out very directly in a pre-*Mabo (No 2)* land rights claim in *Miliripuum v Nabalco Pty Ltd and the Commonwealth* (the 'Gove Land Rights Case').[57] Several aboriginal clans brought a claim in relation to possession and enjoyment of areas of Arneham land over which the Commonwealth government had granted mining leases to Nabalco. Relief was sought on the basis that the clans had occupied the areas from time immemorial, as of right. Under a doctrine of communal native title, the clans contended that their rights under native law were capable of recognition by the common law.

Following extensive evidence as to the customs, beliefs and social organisation of the Aboriginal people, it was established at a factual level that there existed a relationship with traditional lands that was recognisable as a system of laws. Although the judgment recognises the complexity of the plaintiffs' relationship to land,[58] Blackburn J felt himself bound by the decision in *Cooper v Stuart*,[59] concluding:

> The Crown is the source of title to all land; . . . no subject can own land allodially, but only an estate or interest in it which he holds mediately or immediately of the Crown.[60]

The claim that indigenous interests survived the acquisition of sovereignty was thus unsuccessful[61] and was not appealed.[62] The common law declared by Blackburn J did not recognise the relationship of the clans to the Arneham lands as a recognisable right of property or as conforming to an interest in land under the relevant land acquisition legislation. Blackburn J observed that the land did not belong to the clan; rather the clan belonged to the land.[63] Accordingly, the rights did not meet the indicia of property and ownership. By contrast, it was held that the 'source of entitlement to land' of the Yolongu people was fundamentally spiritual—it was not ownership.[64]

While the precedents that so closely bound Blackburn J were displaced in *Mabo (No 2)*, the need to measure native title rights against the standard of property 'ownership' has largely persisted, despite frequent judicial

---

[57] Note 55 above, 151–65.
[58] *Ibid*, 270.
[59] *Cooper v Stuart* (1889) 14 App Cas 286 [1888] AC.
[60] Note 55 above, 245.
[61] *Ibid*, 267.
[62] For a discussion of the case, see P Watson, 'The *Gove Land Rights* Case: Hard Cases Make Hard Law' (1994) 1 *Canberra Law Review* 97.
[63] See Lane, note 6 above, 18.
[64] *Ibid*.

exhortations against adopting 'the language of the common law property lawyer'[65] and despite the acknowledgement that 'the unstated assumptions of exclusivity in concepts such as "ownership" and "possession" may require examination.'[66]

Native Title as Title?

Indeed, in *Mabo (No 2)* the court used a variety of language to refer to the interests held by the Meriam people. Janice Gray notes:

> *Mabo v Queensland (No 2)* failed to offer one conclusion on the question of the nature of native title. Indeed it was variously described native title as 'propri-etary' 'personal', 'usufructuary', 'sui generis' as affording a 'permissive occu-pancy', and perhaps as 'possessory'. More recently it has been described as being a 'bundle of rights'.[67]

But whether native title does or should accord to the Western concept of property is problematic. While this equivocation parallels a similar trend in models of real property, what emerges most strongly is a move away from a broadly conceived and holistic view of indigenous interests.

Despite strong arguments in favour of indigenous possessory title in the academic literature[68] and an admittedly rather equivocal finding by Toohey J in *Mabo (No 2)*,[69] the view that native title may equate to a form of possessory title or title by occupation has not been readily accepted in Australian law. This uncertainty did not affect the outcome of *Mabo*: the Court declared that the plaintiffs were 'entitled as against the whole world to possession, occupation, use and enjoyment of Mer'.[70] The title was clearly outside the common law's tenurial system, but it encompassed rights that were recognised and protected by the common law.[71] In fact, the title was said to be sui generic,[72] but as noted, the precise nature of the title and where it sat within the broader property system was unclear. Was it proprietary, or was it merely a usufructuary right?[73] Was it a right to exclusive occupation, or was it a lesser right—and if so, what did that right conceptually entail? The third element of the decision dealt with protection

---

[65]   *The Commonwealth v Yarmirr* 2001 208 CLR 1, 2.
[66]   Lane, note 6 above, 13.
[67]   Gray, note 5 above, 1 (footnotes omitted).
[68]   K McNeil, 'Aboriginal Title and Aboriginal Rights: What's the Connection?' (1977) 36 *Alberta Law Review* 117; and N Pearson, note 15 above, 83.
[69]   *Mabo (No 2)*, note 1 above (Toohey J).
[70]   *Ibid*, 76 (Brennan J).
[71]   *Ibid*, 58 (Brennan J).
[72]   *Ibid*, 59 (Brennan J).
[73]   *Ibid*, 112–13 (Deane and Gaudron JJ).

of the rights that were said to attract proprietary remedies, although protection would not occur if it was contrary to 'natural justice, equity or good conscience'.[74]

Since *Mabo (No 2)*, however, there has been much greater reluctance to accord native title the status of 'ownership' or possessory title. This reluctance to equate indigenous relationships with land to real property forms of ownership is significant Its significance lies in terms of 'what gets lost in translation' from the raw datum of indigenous relationships with country to their recognition by the common law. It is anomalous that on the one hand native title claimants often are denied the more expansive definition of a title acquired by occupation and possession but must still meet high evidentiary thresholds that require a minute detailing of the physical practices of occupation and possession regarded as traditional law and custom.[75] Indeed, indigenous leader Noel Pearson, commenting on post-*Mabo* cases, has argued:

> Contrary to recent decisions of the High Court, the common law of native title recognises that indigenous people in occupation of land are entitled to possession where the Crown has declined to expropriate their title by act of State constituting the acquisition of sovereignty.[76]

This view relies on the seminal work on common law aboriginal title by Kent McNeil,[77] with the qualification that possessory title is not a claim apart from native title and that indigenous people have an allodial title rather than a fee simple.[78] Pearson, drawing primarily on the leading judgment of Justice Brennan in *Mabo (No 2)* argues that later High Court decisions[79] interpreting section 223 of the Native Title Act (C'th) have fundamentally misapplied the common law. He develops a distinction between the concept of possession and occupation providing an underlying 'title' for indigenous people on the one hand, and the pendant rights or 'incidents' that are evidenced by traditional laws and customs on the other

---

[74] *Ibid*, 61 (Brennan J).

[75] Pearson, note 15 above, 95. See also ss 223 of the Native Title Act (1993).

[76] Pearson, note 15 above, 83.

[77] McNeil has argued that Brennan J's decision in *Mabo* in effect was recognising a proprietary title based on exclusive and prior occupation: K McNeil, 'The Relevance of Traditional Laws and Customs to the Existence and Content of Native Title at Common Law' in K McNeil (ed), *Emerging Justice? Essays on Indigenous Rights in Canada and Australia* (Houghton Boston Printers, 2001) 416, 420–3, 435. Note that Strelein has taken a slightly different approach, suggesting that Brennan J's characterisation of the title allows for a 'continuum of interests to accommodate non-possessory rights': L Strelein, 'Conceptualising Native Title' (2001) 23 *Sydney Law Review* 95, 115.

[78] For an argument that native title should be regarded as an allodial form of title, see S Hepburn, 'Feudal Tenure and Native Title: Revising an Enduring Fiction' (2005) 27 *The Sydney Law Review* 49.

[79] *Commonwealth v Yarmirr* (2000) 168 ALR 426 (hereinafter '*Yarmirr*'); *Western Australia v Ward* (2002) 191 ALR 1 (hereinafter '*Ward*'); *Members of the Yorta Yorta Aboriginal Community v Victoria* [2003] 194 ALR 538 (hereinafter '*Yorta Yorta*').

hand. This distinction is a familiar one in Canadian indigenous law and jurisprudence, particularly following *Delgamuukw v British Columbia*.[80] Therefore any focus upon the details of traditional laws and customs is misguided:

> The foundation of native title is possession arising from occupation—not the detail of traditional laws and customs. These decide who is entitled to the possession and it governs the internal allocation of rights, interests and responsibilities among the members of the native community—but they do not determine the content of the community's title, which is possession.[81]

Indigenous communal title does not equate in any simplistic manner to 'idiosyncratic laws and customs'.[82] Yet it has been proven difficult to displace an increasingly narrow construction of native title premised on the approach that

> Native title has its origin in and is given its content by the traditional laws acknowledged by and the traditional customs observed by the indigenous inhabitants of a territory. The nature and incidents of native title must be ascertained as a matter of fact by reference to those laws and customs.[83]

In the succession of cases after *Mabo (No 2)*, there has been a continual iteration of a necessary link between a community's relationship with land and water as defined by reference to traditional laws and customs, which form 'the bridgehead to the common law'.[84] This formulation, expressed in section 223 of the Native Title Act (1993), emphasises that entitlement is premised upon an interest that has a constitution in and is in accordance with traditional laws and customs.[85]

While there were strong indications of a progressive limitation on the scope of native title, some ambiguity nonetheless still surrounded the exact legal nature and incidents of native title until a trilogy of test cases by the Australian High Court in 2002.[86] Brennan argues that, in various ways, these three test cases approached fundamental issues that remained outstanding about the character of native title interests, including:

> Whether native title is genuinely a 'title' akin to ownership, the kind of interest western law would appropriately translate into freehold title, or whether it is a

---

[80] *Delgamuukw v British Columbia* [1997] 3 SCR 1010. For a discussion of the case, see S Dorsett and L Godden, *A Guide to Overseas Precedents of Relevance to Native Title* (Canberra, Aboriginal Studies Press, 1998) and M Tehan *Delgamuukw v British Columbia* (1998) 22 MULR 763, 782.

[81] Pearson, note 15 above, 94.

[82] *Ibid*, with reference to Gummow J in *Yanner v Eaton* (1996) 187 CLR 1, 176.

[83] *Mabo (No 2)*, note 1 above, 64 (Brennan J).

[84] *Yanner v Eaton* (1999) 166 ALR 258, 278 (Gummow J).

[85] *Wik*, note 4 above, 176 (Gummow J).

[86] *Wilson v Anderson* (2002) 213 CLR 401 (hereinafter '*Wilson*'); *Ward*, note 79 above; and *Yorta Yorta*, note 79 above.

lesser interest or indeed a collection of severable rights easily capable of disaggregation (and hence extinguishment).[87]

The conclusion reached in an analysis of these cases was that:

> Proceeding on a mistaken view of Parliament's intention [ie, in interpreting the Native Title Act (1993)] . . . the court treated native title as an accumulation of rights, in which the unifying notion of a title plays a weak and uncertain role. It defined tradition, continuity and connection in ways that make native title extremely difficult to establish and which artificially limit the kinds of rights that may be recognised.[88]

The progressive limitation of indigenous interests in land to a model of discrete rights that must be sourced back to a factually identifiable custom or tradition through a physical chain of connection has major ramifications for how native title is conceived in its interrelationship with real property forms.

Limiting Native Title Rights: An Incomplete Translation

The increasing restriction on the type and range of rights that can be recognised by law as native title was foreshadowed by Justice North in *Ward v Western Australia* at the federal court level.[89] In that instance, the majority judges held that the right to maintain, protect and prevent the misuse of cultural knowledge is not 'a right in relation to land of the kind that can be the subject of determination'.[90] Rather, that right is 'a personal right residing in the custodians of the cultural knowledge'.[91] By contrast, the dissent judgment noted that native title is not merely about a physical connection to the land but also encompasses the idea of a cultural, spiritual and social connection to the land.[92] Justice North stated:

> The secular and spiritual aspects of the aboriginal connection with the land are twin elements of the rights to land. Thus the obligation to care for country has a secular aspect—burning the land—and a spiritual aspect, acquiring knowledge of ritual.[93]

The corollary of such an approach is that the legal conception of native title should entail the recognition of a broad range of customary traditions, cultural practices and social values that pertain to a given place—akin either to an underlying title or at least to a bundle of rights sufficiently

---

[87] Brennan, note 39 above, 211.
[88] *Ibid*, 209.
[89] *Western Australia v Ward* (2000) 170 ALR 159
[90] *Ibid*, 321, (Beaumont and Von Doussa JJ).
[91] *Ibid*.
[92] *Ibid*, 376 (North J).
[93] *Ibid*.

'aggregated' to encompass possessory incidents. However, as noted, the dominant trend in recent case law has been not only to narrow down the range of rights that can be acknowledged, but also to require physical connection to determine the scope of the spiritual aspects.[94] The persistent trend in recent judicial reasoning with regard to the requisite evidence of traditional customs and laws has been to conceive narrowly the point of connection embraced by such customs and laws.[95] While the majority in *Western Australia v Ward* declined to express a decided view on when a 'spiritual connection' with the land would be sufficient,[96] there was an emphatic rejection that a connection could continue in the absence of a traditional presence upon the land in *Yorta Yorta.*[97]

Further, the reluctance to accord a possessory title interest to native title has clear ramifications for how indigenous relationships with land and water are translated into the settler legal system. In terms of the questions raised in this chapter it is crucial. Arguably what is translated or extracted by law from indigenous relationships with a country is an incomplete and partial entity that fails to capture the holistic and diverse character of that relationship. The irony is that despite repeated reference to traditional law and customs, the focus on factually ascertaining separate 'rights' limits the extent to which a native title interest can retain its cultural integrity, despite what at first blush appears to be a culturally sensitive approach to judicial interpretation.[98]

Property as Right

The view emerging from recent native title jurisprudence is consistent with the conception that native title is in tension with the measure of property. The double movement is maintained as native title becomes constructed as

---

[94]   Strelein, note 77 above, 113.
[95]   The line of *Yorta Yorta* cases from the first-instance decision of Olney J to the High Court majority judgment clearly demonstrates this trend.
[96]   *Ward*, note 79 above (Gleeson CJ Gaudron, Gummow and Hayne JJ).
[97]   *Yorta Yorta*, note 79 above, 554, 558 (Gleeson CJ, Gummow and Hayne JJ). *Cf* the dissent of Kirby and Gaudron JJ. See further at 555: '[T]he difficulty of that analytical task should not be understood, however, as denying the importance of recognising two cardinal facts. First, laws and customs and the society which acknowledges and observes them are inextricably interlinked. Secondly, one of the uncontestable consequences of the change in sovereignty was that the only native title rights or interests in relation to land or waters which the new sovereign order recognised were those that existed at the time of change in sovereignty.'
[98]   For example, a determination must set out details of rights that make up native title and other rights and how they are to interact: Native Title Act (Cth) (1993) s225. The manner and form of interaction is often left to agreement, confirming the trend towards regulation by private contract, discussed later in this chapter. The problematic aspect is explored in depth by K Barnett, '*Western Australia v Ward*: One Step Forward and Two Steps Back: Native Title and the Bundle of Rights Analysis' (2000) 24 *MULR* 462.

a bundle of rights that require physical confirmation of community custom but paradoxically cannot be equivalent in status to real property. Ironically though, the origin of the bundle of rights analogy in property law is itself the Hohfeldian model of inter-subjective rights and duties.[99]

Hohfeld, drawing upon earlier jurisprudential theories such as that of Austin, developed a system for categorising legal powers in terms of inter-subjective rights and duties, privileges and immunities. For example, when one has a property right, then the corresponding inter-subjective duty is that other persons should not interfere with that right. Over time, the more complete system enunciated by Hohfeld was displaced in favour of the more limited concept that is typically designated as the bundle of rights.[100] Under this approach, rights embedded in the relationships between people are emphasised, and the empirical referents drop out of the property 'picture'.[101] Concurrently, the view that these rights exist between particular persons or groups of peoples has become extenuated in favour of a generic and free standing right that did not acknowledge its situated context.

To know the parameters of property law within Australia, we are therefore directed not to turn to the empirical facts of land and waters, to what by instinct and by dint of visceral relationship[102] we would imagine should ground this order. We were disabused at least a century ago: property is not possession, not things—especially not fugacious substances such as water, which elude the parameters of Western possessory intention and control.[103] Property is not land; not running water and sunlight; not a longing for country and the need to be possessed by it.[104] For property is Right[105]—or perhaps more consistently with common law doctrine, it is a bundle of rights.

---

[99] W Hohfeld, *Fundamental Legal Conceptions as Applied in Judicial Reasoning* (Yale, Yale University Press, 1923).

[100] Again this trend toward supposedly abstract rights is muddied by the clear acceptance that these powers must operate between discrete groups of people—even if there is one large group known as 'all the world' but the property rights holder.

[101] The term 'picture' is used here with reference to the arguments developed by Penner: that property is a language picture. See Penner, note 26 above, 711.

[102] See Gray, who argues that property has its origins in part in the need for possession and control of things by which we first separate ourselves as individuals from the surrounding world: K Gray, "Equitable Property' (1994) *Current Legal Problems* 157, 158–9.

[103] On the need for possession and control of 'natural things', see *Yanner v Eaton*, note 29 above, 264.

[104] For example, see Justice Blackburn's reasons above for denying a property status as a result of finding that an aboriginal clan 'belonged to the land' and did not exhibit exclusive control. *Miliripuum v Nabalco Pty Ltd and the Commonwealth (Gove Land Rights Case)* (1971) 17 FLR 141, 151–65.

[105] G Hegel, *Philosophy of Right*, TM Knox (trans) (Oxford, Oxford University Press, 1952).

And the rights so bundled, endure and subsist through time—enforceable against all the world as a right *in rem*.[106] For this is the particular character of real property when constructed as a freestanding right, that it need not be limited by the perversities of the material, nor tied to the vagaries of context. Once land and water are reduced to doctrinal models at law, then it is possible only to 'read' these material forms through the measure of their legal representation.[107] What we call 'property' becomes knowable only as a representation of right or a power of control. In particular, this normative function for property law has provided an ordering mechanism for economic and moral spheres.[108] Recognition of this facet of property law is not new and has formed the basis for wider critiques of property.[109]

In this manner, property as right and power has progressively become largely unfettered from both the aristocratic chains of genealogical and family identity and the physically embedded status of possession.[110] To designate property as a bundle of rights employs 'language . . . used to describe proprietary interests, even sovereign interest as an abstract expression'.[111] Indeed, the most widely accepted theory of property as a bundle of rights readily acknowledges that the content of the bundle has varied at particular historical junctures, but the bundle of rights remains an autonomous entity.[112]

Nonetheless, some oscillation continues as the bundle of rights has not entirely lost its relational character.[113] However, the analogy now predominately serves to reinforce the idea of property as pertaining to an object over which an individual has control:

> [P]roperty does not refer to a thing: it is a description of a legal relationship with a thing. It refers to the degree of power that is recognised in law as a power permissibly exercised over the thing.[114]

Property, then according to this account exists as a dynamic, socially mandated form of control over valuable resources, prefaced upon the capacity to exclude others.[115]

---

[106] For a discussion of the right in rem principle, see *King v David Allen* [1916] 2 AC 54.
[107] Hachamovitch, note 42 above, 95.
[108] C Rose, 'Property as Wealth, Property as Propriety' (1991) 33 *Nomos* 223, 232–41.
[109] Murphy and Roberts, note 53 above, 9.
[110] See the refutation by Simmonds of the arguments in favour of conceptions of private property to the effect that property should be distinguished from possession. AJ Simmonds, 'Historical Rights and Fair Shares' (1995) 14 *Law and Philosophy* 149,184.
[111] Strelein, note 77 above, 105.
[112] Penner, note 26 above, 712.
[113] Strelein, note 77 above, 105.
[114] *Yanner v Eaton*, note 29 above, 264.
[115] *Ibid*, 265.

Beyond the irreducible constraints imposed by the idea of excludability, 'property' terminology is merely talk without substance—a filling of empty space with empty words.[116]

In this manner, property seeks to prescribe a space of exclusivity.[117] Yet these rights do not need the anchor of connection to lands and waters.[118] The points of connection in property law have been largely, although not entirely, emptied of factual content and local reference; they subsist as images transfixed in the symbolic order of the map, certificate of title and, more latterly, the database, all of which comprise the systems of registration of property.[119] Such transformation to the surfaces of the written and digitalised image renders property the 'ideal object of transmission'.[120] Property in the modern commercial order has now become both the object and the subject of alienability.

This capacity for alienability has been further enhanced by the advent of registration systems such as the Torrens title. Land registration systems have taken real property title out of the realm of the private commerce that traced through the lineaments of hereditary, family and contractual relationships.[121] Property is no longer grounded in a normative system that recognises local rules of recognition and empirical fact but is instead abstracted as an ideal form in the public instruments of title that now denote real property interests. Registration of title provides its own fixed point of abstract reference in the notion of indefeasible title.

Thus, no longer is it necessary to locate real property ownership by reference to a cultural and social history of occupation and possession and to evidence it in a material manner.[122] The boundaries and divisions of possessory control, the markers of ownership, have become generic and transmissible in law through the smooth interchanges of bureaucratic forms and instruments that circumscribe the relationships between those people who have the control of lands and waters and those who can

---

[116]   Gray, note 19 above, 256.

[117]   See the discussion of Hohfeld's conception of property as an abstract relation that exists through time as a set of rights, powers, privileges and immunities that may subsist between or against other persons in *Wily v St George Partnership Banking Ltd* (1999) 161 ALR 1 (Finkelstein J).

[118]   For a discussion of land that is transmitted as an 'ideal' via 'instruments' see Hachamovitch, note 42 above, 85.

[119]   For a discussion of how registration of property is predicated upon a remove from the 'local memory of place', see A Pottage, 'The Originality of Registration' (1995) 15 *Oxford Journal of Legal Studies* 371.

[120]   Hachamovitch, note 42 above, 42.

[121]   A Pottage, 'The Measure of Land' (1994) 57 *Modern Law Review* 361.

[122]   It is true that certain property rights in land still accrue or disappear in a factual or material manner by the operation of longstanding common law principles: for example, possessory title itself leading ultimately to an adverse possession title and accretion and erosion. However, we consider these are no longer the dominant form of acquisition or enjoyment of property in land.

exclude others. If property as right is understood in this light, then its distance from what the law now recognises as native title is enhanced. Given this trajectory for the development of real property law as an abstract or jurally defined bundle of rights, it is extremely problematic to translate native title into such a conceptual and doctrinal framework.

Native Title as Right?

Native title, now increasingly constructed at law as the merely 'factual', is distinguished by the need for communal presence and traditional content. Property law by contrast creates an autonomous transcendent 'right' for real property interests from which every present (ie, factual) subject can be absent. Therefore, property is not merely 'a category of illusory reference'[123] defined against varying concentrations of power. Property law creates the very categories of exclusion and inclusion—presence and absence. Any meaning given to property is not just empty; it is always prefaced upon a reference to a present, known only through its absence, against which its meaning is to be understood. That exclusionary divide, as found in recent juridical conceptions of property and native title,[124] precipitates a growing disjunction between settler real property and native title.[125] It constitutes native title as a collection of rights that increasingly have lost their reference to Western proprietary-type characteristics in favour of either a non-commercial spiritual 'guardianship' or some form of rights of access and use, which typically fall well short of title and ownership. Native title, as the legal model for structuring indigenous relationships with country appears to be an increasingly narrow and vulnerable 'interest'.

Moreover, the distinctions between native title and real property interests reinforce that native title is a vulnerable right, as shown very directly in *Ward*. By providing that native title rights can be extinguished one by one,[126] together with the view that certain Crown reservations and vestings extinguish native title completely,[127] the decision has overturned many views about extinguishment deriving from *Mabo (No 2)*.[128] The result, in combination with restrictive interpretations on what is recognised, means that native title will now not exist at all, or at best, only minimal native title rights will now exist on much Crown land and Crown tenures, where previously native title was held to be capable of coexistence.

---

[123] Gray, note 102 above, 53.
[124] Strelein, note 77 above.
[125] The reference here is to the idea of property as 'natural' right, ie, given right.
[126] The consequence of its finding that the title is a 'bundle of rights'.
[127] *Ward*, note 79 above, 78–80.
[128] *Mabo (No 2)*, note 1 above, 69–70 (Brennan J).

In summary, the combined effect of the Native Title Act and recent cases has been to dramatically reduce the scope of native title rights, the land available for claim, the numbers of indigenous people who might successfully claim native title and consequently the breadth of coverage of the various rights flowing to native title holders under the future acts regime, the key enforcement mechanism in the Native Title Act. What has emerged as the legal artefact of native title is a much diminished vehicle for expression of indigenous systems of law and interests in land.[129] The high degree of vulnerability of native title to extinguishment and the stringent tests for recognition stand in marked contrast to the highly protected forms of real property.

Translation to a Market Economy?

Given these very different means for realising indigenous and settler rights, a decade after *Mabo (No 2)* it has been acknowledged that the scheme for recognition and protection of indigenous interests in land in its interaction with the real property tenurial system is not working well for many indigenous people.[130] Consequently, there has been a move away from litigated outcomes to an agreement-based model for resolution of conflicts over claims to land and resources.[131] Against this background, questions arise not only about how indigenous peoples' relationships with land can be realised in tension with the settler legal system, but also about the particular character of those interests and their potential for market alienability.

Accordingly, the parameters of the discussion have shifted to include not just issues about land 'rights' but also how land may be used to stimulate 'development'. Of course, these latter issues are integral to any claim for land, and it is artificial to separate them. Nonetheless, many of the debates surrounding the need for aboriginal communities to adopt a commercial orientation to landholding assume that issues surrounding the legal character of native title and its transmission to Western settler property frameworks can be accomplished without fundamentally changing the

---

[129] M Tehan, 'A Hope Disillusioned, An Opportunity Lost? Reflections on Common Law Native Title and Ten Years of the Native Title Act' (2003) 27 *MULR* 523, 571.

[130] Brennan, note 39 above.

[131] For discussion of this trend, see Tehan, note 129 above, 45; and Hiley and Levy, note 24 above. For critical comment, see: M Tehan and D Llewellyn, '"Treaties", "Agreements", "Contracts" and "Commitments": What's in a Name? The Legal Force and Meaning of Different Forms of Agreement Making' (2005) 7 *Balayi: Culture, Law and Colonialism* 1; C O'Faircheallaigh, 'Implementing Agreements between indigenous Peoples and Resource Developers in Australia and Canada' (Research Paper No 13, School of Politics and Public Policy, Griffith University, 2003); F Flanagan, 'Pastoral Access Protocols: The Corrosion of Native Title by Contract' (Issues Paper No 19, vol 2, Canberra, AIATSIS, 2002) 5.

nature of indigenous relationships with land. Far from being unproblematic, we suggest that these calls for a 'second translation' of native title require close examination, particularly as the trends toward far-reaching changes to the forms of indigenous landholding to precipitate economic and social development continue to gather momentum.[132]

Proposals to adopt market-based and individual models for indigenous land 'ownership' have not emerged in isolation. Rather they form part of the general government approach to indigenous affairs, dominated by notions of 'practical reconciliation' and individual responsibility, expressed through such policy instruments as Shared Responsibility Agreements (SRAs) and Regional Participation Agreements.[133] Earlier rationales for indigenous land rights based upon a desire to give effect to cultural integrity and human rights are increasingly displaced in favour of 'practical reconciliation', which is aligned with ideas of formal equality, mutual obligations and social/economic development.

In late 2004 and early 2005, the focus of many proposals was to create various forms of individual interests over indigenous communal land. For example, 'Building Indigenous Capital: Removing Obstacles to Participation in the Real Economy'[134] articulated the view that one of the major causes of social dysfunction in indigenous communities is dependence on passive welfare and alienation from the 'real economy'. Drawing on de Soto's work,[135] authors Pearson and Kostakidis-Lianos reoriented Pearson's earlier views to argue for an increase in the fungibility of indigenous landholding, which was described as 'dead capital'.[136] Indigenous landholding structures, it appears,

> lock out indigenous people from the Australian property system that enables capital formation' [as all] assets in the form of lands, housing, infrastructure, buildings, enterprises etc are inalienable and as a result have no capital value.[137]

Legal and structural barriers to engagement in the real economy were seen by the authors as contributing to the ongoing social and economic poverty of indigenous people.[138] Part of the proffered solution is to remove the barriers to alienability of indigenous interests that prevent such participation. It is anticipated that this will enable assets 'to be represented in abstract forms—forms which can be leveraged, divided and combined to

---

[132] S Bradfield, 'White Picket Fence or Trojan Horse? The Debate over Communal Ownership of Indigenous Land and Individual Wealth Creation' (2005) 3(3) *Land, Rights, Laws: Issues of Native Title* (Canberra AIATSIS).
[133] Bradfield, note 132 above, 2–3.
[134] Pearson and Kostakidis-Lianos, note 9 above.
[135] de Soto, note 9 above.
[136] Pearson and Kostakidis-Lianos, note 9 above.
[137] *Ibid*, 3.
[138] *Ibid*.

create capital'.[139] The apparent parallel of this view, with the trajectory of Western property development, is clear. There is a specific attempt to align indigenous interests with a move to abstract, fungible, real property rights to promote development.

These arguments emerging from many indigenous communities also resonate with a revised government policy on indigenous affairs and the dismantling of much of the existing indigenous governance structures. For the Australian Prime Minister, the idea was to create 'a more entrepreneurial indigenous culture'[140] in which market forces play a role in ensuring the economic viability of local indigenous communities. The relevant Minister put the case thus: 'being land rich but dirt poor isn't good enough.'[141] Others saw communal land tenure not only as an impediment to the process of land transfer, which was seen as the basis for improved socio-economic sustainability,[142] but varyingly as a 'socialist experiment'[143] similar to communism,[144] and it was said that 'nowhere in the world has communal land ownership ever led to economic development.'[145] Yet rigorous, in-depth examination of the suggested link between individualising indigenous land titles and economic development is only now commencing.[146]

The response from some indigenous leaders to these developments that emphasise individual title was to emphasise the false dichotomy between individual wealth creation and long-term community and cultural integrity. Accordingly, more recent government proposals to stimulate aboriginal socio-economic development based upon 'reforms' to indigenous landholding have now recognised, at least at the rhetorical level, the importance of retaining an underlying communal form of landholding.[147] The reform model now appears to concentrate upon allowing some enhanced form of

---

[139]   *Ibid.*

[140]   Quoted in Bradfield, note 132 above, 3.

[141]   Senator A Vanstone MP, Minister for Immigration and Multicultural and indigenous Affairs, 'Address to National Press Club', 23 February 2005 <http://www.atsia.gov.au//_minister///_02_2005_pressclub.aspx> 17 March 2006.

[142]   Bradfield, note 132 above, 2.

[143]   Hughes, note 10 above.

[144]   C Pearson, 'Case to Put Lands Right', *Weekend Australian*, 11 December 2004, 18, cited in Bradfield, note 132 above, 2.

[145]   *Ibid.*

[146]   It is not within the scope of this chapter to examine these arguments and justifications in detail. As noted, the desirability and some consequences of individualising title is examined by M Stephenson in this volume. For further critical comment, see 'Social Justice Report 2005', note 11 above; and P Lee, 'Individual Titling of Aboriginal Land in the Northern Territory: What Australia can Learn from the International Community' (2006) 29 *University of New South Wales Law Journal* (forthcoming).

[147]   A Ridgeway, 'Addressing the Economic Exclusion of Indigenous Australians through Native Title', The Mabo Lecture, National Native Title Conference, Coffs Harbour, April 2005.

individual dealing with indigenous land rather than individual title per se, while retaining the underlying communal land.[148]

Much of the agitation for individual autonomy over aboriginal communal land has been directed primarily to legislative schemes, particularly as the Australian federal government is able to implement its policy directly in the Northern Territory,[149] notwithstanding that the capacity to use lands for security arguably already exists.[150] However, the suggested approach is not limited in its application to statutory land rights schemes. Given the extent of native title claims that will need to be resolved in the near future and the many existing determinations, it is imperative to consider also whether communal native title interests are amenable to individual title or some lesser form of alienability. Some of the practical and implementation issues that may arise in the second stage of translating native title into some form of individual interest are now considered.

PRACTICAL DIFFICULTIES OF SECOND-STAGE TRANSLATION

Current Indigenous Land-holding Arrangements

'Today the "indigenous estate"—those lands that are owned or controlled by indigenous people—makes up approximately 20% of the Australian continent.'[151] The current patterns of indigenous landholding create a diverse patchwork, with statutory land rights regimes coexisting with older style trust and corporation models of landholding. There are different titling schemes in each Australian jurisdiction, which in turn, attract different regimes for regulation and management of indigenous land and resources. Moreover, many of these forms are potentially overlain by or intersect with native title claims and processes under the Native Title Act (1993), as well as rights of access to land and waters deriving from broader agreement-making and aboriginal cultural heritage protection.[152] Native title may exist on some of this land, either because there has been a native title determination under the Native Title Act (1993) or because native title

---

[148] Aboriginal Land Rights (Northern Territory) Amendment Bill (2006), which retains an underlying communal title while allowing for 99-year leases of whole communities. See 'Report of the Senate Community Affairs Committee on the Aboriginal Land Rights (Northern Territory) Amendment Bill 2006', note 11 above.

[149] Legislative schemes vary enormously in their scope and objectives. Some schemes, such as the Pitjantjatjara Land Rights Act (SA) (1981), seek to give material form to the cultural and spiritual relationship of aboriginal people to their lands and waters. Other schemes, such as the land rights scheme operative in New South Wales, do not give priority to traditional cultural association with land: see 'Social Justice Report 2005', note 11 above.

[150] *Ibid.*

[151] Bradfield, note 132 above, 3.

[152] Langton et al, note 15 above, ch 1.

has not been extinguished.[153] The complexity of the spatial distribution of native title holdings is further complicated by the diversity of the rights comprising native title.

Can Native Title Equate to Western Forms of Security?

The nature of the 'rights' enjoyed under native title varies enormously, as these rights are held to give effect to traditions, laws and customs determined on a case-by-case or negotiated basis. Thus despite formal recognition within the Australian legal system and the potential extent of areas over which native title exists, the rights in terms of empirical impact leave much less physical imprint upon the Australian nation than does settler real property. Native title rights do not leave the same permanent marking and record of occupation of the land as do the more purportedly 'abstract' forms of settler property. The patterns that reveal the lived experience of people are skewed toward the dominant Western tenurial system. The courts have consistently translated native title in terms of practices, for example, rights of access to sacred sites under a particular claim, or traditional fishing and hunting rights protected under section 211 of the Native Title Act (1993); but these do not significantly alter the land and water. Land and indigenous peoples, it seems, are to remain in a 'natural' state.

To date, and perhaps increasingly so after *Ward* and *Yorta Yorta*, native title rights are not recognised as including those lived experiences that markedly transform the landscape, such as commercial fishing or mining and—most emphatically—urban development. The physical ordering of the Australian continent remains predominately demarcated by longstanding settler real property rights. The Australian legal system has so configured the construct of native title, reading its presence against the category of property ownership,[154] as to preserve intact the Australian dream of ownership. As Justice Merkel observed in 2006 in *Ruibibi Community v State of Western Australia*,[155]

> I have some concern as to how a right to exclusive possession and occupation can operate in a practical way in urban and other areas in common use by the general community. However . . . the difficulty in the practical enforcement of a native title right is not a proper ground for denying its existence.[156]

---

[153] *Fejo v Northern Territory* (1998) 195 CLR 96.

[154] Within Australia, the rules on the extinguishment of native title mean that a fee simple interest (ie, what is commonly known as 'private property') will always extinguish native title rights. See *Fejo ibid* and S Dorsett, '"Clear and Plain Intention": Extinguishment of Native Title in Australia and Canada Post-*Wik*' (1997) 6 *Griffith Law Review* 1.

[155] [2006] FCA 82.

[156] *Ibid*, para 117.

Moreover, extensive exclusive possession rights as part of native title are not common. Of the fifty-six native title determinations in which native title was found to exist to 13 March 2006,[157] only thirty-six have included a grant of rights equivalent to exclusive possession or some form of 'underlying title'. Although this is a seemingly high proportion, typically it is only in very remote areas such as desert regions or in the Torres Strait islands that native title might consist of exclusive possession type rights. Furthermore, when grants of exclusive possession are made, they tend to cover small pockets in wider areas surrounded by much larger areas of non-exclusive rights.[158] In many cases, native title amounts to significantly less than exclusive possession.

If native title is understood as a loosely connected bundle of rights, not defined against an underlying unifying title, then the capacity to 'translate' it into a real property 'equivalent' is questionable. It is difficult to imagine how rights that do not include some underlying title or possession but are regarded as more in the character of incidents or rights of access or use (usufructary perhaps) might provide a sufficiently robust and defined interest to support secured lending by financial institutions.

Thus while native title is framed against the bundle of rights model of ownership, given the narrow range of 'interests' accorded under most determinations, native title in reality may not function in an equivalent sense to Western property ownership as a basis for capital accumulation. If native title is to provide a catalyst for economic development, it will require at the very least an innovative approach to defining security interests and 'ownership'.

'Remnant Lands, Remnant Rights'[159]

While *Mabo (No 2)* is widely regarded as a landmark decision, a close examination of its doctrinal foundations reveals a compromise.[160] The compromise is a reminder of the difficulty that the law has had in

---

[157]   81 in total, 48 by consent, 17 litigated.

[158]   For information on native title determinations see National Native Title Tribunal website <www.gov.au> 17 March 2006.

[159]   Pearson argues that this is all native title has been about, but it is an especially apt description of the current state of indigenous native title rights since the decisions of the High Court in *Ward, Wilson v Anderson* and *Yorta Yorta*: N Pearson, 'Where We've Come from and Where We're at with the Opportunity that is Koiki Mabo's Legacy to Australia', Mabo Lecture, Native Title Conference, Alice Springs, 3 June 2003 < http://www.capeyorkpartnerships.com////mabo-lecture-3-6-03.pdf > 21 November 2006, 3–4.

[160]   In *Mabo (No 2)*, Brennan J held that native title could only be recognised if it did not fracture the skeleton of property law principles, ie, the doctrine of tenure and estates derived from English common law. See Bartlett, note 6 above.

assimilating native title to Western concepts of ownership.[161] The compromise is effected in recognising native title, while leaving substantially intact the historical grant of private real property titles over 204 years:

> Even if those titles were gained in circumstances of regret and denial of right, the Court said that the accumulation of these many millions of titles over two centuries could not now be disturbed . . . Let me put it colloquially: the whitefellas get to keep everything they have accumulated, the blackfellas should now belatedly be entitled to whatever is left over.[162]

That 'blackfellas' get *'whatever is left over'* is becoming ever more apparent,[163] despite the growth in the indigenous estate. The restricted scope of the nature of the interests that are recognised as native title (ie, often not regarded as a title at all) is exacerbated when consideration is given to the location of areas of successful native title claims.

Figure 12.1 is a map illustrating the extent of native title determinations up until December 2006. The lack of determinations in closely settled areas around capital cities and in the prime urban, industrial and agricultural areas of the southeast and southwest of the country is obvious from this map. Native title is most visible in locations that white settler society has deemed marginal. In this manner, native title rights are excluded from the commercial and economic realm distinguished by 'private' property ownership.[164] Furthermore, the distance between property and native title is emphasised by a consistent refusal in recent cases to consider native title as comprising rights of a commercial nature, such as rights to trade.[165] Such findings of 'fact' further highlight the exclusion of native title from the commercial market order of real property.[166] It is ironic, given the consistent refusal to accord to native title a realistic commercial content in any way approaching settler property interests, that there should be such a serious call for 'land' in and of itself to become the basis for the economic development of indigenous communities.

---

[161] See Lane, note 6 above, 17–18 on the idea that native title cannot accord with a Western model of property that requires recognition of surplus value.

[162] N Pearson, 'The High Court's Abandonment of "the Time-honoured Methodology of the Common Law" in its Interpretation of Native Title in *Mirriuwung Gajerrong* and *Yorta Yorta*', Sir Ninian Stephen Annual Lecture, University of Newcastle Law School, 17 March 2003 <http://www.capeyorkpartnerships.com///.doc> 21 November 2006, 3–4.

[163] *Ibid.*

[164] Hachamovitch, note 42 above, 101.

[165] Langton and Palmer argue that such a finding in *Yarmirr* was arrived at in the face of a large body of scholarship and empirical research clearly demonstrating that trading occurred between Aboriginal and Malaccan peoples: Langton and Palmer, note 16 above.

[166] In this regard, Detmold argues: 'At the bottom of the desires there was a vast difference of perception of what land was and what it was to desire it; these differences reflect more immediately in the differing conceptions of legal title than desire itself does, and constitute a much greater problem of lawful reconciliation.' M Detmold, 'Law and Difference: Reflections on the *Mabo* Case' (1993) 15 *Sydney Law Review* 159, 160.

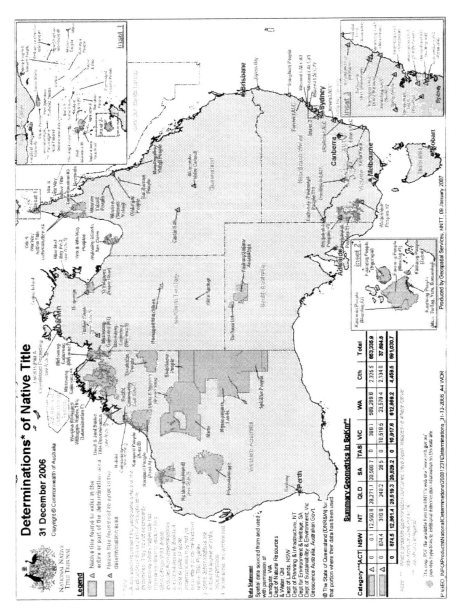

The map shows native title determinations (ie finalised proceedings) as of December 31, 2006. The map is derived from the National Native Title Tribunal (Australia) and the authors gratefully acknowledge the permission given by the national native tribunal for the use of this data.

At a more obvious level, much of the indigenous estate is in rural and remote regions where there are major structural issues relating to socio-economic development and sustainability. The problems of rural decline and limited economic opportunity are not limited to indigenous communities. Thus it is important to question whether the diagnosis of the problem as a lack of 'development' is adequate and whether the proposed solution would be effective given the particular economic and geographical factors at work in rural and remote communities.[167]

In remote communities it is questionable whether land has any intrinsic economic value apart from the resources that it may contain. Moreover it is questionable whether commercial lenders are prepared to accept remote land as security, even without the problems inherent in defining the precise nature of the native title rights to form the basis of the security. If commercial lenders do accept land as security, how is the security to be redeemed or converted: by exercising a power of sale? Is there a market in these locations? To whom would the security revert? Who would buy it on the open market? What might the impact be on indigenous communities as the indigenous estate passes from indigenous hand?[168] At a wider level, it remains an open question whether incentive-based market arrangements will work to achieve the desired outcome of transferring indigenous capital into the real economy.[169] Even if it works elsewhere, whether it will work in the specific cultural environments of indigenous communities remains open. If all these uncertainties are overcome, will there be a sufficient trickle-down effect to enhance substantially the social and economic viability of communities?[170]

Regulating and Managing Native Title Interests: Another Layer of Complexity

Another facet of any translation of native title into the mainstream of real property equivalence and market alienability is the interface with wider governance regimes. While some aboriginal lands may be explicitly

---

[167] M Gratten, 'Individual Approach to Land Rights Only Half the Answer', *Sun-Herald*, 10 April 2005. See generally, J Taylor and O Stanley, *The Opportunity Costs of the Status Quo in the Thamarrurr Region* (Canberra, Centre for Aboriginal Economic and Policy Research ANU WP28, 2005).

[168] See J Altman and M Dillon, 'A Profit Related Investment Scheme for the Indigenous Estate' (Centre for Aboriginal Economic and Policy Research ANU Discussion Paper 27, Canberra, 2004).

[169] R Home and H Lim (eds), *Demystifying the Mystery of Capital: Land Tenure and Poverty in Africa and the Caribbean* (London, Cavendish, 2004).

[170] For a discussion of the need to address land and poverty, see K Deininger, 'Land Policies for Growth and Poverty Reduction' (World Bank Policy Research Report, WB and OPU, 2003).

excluded from such regulatory requirements, little attention has been directed at examining the interface between regimes, such as planning and development control, heritage protection and the moves toward individual dealing with communal lands.

As we have noted, on one hand the problem of second-stage translation is exacerbated by the complexity of indigenous landholding structures determined on a case-by-case basis.[171] On the other hand, complications exist with respect to the complexity of the governance system over indigenous landholding. A central justification for a communal landholding system is the facilitation of environmental and cultural protection for the lands that fall within such a system. Proponents of greater individual autonomy over indigenous landholding see these as insufficient justifications for maintenance of the current system, given that indigenous communities are under great stress. Against such supposedly compelling imperatives, regimes of environmental protection, development control and cultural heritage protection are seen as extrinsic to questions of property 'dealing'. Accordingly, the barriers to alienability and capital formation are conceived only on a narrow basis that tends to eclipse the other rationales for communal landholding, such as cultural heritage protection.[172] Arguably, though, these rationales that typically are given legal effect through heritage and planning regimes are central to questions about the use and access 'controls' that in many instances are all that may remain of native title rights according to the courts. Moreover, questions of the ultimate use of land, if it is to furnish a basis for capital accumulation, have been given far less attention than questions of land title and the facilitation of alienability—although we suggest that these two aspects are integrally related and go to the heart of some of the issues of socio-economic and cultural sustainability.[173] The value of land for commercial security purposes is of course integrally tied to the manner in which that land can be utilised.

Finally, there are issues relating to land registration and recording of land transactions that in many senses underpin the fungibility of property.

---

[171] Questions such as who controls the rights and over what entity the rights are exercised are obscured by the bundle of rights model. The model assumes that the question of exactly which subject controls these rights is immaterial. However these are vital questions for a communal title and for the communities who exist in relationship with each other and with lands and waters. The living systems of land law that survived the acquisition of sovereignty for 218 years are unlikely to quickly dissipate. For a discussion of the living land law, see DB Rose, *Nourishing Terrains: Australian Aboriginal Views of Landscape and Wilderness* (Canberra, Australian Heritage Commission, 1996).

[172] T Calma, Social Justice Commissioner, 'Plenary Address', Native Title Conference, Coffs Harbour, 2005.

[173] For a discussion of the interface between aboriginal landholding and planning law, see S Dorsett and L Godden, 'The Interaction of Planning Law and Native Title' (2000) 17 *EPLJ* 374.

Registrations systems have proven most adaptable in accommodating various forms of proprietary interest from share registers to water rights registers.[174] However, the scale and complexity of what might be termed a third translation—adapting the current systems for recording native title interests to land registration systems, such as the Torrens title system— should not be underestimated.[175] However without such a third-stage 'translation', there may be particular impediments to enhancing the possibilities of native title functioning either as a security interest or as a readily alienable interest.

CONCLUSION

The foregoing discussion has considered the two-step translation of indigenous relationships with land and waters into a purported proprietary framework. The initial translation process has been characterised by an emasculation of that relationship from a holistic interface with country to the 'recognition space' of the common law. The first step is premised on the assumption that indigenous peoples get 'what is left over' once settler property has been secured. The stripping away of the cultural integrity components of the indigenous relationship except for those elements that can be physically manifested, together with the pinioning of native title in the factual and thereby uniquely vulnerable realm, operates as a double movement seemingly measuring native title by the bundle of rights property formula but ultimately creating it as a lesser 'interest' than real property 'ownership'.

The second step of the translation for native title to a market-oriented interest remains to be fully realised, and its feasibility is, we suggest, highly contingent upon the outcomes of the first translation. Recent trends in the recognition and extinguishment of native title have produced a narrowing of the legal and empirical character of native title. *Mabo (No 2)* offered prescience regarding property status for indigenous landholding, which later native title jurisprudence has progressively redefined as a form of lesser 'right'. This redefinition has increasingly moved native title away from possessory and title-based models of property toward forms that appear to replicate not a proprietary status for native title but a contractual one. The bundle of rights that now comprise native title in many instances

---

[174] M Young and J McColl, 'Robust Separation: A Search for a Generic Framework to Simplify Registration and Trading of Interest in Natural Resources' in Land and Water Australia, *Property Rights and Responsibilities: Current Australian Thinking* (Canberra, Land and Water Australia, 2002) 55.

[175] Technically, it is possible simply to transfer interests recorded in the Native Title Tribunal register to a Torrens title register; however, the *legal effect* of such a transfer has not yet been determined.

appears to align more with rights realised through a contractual or negotiated relationship in regard to questions about the use of and access to lands and waters. A change to market processes may ultimately be embraced by those who hold this diminished form of 'title'—if other circumstances, such as the realisation of security value, are conducive. However, such a translation process to commercial forms should not be presumed to accord with a more holistic recognition of the scope of indigenous peoples' landholdings in Australia.

A similar pattern of change in the nature of landholding has effects on customary and indigenous landholding across many countries. There are global and historical dimensions of the move to transform patterns of landholding that are based in cultural relationships, localised control over land and resources and inalienabilty into a network of contractual and economic relationships. Native title in Australia, although in many regards not conceived as a direct equivalent for settler real property interests, nonetheless may still follow a similar trajectory to Western real property. However, the difficulties and problems inherent to this process should not be ignored in the rush to embrace 'contractualism'.

13

Individual Title versus Collective Title in Australia: Reflections on the North American and New Zealand Experiences of Indigenous Title to Land

M A STEPHENSON*

I. INTRODUCTION

THIS CHAPTER WILL explore and critically evaluate one of the significant contemporary debates in Australia today: issues relating to individual title and collective ownership of indigenous lands. At a time when the Australian government is considering reforms regarding indigenous title to land, the question of how that title is to be held is paramount for indigenous Australians. Proposals have emerged to convert indigenous communal landholdings into individual, alienable forms of title and to open up indigenous landholding regimes.[1] These proposals have more recently been reviewed, and consideration has been given to retaining the underlying indigenous communal title while allowing individual dealings with land.[2]

---

* Senior Lecturer in Law, T.C. Beirne School of Law, University of Queensland, Australia.

[1] See N Pearson and L Kostakidis-Lianos, 'Building Indigenous Capital: Removing Obstacles to Participation in the Real Economy' (Cape York Institute for Policy and Leadership Viewpoint paper, July 2004) <http://www.cyi-staging.net/.aspx?article=EG088DQNZMZG1O33R3IN> accessed 27 February 2006; and A Vanstone, Minister for Indigenous Affairs, 'Being Land Rich and Dirt Poor is Not Good Enough' (Address to the National Press Club, February 2005).

[2] Prime Minister, 'Address to National Reconciliation Planning Workshop' (May 2005), in which he outlined his view that inalienable and communal indigenous land should be retained.

The individualising of indigenous land titles has been promoted as a means to encourage economic development.[3] In 2006 the Commonwealth government introduced the first of the proposed changes with a Bill to amend the Aboriginal Land Rights (Northern Territory) Act (1976), which would allow for the leasing of aboriginal land held under that legislation.[4] With approximately 20 per cent of the land in Australia owned or controlled by indigenous peoples, it is an appropriate time to consider and review management regimes and alternative forms of tenure that could be appropriate for Australian indigenous lands.[5]

Issues that must be faced in considering the merits of collective rights versus individual rights to indigenous lands, include the following:

- What are the consequences of individualising indigenous title?
- Should indigenous individual titles be alienable?
- How will future indigenous generations deal with the consequences of the individualisation of indigenous title?
- Who should make the decision as to whether indigenous title is to be collective title or individual: the government, the community or individual members of that community?

[3] H Hughes, 'The Economics of Indigenous Deprivation and Proposals for Reform' (Centre for Independent Studies Issues Analysis No 63, 2005); H Hughes and J Warin, 'A New Deal for Aborigines and Torres Strait Islanders in Remote Communities' (Centre for Independent Studies Issues Analysis No 54, 2005). Hughes and Warin state: 'nowhere in the world has communal land ownership ever led to economic development' 1. H de Soto, *The Mystery of Capital: Why Capitalism Triumphs in the West and Fails Everywhere Else* (New York, Basic Books, 2000); A Vanstone, 'Initiatives Support Home Ownership on Indigenous Land' (Press Release, 5 October 2005).

[4] The Aboriginal Land Rights (Northern Territory) Amendment Bill 2006 was given Royal Assent and became an Act on 5 September 2006.

[5] S Bradfield, 'White Picket Fence or Trojan Horse? The Debate over Communal Ownership of Indigenous Land and Individual Wealth Creation' (2005) 3 *Land, Rights, Laws: Issues of Native Title*, issues paper no 3 ; JC Altman, C Linkhorn and J Clark, 'Land Rights Development Reform in Remote Australia' (Centre for Aboriginal Economic Policy Research, Oxfam Australia and Australian National University, Discussion Paper No 276/ 2005); N Watson, 'Privatisation versus Communal Lands' (2005–06) 80 *Arena Magazine* 10; The Aboriginal and Torres Strait Islander Social Justice Commissioner, 'Promoting Economic and Social Development through Native Title' 2004 2 *Land, Rights, Law: Issues of Native Title*, issues paper no 28; T Calma (Aboriginal and Torres Strait Islander Social Justice Commissioner), *Native Title Report 2005* (No 4/2005); National Indigenous Council, 'Indigenous Land Tenure Principles' (2005); A Ridgeway, 'Addressing the Economic Exclusion of Indigenous Australians through Native Title' (*Mabo* Lecture, National Native Title Conference, 2005); P Lee, "Individual Titling of Aboriginal Land in the Northern Territory: What Australia Can Learn form the International Community" (2006) *University of New South Wales Law Journal* 22, 36 and see generally re land reform of customary tenures J Fingleton, "Privatizing Land in the Pacific: A Defence of Customary Tenures", The Australia Institute, Discussion Paper No 80, June 2005; K Deininger and H Binswanger, "The Evolution of the World Bank's Policy" in A de Janvry et al (eds), *Access to Land, Rural Poverty and Public Action* (2001) 407, 418-419. In the Northern Territory, 44% of land is in aboriginal ownership.

- Would individualisation of title necessarily result in increased economic benefits and private home ownership for indigenous peoples in Australia?
- What alternative models of indigenous landholding might work in the Australian context?

To aid in the assessment of these issues, the focus of this chapter will be on experiences in the differing forms of indigenous land tenure in North America and New Zealand. First, the chapter will examine and analyse the past experiences of individualising communal indigenous title in North America and the 'individualisation' of Maori title in New Zealand. Secondly, the chapter will explore alternative forms of landholdings on First Nations reserve lands in Canada under the Canadian Indian Act (1876) and then review Maori land in New Zealand. Thirdly, land held under comprehensive claims agreements in Canada, such as the freehold model under the Nisga'a Agreement (1998), will be considered. Fourthly, the corporate model of indigenous landholding in the Alaska Native Claims Settlement Act (1971) will be discussed. The impact of each of the above forms of indigenous landholdings will be critiqued and an assessment undertaken in order to establish what lessons can be learnt for the management of indigenous lands in Australia.

II. CURRENT FORMS OF INDIGENOUS LANDHOLDINGS IN AUSTRALIA, THE USA, CANADA AND NEW ZEALAND

Current forms of indigenous land tenure in the different jurisdictions will be briefly outlined by way of comparison.[6]

A. Australia

Australia was settled on the basis that aboriginal people had no title to the lands on which they had lived for generations. Although each State has passed protectorate legislation that designates reserve lands for indigenous peoples, aboriginal control over these lands has been absent.

1. Land Rights Schemes

In 1976 the Commonwealth government passed the first significant land rights legislation, the Aboriginal Land Rights (Northern Territory) Act

---

[6] S Dorsett and L Godden, 'A Guide to Overseas Precedents of Relevance to Native Title' (AIATSIS, 1998).

(1976) (Cth),[7] which provided statutory schemes for the transfer of land to aboriginal peoples. All States, except Western Australia and Tasmania, subsequently passed land rights legislation that allows for the granting and holding of title to indigenous lands.[8] In most of these land rights schemes, the tenure granted to the indigenous landholders is an inalienable fee simple.

2. Native Title

In Australia, common law recognition of native title commenced with the 1992 Australian High Court decision in *Mabo v State of Queensland (No 2)*.[9] The Court found that native title is recognised by the common law and that indigenous inhabitants have rights to their traditional lands. The Commonwealth government's legislative response to the High Court's decision in *Mabo* was to enact the Native Title Act (1993) ('NTA'), section 223 of which defines native title as a collective and communal title. Rights recognised under native title are communal rights enjoyed by the whole community, but individual title rights can also be recognised.[10] Once a determination of native title is made, the NTA requires that the native title be held and managed by a body corporate.[11]

The nature and content of native title in Australia varies widely. In many instances native title can amount to an exclusive possession interest in land, while in other cases it is a free-standing right of user of the land. Native title in Australia is inalienable except by surrender to the Crown, which has the right to extinguish this title.[12] Native title does not include mineral rights.[13] Thus, in Australia today there is a range of indigenous landholdings, including statutory land rights schemes and native title. This mix of titles frequently intersects and overlaps, making the management and regulation of indigenous lands extremely complex.[14]

---

[7]   M Tehan and L Godden, 'Analyzing Aboriginal Land Tenure and its Intersection with Economic, Social and Cultural "Sustainability" for Australia's Indigenous Peoples' (Australasian Real Property Law Teachers Conference, Vanuatu, 2005).

[8]   Aboriginal Land Rights Act (1983) (NSW); Aboriginal Lands Act (1970) (Vic); Aboriginal Land Act (1991) (Qld); Torres Strait Islander Land Act (1991) (Qld); Pitjantjatjara Land Rights Act (1981) (SA); Maralinga Tjarutja Land Rights Act (1984) (SA).

[9]   (1992) 175 CLR 1 ('*Mabo*').

[10]   NTA (1993) s 223(1) defines native title to include communal, group or individual rights.

[11]   *Ibid*, s 24DD and Native Title (Prescribed Body Corporate) Regulations (1999).

[12]   *Mabo*, note 8 above, 64.

[13]   *Western Australia v Ward* (2002) 213 CLR 1, 186.

[14]   For example, Aboriginal Land Act (1991) (Qld) s 71.

B. The United States

When North America was settled, British imperial policy (as evidenced in the 1763 Royal Proclamation) was to give limited recognition of aboriginal titles to traditional lands. Private individuals were prohibited from purchasing Indian lands, and the sale of Indian land could be made only to the Crown. In 1823 the United States Supreme Court in *Johnson v McIntosh*[15] recognised that the lands that had traditionally been occupied by the Indian tribes since time immemorial were held as 'Indian title'. 'Indian title' is generally a communal title, but individual rights can be recognised;[16] it also includes mineral and timber rights.[17]

In *Johnson v McIntosh*, the court also affirmed that the doctrine of discovery applied in the US, meaning that the sovereign (the United States) gained *ultimate dominion* over the land. However, this right was subject to 'Indian title', the Indian right of occupancy.[18] Discovery also gave the discoverer (the federal government) the exclusive right to extinguish Indian title.

The United States 1990 census showed that there were then 555 federally recognised Indian tribes and 287 reservations, which comprised 22.68 million hectares and are held on trust by the United States for Native Americans.[19]

C. Canada

Canadian aboriginal lands include not only aboriginal title lands but also reserve lands under the Indian Act 1876. In addition, there are 'modern treaty' lands, the subject of comprehensive claims treaties. In other words, there is no single model of property rights for indigenous Canadians.

1. Aboriginal Title Lands

Australia and Canada share similar jurisprudence in the recognition by the common law of traditional rights to the traditional lands of indigenous people. In Canada, the Supreme Court in the 1972 decision in *Calder v*

---

[15]   21 US 543 (1823). For an analysis of *Johnson v McIntosh*, see L Robertson, *Conquest by Law: How the Discovery of America Dispossessed Indigenous Peoples of Their Lands* (New York, Oxford University Press, 2005).

[16]   *Sac & Fox Tribe of Indians* 383 F 2d 991 (1967); *United States v Dann*, 873 F 2d 1189 (1989). At 1196, it was considered that no theoretical reason existed to prevent an individual aboriginal title being established.

[17]   *United States v Shoshone Tribe of Indians* 304 US 111 (1938).

[18]   *Lac Courte Oreilles Band of the Lake Superior Chippewa Indians v Voight* 700 F2d 341 (1983).

[19]   Dorsett and Godden, note 5 above, 12 .

Attorney General of British Columbia[20] confirmed that aboriginal title existed at common law. However, the nature of aboriginal title remained unclear until 1997, when the Supreme Court decided *Delgamuukw v British Columbia*,[21] where it was recognised that aboriginal title is a communal title vested in the indigenous community and is a right to the land itself.[22] Despite aboriginal title being recognised as a possessory title, certain limitations were outlined. One of these was that aboriginal title is inalienable except by surrender to the Crown.[23]

2. Reserve Lands (Treaty Lands) under the Indian Act 1876

Canadian reserves total around 3 million hectares.[24] The Crown retains the underlying title and ownership. Reserve lands were set aside for the use and benefit of the Indians under treaties made between First Nations peoples of Canada and the Crown. Indian property rights on reserves are treated as collective rights by the Indian Act 1876.

3. Negotiated Agreement Lands

Federal policy was originally not to recognise Indian land claims outside Indian reserves. This changed with the *Calder* decision in 1973.[25] New federal policy declared that negotiations with First Nations peoples who were able to establish their traditional interests in lands would be conducted, and compensation or benefits in exchange for those interests would be provided.[26] Negotiations have resulted in the settlement of several comprehensive land claims agreements with First Nations peoples in the North West Territories and in British Columbia. Unique models of land tenure are contained in some agreements, such as the Nisga'a Agreement (1998), which will be discussed further below.

---

[20] [1973] SCR 313 ('*Calder*').
[21] (1998) 153 DLR (4th) 193 ('*Delgamuukw*').
[22] *Ibid*, 243–4 and 252. Ownership of minerals, forest products and other natural resources is part of aboriginal title (247).
[23] *Ibid*, 247.
[24] Dorsett and Godden, note 5 above, 14.
[25] [1973] SCR 313.
[26] Canadian First Nations hold approximately 6% of the total land mass of Canada.

D. New Zealand

In New Zealand, treaties of cession were the foundation of legal sovereignty by the settler nation.[27] In 1840 the Treaty of Waitangi was signed, and according to the English text version of the Treaty, sovereignty (*kawanatanga*) passed to the British Crown (and subsequently to the New Zealand government).[28] Under the Treaty the British Crown's right to govern New Zealand was dependent upon the Crown's meeting its obligations to the Maori peoples under the Treaty Articles. The Treaty guaranteed the *tino rangatiratanga* (sovereignty) of the Maori, and they thus retained authority to control their lands according to tribal customs.[29] The Treaty gave the Crown the preemptive right to purchase lands surplus to the Maori tribes' requirements.[30]

In 1975 the Waitangi Tribunal was established pursuant to the Treaty of Waitangi Act (1975). The Tribunal's function is to hear and report on Maori claims that they have been 'prejudicially affected' by Crown actions, past or present, and that conflict with the principles of the Treaty of Waitangi.[31] The Tribunal's general jurisdiction is recommendatory.[32] A process of direct negotiation with Maori to settle claims resulting in Deeds of Settlement has also been established.[33]

Little Maori customary land remains in New Zealand.[34] Maori lands comprise mostly Maori freehold land and some Maori reserved land. Today Maori lands consist of about 1.5 million hectares, or 6 per cent of the total area of land in New Zealand.[35]

1. Maori Customary/Aboriginal Land

Customary land is defined in the Te Ture Whenua Maori/Maori Land Act (1993) ('TTWMA') as land held 'by Maori in accordance with *tikanga* Maori'.[36] '*Tikanga*' has been described as 'the norms that maintain law

---

[27] R Boast, A Erueti, D McPhail, and NF Smith, *Maori Land Law*, 2nd edn (Wellington, NZ, LexisNexis, 2004).

[28] Treaty of Waitangi (1840) art 1. The Maori text speaks of granting a right of governance—not sovereignty.

[29] *Ibid*, art 2.

[30] *Ibid*; *R v Symonds* (1847) NZ PCC 387.

[31] Treaty of Waitangi Act (1975) s 6.

[32] *Ibid*, s 6(3). The Tribunal cannot recommend that the Crown return private land to Maori ownership.

[33] Boast, note 26 above, 14–20.

[34] Apart from foreshore and seabed customary rights, today customary title will generally comprise small areas of land previously overlooked or areas where survey errors occurred.

[35] Altman, note 4 above, 23.

[36] TTWMA (1993) s 129(2)(a).

and order in Maori customary society'.[37] Little customary Maori land title exists in New Zealand today. The keybut not the only reasons for this were that, first, the Crown, through its rights of pre-emption of Maori title, acquired significant sections of Maori lands prior to 1862. By 1862, approximately two-thirds of customary Maori title, including most of the South Island, was no longer owned by Maori.[38] Secondly, the Native Lands Acts were passed.[39] This legislation established a process by which Maori could, where the customary title was recognised by the Native Land Court (and later the Maori Land Court), convert their land from customary title to freely alienable Maori freehold title.[40]

In 2003 the Court of Appeal in A-G v Ngati Apa[41] found that the Maori Land Court's jurisdiction extended to making a determination that the foreshore and seabed is Maori customary land. However, the effect of the decision was reversed by the enactment of the Foreshore and Seabed Act (2004) ('FSA'), which replaced the Maori Land Court's jurisdiction to determine customary title with a statutory jurisdiction to determine 'territorial customary rights orders'[42] and 'non-territorial customary rights orders',[43] which together confer rights to carry out recognised customary activities.[44] A territorial customary rights order equates with aboriginal/customary title at common law. To obtain such an order, claimants must prove exclusive use and occupation of the area. Non-territorial customary rights orders are restricted to minor site-specific activities and will generally exclude fishing rights.[45]

---

[37] Boast, note 26 above, 41.

[38] Ibid, 66–7.

[39] Native Lands Act (1862) (NZ); Native Lands Act (1865) (NZ) (hereinafter, 'Native Lands Acts').

[40] The Maori Land Court was established under TTWMA (1993) ss 131(1) and 129(1): Boast, note 26 above, ch 5.

[41] [2003] 3 NZLR 643 ('Ngati Apa'). See: R Boast, 'Maori Proprietary Claims to the Foreshore and Seabed after Ngati Apa' (2004) 21 New Zealand Universities Law Review 1; PG McHugh, 'Aboriginal Title in New Zealand: A Retrospect and Prospect' (2004) 2 New Zealand Journal of Policy and International Law 1; J Ruru, 'What Could Have Been: The Common Law Doctrine of Native Title in Land under Saltwater in Australia and New Zealand' (unpublished paper, University of Dunedin, 2005); S Dorsett, 'Making Strategic Choices: Claiming Territorial and Non-territorial Customary Rights under the Foreshore and Seabed Act' (forthcoming 2006) McGill Law Journal.

[42] FSA (2004) s 32(1).

[43] Ibid, ss 49(2) and 50–2.

[44] S Dorsett and L Godden, 'Interpreting Customary Rights Orders under the Foreshore and Seabed Act: The New Jurisdiction of the Maori Land Court' (2005) 36 VUWLR 229.

[45] FSA (2004) ss 50(b)(i) and 49(1)(a)(b). Non-territorial customary rights orders can be made only regarding a 'use, activity or practice' that 'is and has been since 1840, integral to tikanga Maori'.

2. Maori Freehold Land

Maori freehold land is customary Maori land that the Maori Land Court (or its predecessor the Native Land Court) has determined ownership by the traditional Maori owners by way of freehold order.[46]

3. Maori Reserved Land

Some lands acquired by pre-emptive purchase deeds have ultimately become Maori reserved land. 'Maori reserved land' is a not a formal category. It is a term used to cover various lands that are subject to the Maori Reserved Land Act (1955).[47] It includes some Crown lands reserved for Maori and some freehold land that pre-dates the establishment of the Maori Land Court.[48]

E. General Differences between Western and Indigenous Land Title

In the four jurisdictions referred to above, United States, Canada, Australia and New Zealand, we see a dual regime of indigenous property rights (Indian/aboriginal/Maori/native title) and Western property rights in relation to land. Key differences between Western and indigenous notions of property include the following. First, unlike most Western title, indigenous title is inalienable except to the Crown by the Crown's pre-emptive right. This means that in none of the above jurisdictions can indigenous title be sold or traded privately. In addition, the mortgaging of indigenous title to land may not be possible. A commercial mortgage of an inalienable title would be of little value or interest to a mortgagee. A restriction on mortgaging could make the direct development of indigenous land by indigenous peoples difficult.

Furthermore, unlike most Western land tenures, indigenous title is in general liable to extinguishment by Crown/government action. In addition, unlike the Western model of private landholding, indigenous tenure is

---

[46] TTWMA (1993) s 129(2.See the discussion below in relation to customary Maori lands. Maori land in New Zealand is a separate and different form of tenure to the freehold title granted by the Crown. This is the most important category of Maori land today. See Robertson, B "Maori Land Tenure – Issues and Opportunities", *New Zealand Institute of Surveyors Annual Conference*, Auckland, 2004, 3; Boast, note 27 above, ch 4 and ch 5.

[47] Boast, note 27 above, 66 and ch 14. This land is also governed by the Maori Reserved Land Amendment Act 1997. Certain Maori reserved land has been held under perpetually renewable leases which made it difficult for the Maori owners to utilise or occupy their lands.

[48] Boast, note 27 above, ch 14.

generally a communal or collective title.[49] In the above jurisdictions indigenous title generally allows for the recognition of individual interests in communally owned land.

II. INDIVIDUALISING INDIGENOUS TITLE TO LAND

A. The American Allotment System

In the latter part of the nineteenth century there was increasing dissatisfaction with Indian reservation policies in the United States. Tribal economies were not successful, and many Native Americans were living in poverty. Congress was looking to resolve these issues and therefore passed several Acts that divided the communal reservations of Indian tribes into individual parcels of land, referred to as 'allotments'.[50] The first of these Acts was the General Allotment Act (1887) ('Allotment Act').[51]

Individualisation of Indian title to land (allotment) was generally promoted by those sympathetic to the Indians. The allotment legislation may have been well intentioned and many supporters believed that, if individual Native Americans had title to land that they could cultivate, economic self-sufficiency would follow. It was further believed that this would in turn create Native American middle-class farmers, thereby assisting the assimilation of the indigenous population into American culture.[52] Some who were unsympathetic to Native Americans and who resented the vast areas of 'Indian lands' that were unavailable to non-Native settlers welcomed the legislation as a way of breaking up the tribal land mass and freeing up new lands for white settlement.[53] In other words, the allotment legislation can be seen as an attempt to destroy tribal culture by dismantling tribal landholdings, and unsurprisingly, allotment was frequently forced on the tribes without their consent.[54] However, Congress sought to obtain the agreement of individual tribes with the passage of the Allotment Act.

Under the Allotment Act, portions of reservation land were allotted to individual Native Americans. Allotments of 160 acres were to be made to

---

[49] Indigenous property is not analogous to Western forms of collective ownership because indigenous title is not an alienable or inheritable interest in communal property.

[50] WC Canby, *American Indian Law in a Nutshell*, 3rd edn (St Paul, West, 1998); DH Getches, CF Wilkinson and R Williams, *Cases and Materials on Federal Indian Law*, 4th edn (St Paul, West, 1998) ch 4, 140–85; RN Clinton, NJ Newton and M Price, *American Indian Law: Cases and Materials*, 3rd edn (Charlottesville, Michie, 1991); F Cohen, *Handbook of Federal Indian Law* (New York, AMS Press, 1972); and *Hodel v Irving* 481 US 704 (1987).

[51] 24 Stat 388; 25 USC 331 (Dawes Act).

[52] *Solem v Bartlett*, 465 US 463 (1984); Canby, note 48 above, 19.

[53] Canby, note 48 above, 19–20.

[54] *Lone Wolf v Hitchcock* 187 US 553 (1903).

each head of a household, 80 acres to individuals and 40 acres to minors. Double allotments were made where land was suitable for grazing. Title to the allotted land was to remain in the United States in trust for 25 years. This meant that the allotted lands could not be sold for 25 years, but at the end of that period the allotted land was transferred to the individual Native Americans in fee simple. The trust period was intended to protect allottees from improvident sales to non-Native settlers and also from immediate State taxation. In addition, this 25-year period was designed to allow time to encourage Native Americans to learn agricultural skills that could be used on their lands.[55] Furthermore, the Allotment Act authorised the Secretary of the Interior to negotiate with the tribes for disposition of all 'excess' lands remaining after the allotments. This 'surplus' land was sold to white settlers.

The Allotment Act was the first legislation concerning Native Americans that affected the internal affairs of nearly all tribes in the United States,[56] and its legacies are well documented.[57] Because the allotment system was designed to bring Native Americans into non-Native culture, its administration effectively destroyed many tribal traditions and tribal influences. Key problems with allotment included the loss of traditional lands, the checkerboarding of landholdings on reserve lands, fractionalisation of tribal lands, the loss of cultural identity including governing ability, economic difficulties and bureaucratic costs.[58] Frequently, Native Americans were uninterested in farming or, especially in the cases of minors, the elderly or the infirm, were incapable of working the land. To prevent land

---

[55] Allotment Act (1887) s 148. The Burke Act (1906) 34 Stat182 allowed the transfer of the fee patent to 'competent Indians' prior to the trust period expiring.

[56] Indian reservations in the West, established late in the allotment period, largely escaped allotment.

[57] See for example: JV Royster, 'The Legacy of Allotment' (1995) 27 *Arizona State Law Journal* 1; SL Leeds, 'The Burning of Blackacre: A Step Toward Reclaiming Tribal Property Law' (2001) 10 *Kan J L & Pub Policy* 491; KR Guzman, 'Give or Take an Acre: Property Norms and the Indian Land Consolidation Act' (2000) 85 *Iowa L Rev* 595; JA Shoemaker, 'Like Snow in the Spring Time: Allotment, Fractionalisation, and the Indian Land Tenure Problem' (2003) *Wisconsin L Rev* 729; EAC Thompson, '*Babbitt v Youpee*: Allotment and the Continuing Loss of Native American Property and Rights to Devise' (1997) 19 *Hawaii L Rev* 265; KH Bobroff, 'Retelling Allotment: Indian Property Rights and the Myth of Common Ownership; (2001) 54 *Vanderbilt L Rev* 1559; CG Hakansson, 'Allotment at Pine Ridge Reservation: Its Consequences and Alternative Remedies' (1997) 73 *N Dakota L Rev* 231; MM Lindo, '*Youpee v Babbitt*: The Indian Land Inheritance Problem Revisited' (1997) 22 *American Indian L Rev* 223; MD Poindexter, 'Of Dinosaurs and Indefinite Land Trusts: A Review of Individual American Indian Property Rights amidst the Legacy of Allotment' (1994) 14 *Boston College Third World Law Journal* 53; and JR Fitzpatrick, 'The Competent Ward' (2003) 28 *American Indian L Rev* 189.

[58] Bobroff, note 55 above, 1607.

lying idle, leasing of allotment lands was introduced,[59] even though leasing (generally to white settlers) was seen as undermining the allotment policy objective—promoting self-sufficiency among the Native Americans.[60] The allotment policy lasted from 1887 to 1934, when allotment ended with the passage of the Indian Reorganization Act (1934).[61]

1. The Effects of the Allotment Policy

Allotment policy in relation to Indian lands was disastrous on a number of levels. The general effect was a separation of Native Americans from their traditional lands. As a result of allotment there was a reduction in the total amount of Native American land from 138 million acres in 1887 to 48 million acres in 1934. Of the 48 million acres that remained, some 20 million were desert or semi-desert.[62] Indian lands were lost both by the sale of allottee lands (after the 25-year trust period expired) and by the sale of tribal 'surplus' lands. After 25 years, the allottees who received fee simple titles were subject to state property taxes, and many forced sales resulted from non-payment of these taxes. The availability of the land as security meant Native Americans lost their land owing to defaults.[63] Moreover, many of the sales to non-Indians were on terms disadvantageous to the Indians. The allottees were frequently left with neither their lands nor with any benefits from its disposition.

In the long term, the failure of allotment became increasingly clear as successive generations inherited the allotted lands. The Allotment Act subjected the allotted lands to state intestacy laws, which resulted in highly fractionalised ownership. For example, a 160-acre parcel held by multiple owners was unworkable. Where the land remained in trust (after allotment ended), this land was often inalienable and not capable of partition. Fractionalisation of lands occurred because the restrictions on alienation required the division of property among intestate heirs.[64]

The fractionalisation problems only compounded over time. As each allotment owner often had more than one heir, the problems inevitably increased with the passing of generations. Allotment thus resulted in expensive bureaucratic land administration processes and increased transactional costs. Identifying, locating and obtaining consent from allotment

---

[59] A leasing amendment was made to the Allotment Act in 1891. See 26 Stat 794, 794-96 (1891); Cohen, note 48 above, 227–9; Poindexter, note 55 above, 65 – 70; J A McDonnell, *The Dispossession of the American Indian 1887-1934* (Indiana University Press, Bloomington and Indianapolis, 1991, ch4 and ch5).

[60] *Hodel v Irving*, 481 US 704, 707.

[61] 25 USC 461.

[62] Canby, note 48 above, 21; Cohen, note 48 above.

[63] Hakansson, note 55 above, 234–6.

[64] Shoemaker, note 55 above, 730.

co-owners proved inefficient and unwieldy.[65] Fractionalisation frequently rendered lands unusable as farmland due to their small size and limited revenue potential. In addition, the checkerboard areas of alternative Indian and non-Indian land (on the Indian reserves) made sizeable farming or grazing projects impracticable. Fractionalisation has been said to amount to a constructive dispossession of land despite paper title records showing the land as being held by Native Americans.[66] By denying Native Americans tangible benefits from their lands, allotment has undoubtedly contributed to the poverty of Native Americans generally.[67]

2. The Meriam Report (1928) and the End of the Allotment Policy

By 1928 allotment was recognised as a failure. Congress commissioned a report, known as the 'Meriam Report',[68] to document the failure of federal Indian policy during the allotment period. This report provided part of the impetus for subsequent extensive changes in federal policy. The report indicated that poverty among Native Americans was widespread; administrative abuse on reservations was also rampant. Furthermore, the report noted the extensive difficulties in administering fractionalised property such as that produced by the allotment system.

Eventually, in recognition of the need to protect what remained of the tribal lands, Congress passed the Indian Reorganization Act (1934) ('IRA').[69] This Act ended allotment, prohibited alienation of Indian lands and set up a fund for economic development. However, the Act did not expressly repeal the Allotment Act but rather prevented the issuing of new allotments and provided for the extension of the trust status of existing allotments (indefinitely).[70] The IRA authorised the Secretary of the Interior to restore to tribal ownership any 'surplus' lands acquired from the tribes under the Allotment Act, provided third parties had not acquired rights in that land. In addition, the IRA gave the tribes power to organise and adopt a constitution to vest certain rights in the tribe, for example, power to

---

[65] Guzman, note 55 above, 608.

[66] Shoemaker, note 55 above, 749.

[67] *Ibid.* The failure of individualization of title to produce economic success in farming is discussed in R B Bateman, "Talking with the Plough: Agricultural Policy and Indian Farming in the Canadian and U S Prairies" (1996) (2) *The Canadian Journal of Native Studies* 211, at 217-9.

[68] L Meriam, 'The Problem of Indian Administration' (Institute for Government Research, 1928) 40–1.

[69] 25 USC 461. Getches, note 46 above, 191–203.

[70] The *Indian Reorganization Act* extended the trust status of all allotments which were held in trust in 1934, when this Act was passed, for an indefinite period of time. Much allotted Indian land continues to remain in trust status today. See Canby, note 8 above , at 270; R A Monette, "Governing Private Property in Indian Country: The Double-Edged Sword of the Trust Relationship and Trust Responsibility Arising out of Early Supreme Court Opinions and the *General Allotment Act*", (1995) 25 *New Mexico Law Review*, 35.

prevent the sale of land.[71] The policy aim of the IRA was to encourage tribal self-government and revitalise Indian culture.

3. The Continuing Legacies of the Allotment Policy

The end of the allotment policy did not end the problems brought about by allotment. In the 1960s the US government undertook studies of allotted trust lands, and these studies reported that half of the allotted trust lands were held in fractionated ownership. Three million acres were held by more than six heirs to a parcel.[72] In an effort to deal with the problems of fractionalised ownership, Congress eventually passed the Indian Land Consolidation Act (1983) ('ILCA').[73]. It was hoped that this legislation would prevent the problem from compounding further, by forbidding small, undivided interests in Indian lands to be passed on after the death of an owner. Section 207 of the ILCA provided for the escheat of small undivided property interests that were unproductive during the year preceding the owner's death. No provision was made in this statute for the payment of compensation to the owners of the interests covered by section 207.

This provision was challenged in the case of *Hodel v Irving*,[74] in which the Supreme Court found that the regulation represented an unconstitutional 'taking' of property without just compensation.[75] Congress amended the ICLA; however, the Supreme Court reached a similar decision in *Babbit v Youpee* in 1997.[76] As a result, the American Indian Probate Reform Act was passed in 2004.[77]

Debates continue about how best to resolve the aftermath of allotment and what reforms might be implemented. Suggestions include the conversion of unrestricted allotments from fee simple to trust status and the enactment of tribal laws to prohibit tribal members from selling their real property interests to non-members.[78] The adverse legacies from the allotment and individualisation of indigenous land title policies of the 1880s continue to require remedial action in the USA well over a century after their introduction. Clearly these are policies that other countries should be hesitant to replicate.

---

[71] IRA (1934) s16.
[72] Hearings on the HR 1113.
[73] 96 Stat 2519; 25 USC 2206.
[74] 481 US 704 (1987).
[75] Leeds, note 55 above, 492.
[76] 117 US 727 (1997). Thompson, note 55 above, 267. See amended ICLA 26 *USCA* 2206 (1984).
[77] 118 Stat 1773 (2004).
[78] Leeds, note 55 above, 496.

B. Allotment in Canada

In Canada, individual ownership of indigenous lands was also promoted in the latter part of the 1880s.[79] Legislation, allowing for the individual allotment of reserve lands, was passed which mirrored the policies behind the United States *Allotment Act*.[80] However, agreement of the Band Council was required prior to individual titles being issued and by the 1890s these policies had been largely reversed.[81] Generally, no wide spread 'allotment' and no substantial loss of Indian lands from the Indian reserve land system occurred in Canada.

[79] Report of Commissioner Reed 1889, *Canada Sessional Papers* (No 12) (1890) 165. Hayter Reed, Commissioner for the North West Territories, stated 'The policy of destroying the tribal ... system is assailed in every possible way and every effort made to implant a spirit of individual responsibility, instead'.

[80] For example, in 1857 the *Gradual Civilization Act* entitled "enfranchised" indigenous men to an individual allotment of 50 acres of Indian reserve land. This allocated land was ultimately to be removed from the Indian reserve system and held in fee simple. Band Councils could refuse to allot land to individual members and most were reluctant to do so. However, in 1884 this power to assign individual allotments was vested in the Superintendent General of Indian affairs. See R Metcs and CG Devlin, "Land Entitlement Under Treaty 8", (2004) 41 *Alberta Law Review*, 951; Canadian Royal Commission "Looking Forward, Looking Back," Report of the Royal Commission on Aboriginal Peoples, (Canada Communications Group Publishing, Ottawa, Canada, 1996) 145 -148 and 271- 287; S Carter, *Lost Harvests: Prairie Indian Reserve Farmers and Government Policy*, McGill University Press, Montreal 1993.

[81] The 1876 *Indian Act* provided for individual allotments of reserve lands to be made by Band Councils to Indians who held "location tickets". To further promote individual titles the *Indian Act* was amended in 1879 to allow the Superintendent General (and not the Band Councils) to order a reserve to be surveyed and divided into lots to enable the issuing of "location tickets". However, such land continued to remain within the Indian Reserve system and the "location ticket" indicated only that the holder had a right of lawful possession. (See Canadian Royal Commission "Looking Forward, Looking Back, note 80 above, t 279). Hayter Reed, Indian Commissioner for the North West Territories, in his annual report in 1888, declared that the Western Indian Reserves were to be surveyed and subdivided into separate individually run farms. Reserves were subdivided into 40 acre lots. Many reserves were surveyed but only a few reserves were actually subdivided. In the 1890s, after a change of government, the program of subdividing Indian reserves ceased. See Metcs and Devlin, above note 80; Carter above note 80, ch6 ; Miller J, *The Canadian Campaign to turn Aboriginal Peoples into Agrarian Societies*, unpublished, University of Saskatoon, 2006; Bateman R B, "Talking with the Plow : Agricultural Policy and Indian Farming in the Canadian and U S Prairies," (1996) (16) (2) *The Canadian Journal of Native Studies* 211, at 217-9.

C. The Maori Experience of Individualising Title

Past experiences in New Zealand demonstrate patterns of significant loss of Maori customary title lands. Much customary title was lost through Crown purchase, but a significant proportion of the balance was 'individualized'.[82]

Originally Maori title was alienable only to the Crown.[83] Waiver of the Crown's right of pre-emption was set out in the preamble to the Native Lands Act (1862).[84] This Act and the later Native Lands Act (1865) allowed Maori customary title to be converted to a Crown grant in freehold.[85] The Native Land Court determined ownership of Maori lands by conducting investigations into customary lands. If the traditional owners could prove that in Maori law they were the owners, they would be issued with a court certificate of title, which could be exchanged for a Crown granted freehold. The Maori who were confirmed as land owners by the court had power to deal freely with the lands. The Native Lands Acts thus promoted direct land dealings between Maori and private purchasers, therefore allowing sales of traditional Maori land to non-traditional owners.[86]

One consequence of the Native Lands Acts was to facilitate the demise of collective rights of Maori land ownership and to promote 'individual' land tenures. Maori customary title was effectively 'individualised' as title could either be held in common or divided by shareholdings. This has been a matter of concern for the Maori, as Maori conceptions of 'ownership' have never accorded with the notion of individual title. As a result of the Native Lands Acts, individual owners of freehold land had the power to act independently of community interests and divide communal lands into individual titles, which were then dealt with separately and frequently alienated. Other policies and practices promoted by the Acts also contributed to the loss of Maori lands.[87] Although the government policy behind

[82]   Boast, note 26 above; DV Williams, 'Te Kooti Tango Whenua' The Native Land Court, 1864–1909 (Wellington, Haia Publishers, 1999); P McHugh, The Maori Magna Carta: New Zealand Law and the Treaty of Waitangi (Oxford, Oxford University Press, 1991); and Altman, note 4 above, 23.

[83]   Treaty of Waitangi (1840) art 2; Land Claims Ordinance (1841).

[84]   Affirmed New Zealand Constitution Act (1852) (Imp) s 73.

[85]   Native Lands Act (1862) ss 2, 7 and 8; and Native Lands Act (1865) ss 5 and 46.

[86]   Boast, note 26 above, ch 4.

[87]   The high costs of court fees and surveyor's costs meant that many Maori incurred debts in bringing land before the Court, which increased the need for cash, which in turn resulted in land sales. Failure to pay fees was at one time designated as a registered charge upon the land. If survey fees were unpaid, a Crown Grant could issue directly to the surveyor, who could hold it as a lien over the land. Partition orders were encouraged by the Native Lands Acts: Altman, note 4 above.

the passage of the early Native Lands Acts was not directed at the demise of Maori customary title, this has clearly been the result.[88]

D. Lessons for Australia

The individualisation of indigenous title has resulted in the significant loss of traditional customary indigenous lands in both the USA and New Zealand. To many Native Americans, allotment meant not only loss of property but also loss of the ability to effectively regulate, manage and direct activities within reservations. From 'individualisation' experiences in both the USA and New Zealand it is apparent that the allotting of individual fee simple titles to indigenous landholders will not necessarily achieve economic advantage for the indigenous title holders.

When individual indigenous title owners have the power to act independently of community interests and deal with their share of communal lands as individual titles, such titles are most vulnerable to alienation. Thus a principal lesson for Australia is that the indigenous community's complete title should never be individualised or made freely alienable.

However, it is suggested that some parts or a percentage of an indigenous community's traditional lands could be freely alienable and individualised as 'privatised land'. With this land an indigenous community could participate in commercial development in the same way that non-indigenous landholders do. At the same time, it would guarantee that some traditional title is preserved. Decisions about individualising title should be made by the indigenous peoples concerned, not superimposed as policy directives from government.

Whenever possible, communal underlying title to indigenous lands should be preserved. An indigenous community's collective decision-making powers should be preserved, even when part of the land is 'privatised', 'individualised' or made freely alienable. In addition, issues of liability of lands for taxation as well as succession rights and intestacy rules to indigenous property need to be addressed. Finally, careful planning will be needed to avoid the 'checkerboarding' of differing tenures on indigenous traditional lands.

---

[88] Boast, note 26 above, 72.

III. DIFFERENT FORMS OF INDIGENOUS LANDHOLDINGS

A. Canada

Indian reserve lands were set aside under treaties for the use and benefit of the people of the First Nations. Through the Indian Act 1876[89] the federal government administers and manages reserve lands and certain aspects of the lives of those who live thereon. This Act gives the Minister for Indian Affairs and Northern Development broad powers to control Indian lands, assets and moneys. The Crown retains the underlying title and ownership of Indian reserves.

Canadian policy has treated Indian property rights as collective rights. However, Indian reserves have not functioned solely as collective property regimes. Although Band Councils control reserve lands as collective property, individual property rights of the First Nations peoples who live on reserve lands have been recognised and exist within this system.[90] These individual property rights are not in the form of fee simple but rather exist as four different but overlapping regimes of private property rights:

1. Traditional customary rights to land;
2. Certificates of possession under the Indian Act 1876;
3. Rights under the First Nations Land Management Act (1999); and Leases.

1. Traditional Customary Rights on Reserve Lands

In Canadian Indian reserves it is not uncommon for First Nation families to hold land as a form of customary private property. Band Councils allocate land on the basis that a family had lived there for a lengthy period of time or on the basis that the land was inherited from their ancestors.[91] Such land allocations give the allocatee lawful possession of specified land in the Indian reserve. These customary holdings cannot be sold but can be left as inheritance. No legal recognition is given to customary holdings;

---

[89]   RSC (1985) c I-5. S Imai, *The 2005 Annotated Indian Act and Aboriginal Constitutional Provisions* (Toronto, Carswell, 2004).

[90]   T Flanagan and C Alcantara, 'Individual Property Rights on Canadian Indian Reserves: A Review of the Jurisprudence' (2005) 42(4) *Alberta Law Review* 1019; T Flanagan and C Alcantara, 'Individual Property Rights on Canadian Indian Reserves' (2004) 29(2) *Queens Law Journal* 489; T Flanagan and C Alcantara, 'Individual Property Rights on Canadian Indian Reserves: Public Policy Sources' (Fraser Institute Occasional Paper No 60, 2002); C Alcantara, 'Certificates of Possession and First Nations Housing: A Case Study of the Six Nations Housing Program' (2005) 20(2) *Canadian Journal of Law and Society* 183; D Kydd, *Indian Land Holdings on Reserve* (Vancouver, Native Programs, 1992) 1; C Notzke, *Indian Reserves in Canada* (Marburg, Lahn, 1985) 53; and S Imai, *Aboriginal Law Handbook*, 2nd edn (Toronto, Carswell, 1999).

[91]   Flanagan and Alcantara (2005), note 86 above, 1038–40.

neither the Indian Act 1876 nor the federal government recognises such title. Nonetheless, Band Councils continue to allocate land without Ministerial approval.[92]

To date, Canadian courts have failed to enforce customary property rights on reserve lands.[93] Customary property rights on Indian reserves are therefore an uncertain, insecure and unprotected form of tenure. With no formal recording of customary interests, boundaries between the plots of land are not always clearly defined, and disputes frequently arise. With courts generally reluctant to deal with such issues, there is often no legal recourse available to customary rights holders. If a Band decides to re-possess lands, then again customary rights holders would have no legal recourse.

Despite the uncertainties and insecurities of this form of tenure, Flanagan and Alcantara consider that such property rights have had a measure of effectiveness.[94] Many First Nations peoples 'dwell in houses and operate farms, ranches and other businesses based on such rights'.[95] On occasion, Bands have arranged for customary title to be used to obtain mortgages for the individual Band members.[96] Despite the limitations of such title, for many Bands, it is not cost-effective to establish and maintain a formal system of individual property rights where reserve land has marginal value.[97]

In Australia, the court in *Mabo* held that individual customary property rights can be recognised within a communal native title.[98] To date it is unclear whether such recognition has been widely afforded, as this is a matter for the indigenous communities concerned. It is suggested that management of customary property rights would be better served by formalising a system for dealing with such rights. Issues faced by the holders of customary individual title on native title land would probably be similar to those occurring in Canadian reserve lands.

2. Certificates of Possession on Indian Reserve Land

Individual Indian Band members can acquire rights of exclusive possession of specific areas of Indian reserve land under the Canadian Indian Act.[99] This form of property right is known as a certificate of possession. Over

---

[92] Notzke, note 86 above, 48–9.
[93] *Ibid.* In *Joe v Findlay* (1981) 122 DLR (3d) 377 reserve land was found to be held in common by the band as a whole and not by individual members.
[94] Flanagan and Alcantara (2002), note 86 above, 8.
[95] *Ibid.*
[96] *Ibid.*
[97] *Ibid*, 8–9.
[98] *Mabo*, note 8 above.
[99] Indian Act (1876) ss 20–8. See Imai, note 85 above.

100,000 certificates have been issued on 288 Indian reserves in the last 125 years.[100] A certificate of possession is proof of a lawful right to possession of land.[101] The process is as follows. Lawful possession must first be allotted and approved by the Council of the Band.[102] The Minister must approve the allotment prior to a legal interest being created. The Minister has discretion to withhold approval of a certificate of possession.[103] When an allotment is approved, a certificate of possession is issued. Certificates of possession can be held only by First Nations members.[104] The Indian Lands Registry system is authorised by the Indian Act 1876to record details of all landholding documents on reserve lands, including certificates of possession (as well as other transactions such as transfers and leases).[105]

A holder of a certificate of possession acquires rights (to the subject land) that generally equate with private property rights.[106] However, the legal title remains with the Crown.[107] Property rights under a certificate of possession are not the equivalent of a fee simple.[108] The holder of a certificate of possession can bring an action for trespass.[109] Land held under a certificate of possession can be subdivided or left under a will and is exempt from taxation. Canadian courts will hear disputes and are prepared to enforce the rights established under the system of certificates of possession.[110]

A key limitation placed on certificates of possession is that alienation is restricted within the Band.[111] Certificate of possession lands can therefore be sold only to other Band members.[112] These lands cannot be mortgaged.[113] Such restrictions limit the usefulness of certificates of possession and increase the difficulties for business ventures and economic development projects as well as making it difficult for individuals to construct housing on the reserve.[114] However, some Bands have successfully secured mortgages for Band members for private homeownership on certificate of

---

[100] Flanagan and Alcantara (2002), note 86 above, 10.
[101] Indian Act (1876) s 20(2).
[102] *Ibid*, ss 20(1) and 22.
[103] *Ibid*, s 20(4).
[104] *Ibid*, s 20(2).
[105] *Ibid*, ss 21 and 55. Failure to register a certificate of possession could result in the invalidity of subsequent dealings: *Cooper v Tsartlip* [1997] 1 CNLR 45.
[106] *Westbank Indian Band v Normand* [1994] 3 CNLR 197.
[107] *Simpson v Ryan* (1996) 106 FTR 158.
[108] *Boyer v Canada* (1986) 4 CNLR 53.
[109] *Watts v Kincolith Indian Band Council* [2000] FCJ No 470.
[110] *Westbank Indian Band v Normand* (1994) 3 CNLR 197.
[111] Imai, note 85 above, 46.
[112] Indian Act (1876) ss 24 and 28.
[113] *Ibid*, s 29.
[114] Flanagan and Alcantara (2002), note 86 above, 12.

possession lands.[115] One method allows a holder of a certificate of possession formally to transfer the certificate to the Band as collateral.[116] The Band signs a guarantee with the mortgagee whereby the Band assumes the mortgage in the event of a default. The certificate is returned to the owner only after the mortgage is repaid. In case of default, the Band can retake the land because it has the certificate.[117] A further limitation of certificates of possession is that if a First Nations member ceases to be entitled to reside on a reserve, possession of reserve lands reverts to the Band.[118]

The Indian Act 1876 includes no provisions as to forced sale or partition of certificate of possession lands, division of property in divorce proceedings, or succession and the disposition of certificates of possession in wills. In the absence of statutory guidelines, such issues are dealt with by the courts. This has resulted in a body of inconsistent case law.[119]

Despite their limitations, certificates of possession are potentially a means of dealing with the individual indigenous property interests on indigenous lands in Australia. Certificates of possession ensure the preservation of underlying collective title while allowing for the recognition of a form of individual property right. The use of certificates of possession avoids issues of alienability of title and loss of title for future generations. Canadian experiences demonstrate that with some creativity, mortgages on individual land parcels are achievable. A registry system of indigenous land title would be appropriate.

3. The First Nations Land Management Act (1999)

Property rights are recognised on Canadian Indian reserve lands under the First Nations Land Management Act (1999) ('FNLMA'). This legislation enables First Nations to comprehensively manage their lands without the need for Ministerial or Department of Indian Affairs approval. Pursuant to this legislation a Band can draft its own land code, establish its own land registry, formulate its own regulations (for example, the division of matrimonial property post-divorce and the devise of reserve interests) and administer leasing on reserves.[120] FNLMA offers Bands a secure system for land management, a means to avoid the delays associated with the

---

[115] *Ibid*, 12; Alcantara, note 86 above, 190–6. The Six Nations have established a system of revolving loan funds with a major Canadian bank to provide individual mortgages for member housing.

[116] Indian Act (1876) s 24.

[117] Flanagan and Alcantara (2002), note 86 above, 12.

[118] Indian Act (1876) s 25(1)(2).

[119] *Derrickson v Derrickson* [1986] 1 SCR 285; *Paul v Paul* [1986] 1 SCR 306: *Francis v Canada* [2000] FCJ No 848.

[120] Alcantara, note 86 above, 199–200.

Department of Indian Affairs and an escape from certain provisions in the Indian Act 1876.[121] Certificates of possession can continue to be issued under FNLMA.

One disadvantage of FNLMA is that Bands cannot create property interests that amount to ownership in fee simple.[122] Title holders are unable to transfer their interest to non-Band members and off-reserve purchasers. This regime is unlikely to improve the scope of private property rights in reserve lands.[123] Another downside to FNLMA is that First Nations are required to accept responsibility for land management and associated costs, such as land surveys, satisfying environmental requirements and various administration and legal expenses. Flanagan and Alcantara consider that the FNLMA is viable only for those First Nations communities with adequate financial resources.[124]

As a result, in Australia, without significant government funding, similar community administered land management systems would be viable only for a few Australian indigenous communities with sufficient financial resources.

4. Leases on Indian Reserves

The Canadian Indian Act 1876 allows leases to be granted on a Band's collective land as well as on individually controlled reserve land. Short-term leases or 'permits' may be granted for residential use or occupation for less than one year.[125] Leases longer than one year require Band council consent.[126] Neither Band councils nor individual title holders can lease reserve land to non-Indians without Ministerial consent.[127]

Long-term leases of reserve lands are possible.[128] A Band can 'surrender' or 'designate' land to the federal government for the purpose of leasing. This process is used for leasing commercial developments, such as the construction of shopping centres and the development of natural resources on Indian land.[129] The Surrendered and Designated Lands Register records details of transactions relating to lands that have been surrendered for sale

---

[121]   *Ibid*, 200.
[122]   FNLMA (1999) s 4.2.
[123]   Flanagan and Alcantara (2002), note 86 above, 16.
[124]   *Ibid*.
[125]   S 28(2). See Imai, note 85 above, 47.
[126]   Indian Act (1876) s 53.
[127]   *Surrey v Peace Arch Enterprises Ltd* 1970 (74) WWR 380. Imai, note 83 above, 106.
[128]   Indian Act (1876) s 38(2).
[129]   Reserve land cannot be mortgaged under s 89(1) of the Indian Act 1876. Thus it is difficult to obtain financing for reserve land projects. 1988 amendments allow a leasehold interest in designated lands to be mortgaged (s 89(1.1)). However, the Minister's consent is required prior to leasehold being mortgaged (s 54).

or designated for leasing.[130] Surrender can be absolute or by 'designation'.[131] An absolute surrender extinguishes the First Nation's interest in the land.[132] Surrender by 'designation' is common in commercial leasing and it is frequently conditional, thus enabling a Band to negotiate terms directly with developers.[133] It is not uncommon for a Band to negotiate the lease terms with the developer prior to the government designating the reserve land. In this way the indigenous community accepts responsibility for the terms of the agreement. The government then leases on the same terms and conditions to the developer. The Minister is bound to act in accordance with the terms of the surrender.[134]

The Indian Act gives Bands an absolute veto regarding commercial development. A Band can refuse to surrender its land or can surrender only on stipulated conditions.[135] In this way tribes retain control of commercial developments. After ,surrender the government enters into a contract in the form of a lease with the developer.[136] First Nations are not a party to that lease. The lease agreement usually specifies that the designated land is to be returned to the Indian community as soon as the designated use ceases.[137] Leases are drafted on the basis that all the benefits go to the Indian tribe. Surrenders under the Indian Act 1876 are not surrenders in the usual conveyancing sense.[138]

A certificate of possession owner can grant a long-term lease, but this must be done through the Department of Indian Affairs.[139] Profits from such leases go to the individual holder of the certificate of possession, and the Band receives no revenue.[140] Such leases have been granted for 99 years to companies who have built gated communities and residential neighbourhoods. After 99 years the land reverts to the holder of the certificate of possession.[141]

In Australia, the 'designated lands' leasing system for commercial development has potential for application to indigenous lands. Long-term leases allow for economic development while preserving the reversionary interest, the underlying communal title, for the traditional owners. This model has been utilised successfully for commercial development on

---

[130] Indian Act (1876) s 55.
[131] *Ibid*, ss 37–41.
[132] *Ibid*, s 38(2).
[133] *Ibid*, s 53(1).
[134] *Ibid*, s 53(3).
[135] *Ibid*, s 53.
[136] *Ibid*, s 57.
[137] *Ibid*, ss 37–41 and 53–60.
[138] *Surrey v Peace Arch* (1970) 74 WWR 380.
[139] Indian Act (1876) ss 58(1)(b) and 58(3). See Imai, note 85 above, 61 and 71.
[140] Indian Act (1876) s 58(2).
[141] Flanagan and Alcantara (2002), note 86 above, 21.

Canadian Indian reserves and furthermore encourages indigenous communities to participate in development by allowing communities to negotiate lease terms directly with developers. 'Designated leasing' is therefore one method by which commercial and economic development could take place on indigenous lands in Australia without making that indigenous title freely alienable.

B. New Zealand

Land remaining in Maori ownership and control today is mainly 'Maori freehold land',[142] which the Maori Land Court has determined ownership by freehold order.[143] Maori land is regulated by the Te Ture Whenua Maori Act/Maori Land Act (1993) ('TTWMA'). This Act promotes two principles: first, ownership of Maori land should be retained by Maori; and secondly, effective management, development and occupation by Maori owners of their land is to be encouraged.[144] The TTWMA rejects the individual title approach to land management of previous legislative regimes—in other words, 'the English system of individual freehold title'[145]—in favour of collective approaches. As one commentator notes, the passage of the Act was the first time that 'the collective ownership characteristics of Maori land were officially recognized and its continuance as a permanent tenure accepted'.[146]

Although Maori land has effectively been 'individualised', it remains multiply-owned and collectively managed. Succession rights to the interests of deceased owners have resulted in large numbers of multiple owners for much Maori land.[147] In addition, Maori land has also been subdivided over the years, and this has resulted in blocks of small, uneconomic parcels of land.[148]

1. Dealing with Maori Land

How can the interests of individual owners be accommodated in a multiply-owned and collectively managed Maori land title? For example, when some owners choose to occupy multiply-owned land and others do not, or when only some owners wish to raise finance, what options exist?

---

[142] Hereafter 'Maori land'.
[143] TTWMA s 129(2).
[144] Calma, note 4 above, 104.
[145] Robertson, note 46 above, 2.
[146] *Ibid.*
[147] Many Maori Land Court orders of 'individual titles' were made in favour groups of Maori families as well as individual landholders. Boast, note 26 above, 155.
[148] Robinson, note 141 above, 4.

One option is partition: the Maori Land Court has jurisdiction to order partition of Maori freehold land to provide an owner with a dwelling site.[149]

Owners of Maori land can also lease their land to another Maori for housing purposes.[150] Leases over 52 years require Maori Land Court approval and the consent of at least '50% of the beneficial freehold interest in the land'.[151] In addition, all leases must be noted by the Maori Land Court Registrar.[152] Claims based on the contractual terms of the lease, such as non-payment of rent, can be brought before the Maori Land Court or the High /District Court.[153]

A third method for dealing with multiply-owned and collectively managed Maori land title makes use of occupation orders. Occupation orders provide for exclusive possession of all or part of land used for dwellings. The Maori Land Court can issue an occupation order in favour of an owner for either a specified period or for the term of a person's life. Interests in occupation orders may pass on succession.[154] Multiple orders can be made in relation to different areas in one title. No fragmentation/ division of title occurs, as only a sketch plan (not survey plan) is required. Orders must stipulate whether rights to buildings pass to the land owner after the order expires.[155]

2. Financing Housing

How is finance raised on multiply-owned Maori land? If the Maori land owners are a family/tribal unit who also operate as a single economic unit, then the land can be mortgaged to obtain a loan. The Housing New Zealand Corporation (HNZC) offers loans to tribal groups with some unique security arrangements. Security comprises the buildings on the land and not the land itself.[156] HNZC requires that the house (usually single-storey) be built close to a road. In the event of loan default, the house can easily be removed.[157] HNZC also arranges low-interest loans from the Housing Innovation Fund to fund community projects, for example housing community elders.[158]

---

[149]   TTWMA (1993) s 287. See Boast, note 26 above, ch 10.
[150]   TTWMA (1993) ss 146–7. See Boast, note 26 above, ch 12.
[151]   TTWMA (1993) ss 150C and 150C(1)(b).
[152]   Altman, note 4 above, 25.
[153]   TTWMA (1993) s 18(1)(d).
[154]   *Ibid*, ss 328 and 296. See Boast, note 26 above, 203.
[155]   Altman, note 4 above, 25.
[156]   *Ibid*, 34 and 25.
[157]   *Ibid*.
[158]   *Ibid*.

3. Recording of Maori Lands

Although the TTWMA requires Maori land to be brought under the New Zealand land registry system for general lands,[159] much Maori land remains unregistered in this system.[160] However, the Maori Land Court functions as a registry of Maori land, even though no formal 'Maori land system' exists.[161] In reality, a plural system of recording land titles operates in New Zealand—the Maori Land Court alongside the Land Registrar.[162] Unfortunately, some of the records of the Maori Land Court in relation to the ownership of Maori lands are incomplete, and not all parcels of land have been adequately surveyed.[163]

4. Managing Maori Title

To ameliorate the loss of traditional lands and facilitate land dealings, today tribal groups are encouraged to vest traditional landholdings in trustees for the benefit of the whole community or in Maori Corporations.[164] Currently the New Zealand Law Reform Commission is developing a legal framework for a new form of Maori legal entity to manage communally owned assets on behalf of tribal groups.[165]

5. Lessons for Australia

The New Zealand experience demonstrates that management of 'individualised' indigenous lands is a complex endeavour, in part because of the collective nature of the individual title. However, the Maori experience also demonstrates that dealing successfully with the individual interests of owners in a multiply-owned title is possible. A proper recording system of collectively managed indigenous title is essential, and the development of a new entity to manage communally owned assets could prove invaluable.

---

[159] TTWMA (1993) s 123. See Robinson, note 140 above, 3; and Boast, note 26 above, 257–9.

[160] Many titles were never registered, while others were incapable of registration: Robinson, note 141 above, 3; Boast, note 26 above, 257.

[161] TTWMA (1993) s 127. See Boast, note 26 above, 258.

[162] If conflict occurs, the Land Transfer Act (1952) records override Maori Land Court records.

[163] Robinson, note 141 above, 4.

[164] Altman, note 4 above; Boast, note 26 above, chs 8 and 11.

[165] See the Te Puni Kōkiri (Ministry of Maori Development) website <http://www.tpk.govt.nz///.asp> accessed 1 December 2006.

IV. INDEPENDENT, COMPREHENSIVE LAND CLAIMS

A. The Nisga'a Agreement

Another form of landholding by First Nations in Canada is the rights that exist pursuant to the Nisga'a Final Agreement (Treaty), which was signed and ratified in 1998 by the Nisga'a peoples of British Columbia and both the provincial and federal governments.[166] It is a modern-day indigenous self-government agreement. The Nisga'a Treaty settled land claims in the Nass River Valley in north-western British Columbia, by an agreement that included certain lands to be held by the Nisga'a peoples, while other lands and resources, originally claimed, remained under the Canadian legal system. The Nisga'a government is integrated into the Canadian constitutional system. The laws governing the Nisga'a Nation include the Treaty, the Nisga'a Constitution and Nisga'a law. The Treaty comprehensively deals with most areas of the life of the Nisga'a Nation.

1. Nisga'a Lands

Nearly 2,000 square kilometres of land are confirmed as 'Nisga'a lands'.[167] They are comprised of Nisga'a public lands, Nisga'a private lands and Nisga'a village lands. Nisga'a lands that are not designated for a specific purpose or particular use are 'Nisga'a public lands'.[168] The Nisga'a Nation owns the fee simple to the surface and subsurface of the Nisga'a Lands, including lands within certain existing Indian reserves.[169] In addition, the Nisga'a Nation also holds private ownership of 1,500 hectares of additional lands, which are classified as 'Nisga'a Fee Simple Lands'. This includes 18 Indian reserves not included as 'Nisga'a Land'. The Nisga'a government has full ownership of these lands (but not legislative jurisdiction).[170]

The Nisga'a Nation owns the forests on their lands and the mineral resources on or under their lands but not those under submerged lands.[171]

---

[166] See: D Sanders, 'We Intend to Live Here Forever: An Analysis of the Nisga'a Treaty' (1999) 33 *UBCLR* 103; L Dufraimont, 'Continuity and Modification of Aboriginal Rights in the Nisga'a Treaty' (2002) 35 *UBCLR* 455; and T Calma (Aboriginal and Torres Strait Islander Social Justice Commissioner), *Native Title Report 2004.*

[167] Nisga'a lands do not come under the Indian Act 1876, nor do they come within federal jurisdiction over 'Lands reserved for the Indians' (s 91(24) of the Constitution Act (1867)).

[168] Nisga'a Final Agreement (1998) ch 1, para 1.

[169] *Ibid*, ch 3, para 3.

[170] *Ibid*, paras 49, 50, 51 and 63.

[171] *Ibid*, ch 5, paras 3 and 19.

Rules for Nisga'a management of Nisga'a Lands have been established.[172] Neither the federal land registries nor the British Columbia Torrens system automatically applies to Nisga'a lands.[173] The Nisga'a government may, however, register parcels of Nisga'a land under the provincial Land Title Act (BC).[174]

The Nisga'a First Nation has taken a unique approach to the alienation of Nisga'a lands. The Nisga'a Agreement permits, under certain conditions, the alienation of traditional Nisga'a Lands that are held in fee simple.[175] Nisga'a Lands may be transferred to either Nisga'a or non-Nisga'a persons.[176] However, disposal of Nisga'a land does not mean that the land ceases to be Nisga'a land.[177] Any purchaser of Nisga'a lands acquires a freehold title; but the Crown is obliged to re-transfer to the Nisga'a Nation any estate or interest in Nisga'a lands that reverts to the Crown.[178] Moreover, alienation under the Treaty must occur in accordance with Nisga'a law, traditions and customs.[179] Nisga'a law can be found in stories and songs as well as in other forms. Nisga'a law prevents land that is of particular cultural significance being alienated. Furthermore, the Nisga'a Agreement guarantees that the proper decision-making processes, which form part of the broader governance structures, are utilised in making decisions regarding the alienation of Nisga'a Lands.[180] All decision-making processes and governance structures are contained in the Constitution. The Nisga'a government has the power to create or transfer interests in Nisga'a Lands without the need for the consent of the Canadian federal government or the provincial government.

2. Lessons for Australia: The Nisga'a Agreement (1998)

Self-governing agreements like the Nisga'a Treaty are yet to be achieved in the Australian context. It is too early to assess the effectiveness of this model of indigenous landholdings and alienability of indigenous lands in British Columbia. However, the Nisga'a Agreement provides an example of alienation of indigenous land that takes place without a government legislating to transform indigenous lands to alienable freehold. Moreover,

---

[172] For example, timber extraction and forest management must meet provincial standards.
[173] Nisga'a Final Agreement (1998) ch 4, para 1.
[174] *Ibid*, paras 2 and 5. Land Title Act (BC) [RSBC 1996] ch 250.
[175] *Ibid*, ch 3, paras 3–8.
[176] *Ibid*, para 4(a)(b).
[177] *Ibid*, para 5.
[178] *Ibid*, para 7.
[179] *Ibid*, para 3.
[180] *Ibid*, ch 11.

this Agreement is an example of indigenous peoples establishing decision-making processes and governance structures that are specific to and appropriate for their community, so that they can deal effectively with issues such as the alienation of their lands.[181]

B. The Alaska Native Claims Settlement Act (1971)

The history of native land claims in Alaska dates back to 1867, when the natives there protested Russia's sale of Alaska to the United States, arguing that they were the owners of the land.[182] When Alaska became a state in 1958 the Statehood Act renounced all Alaskan native property rights, although aboriginal title remained unextinguished. However, the discovery of oil in Alaska in 1969 gave the impetus for a new era regarding native land.[183]

In 1971 the Alaska Native Claims Settlement Act ('ANCSA') was enacted.[184] Pursuant to this legislation the Indians, Eskimos and Aleuts of Alaska[185] were granted title to 44 million acres of land and were paid $962.5 million in compensation for the extinguishment of their claims to aboriginal title and aboriginal rights to hunt and fish on ancestral lands.[186] The Alaska natives supported the ANCSA at the time of its passage and believed that the agreement would protect their subsistence-based economy and their traditional lands for future generations.[187] In 1983 Thomas Berger was appointed by the Inuit Circumpolar Conference (Eskimos from Alaska, Canada and Greenland) to conduct the Alaska Native Review

---

[181] Calma, *Native Title Report 200*, note 167 above, 9.

[182] T Berger, *Village Journey: The Report of the Alaska Native Review Commission* (New York, Hill and Wang, 1985) 22–4.

[183] M Hirschfield, 'Alaska Native Claims Settlement Act' (1992) 101 *Yale Law Journal* 1331, 1333.

[184] 85 Stat 668.

[185] Hereafter 'Alaskan natives'.

[186] ANCSA (1971) ss 1605(a), 1611 and 1603(b).

[187] Hirschfield, note 179 above, 1331; MJ Ward, 'Indian Country and Inherent Tribal Authority: Will They Survive ANCSA?' (1997) 14 *Alaska Law Review* 443; J Alloway and B Mallott, 'ANCSA Unrealized: Our Lives are Not Measured in Dollars' (2005) 25 *J of Land Resources & Environmental Law* 139; DM Blurton, 'ANCSA Corporation Lands and the Department Indian Community Category of Indian Country' (1996) 13 *Alaska Law Review* 211; H Kendal-Miller, 'ANCSA and Sovereignty Litigation' (2004) 24 *J of Land Resources & Environmental Law* 465; S Colt, 'Alaska Natives and the "New Harpoon": Economic Performance of the ANCSA Regional Corporations' (2005) 25 *J of Land Resources & Environmental Law* 155.

Commission and review the ANCSA.[188] His Report found serious problems with both the terms of the ANCSA and their implementation.[189]

1. The ANCSA Settlement and Corporate Structure

Pursuant to the ANCSA and the Alaska National Interest Lands Act
(1980), Alaskan lands were divided between government (both federal and
state) and the Alaskan natives. Federal government reserves included 197
million acres of land, approximately sixty per cent of Alaska. The state
selected 124 million acres, about thirty per cent of Alaska. Native Alaskans
obtained 44 million acres of land, about ten per cent of the state.[190]

Land allocated to the native Alaskans is held by native corporations as a
fee simple title.[191] The ANCSA divided Alaska into twelve geographic
regions, and each region incorporated, creating twelve regional companies.[192] Every Native Alaskan received one hundred shares of stock in
one of those regional corporations.[193] Native villages within each region
also incorporated. This created over two hundred village companies.
Natives enrolled in the relevant village acquired one hundred shares each
in that village's company.[194] Village companies selected 22 million acres of
land. Regional corporations selected 18 million acres of land. The remaining land was distributed to native groups outside the main provisions of
the ANCSA.

No river, water or offshore rights of native Alaskans were recognised
under the ANCSA.[195] Village landholdings comprise surface title only.
Regional landholdings include subsurface rights to the entire 44 million
acres.[196] Exclusive rights of native Alaskans to fish, hunt, trap and gather
were secured to only 10 per cent of Alaska.[197] Today Native Alaskans no
longer hold common law aboriginal title to their traditional lands: all
Alaskan ancestral lands are the property of native corporations.

Under the ANCSA, responsibility for land and money is divided between
regions and villages. Village corporations administer the land while the
regional corporations control the monetary benefits. A complex profit-
sharing arrangement requires each region to divide 70 per cent of their

---

[188] Berger, note 178 above, 26 and 60.
[189] A 1985 Department of the Interior study found serious limitations on the benefits of
this ANCSA settlement: HR REP No 31.
[190] *ANCSA* (1971) s 1603(b).
[191] *Ibid*, s1613(a)(e)(f). See Berger, note 178 above, 88.
[192] A thirteenth regional corporation was established for non-resident native Alaskans:
ibid, s 1606(c).
[193] *Ibid*, s 1606(g).
[194] *Ibid*, ss 1606 and 1607. See Berger, note 178 above, 24.
[195] Berger, note 178 above, 61.
[196] *ANCSA* (1971) s 1613(e).
[197] Berger, note 178 above, 162.

profits from timber and subsurface resources among all twelve regional corporations.[198] Village consent is required for any subsurface development within village boundaries.[199] Although villages were supposed to be autonomous, the power of the regional corporations seriously limited that autonomy.[200]

The ANCSA excluded from automatic corporate ownership 'every Native child born since December 18, 1971, the date of the Act's passage. Thus, native Alaskans born after that date had no legal interest in the native corporations or the corporations' native landholdings.[201] The 1987 ANCSA amendments altered this.[202] Corporations now have the ability to expand shareholders by amending the articles of incorporation and to issue stock to new native Alaskans.[203]

2. Alienability of Title

Native land is potentially alienable.[204] The ANCSA stipulated that for the first twenty years after the passage of the Act (ie, until 1991), voting shareholders must be Alaskan natives,[205] and shares were not saleable until after that. Saleable shares allow for the possibility of corporate takeovers[206] and for the possibility that non-natives could purchase shares and thus acquire interests in ancestral lands.[207] Accordingly, traditional ancestral lands could potentially be lost through sale, bankruptcy, corporate takeovers, corporate failure and presumably through mortgage defaults.[208]

It was clear that traditional native Alaskan lands were not secure under the ANCSA. Native Alaskans sought to protect their assets post-1991 and to ensure control over corporate membership.[209] Congress responded by enacting the ANCSA Amendment Act in 1987.[210] The amendments offered native corporations a choice in extending alienability restrictions indefinitely. Corporations can 'opt-in', 'opt-out' or 'recapitalise'. If a corporation opts-in, transferability restrictions terminate unless shareholders vote to

---

[198] ANCSA (1971) s 1606(i).
[199] *Ibid*, s 1606(f).
[200] Hirschfield, note 179 above, 1337.
[201] ANCSA (1971) s 1604(a).
[202] 101 Stat 1788; 43 USC 1601 (1988).
[203] ANCSA (1988) s 1606(g)(i)(B).
[204] *Ibid*, s 1620(1)). See Berger, note 178 above, 85 and 99.
[205] ANCSA (1971) s 1606(h)(2(c).
[206] Berger, note 178 above, 96.
[207] ANCSA (1971) ss 1606(h)(1)(B) and 1629(C).
[208] Berger, note 178 above, 6 and 85.
[209] Hirschfield , note 179 above, 1338; JT London, 'The 1991 Amendments to the Alaska Native Claims Settlement Act: Protection for Native Lands?' (1989) 8 *Stanford Environmental Law Journal* 200, 211–12.
[210] 101 Stat 1788; 43 USC 1601.

continue them. If a corporation opts-out, transferability restrictions continue until the shareholders vote to eliminate them. Alternatively, corporations can recapitalise by issuing different classes of shares with different voting rights.[211] Furthermore, the amendments allow assets of ANCSA corporations to be transferred to trusts to protect corporate lands from business risks.[212]

3. The Failure of the Corporate Model of Landholding under the ANCSA

The corporate ANCSA model has not proved effective for managing indigenous lands in Alaska. Most corporations have failed to pay significant dividends. Factors contributing to corporate failure include the high costs of corporate compliance and professional advice and delays in the original transfer of land to regions and villages.[213] The absence of commercial experience among native Alaskan communities also resulted in poor management.[214] Additionally, the potential economic benefits of Alaskan tundra land are limited, except where significant oil and timber resources exist. Furthermore, many native Alaskans when selecting lands under the ANCSA rejected lands traditionally used for subsistence in preference for lands that were at the time considered more suitable for economic development.[215] However, any subsequent improvements in native housing, health and education can be attributed to increases in public capital expenditure, not from profits from the ANCSA lands.[216] One writer has identified the omission of larger conceptual issues from the ANCSA as the major reason behind the failure of the Alaskan model of indigenous landholdings.[217] Native lands are about heritage, community and native identity—not about land that has been effectively privatised in corporations.[218]

4. Lessons for Australia: Corporate Title

The ANCSA model is of interest to Australia because it represents a unique form of indigenous landholding. It is clear that corporate title, at least in the form utilised in the ANCSA scheme, is not the answer to economic development of indigenous lands. Economically, traditional indigenous lands in Alaska and Australia offer little commercial benefit to the

---

[211] ANCSA (1987) s 1606(g)(B). See Hirschfield, note 179 above, 1343.
[212] ANCSA (1987) s 1629(e). See Hirschfield, note 179 above, 1343.
[213] Hirschfield, note 179 above, 1339.
[214] Berger, note 178 above, 49.
[215] *Ibid*, 34.
[216] *Ibid*, 43.
[217] Hirschfield, note 179 above, 1338–41.
[218] *Ibid*.

indigenous communities who live on them. As in Alaska, many traditional indigenous lands in Australia have value only insofar as indigenous culture dictates. One lesson is clear: traditional indigenous connections must be respected in any model of landholding introduced for Australia indigenous lands. Moreover, in terms of indigenous corporate governance, similar problems regarding a lack of business acumen and the onerous reporting requirements of the Corporations Act (2001) (Cth) could also arise in Australia if a title scheme similar to the ANCSA were to be introduced.

V. CONCLUSION

To briefly summarise the lessons in this review of the North American and New Zealand experiences: it is clear that the consequences of individualising indigenous title have in two jurisdictions (the USA and New Zealand) resulted in loss of traditional lands. It is obvious from the US allotment model that allocating discrete and freely alienable portions of indigenous lands to individual allottees may result in significant loss of indigenous landholdings. Preservation of the underlying communal/traditional title is vitally important. Other property interests can be created without necessarily compromising that underlying title, for example, the leasing of reserve lands and certificates of possession, which support individual title, as evidenced in Canada.

Individualisation of title has not necessarily resulted in increased economic benefits for the indigenous peoples affected. Future indigenous generations will be faced with the consequences of individualising indigenous title if free alienability is permitted. This should be a prime consideration in relation to any new forms of tenure being reviewed. It is the indigenous communities who should decide whether indigenous land should be held collectively or individually. This process should never be imposed by a paternalistic government. Significant loss of traditional title in Australia could mean a return to pre-*Mabo* days, when indigenous communities had to search for new land rights.

Converting all indigenous landholdings to one form of title only, for example an alienable fee simple, is not a satisfactory model. A system involving a mixed portfolio of landholdings is preferable. For example, a significant portion of traditional lands, where the underlying collective title of communities is intact, should be preserved for common benefit and use and for future generations. On the other hand, some land should be available for commercial development, and this land may need to be freely alienable. Again, the underlying collective title of communities should be preserved to allow for communal decision-making in relation to this land.

Alternative models of indigenous landholding that might be effective in the Australian context include property rights recognised on Canadian reserves, for example, certificates of possession, which recognise individual property rights, and the leasing by designation, whereby the underlying communal title is preserved. The introduction of new models of indigenous land tenure will also need to be supported by a land registration system for recording titles and transactions. Should this be a separate registration system for indigenous lands or be included within existing systems?

This chapter has tried to make clear that prior to embracing and implementing any significant land reforms regarding indigenous land tenure in Australia, we must give serious consideration to the implications that flow from the proposed changes. Furthermore, wider issues about these new indigenous land tenure models will need to be addressed. For example, what succession laws should be applied—customary/traditional or Western? How will the property be dealt with on intestacy or divorce?

Brennan J in *Mabo*[219] noted that the common law of Australia should not be frozen in an age of racial discrimination. Likewise, traditional title lands must not be frozen in an age of subsistence economics and isolated from opportunities for commercial development. The issue is how best to achieve this while protecting indigenous culture. It seems that a 'balanced portfolio' of landholdings is appropriate for promoting an economically successful future for indigenous communities while at the same time preserving traditional customary title and the land heritage that these communities share.

---

[219]   (1992) 175 CLR 1.

Index

.